Advocacy in Negotiation and Mediation

A Practical Approach

G. Nicholas Herman

Adjunct Professor of Law
Campbell University School of Law
North Carolina Central University School of Law

Carolina Academic Press
Durham, North Carolina

LIBRARY OF CONGRESS CATALOGING-IN-PUBLICATION DATA

Names: Herman, G. Nicholas, author.
Title: Advocacy in negotiation and mediation : a practical approach / by G. Nicholas Herman.
Description: Durham, North Carolina : Carolina Academic Press, [2021]
Identifiers: LCCN 2021035349 (print) | LCCN 2021035350 (ebook) | ISBN 9781531023263 (paperback) | ISBN 9781531023270 (ebook)
Subjects: LCSH: Dispute resolution (Law)--United States. | Negotiation--United States. | Mediation--United States.
Classification: LCC KF9084 .H464 2021 (print) | LCC KF9084 (ebook) | DDC 347.73/9--dc23
LC record available at https://lccn.loc.gov/2021035349
LC ebook record available at https://lccn.loc.gov/2021035350

Carolina Academic Press
700 Kent Street
Durham, North Carolina 27701
(919) 489-7486
www.cap-press.com

Printed in the United States of America

This book is dedicated to Bob and Jennifer Forsman

Contents

Acknowledgment xvii

Preface xix

Chapter One
Learning Negotiating and Mediating 3
§1.01 The Importance of Negotiating and Mediating 3
§1.02 "Learning by Doing" and the Role of This Book 4

PART I NEGOTIATION

Chapter Two
Introduction and Academic Approaches to Negotiation 7
§2.01 Introduction 7
§2.02 Academic Approaches to Understanding Negotiation 8
§2.03 Game Theory and the Prisoner's Dilemma 8
§2.04 Economic Approaches 12
§2.05 Anthropological & Sociological Approaches 17
§2.06 Psychological Approaches and Factors 22
[1] Risk Aversion or Risk Tolerance 22
[2] Reference Points and Framing Effects 24
[3] Sunk Costs 26
[4] Reactive Devaluation 27
§2.07 Translating Academic Approaches into Practice 28

Chapter Three
Negotiating Models, Strategies, and Styles 29
§3.01 Introduction 30
§3.02 The Adversarial Model 30
§3.03 The Problem-Solving Model 33
§3.04 Factors Affecting the Utility of the Adversarial and Problem-Solving Models 35
[1] The Nature of the Dispute or Problem 35
[2] The Other Side's Negotiating Approach 36
[3] Differences in Bargaining Leverage 37
[4] Future Dealings Between the Parties or Negotiators 37
[5] Pressures to Reach an Agreement 38
§3.05 Negotiating Strategies and Styles 38
§3.06 Competitive (Hardball) Style 38
§3.07 Cooperative (Softball) Style 39
§3.08 Competitive-Cooperative (Hardball and Softball) Style 40
§3.09 Choosing a Negotiating Style and Strategy 40
§3.10 Style and Strategy Combinations 41
[1] Competitive and Adversarial 41
[2] Cooperative (or Competitive-Cooperative) and Adversarial 41
[3] Competitive and Problem-Solving 42
[4] Cooperative (or Competitive-Cooperative) and Problem-Solving 42
§3.11 The Overall Importance of Flexibility and Credibility 42
§3.12 Summary of Style and Strategy Characteristics, Advantages, and Disadvantages 43

Chapter Four
Ethical Considerations in Negotiation and Settlement 49
§4.01 Introduction 49
§4.02 Attorney's Authority to Settle and Advising the Client 50
§4.03 Aggregate Settlements 52
§4.04 Contingent Fees 54
§4.05 Example of Contingent Fee Contract 58
§4.06 Truthfulness in Negotiating 59
§4.07 Civility in Negotiating 63
§4.08 Threatening Criminal Prosecution in Negotiating 65

Chapter Five
Negotiating Tactics and Techniques 67
§5.01 Introduction 68
§5.02 Abdication 69
§5.03 Adjournment or Caucus 70
§5.04 Anger/Aggressiveness 70
§5.05 Asymmetrical Time Pressure 70
§5.06 Blaming or Fault Finding 71
§5.07 Bluffing 71
§5.08 Boulwarism 72
§5.09 Coalition 72
§5.10 Company Policy Excuse 72
§5.11 Deadlines 73
§5.12 Delay 73
§5.13 Dodging the Question Through Blocking Techniques 74
§5.14 Draft Document or Single Negotiating Text 74
§5.15 Escalating Demands 75
§5.16 Excessive Initial Demands/Offers 75
§5.17 Face Saving 76
§5.18 Fait Accompli 76
§5.19 False Demands 77
§5.20 False Emphasis 77
§5.21 False Multiple Concessions 77
§5.22 False Scarcity 78
§5.23 Floating Trial Balloons and Bracketing 78
§5.24 Good Guy-Bad Guy Routine/Mutt and Jeff 79
§5.25 Lack of Authority or Limited Authority 80
§5.26 Little Ol' Country Lawyer 80
§5.27 Lock-In Positions 81
§5.28 Low-Balling 81
§5.29 Misstatement 82
§5.30 Nibbling 82
§5.31 Off-the-Record Discussions 82
§5.32 Personal Attacks 83
§5.33 Playing Dumb 83
§5.34 Preconditions or Conditional Proposals 83
§5.35 Problem Solving 84

§5.36 Publicity 84
§5.37 Questions to Facilitate Agreements 86
§5.38 Questioning by Socratic Method 87
§5.39 Reversing Position 88
§5.40 Salami 88
§5.41 Snow Job/Alleged Expertise 88
§5.42 Splitting the Difference 89
§5.43 Surprise 89
§5.44 Take-It-or-Leave-It 90
§5.45 Threats 91
§5.46 Timing 91
§5.47 Two Against One 92
§5.48 Walkout 92
§5.49 Word Smithing 92
§5.50 Dealing with Disingenuous or Inappropriate Tactics or Techniques 93
[1] Rule the Tactic or Technique Out of Bounds Before Negotiations Start or When It Arises During the Negotiation 94
[2] Deflect the Tactic or Technique by Ignoring It 95
[3] Expressly Expose the Tactic or Technique 95
[4] Respond to the Tactic or Technique in Kind 95

Chapter Six
Valuing Cases for Negotiation and Settlement 97
§6.01 Introduction 97
§6.02 Target and Resistance Points 98
§6.03 Intuitive "Case Worth" Analysis 100
§6.04 Rule-of-Thumb Valuation 102
§6.05 Computer-Generated Valuation 102
§6.06 Traditional Economic Analysis 103
§6.07 Fair Settlement Range Formula 107
§6.08 Analysis of the Client's Motivations and Aversion to Risk 109
§6.09 Adopting a Holistic Analysis and Advising the Client 111
§6.10 Example of Holistic Analysis 114

Chapter Seven
Preparing for Negotiation 123
§7.01 Introduction 124
§7.02 Information to Obtain 124
[1] Information from the Client 125
[2] Information About the Other Party 125
[3] Information About the Opposing Negotiator 126
[4] Information About the Law 126
[5] Other Information 126
§7.03 Preparing a Negotiation Preparation Outline 127
[1] Step 1: From the Perspective of Each Party, Make a List of Information to Obtain, Information to Reveal, and Information to Protect 127
[2] Step 2: Make a List of Each Party's Interests 128
[3] Step 3: Make a List of Each Party's Primary Objectives, Secondary Objectives, and Incidental Objectives (To Exchange) 129
[4] Step 4: Make a List of Possible Solutions for Each Party (From Most Preferred to Least Preferred) 129
[5] Step 5: Make a List of Each Party's Best Alternatives to a Negotiated Agreement (BATNA) 130
[6] Step 6: Make a List of Each Party's Factual and Legal Leverage Points (Strong and Weak) 130
[7] Step 7: Identify Each Party's Potential Target and Resistance Points 131
[8] Step 8: Identify Each Party's Negotiating Strategy: Adversarial or Problem-Solving 131
[9] Step 9: Identify Each Party's Negotiating Style: Competitive (Hardball), Cooperative (Softball), or Competitive-Cooperative (Hardball and Softball) 132
[10] Step 10: Make a List of Each Party's Offers or Proposals in the Order They May Be Presented 132
[11] Step 11: Consider Each Party's Particular Tactics 133
[12] Step 12: Revise All of the Foregoing Matters Throughout the Negotiating Process 134

§7.04 Format for Negotiation Preparation Outline 134
§7.05 Illustration of Negotiation Preparation Outline (Adversarial Approach) 136
§7.06 Illustration of Negotiation Preparation Outline (Problem-Solving Approach) 142
§7.07 The Role of the Client and Advising the Client 148

Chapter Eight
Negotiating in Writing and Over the Telephone 149
§8.01 Introduction 150
§8.02 Negotiating in Writing—Advantages and Disadvantages 150
§8.03 Techniques for Effective Correspondence 151
[1] Send a Letter by Registered or Certified Mail 151
[2] Copy the Email or Letter to Other Persons 151
[3] Identify Your Authority to Represent 151
[4] Adopt an Appropriate Style and Tone 151
[5] Highlight the Pertinent Facts and Law 152
[6] Convey a Specific Proposal or Course of Action 153
[7] State a Time Frame for Action and Consequences for Inaction 153
§8.04 Illustration of a Demand Letter 154
§8.05 Settlement Brochures 156
[1] Introduction to Brochure/Cover Letter 157
[2] Statement of Facts and Liability 157
[3] Summary of Medical Treatment 158
[4] Summary of Lost Earnings 158
[5] Summary of Pain and Suffering and Permanent Injury 158
[6] Damages Summary and Initial Demand 159
§8.06 Illustration of Settlement Brochure (Personal Injury Case) 160
§8.07 Negotiating Over the Telephone—Advantages and Disadvantages 168
§8.08 Techniques for Effective Telephone Negotiations 169
[1] Do Not Commit Yourself Unless You Are Prepared 169
[2] Do Not Be Afraid to Be "Unavailable" 169
[3] Use a Preparation Negotiation Outline 170
[4] Adjust the Pace and Tone of Your Voice 170
[5] Do Not Be Afraid to Call Back 170

Chapter Nine
Negotiating Face to Face 171
§9.01 Introduction 172
§9.02 With Whom to Negotiate 173
§9.03 When to Negotiate 174
§9.04 Where to Negotiate 174
§9.05 Who Should Attend the Negotiation 175
§9.06 Setting the Tone 176
§9.07 Setting the Agenda 177
§9.08 Reading Body Language 179
§9.09 Exchanging Information 180
§9.10 Obtaining Information 181
[1] Ask Broad, Open-Ended Questions When Seeking Maximum Information 181
[2] Use Silence, Encouragement, and Questions That Call for Elaboration 182
[3] Listen Intently and Patiently 182
[4] Ask Specific Questions to Clarify, Pin Down, and Confirm Information 182
[5] Insist upon the Necessity of Receiving Crucial Information 183
§9.11 Protecting Information 183
[1] Ignore the Question and Change the Topic 183
[2] Answer the Question by Asking Another Question 184
[3] Answer the Question by Answering Another Question 184
[4] Over-Answer or Under-Answer the Question 184
[5] Rule the Question Out of Bounds 184
§9.12 Revealing Information 185
§9.13 Adversarial Bargaining 185
[1] Making Offers 186
[a] Who Should Make the First Offer 186
[b] When to Make the First Offer 187
[c] The Amount of the First Offer 187
[d] Communicating Offers 188
[2] Making Counteroffers 188
[3] Making Concessions 189
[a] When to Make Concessions 189
[b] Concession Strategy 189

[c] Communicating Concessions 193
[4] Forms of Persuasion 194
[a] Argument 194
[b] Exhibits 195
[c] Emotional Appeals 195
[d] Threats and Promises 196
§9.14 Problem-Solving Bargaining 197
[1] Identifying and Sharing Interests or Needs 197
[2] Brainstorming for Solutions 198
[3] Making Problem-Solving Offers, Counteroffers, and Concessions 199
§9.15 Combining Adversarial and Problem-Solving Bargaining 200
§9.16 Concluding the Negotiation 202

Chapter Ten
Negotiating During Civil Litigation 205
§10.01 Introduction 205
§10.02 General Considerations About Preparation 206
§10.03 General Considerations About Pretrial Strategy and Style 206
§10.04 Filing the Complaint and Answer 208
§10.05 Using Discovery 210
§10.06 Making Offers of Judgment 212
§10.07 Using Timing and Deadlines 213
§10.08 Using Pretrial Settlement Conferences 215
§10.09 Settling at the Last Minute 216
§10.10 High-Low Agreements 217
§10.11 Collaborative Law Agreements 218

PART II **MEDIATION**

Chapter Eleven
The Mediation Process and Mediator Styles and Strategies 223
§11.01 Introduction 223
§11.02 The Mediation Process, in General 225
§11.03 Facilitative v. Evaluative Mediation 228
§11.04 Mediator Styles and Strategies 229

Chapter Twelve
When to Mediate, Choosing a Mediator, and Mediator Tactics and Techniques 233
§12.01 What Cases to Mediate and When to Mediate 233
[1] Factors That Favor Mediation 234
[2] Factors Unfavorable to Mediation 235
§12.02 Choosing a Mediator 236
§12.03 Mediator Tactics and Techniques 237
[1] Tactics and Techniques Drawn from Traditional Negotiating 237
[2] Tactics and Techniques for Obtaining Information 239
[3] Tactics and Techniques for Generating and Discussing Potential Solutions 240
[4] Tactics and Techniques for Assessing, Selecting, and Communicating Specific Proposals 241
[5] Tactics and Techniques for Creating Movement in the Negotiations 242
[6] Tactics and Techniques for Forging and Finalizing the Terms of an Agreement 244

Chapter Thirteen
Preparing for Mediation 245
§13.01 Preparing a Mediation Preparation Outline 245
§13.02 Holding a Pre-Mediation Conference with the Mediator or Between Counsel 247
§13.03 Who Should Attend the Mediation 248
§13.04 Preparing the Client for Mediation 250

Chapter Fourteen
Effective Advocacy During Mediation 253
§14.01 Introduction 253
§14.02 Preparing a Pre-Mediation Submission 254
§14.03 Making the Opening Statement 256
§14.04 Using the Private Caucuses 259
[1] Assist the Mediator in Obtaining Information 260
[2] Discuss the Strengths and Weaknesses of the Case 261
[3] Invite the Mediator's Perspectives About the Case 262

[4] Listen to the Mediator's Cues and Clues 263
[5] Specify Confidential Information 263
[6] Make Reasonable Settlement Offers Supported by Sound Reasons 264
[7] Do Not Disclose Your Bottom Line Up Front 264
[8] Confer Alone with the Mediator and Opposing Counsel, If Necessary 265
[9] Be Patient with the Process and Take Time to Confer Privately with Your Client 265
§14.05 Concluding the Mediation 266

Appendix A
Negotiation & Mediation Role Plays 267
(1) Bloch & McDonald (Premarital Agreement) 268
(2) Bloch v. Bloch (Separation Agreement) 270
(3) Daye v. City of Rexford (Employment Discrimination) 276
(4) French v. Goff (Automobile Personal Injury) 281
(5) Hillsborough v. Hughes (Condemnation Case on Appeal) 285
(6) Joseph v. Peters (Medical Malpractice) 289
(7) Kegnim v. Drake (Automobile Personal Injury) 290
(8) Lowe v. Interstate Feed Cooperative, Inc. (Wrongful Employment Discharge) 293
(9) Mann v. Parsons University Medical Center (Nursing Malpractice) 296
(10) Martel v. Simba (Unfair Debt Collection) 298
(11) Monolith v. Sat-Lith (Breach of Covenant Not to Compete) 302
(12) Seaver v. Excellent Pet Foods Co. (Breach of Distributorship Agreement) 305
(13) Solomon Clinic v. Carr (Breach of Employment Contract) 314

Appendix B
General Suggestions to Mediators for How to Mediate a Case 325
[I] Introductions and the Mediator's Introductory Remarks 325
[II] The Parties' Opening Statements 327
[III] Private Caucusing 328
[IV] Concluding the Mediation 329

Index 331

Acknowledgment

The author gratefully acknowledges Professor Emeritus Mark W. Morris, for his selfless review and contributions to this work.

Preface

This book replaces a previous work, titled *Legal Counseling, Negotiating, and Mediating: A Practical Approach*. The new book focuses exclusively on advocacy in negotiating and mediating because these skills are now typically taught in a course that is separate from a course on the skills associated with legal counseling. The new book, however, covers the lawyer's counseling function as it specifically pertains to negotiating and mediating.

Most of the literature on negotiating and mediating falls into one of three categories: the academic literature, the practice literature, or the lay literature. The academic literature, largely drawn from the disciplines of psychology, economics, and sociology, is often highly conceptual and theoretical. The practice literature is largely based on professional experience and thus is highly anecdotal and sometimes lacks discussion of ethical and legal ramifications. The lay literature, particularly on negotiating, is typically aimed at providing general advice about how to improve one's interpersonal relationships and negotiate in everyday affairs. Within all three categories, albeit to varying degrees, there are many works that are insightful, thought provoking, and useful.

However, a common criticism of much of the literature is that, upon close reading, what often sounds good and even may be quite interesting, frequently is not very helpful in terms of teaching one *how* to engage in effective negotiating, and mediating. For example, notable exceptions aside, a good bit of the academic literature is quite difficult to understand and tends to supplant reality with heuristic simulations of limited utility. Similarly, the practice literature often places too much reliance on personal "war stories" that are not representative of the most common situations encountered in practice, and the lay literature tends to be dominated by general shibboleths and postulates that are often too abstract to apply in a meaningful way. Thus, there is a need to heed these criticisms to take a more understandable, realistic, and practical approach in writing about negotiating and mediating.

This book tries to do that. Two factors shape its content. First, the topics at hand are, at bottom, "practical skills" that are integral to effective legal representation. Second, while most law students will become practicing lawyers, some will become judges, academicians, or will use their law degree in business or other professions. Therefore, the book strives to be eminently practical in the descriptive and prescriptive treatment of these skills, including the ethical and client-counseling ramifications. At the same time, it is important to encourage broader and more creative thinking by discussing some of the more important theoretical approaches to negotiation. The primary goal in this effort, however, is to emphasize a blend of theory and practice that is most *meaningful and useful* to effective client representation in negotiating and mediating.

Advocacy in Negotiation and Mediation

Chapter One

Learning Negotiating and Mediating

SYNOPSIS

§1.01 The Importance of Negotiating and Mediating
§1.02 "Learning by Doing" and the Role of This Book

§1.01 The Importance of Negotiating and Mediating

Courses in negotiating and mediating are viewed by some law professors as "soft" courses in contrast courses in doctrinal or statutory law such as constitutional law, torts, property, civil procedure, criminal law, contracts, and the like. This may be true in the sense that, while courses in substantive law require you to learn complex legal rules whose proper application to myriad factual situations often depends upon rigorous legal analysis and an appreciation of nuances in the law and the facts, courses in negotiating and mediating generally do not focus on these matters. Instead, the focus is on learning and applying the processes and techniques, including pertinent ethical and counseling considerations, that effective lawyers use in advising their clients and helping them to resolve their legal problems or disputes without litigation. As such, negotiating and mediating courses are sometimes thought of as being heavy on "how to" mechanics and light on intellectual substance.

However, it is a mistake to think that legal negotiating and mediating involve purely mechanical skills that are separable from knowledge of the substantive law and intellectual legal skills. This is because your knowledge of the law and your ability to engage in legal analysis largely shape the content of your advice to a client and your representation in negotiations and mediations. Negotiating and mediating courses thus do not intend to downplay knowledge of the law and legal-reasoning skills. They are taught with the assumption that you will bring that knowledge and those skills to your learning about negotiating and mediating, that you deploy them in activities that simulate the actual practice of law. The intent is, as it is often said, to help "bridge the gap between theory and practice."

The importance of negotiating and mediating is underscored by the fact that the vast majority of disputes between opposing clients are resolved by negotiation, mediation, or some other dispute resolution process. Trials are rare. Moreover, negotiations are integral in most transactional-law contexts. Thus, effective legal representation requires effectiveness in negotiating and mediating.

§1.02 "Learning by Doing" and the Role of This Book

In broad terms, negotiating involves the processes and techniques used in trying to resolve your client's disputes or common problems with another party in order to reach a satisfactory agreement. It may be helpful to think of two kinds of negotiations in which lawyers are most often involved: deal-making on the one hand and resolving legal disputes on the other. Mediating involves negotiating through an informal, non-adversarial dispute resolution process, in which a neutral third party encourages and facilitates the parties to voluntarily resolve their dispute. Mediation is assisted negotiation.

The best way to learn the concepts, skills, and processes of negotiating and mediating is to "just do it," under the guidance and critique of your professor and fellow students. This "learning by doing" approach is also used in teaching trial practice and other practical skills such as interviewing and counseling.

This book is designed for use in connection with this "learning by doing" approach. The main text will provide you with the processes, concepts, and techniques involved in negotiating and mediating, along with illustrations of how various concepts and techniques may be applied. The Appendix contains role plays that may be used in conducting simulated negotiating and mediating sessions from which you can develop your own effectiveness in these practical skills.

Part I

Negotiation

Chapter Two

Introduction and Academic Approaches to Negotiation

SYNOPSIS

§2.01 Introduction
§2.02 Academic Approaches to Understanding Negotiation
§2.03 Game Theory and the Prisoner's Dilemma
§2.04 Economic Approaches
§2.05 Anthropological and Sociological Approaches
§2.06 Psychological Approaches and Factors
[1] Risk Aversion or Risk Tolerance
[2] Reference Points and Framing Effects
[3] Sunk Costs
[4] Reactive Devaluation
§2.07 Translating Academic Approaches into Practice

§2.01 Introduction

Negotiation is a process in which parties try to resolve their differences or common problems in order to reach some mutually satisfactory agreement. Of course, parties routinely negotiate in a non-dispute context when they seek to engage in a business relationship for the sale of goods or services or to consummate a transaction. When a dispute is involved, parties almost always initially seek to resolve their differences through negotiation, and it is estimated that over 90% of all lawsuits are settled.

The sections below summarize some of the traditional academic approaches to negotiation. These conceptual and theoretical approaches, drawn from a variety of academic disciplines, underscore the complexity of negotiating as a form of human behavior. Together, they help—in part—to describe this unique behavior in ways that help us to understand *why* certain negotiations are successful when others are not and *how* we might be more effective in negotiating. The last section of this Chapter makes this point by providing a perspective about the utility of various academic approaches to the real-life practice of successful negotiations.

§2.02 Academic Approaches to Understanding Negotiation

For many years, academicians have studied the process of negotiation from the perspectives of disciplines such as economics, anthropology, sociology, psychology, and game theory. Provided below is a selected, and by no mean exhaustive, summary of some of the most often-cited multi-disciplinary commentary about negotiating. We intend this very brief summary as a useful introduction to the overall subject of negotiating. It may also serve as a point of departure for students and lawyers thinking more deeply and creatively about the subject and the craft of negotiating.

§2.03 Game Theory and the Prisoner's Dilemma

Game theory[1] is an experimental tool used by a number of theorists to study negotiation.[2] Probably the most widely known game used in teaching negotiation is the "Prisoner's Dilemma." While there are many variations of this game, it typically involves two persons (*e.g.*, Smith and Jones) who are taken into custody by the police and charged with a serious felony.[3] Smith and Jones are separated from one another for purposes of interrogation, and each must

1. The seminal work on game theory is J. Von Neumann & O. Morgenstern, *Theory of Games and Economic Behavior* (1944).

2. *See D. Pruitt, Negotiation Behavior*, 102–110 (1981); H. Raiffa, *The Art and Science of Negotiation*, 123–126 (1982); *see generally*, A. Rapoport, *Two-Person Game Theory: The Essential Ideas* (1966).

3. *See* E. McGinnis, *Social Behavior: A Functional Analysis*, 417–418, 423–424 (1970).

decide whether to confess to the felony and turn State's evidence against the other or not to confess. Both prisoners know that if neither confesses, the State will not have enough evidence to convict them of the felony and each will receive only a 1-year sentence for a misdemeanor. If both confess (*i.e.*, plead guilty so that there is no need for one to turn State's evidence against the other), both will go to jail for the felony but will receive a reduced sentence of 7 years in return for pleading guilty. However, if one confesses and the other does not (*i.e.*, one turns State's evidence and the other does not confess and pleads not guilty), the former will be released and the latter will go to jail for 10 years. Thus, each prisoner's choice of confessing or not confessing will result in different outcomes depending not only upon his own decision, but also upon the decision made by his fellow prisoner. Because the prisoners are not permitted to communicate with one another, neither knows what the other will do.

The different outcomes or "payoffs" may be illustrated by the following matrix:

		Jones	
		Does not Confess	Confesses
Smith	Does not Confess	Smith gets 1 year Jones gets 1 year	Smith gets 10 years Jones is released
	Confesses	Smith is released Jones gets 10 years	Smith gets 7 years Jones gets 7 years

The "dilemma" faced by Smith and Jones is that while both will be better off if neither confesses (*i.e.*, each gets 1 year) than if both confess (*i.e.*, each gets 7 years), neither wants to be the "sucker" who pleads not guilty when the other has confessed and turned State's evidence (*i.e.*, the "sucker" will get 10 years). Thus, without being able to communicate with one another, the incentives tend to pressure both into confessing such that "the pursuit of self-interest leads to a poor outcome for all"[4] (*i.e.*, each prisoner ends up with a 7-year jail term).

This result is apparent when one considers the various alternatives available to Smith if Jones confesses on the one hand, or does not confess on the other:

---

4. R. Axelrod, *The Evolution of Cooperation* 7 (1984).

1. Assume Jones confesses: Here, if Smith does not confess, Smith gets a 10-year sentence. If Smith also confesses, then Smith gets a 7-year sentence. Thus, assuming Jones confesses, Smith is better off by confessing.
2. Assume Jones does not confess: Here, if Smith confesses, Smith is set free. If Smith also does not confess, then Smith gets a 1-year sentence. Thus, assuming Jones does not confess, Smith is better off by confessing.

If Jones applied the same analysis *vis a vis* the choices available to Smith, Jones would also conclude that his best option would be to confess.

The Prisoner's Dilemma game illustrates that cooperation and competition are inherent in two-party bargaining. Cooperation is necessary to achieve a voluntary agreement, but competition usually occurs over the terms of a final agreement. Analogizing Smith and Jones as opposing negotiators, if Smith *cooperates* with Jones by *not confessing*, Smith is gambling that Jones is to be trusted to reciprocate by also not confessing. However, Jones might *compete* by *confessing* (*i.e.*, "defecting" as it is called in the game-theoretic nomenclature) and thereby exploit Smith's cooperation such that Jones is released at Smith's expense. Thus, the game suggests that the best outcome for any one negotiator (prisoner) is to engage in competitive behavior (*i.e.*, to confess and serve no jail time) when the other engages in cooperative behavior (*i.e.*, does not confess and receives a 10-year sentence). The game also suggests that if both negotiators engage in cooperative behavior (*i.e.*, both do not confess), a reasonable, albeit less than ideal result occurs (*i.e.*, both get a 1-year sentence). If both engage in competitive behavior (*i.e.*, both confess), the result is largely undesirable for both (*i.e.*, both get a 7-year sentence).

There is extensive literature analyzing what happens when two players repeatedly play the game.[5] One prominent theorist held two computer tournaments in which professional and amateur game theorists submitted computer programs to compete against one another in repeated plays of the Prisoner's Dilemma where the number of rounds was not predetermined. The winner was the simplest of all strategies submitted, "Tit for Tat." Under this strategy, the player started out by cooperating and then did whatever the opposing

5. *See, e.g.*, Roger B. Myerson, *Game Theory: Analysis of Conflict*, 308–310, 337–42 (1991); Jean-Francois Mertens, "Repeated Games," in *The New Palgrave: Game Theory* 205 (1989); R. Duncan Luce & H. Raiffa, *Games and Decisions: Introduction and Critical Survey*, 97-102 (1957).

player did on the previous move. In this way, Tit for Tat used cooperation at first instance, but switched to competitive behavior (defection) in response to competitive moves by the other side.[6]

Along with different variations on the Prisoner's Dilemma, numerous other games and game-theoretic models have been developed to illustrate and analyze the tension between cooperative and competitive behavior.[7] These heuristics necessarily operate within the somewhat artificial "rules of the game." For example, most of the games involve only two parties who are the principals to the negotiation, and thus there is no accounting for the involvement of agents such as lawyers[8] or the involvement of third-party neutrals such as mediators. The games also heavily restrict other circumstances attendant to the negotiation, such as the type and number of potential outcomes or payoffs, the extent to which the players are able to communicate with one another, and the choice of strategies that may be employed (*e.g.*, cooperating or competing by "defecting"). There are usually no time constraints, and the bargainers are only concerned about the instant negotiation to the exclusion of factors such as past or future dealings between the parties, linkage to other transactions or problems faced by the parties, or the effects of establishing precedents through settlements, and the like. Finally, the controls placed over the form of the game may diminish the importance of individual and interpersonal variables such as emotion, irrationality, and the personal situations of the parties, which are often paramount in both deal-making and resolving disputes through negotiation.[9]

For these reasons, some have pointed to the limits of game theory's power to predict real world outcomes or to outline a path to achieving consistently better ones. As one scholar tactfully put it:

---

6. *See* R. Axelrod, *The Evolution of Cooperation* 27–54 (1984); D. Lax & J. Sebenius, *The Manager as Negotiator: Bargaining for Cooperation and Competitive Gain* 157–160 (1986).

7. *See, e.g.*, O. Young, Bargaining (1975) (summarizing various game-theoretic and economic models); James P. Kahan, "Experimental Studies of Bargaining as Analogues of Civil Disputes," (Rand Paper Series, Rand Corp. 1983) (bilateral monopoly game and others); H.M. Kritzer, *Let's Make a Deal* 88–98 (1991) (summarizing various models); J. Rubin & B. Brown, *The Social Psychology of Bargaining and Negotiation* 19–32 (1975) (summarizing various games).

8. *See* R.J. Gilson & R.H. Mnookin, Disputing Through Agents: Cooperation and Conflict Between Lawyers in Litigation, 94 Colum. L. Rev. 509 (1994).

9. *See* H. Scott Bierman & Luis Fernandez, *Game Theory with Economic Applications*, 68–70 (1993); H. Raiffa, *The Art and Science of Negotiation* 3–4, 54 (1982).

> One criticism of [game-theoretic analysis], to put it bluntly, is that it often represents a "painful elaboration of the obvious." In fact, what appears to be obvious in retrospect is frequently less clear before the elaboration. More important, the game theoretic models serve to systematize what are often disparate bits and pieces of common wisdom (and perhaps wisdom that is not so common) and to provide a useful, albeit perhaps only heuristic, framework for thinking about bargaining. Such models also point to the basic fact that negotiations do involve a substantial component of gamesmanship.[10]

§2.04 Economic Approaches

Negotiation has often been viewed through the lens of economic analysis.[11] Such analysis tends to focus on a "cost-benefit" approach to understanding the process and outcomes of negotiations, particularly when money is the predominant or exclusive subject of the negotiation. In negotiations involving business transactions where there is no legal dispute to be resolved, strict economic analysis would propose that straightforward economic considerations dictate the course and outcome of bargaining, based upon the extent to which the parties believe that a deal would be profitable. In the context of negotiations to resolve a legal dispute, economic theory posits that the likelihood of a settlement depends on the extent to which the parties calculate or otherwise perceive that the benefit to be achieved by settling the case outweighs the likely "cost" of resolving the dispute through litigation.

In a transactional negotiation, for example the sale of car, economic analysis predicts that a deal will be made, indeed should be made, if the bottom lines of the parties create a "zone of overlap," where the minimum amount the seller will accept is less than the maximum amount the buyer will pay. In a legal dispute, the calculation is similar but somewhat more complex because the parties must compare the value of a settlement, which is certain, with the uncertain but potentially better outcome that might be had from winning the case in court.[12] In a legal dispute, these bottom-line amounts, often referred

10. H. M. Kritzer, *Let's Make a Deal*, 92–93 (1991).

11. *See* O. Young, *Bargaining* (1975) (summarizing a number of classical economic models).

12. *See generally* Richard A. Posner, An Economic Approach to Legal Procedure and Judicial Administration, 2 J. Legal Studies 399 (1973); Alan E. Friedman, An Analysis of

to as "resistance points," can be the result of calculating an "*expected value*" of the case. This is done by multiplying the gross outcome that could be obtained at trial by the probability of achieving that outcome, and then subtracting (for plaintiffs) or adding (for defendants) the non-shiftable costs that would be incurred in obtaining that outcome ("transaction costs").

For a simple example:

If the Plaintiff estimates that the gross outcome he could obtain at trial is $100,000, that he has approximately a 75% chance of obtaining such a verdict in light of the particular circumstances of the case, and that it will cost him approximately $5,000 in non-shiftable litigation expenses to obtain that verdict, his bottom-line settlement amount or resistance point would be $70,000 (*i.e.*, $100,000 ×.75 = $75,000; $75,000 − $5,000 = $70,000).

On the other hand, the Defendant might estimate that Plaintiff has only a 60% chance of obtaining $100,000 at trial, and that it will cost her (the Defendant) $20,000 in non-shiftable expenses to try the case. Thus, her bottom line or resistance point would be to pay Plaintiff no more than $80,000 to settle the case (*i.e.*, $100,000 ×.60 = $60,000; $60,000 ∓ $20,000 = $80,000).

Here, because the minimum amount the Plaintiff will accept, $70,000, is less than the maximum amount the Defendant will pay, $80,000, a settlement is theoretically possible within the $10,000 zone of overlap between $70,000 and $80,000.

A fundamental difficulty in using this analysis to determine "what the case is worth" lies in accurately predicting the gross amount that a jury might award and the probability that such a verdict would be realized. In addition, the amount of non-shiftable litigation costs in a given case may be quite difficult to estimate. To some extent, these uncertainties may be mathematically taken into account if each party considers a variety of possible jury verdicts (*e.g.*, from $0 to $10,000 to $20,000, etc. up to $100,000), assigns a probability to each (where the total of the percentages equals 100%), multiplies each possible jury verdict by the particular probability assigned to it to arrive at a set of "expected values," and then adds the expected values together to arrive at an overall expected outcome. The same procedure could be followed to arrive at an overall estimate of expected costs. The expected costs would then be subtracted from the plaintiff's expected outcome or added to the expected outcome for the defendant. However, the prophetic accuracy of this method of calculation remains contingent on the accuracy of the probabilities assigned to

---

Settlement, 22 Stanford L. Rev. 67 (1969); John P. Gould, An Economic Analysis of Legal Conflicts, 2 J. Legal Studies 279 (1973).

different possible jury verdicts and cost estimates. Moreover, and perhaps most importantly, the utility of this method is often limited by the unwillingness of the parties or their lawyers, often for good reason, to think of their case in these purely arithmetic terms.

Apart from the difficulty of arriving at an expected value in which the parties can have a high level of confidence, numerous other uncertainties affecting the negotiation and potential settlement cannot be captured in purely economic or mathematical analysis of the case. For example, the extent to which the parties are psychologically willing to gamble on going to trial, commonly referred to as risk aversion or risk tolerance, may have a profound impact on the negotiating process and its outcome. Economic analysis struggles to account for the personal reasons and emotions driving a dispute that might explain why a party would prefer a trial or a settlement of the case. The history of the dispute, the relationship between the parties, and the particular concession behavior of a party during negotiation may significantly affect the attitude and behavior of the other party. In various ways, economic theorists are struggling to incorporate these and other variables into intricate mathematical models in an on-going effort to understand different types of negotiations and their potential outcomes.[13]

The foregoing discussion of economic theory has assumed a type of bargaining that is frequently called "distributive" bargaining, having a "zero-sum" nature. That is, where there is a single issue such as money, the consequence of negotiating is that the more money or gain one side gets, the less the other side gets.[14] Another line of economic theory, however, conceptualizes "integrative" bargaining, having "positive-sum" results. Here,

> ... [in] such bargaining, in which there are two parties and several issues to be negotiated, ... [t]he parties are not strict competitors. It is no longer true that if one party gets more, the other necessarily has to get less; they both can get more. They can cooperate in order to enlarge the pie that they eventually will have to divide.[15]

One way of conceptualizing integrative bargaining is through the model of the so-called "efficient frontier" or "Pareto Optimal Frontier," developed by the

---

13. For an excellent summary of many of these models, *see* Robert D. Cooter & Daniel T. Rubinfield, Economic Analysis of Legal Disputes and Their Resolution, 27 J. Econ. Literature 1067 (1989).

14. H. Raiffa, *The Art and Science of Negotiation* 33 (1982).

15. H. Raiffa, *The Art and Science of Negotiation* 131 (1982).

Italian economist Vilfredo Pareto.[16] This model may be graphically represented as follows:[17]

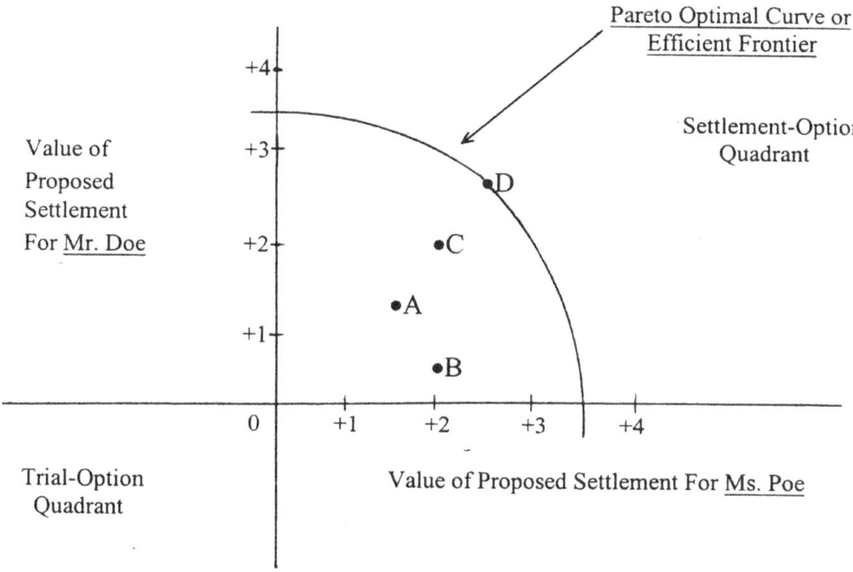

In this graph, the point symbols designated by • with their accompanying letters represent different settlement proposals. The horizontal axis represents increases in the value of a settlement proposal for Ms. Poe in an easterly direction, and the vertical axis represents increases in the value of a settlement proposal for Mr. Doe in a northerly direction. A settlement proposal perceived by one or both of the parties to be of less value than what could be obtained at trial would not give rise to a settlement and would fall within the southwest "Trial Option Quadrant." The parties will only settle the case if a particular proposal falls within the northeast quadrant.

Within this "Settlement-Option Quadrant," there are theoretically three types of settlement proposals that could be made: (1) proposals that are of greater value to one party but simultaneously reduce value to the other party, (2) proposals that are of greater value to one party but do not reduce value

16. *See* H. Raiffa, *The Art and Science of Negotiation*, 138–142, 148–165 (1982).

17. This graph is adapted from the one found in Jonathan M. Hyman, Trial Advocacy and Methods of Negotiation: Can Good Trial Advocates be Wise Negotiators?, 34 UCLA L. Rev. 879 n.34 (1987).

to the other, or (3) proposals that are of *maximum* value to each party without reducing value to any party. The latter settlement proposals are said to be "Pareto-optimal" or most "efficient." That is, at some level, it will not be possible to fashion a settlement that will increase value for at least one party without reducing value to the other, and this level is represented by the "Pareto Optimal Curve or Efficient Frontier." Thus, no settlements exist to the north or east of the curve, but from any position within the area bounded by the curve it is theoretically possible to find a settlement along the curve line that is better for at least one party without reducing value to the other.

For example, if, after Mr. Doe has proposed a settlement of comparable value to both parties at point A, Ms. Poe proposes a settlement at point B which is of greater value to her, the latter proposal will be rejected by Mr. Doe because it reduces the value of the settlement he would have received through proposal A. If either party thereafter proposes a settlement at point C, such a settlement would be more efficient than B because proposal C would increase value for Mr. Doe without decreasing value for Ms. Poe. In this way, proposal C is said to be "pareto superior" to proposals A or B. However, a settlement at point C is not "pareto optimal" in the face of proposal D that would be of yet further value to both parties without reducing value to any one party.

The theory of the efficient frontier is that where the parties are bargaining over a number of issues rather than merely the question of how much money one party will pay and the other will get, an optimal settlement is one that provides the most gain to each party without diminishing the value received by any one of them. The theory presupposes and prescribes that the parties explore and share their various interests, needs, goals, and values underlying the subject matter of the negotiation. In this way, they are more likely to arrive at an optimal settlement that is of greater net benefit to both of them than would otherwise be the case if they engaged in myopic "positional" bargaining without taking into account their underlying interests, needs, goals, and values.

As a simple example, if Ms. Poe and Mr. Doe are in a dispute about custody, child support, and alimony, Ms. Poe's initial position might be that she will have sole "legal and physical custody" of their child, that Mr. Doe must pay her $X in child support, and that he should pay $Y in fault-based alimony each month because he committed adultery. Mr. Poe's initial position might be that he should have sole custody of the parties' child or will pay only $Z in child support if Ms. Poe has custody, and in no event will he pay any alimony notwithstanding his adultery. If the parties essentially maintain these initial positions and limit their bargaining solely to the payment amounts regarding child support and alimony, they might never reach agreement. On the other hand, if they share their underlying interests, needs, goals, and values with one another (*e.g.*, through their lawyers or a mediator), they may be successful in reaching an agreement that each perceives to have more positive-sum than zero-sum aspects. For instance, the parties might agree to have "joint legal custody" of their child with Ms. Poe having primary "physical" custody, and Mr. Doe might agree to pay more in child support than he otherwise was willing to pay (or would statutorily be obligated to pay) in exchange for Ms. Poe's agreement to forego receiving any alimony. In short, these various tradeoffs between the parties will more closely reflect the differing needs and values that the parties place upon parental status, the most appropriate care for their child, the relative importance of admitting fault in the break up of the marriage, and considerations of immediate or longer-term financial security for the child and/or the spouses.

This multi-dimensional approach of integrative bargaining as conceptualized through the search for pareto-optimal settlements has become commonly referred to as "problem-solving" negotiation in contrast to purely distributive, "adversarial" negotiation.[18] The attributes and limitations of each approach have been vigorously debated among scholars.[19] This debate should remind students of negotiation that many negotiations are primarily, if not exclusively, concerned with how much money one party will receive, the "fixed pie," while others present opportunities to achieve greater mutual satisfaction by working together to expand or enlarge the pie by fashioning solutions that place a premium on satisfying both sides' true interests, needs, goals, and values.

§2.05 Anthropological & Sociological Approaches

Much of the anthropological and sociological literature in regard to negotiation has focused on process, identifying and exploring typologies of negotiating that are, for the most part, descriptive. These typologies tend to combine analyses of the structure of negotiations with analyses of different

18. *See generally*, R. Fisher & W. Ury, *Getting to Yes* (1981); C. Menkel-Meadow, Toward Another View of Legal Negotiation: The Structure of Problem Solving, 31 UCLA L. Rev. 784 (1984).

19. *Cf., e.g.*, James J. White, Review Essay: The Pros and Cons of "Getting to Yes" by Roger Fisher & William Ury, 31 J. Legal Education 115 (1981) *with* Roger Fisher, Comment on James White's Review of "Getting to Yes," 31 J. Legal Education 128 (1981).

styles of negotiating used within those structures to explore the interrelationship between the ends and means involved in negotiating.

For example, one prominent anthropologist has developed a seven-phase model of the negotiating process based upon research in a variety of cultural settings.[20] These phases may be summarized as follows:

1. The search for an arena. The negotiators begin by choosing a forum to engage in negotiations, whether that forum is a particular place where discussions are held in person or the circumstances under which the negotiation will take place, *i.e.*, over the telephone, via the internet, or in writing.
2. Composition of agenda and definition of issues. The negotiators decide what issues need to be addressed and the agenda for the negotiation.
3. Establishing maximal limits to issues in dispute. The negotiators limit the key issues and stake out their positions on those issues.
4. Narrowing the Differences. The negotiators begin to narrow their differences, and the negotiation shifts from differences and antagonism to coordination and even cooperation. When multiple issues are involved, differences are narrowed through strategies such as following a simple agenda, focusing on the most important issues, reducing issues to the attributes of a single objective, solving the less difficult issues, and/or considering matters to trade or package deals.
5. Preliminaries to final bargaining. To the extent that the negotiators, in the process of narrowing their differences, identify sub-issues or other matters that need to be resolved to reach an agreement, information is exchanged and these issues are also addressed to bring the negotiators closer to final agreement.
6. Final bargaining. The negotiators close the deal, disposing of the few issues or problems that remain to be resolved.
7. Ritual Affirmation. Upon reaching a final agreement, the negotiators engage in any customary ritual that acknowledges or memorializes it, whether a simple hand shake, elaborate ceremony, or celebration.

---

20. P.H. Gulliver, *Disputes and Negotiations: A Cross-Cultural Perspective* (1979).

This anthropological model was developed from a cross-cultural perspective. In the context of negotiating legal disputes, one scholar has reduced the negotiating process to a series of four stages that roughly complement the phases set out above. Those stages are:

1. "orientation and positioning" (during which the negotiating attorneys establish a relationship and their opening positions);
2. "argumentation" (during which the attorneys present their positions in the light most favorable to their respective side, define the issues, seek to discover the "real" position of the other side, and make concessions);
3. "emergence and crisis" (during which the attorneys recognize that one or both of them must make further concessions to prevent deadlock, further concessions are made, "crisis" is reached when neither side wants to make yet further concessions, and one of the parties either accepts the other's final offer or an impasse occurs); and
4. "agreement or final breakdown" (during which a settlement is formalized if an agreement is reached, or a decision is made to go to trial if no agreement is reached).[21] Taken together, the cross-cultural and legal typologies provide an overall portrait of the major features of the process of negotiating from initial discussions to final agreement.

In addition, much of the sociological literature (and legal literature) has been devoted to identifying key variables or factors that permeate or differentiate negotiations. Among the more important factors that have been routinely discussed include:[22]

- The effects of the location where the negotiation takes place and the particular physical arrangements at the site of negotiations;

---

21. Gerald R. Williams, *Legal Negotiation and Settlement* 70–72 (1983).

22. *See generally*, J. Rubin & B. Brown, *The Social Psychology of Bargaining and Negotiation* (1975); D. Druckman, *Negotiations: Social Psychological Perspectives* (1977); S. Bacharach & E. Lawley, *Bargaining: Power, Tactics, and Outcomes* (1981); A. Strauss, *Negotiations: Varieties, Contexts, Processes and Social Order* 237–238 (1978); H. Raiffa, *The Art and Science of Negotiation* 11–19 (1982); G. Lowenthal, A General Theory of Negotiation Process, Strategy, and Behavior, 31 U. Kan. L. Rev. 69 (1982); C. Menkel-Meadow, Review Essay: Legal Negotiation: A Study of Strategies in Search of a Theory, 4 Am. Bar. Found. J. 927–928 (1983).

- The number of parties involved in the negotiation and whether any coalitions exist;
- The number and complexity of the issues involved in the negotiation;
- The nature of the stakes in the negotiation;
- The effect of time constraints or time-related costs on the parties;
- The relative bargaining power possessed by the parties;
- Whether the negotiations are public or private;
- Whether there are any persons other than the parties ("audiences") to whom the negotiators are beholden or accountable, or whether there are any constituencies that may be affected by the negotiation;
- Whether a third-party neutral assists or intervenes in the negotiation;
- Whether the negotiations are one-shot or multiple events, or are linked;
- The effects on the negotiation of any continuing relationships between the parties or their negotiators after the negotiation is concluded;
- The alternatives available to the parties in the absence of reaching an agreement;
- The personalities of the parties and their negotiators;
- The interests, needs, goals, and values of the parties and their negotiators;
- The extent of information sharing between the parties and their negotiators, and their ability to communicate with one another.

Another major line of research and analysis concerns the impact of the negotiator's *style* or strategy upon his or her *effectiveness* and the outcome of negotiations. Much of this research has attempted to compare the effectiveness of negotiators who adopt a "cooperative" approach to bargaining (*e.g.*, by "seeking common ground" and "communicating a sense of shared interests, values, and attitudes using rational logical persuasion as a means... to reach a fair resolution of the conflict based on an objective analysis of the facts and law..."[23]) with those who employ a "competitive" approach (*e.g.*, by making high initial demands, maintaining a high level of demands during negotiations, making

23. Gerald R. Williams, *Legal Negotiation and Settlement* 53 (1983).

few and small concessions, and having a general high level of aspiration).[24] One study of negotiator "effectiveness" that took into account such matters as the cost of the negotiations, the comprehensiveness of a settlement, the satisfaction of both parties, the quality of the outcome, and fidelity to the accepted "rules of the game," concluded that cooperative negotiators are generally more effective than competitive negotiators. However, the author of this same study ultimately concluded, "neither pattern has an exclusive claim on effectiveness. Use of the cooperative pattern does not guarantee effectiveness, any more than does the use of the competitive pattern. An attorney can be very effective or very ineffective within the constraints of either."[25]

A number of scholars have suggested that a competitive negotiator will achieve better outcomes when pitted against a cooperative negotiator, particularly if the latter does not recognize his counterpart's competitive tactics.[26] This is because, given that competitive negotiators tend to take tougher positions and make fewer concessions, it has been statistically shown that "[h]igh initial demands (relative to stakes) by plaintiffs and low initial offers (again, relative to stakes) by defendants are related to [more positive] success for the relevant side."[27] However, when the negotiators for both sides take the same approach, whether competitive or cooperative, there would not seem to be any theoretical reason why one style should lead to consistently better outcomes when the only issue is money.

---

24. Id. *See also* D. G. Gifford, A Context-based Theory of Strategy Selection in Legal Negotiation, 46 Ohio St. L. J. 41 (1985) (distinguishing "cooperative," "competitive," and "integrative"); G.T. Lowenthal, A General Theory of Negotiation Process, Strategy and Beahvior, 31 U. Kan. L. Rev. 69 (1982) (distinguishing between "competition" and "collaboration"); D. Lax & J. Sebenius, *The Manager as Negotiator: Bargaining for Cooperation and Competitive Gain* (1987) (distinguishing between negotiating to "claim value" and to "create value"); H. Raiffa, *The Art and Science of Negotiation* (distinguishing between "distributive" and "integrative" bargaining).

25. *See* Gerald R. Williams, *Legal Negotiation and Settlement* 18–19 (1983).

26. *See* Gerald R. Williams, *Legal Negotiation and Settlement* 54 (1983); Gary T. Lowenthal, A General Theory of Negotiation Process, Strategy, and Behavior, 31 U. Kan. L. Rev. 82–83, 109–110 (1982); Donald G. Gifford, A Context-Based Theory of Strategy Selection in Legal Negotiation, 46 Ohio St. L. J. 60–62 (1985); Hazel Genn, *Hard Bargaining: Out of Court Settlement in Personal Injury Actions* 48 (1988).

27. H. M. Kritzer, *Let's Make a Deal* 54, 79 (1991).

§2.06 Psychological Approaches and Factors

The psychological theories that are most often drawn upon in the academic literature about negotiating relate to how people communicate with one another and how negotiators can overcome common barriers to effective communication. Another line of psychological theory examines how people make decisions under conditions of stress and uncertainty. Because negotiations usually require parties to make choices under circumstances of risk, some of the more important psychological factors affecting such decision-making are briefly highlighted here.

[1] Risk Aversion or Risk Tolerance

A critical factor in a party's decision whether to settle a legal dispute may be their willingness to gamble that the alternative to settlement—taking the case to trial—will yield a better result than the one on the table in a negotiation or mediation. Risk aversion, or its converse, risk tolerance, is merely an expression of the degree to which a party is psychologically inclined or disinclined to take risk.

In the litigation context, a risk-averse plaintiff is one who theoretically will settle the case for something less than his calculation of the "expected outcome" for the case (*i.e.*, his estimate of the gross outcome that could be obtained at trial multiplied by the probability that the gross outcome will occur). That is, when faced with a final settlement offer, if Plaintiff estimates that there is a 75% chance of obtaining a $100,000 verdict at trial (*i.e.*, an expected outcome of $75,000), he will reduce that expected outcome further by an amount that reflects his aversion to risking a worse outcome at trial. This discount would be in addition to the non-shiftable litigation costs that he would subtract from the expected outcome to arrive at his potential bottom-line settlement amount (resistance point). Similarly, a risk-averse Defendant will theoretically settle the case for something more than her calculation of the expected outcome for the case. That is, along with adding the estimated litigation costs to her calculation of the expected outcome, Defendant will make a further adjustment to the bottom-line settlement amount she is willing to pay to reflect her aversion to risking a worse result at trial. In short, the parties' bottom-line settlement amounts are often adjusted downwards (for plaintiffs) and upwards (for defendants) if they averse to the risks of going to trial.

Of course, a party might be risk neutral or risk tolerant. If a party is risk neutral, that party, in theory, will make no adjustment of the sort described above. If the Plaintiff is risk tolerant, he might adjust his bottom-line settlement demand *upwards*, not downwards; and if the Defendant is a risk preferer, she might adjust her bottom-line settlement offer *downwards*, not upwards. Most significantly, if one party is risk averse and the other is more tolerant of risk, the latter will have an advantage over the former in that the latter will theoretically be able to extract greater concessions from the former than would otherwise be the case.

This advantage frequently exists where one party is a "repeat player" in the type of litigation involved, and the other party is a "one-shot" player.[28] For example, in personal injury cases, an insurance company—which for all practical purposes is the paying defendant in such cases—is a repeat player because it is involved in settling and litigating personal injury claims all the time. On the other hand, the injured plaintiff is a one-shot player. The important difference between the parties is that the insurance company has experience and significant financial resources available to it that may not be available to the plaintiff, particularly if she is represented by an inexperienced lawyer or one who is not willing or able to advance the costs of the litigation. As a repeat player, the insurance company may be risk neutral (or even a risk preferer) because any loss resulting from a particular case will, at some level, be offset by wins in other cases. However, the injured plaintiff may be more risk averse because she has only "one shot" at receiving compensation; there is no averaging out of wins and losses over a series of cases. Thus, if the insurance company has a lower aversion to risk than the plaintiff, the company is likely to hold out for a settlement on its own terms.

A person's risk aversion sometimes depends upon whether the risk is perceived as one of gaining or losing a sum of money. There is growing research to indicate that a party who perceives her situation in terms of losing money will often prefer to gamble to avoid what otherwise would be a sure loss, even if the expected loss from the gamble is larger. On the other hand, a party who perceives her situation in terms of gaining money will usually be less inclined to gamble on obtaining a greater amount, even if the expected gain from the gamble is larger. That is, parties who stand to lose money may have

---

28. *See* D. Wittman, Dispute Resolution, Bargaining, and the Selection of Cases for Trial: A Study of the Generation of Biased and Unbiased Data, 17 J. Legal Studies 322 (1988); M. Galanter, Why the 'Haves' Come Out Ahead: Speculations on the Limits of Legal Change, 9 Law & Society Review 95 (1974).

a tendency to be "loss averse" and risk preferring—more willing to prevent or minimize loss by taking their chances at trial; but parties who stand to gain money are generally more risk averse—less willing to gamble on getting more money at trial.[29]

As an example of this phenomenon, suppose that a person is faced with the choice of (a) a sure gain of $15,000, or (b) an 80% chance of winning $20,000 and 20% chance of getting $0. Here, even though the expected value of choice (b) is $16,000 (*i.e.*, .80 × $20,000 ∓ .20 × $0), most people would choose the sure gain of $15,000. On the other hand, if a person is given the choice of (a) a sure loss of $15,000, or (b) an 80% chance of losing $20,000 and a 20% chance of losing nothing, studies suggest that most people will choose option (b).[30] To the extent this phenomenon is at work in a particular case, it suggests that, absent other factors that might affect the parties' risk preferences, plaintiffs will generally opt to accept a smaller gain through settlement rather than gamble on winning a larger sum at trial, whereas defendants will be more prone to risk a larger possible loss at trial in lieu of incurring a sure, albeit smaller, loss by settling a disputed case.[31]

[2] Reference Points and Framing Effects

Whether one views a matter as a gain or loss largely depends upon one's "reference point" (*i.e.*, the situation from which the gain or loss is measured) and how the matter is "framed" (*i.e.*, whether the issue, problem, or choice

---

29. *See* P. J. van Koppen, Risk Taking in Civil Law Negotiations, 14 Law and Human Behavior 151–167 (1990); Amos Tversky & Richard Thaler, Anomalies Preference Reversals, 4 J. Econ. Perspectives 201 (1990); Amos Tversky, et. al., The Causes of Preference Reversals, 80 Am. Econ. Rev. 204 (1990); Robert H. Mnookin, Why Negotiations Fail: An Exploration of Barriers to the Resolution of Conflict, 8 Ohio St. J. Disp. Res. 243–245 (1993); M. Neal & M. Bazerman, The Effects of Framing and Negotiator Overconfidence on Bargaining Behaviors and Outcomes, 28 Acad. Mgmt. J. 34, 37–38 (1985).

30. *See* G. Goodpaster, Rational Decision-Making in Problem-Solving Negotiation: Compromise, Interest-Valuation, and Cognitive Error, 8 Ohio St. J. Disp. Res. 346–347 (1993).

31. *See* H. M. Kritzer, *Let's Make a Deal* 76 n. 19 (1991). This is not always the case, however. New lawyers are sometimes surprised at the willingness of their personal injury clients to "roll the dice" or "swing for the fences." This may happen when the plaintiff believes that losing her case, no matter how likely, would not change her life in any significant way but winning the case, no matter how unlikely, would have a great impact. It must be remembered that risk is not merely the likelihood of an outcome but the magnitude of its effect.

is presented as a "gain" or "loss").[32] This is also true in negotiating. A party will view a particular proposal as a gain or loss (which, in turn, may affect that party's level of risk aversion) based on that party's reference point—usually his resistance point—and the manner in which the proposal is framed. Thus, negotiators routinely try to induce one another to change their resistance points and risk preferences by "framing" the situation in terms of gain or loss as best suits the negotiators' respective objectives.

For example, in buyer-seller negotiations, the seller may prevail upon the buyer to purchase an item for an amount that the buyer thinks he cannot afford (a loss) by characterizing the purchase as an "investment" (a gain). Similarly, a worker may be convinced to switch jobs in the face of taking a pay cut (a loss) if she is made to see the new job as a stepping stone to greater, long-term career advancement (a gain). On the other hand, a bargainer might seek to emphasize what she stands to lose from a particular proposal in order to induce the other party to forgo a greater gain, or, more frequently, emphasize what the other party stands to lose if she is unwilling to make further concessions. In either case, the overriding effort is to manipulate the other party's perspective on the situation in terms of acquiring gain or incurring loss.

Another implication of framing a proposal as an opportunity to maximize gain (which may cause a party to be risk averse) or minimize loss (which may cause a party to be loss averse) is that a party seeking to maximize gain may take a more cooperative approach to the negotiation to achieve a settlement in preference to going to trial, whereas a party seeking to minimize loss may take a more competitive approach due to a greater willingness to take the case to trial. In adversarial bargaining, where a gain to one side is viewed as a corresponding loss to the other, a party who is loss averse and thus risk-preferring and more competitive is likely to have an advantage in the negotiation if the other party is risk averse and thus more cooperative. On the other hand, the parties might take a problem-solving approach to the negotiation, in which case each would cooperate with one another by viewing the negotiation as an opportunity for both parties to maximize gain and minimize loss. In theory, the potential effects of these different factors on a settlement may be illustrated by the following matrix:

32. *See generally*, D. Kahneman, et. al., *Judgment Under Uncertainy: Heuristics and Biases* (1982); D. Kahneman & A. Tversky, Prospect Theory: An Analysis of Decision Under Risk, 47 Econometrica 263 (1979).

		Jones	
		Maximize Gain	Minimize Loss
Smith	Maximize Gain	Problem Solving Smith is risk neutral & cooperative Jones is risk neutral & cooperative (Better settlement for both)	Adversarial Bargaining Smith is risk averse & cooperative Jones is loss averse (risk preferring) & competitive (Better settlement for Jones)
	Minimize Loss	Adversarial Bargaining Smith is loss averse (risk preferring) & competitive Jones is risk averse & cooperative (Better settlement for Smith)	Problem Solving Smith is risk neutral & cooperative Jones is risk neutral & cooperative (Better settlement for both)

[3] Sunk Costs

A common psychological barrier to rational decision-making under conditions of uncertainty is the tendency to allow past events, which one cannot change, to govern one's choices about the future. In negotiations, this barrier frequently occurs when one or both of the parties becomes entrapped by "sunk costs"—*i.e.*, losses or costs already incurred that the party vainly seeks to recoup in making a choice about settlement or trial.[33]

For example, before attempting to settle a case, the parties may have incurred substantial expenditures in pretrial litigation. If they have become psychologically entrapped by these investments, they may forgo any possibility of settling the case out of a belief that going to trial is the only way to justify or recoup that investment. In this way, the parties may only escalate the conflict, persist in spiraling litigation, and end up sustaining losses that far surpass the benefits of any favorable trial outcome. Conversely, a party may become psychologically entrapped by the time, effort, and resources expended in seeking to settle the case. Unwilling to abandon this investment, the party might irrationally agree upon a settlement that ends up costing far more than the alternative of going to trial.[34]

In short, rational decision-making generally involves an assessment of the benefits that may be realized or losses that may be minimized when looking toward the future, rather than the past. Past events or investments, to the extent

33. *See* Robyn M. Dawes, *Rational Choice in an Uncertain World* 22 (1988).

34. *See* Charles B. Craver, *Effective Legal Negotiation and Settlement* 277–278 (3d ed. 1997).

they are truly "sunk" in the sense that they cannot be realistically recouped through a settlement or some reasonable alternative to a negotiated agreement, should be abandoned unless there is some other, overriding reason to honor those past events or investments.[35]

[4] Reactive Devaluation

The phenomenon of "reactive devaluation" relates to the sometimes-irrational inferences that parties draw from one another's offers or concessions made during negotiations. This phenomenon, which is commonly observed and has been empirically verified, refers to the tendency of a party to devalue a settlement proposal or compromise simply because it originated with the other side.[36] That is, a compromise or concession made unilaterally by a party is often valued less highly than one that is initially withheld and subsequently extracted through reciprocal proposals or concessions. Thus, a party might reject a seemingly gratuitous offer that is beneficial to her by misinterpreting it as a sign of weakness by the other side that warrants yet greater concessions from the other side. This misinterpretation may, in turn, result in a gross miscalculation that causes an otherwise desirable settlement to end in deadlock.

Reactive devaluation is not to be confused with a reasoned assessment about what a party's particular proposal means about his overall approach to the negotiation and concession behavior. For example, depending upon the overall context in which it is made, a unilateral concession may be a good indicator of the conceding party's resistance point. However, to *automatically* devalue a proposal or concession solely because the other side makes it is irrational. Thus, a party who is the recipient of such a proposal should act upon it to the extent it advances her objectives, rather than allow her objectives to be undermined by a gut reaction that is based on purely speculative assumptions about the other side's motives in making the proposal.

If a party is concerned that his proposal may be erroneously devalued by the other side, he might frame it as emanating from some objective criterion such as an independent standard, custom, rule, or measure of damage under applicable law, rather than as stemming from his purely individual intentions. Alternatively, any effect of reactive devaluation is likely to be greatly dimin-

---

35. *See* G. Goodpaster, Rational Decision-Making in Problem-Solving Negotiation: Compromise, Interest-Valuation, and Cognitive Error, 8 Ohio St. J. Disp. Res. 356 (1993).

36. *See* R. H. Mnookin, Why Negotiations Fail: An Exploration of Barriers to the Resolution of Conflict, 8 Ohio St. J. Disp. Res. 246–247 (1993).

ished if the proposal is communicated through a third-party neutral such as a mediator.

§2.07 Translating Academic Approaches into Practice

The foregoing summary of the major academic approaches to understanding negotiation underscores the fact that the study of negotiation is essentially an interdisciplinary field. There is no single discipline or intellectual perspective that has a monopoly on useful insights into the subject, and likewise there is no single theory, model, or typology that is most descriptive and instructive about it. However, taken together, the various academic approaches provide a useful introduction to learning about negotiating because they help us to understand *why* certain negotiations are successful when others are not.

By the same token, the academic approaches are useful from a prescriptive standpoint. That is, understanding the fundamental dynamics of negotiating also tells us a lot about *how* to negotiate effectively. For example, the game-theoretic interplay between cooperation and competition in bargaining implicates the relative merits of employing cooperative or competitive means in achieving problem-solving or adversarial ends to negotiating. The cost-benefit analyses underlying economic theory may be highly useful in valuing a case when choosing between the options of settlement or trial. The social-psychological literature is instructive about effective negotiating styles, tactics, and techniques that may be employed to foster rational decision-making under circumstances of risk and uncertainty. In short, in varying forms and degrees, all of these theoretical approaches may be translated into practical application.

Finally, as indicated at the outset of this Chapter, the academic research may encourage us to push the intellectual envelope to consider more expansive and imaginative approaches to negotiating. This is important because, as in the application of other practical skills, lawyers too often form the habit of adopting a single negotiating approach in client representation. Although a routine approach may be comfortable and workable in many circumstances, the genius of the most effective lawyers is their ability to adopt and adapt to different approaches to negotiation as may be warranted by the particular circumstances of a case. Encouraging this ingenuity is perhaps the most practical contribution of the academic literature.

Chapter Three

Negotiating Models, Strategies, and Styles

SYNOPSIS

§3.01 Introduction
§3.02 The Adversarial Model
§3.03 The Problem-Solving Model
§3.04 Factors Affecting the Utility of the Adversarial and Problem-Solving Models
  [1] The Nature of the Dispute or Problem
  [2] The Other Side's Negotiating Approach
  [3] Differences in Bargaining Leverage
  [4] Future Dealings Between the Parties or Negotiators
  [5] Pressures to Reach an Agreement
§3.05 Negotiating Strategies and Styles
§3.06 Competitive (Hardball) Style
§3.07 Cooperative (Softball) Style
§3.08 Competitive-Cooperative (Hardball and Softball) Style
§3.09 Choosing a Negotiating Style and Strategy
§3.10 Style and Strategy Combinations
  [1] Competitive and Adversarial
  [2] Cooperative (or Competitive-Cooperative) and Adversarial
  [3] Competitive and Problem-Solving
  [4] Cooperative (or Competitive-Cooperative) and Problem-Solving
§3.11 The Overall Importance of Flexibility and Credibility
§3.12 Summary of Style and Strategy Characteristics, Advantages, and Disadvantages

§3.01 Introduction

The current literature about the negotiating process has developed two distinct models of negotiation, and each is helpful in understanding what negotiators do and what they ought to do. Typically, these are denominated the adversarial or competitive model and the problem-solving or integrative model. These models are both descriptive and prescriptive and both are useful in bridging the gap between theory and practice. It is crucial for effective negotiators to be flexible in their approach to the process while maintaining personal and professional credibility. Included here is a summary of these two models, the choices of styles and strategies available to the negotiator, and the characteristics, advantages and disadvantages these choices present.

§3.02 The Adversarial Model

The adversarial model of negotiation (sometimes called "competitive," "zero-sum," "individualistic," or "distributive bargaining") is the most commonly used approach to legal negotiations. It focuses on "winning," that is, on maximizing the likelihood the client will prevail and what the client receives upon prevailing. Each side strives to get as much of the thing bargained for (usually money), and the more one side gets, the less the other side gets. Adversarial negotiators engage in a largely competitive and manipulative process in which a series of concessions is made from initial, polarized positions to arrive at a compromise point which is perceived to be either roughly equivalent to what a court would award or more desirable than taking the risk of what might happen in court.

Adversarial negotiation usually involves five stages. First, each party prepares for the negotiation by establishing her "target" and "resistance" points and estimating the target and resistance points of the other side. A "target point" is the best result a party realistically expects she can obtain, and her "resistance point" is the point below which she will not make any further concessions and will resort to her best alternative to negotiation, such as going to trial. From these target and resistance points, the parties plan their first offers (which are set somewhere beyond their target points) and establish their concession patterns in light of the ultimate "settlement zone" created by the overlap between the parties' resistance points.

For example, if P sues D for personal injuries sustained due to the alleged negligence of D, the parties' target and resistance points, first offers, concession patterns, and settlement zone may look like the following:

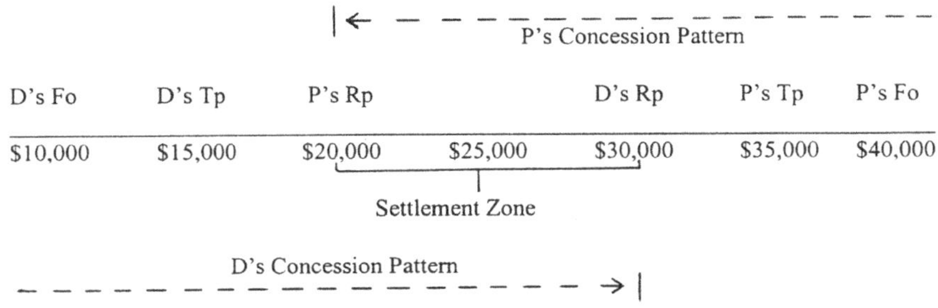

P's Fo = P's first offer
D's Fo = D's first offer
P's Tp = P's target point
D's Tp = D's target point
P's Rp = P's resistance point
D's Rp = D's resistance point

In the second stage, the parties define the issues and often make their first offers or proposals. Third, the parties exchange information in the course of presenting their varying positions and arguments in support of those positions. Fourth, they bargain toward compromise by analyzing and making concessions. And fifth, the parties conclude the negotiation by executing settlement documents or releases if an agreement has been reached, or, if no agreement can be reached, by resorting to their best alternative to negotiation.

The adversarial model is based on four assumptions. First, the model assumes that the parties desire the same goals, items, or values (*e.g.*, money). Second, the model assumes that the parties are in conflict because they are bargaining over the same "scarce" goals, items, or values. Third, it is assumed that the matters to be bargained for are limited to those that a court would award, whether money or something that the law may compel a party to do or not to do. Finally, the model assumes that the best solution is predicated upon a division of and compromise over the goals, items, or values at issue. As summarized by one scholar:

> The adversarial paradigm is based almost exclusively on the simple negotiation over what appears to be one issue, such as price in a buy-

> sell transaction, or money damages in a personal injury or breach of contract suit. The common assumption in these cases is that the buyer wants the lowest price, the seller the highest; the plaintiff wants the money demanded in the complaint and the defendant wants to resist paying as much as possible. Each dollar to the plaintiff is a commensurate loss to the defendant; the same is true with the buyer and seller. Given this description of the paradigmatic negotiation, the negotiator's goal is simply to maximize gain by winning as much of the material of the negotiation as possible. Underlying this general assumption are really two assumptions: first, that there is only one issue, price; and second, that both parties desire equally and exclusively the thing by which that issue is measured, in most cases, money.[1]

Critics of the adversarial model contend that its underlying assumptions and method of negotiating often limit the quality of the solution to the parties' problem or dispute. By assuming that they desire the same goals, items, or values (such as money) and therefore are limited to bargaining over the same scarce resource, the parties may overlook the fact that they really value these goals or items unequally or have completely different goals in mind. When these differences are not taken into account, the parties may fail to consider alternative solutions, such as trading a smaller sum of money for the performance of an act or service by the other side. Moreover, by assuming that the matters to be bargained for are limited to those that a court would award, the parties often limit their solutions to purely "legal" ones without considering extra-judicial alternatives that may better satisfy their goals, values, or needs.

For example, assume a former husband and wife are in dispute about an appropriate increase in the amount of alimony the wife should receive. The wife contends she needs $300 more per month than the husband says he can afford without straining his cash-flow situation. A strict application of the adversarial model may result in the parties splitting the difference at $150 more a month or some other amount they think a court might award. However, if the wife's underlying need for the additional $300 is to allow her to make payments on a new car over a two-year period, and the former husband is the owner of a car dealership, he may be able to give her a car from his inventory in exchange for the wife's agreement to forego a $300 increase in monthly support payments.

1. C. Menkel-Meadow, Toward Another View of Legal Negotiation: The Structure of Problem Solving, 31 U.C.L.A. L. Rev. 784 (1984).

In this way, the wife receives the item that is of greater value to her (the immediate use of a dependable car), and the husband obtains the goal that is most important to him (preserving his future cash-flow situation).

Critics of the adversarial model also contend that the process by which adversarial negotiations are conducted tends to undermine the quality of potential solutions in two ways. First, the process of exchanging offers, counteroffers, and concessions may not be helpful when the parties are faced with multiple issues. Second, the parties often experience adversarial negotiation as argumentative, manipulative, even deceptive, which may inhibit creativity in finding solutions. Even when an agreement is reached, an adversarial negotiation can leave the parties resentful and their relationship damaged.

§3.03 The Problem-Solving Model

The problem-solving model of negotiation (sometimes called "cooperative," "accommodative," "collaborative," or "integrative bargaining") calls upon the negotiator to focus on identifying the interests or needs that underlie the positions taken by the parties in a dispute. This is done to develop a broader range of potential solutions from which an agreement can be fashioned that satisfies as many of the parties' mutual needs as possible. Unlike the adversarial model, which emphasizes maximizing individual gain at the expense of the other side, problem solving emphasizes maximizing the parties' joint gain. Problem-solving negotiators engage in a largely cooperative and collaborative process that strives to create a mutually satisfactory solution that is not necessarily limited to traditional judicial remedies.

The problem-solving model is based on four assumptions. First, the model assumes that the usual objective of obtaining money damages is actually a proxy for more basic interests or needs apart from merely those things that money can buy. Second, the model assumes that the parties' interests or needs are often not mutually exclusive. Third, it assumes that by identifying the parties' underlying interests or needs, the parties can come up with a greater number of possible solutions. And fourth, the model assumes that by exploring a greater number of possible solutions, the parties are more likely to find a solution that mutually satisfies their interests or needs.

The problem-solving model has been described in five stages of so-called "principled negotiation."[2] First, the parties plan for the negotiation by identify-

---

2. *See* R. Fisher & W. Ury, *Getting to Yes* 4, 17–98 (1981).

ing each side's underlying interests or needs. These interests, which essentially constitute the underlying *reasons* for the parties' objectives or goals, are identified in light of the financial situation of the parties, their social and psychological needs, their moral perspectives, and the legal issues in the case.

Second, the parties make a conscientious effort to "separate the people from the problem"—a mindset that attacks the problem, not each other. Instead of focusing on stated "positions," they discuss and share information about each other's interests or needs to see where they are shared or in conflict.

Third, the parties engage in a "brainstorming" session to generate as many solutions as possible that may satisfy the interests or needs of both parties. Fourth, the parties choose the most reasoned solution that maximizes their mutual gain. Concessions might be made by trading off different interests or needs, and, where interests conflict, the parties strive to resolve their differences based on some objective standard (such as market values, expert opinions, customs, industry standards, or the law) which is independent of the naked will of either side. Finally, the parties conclude the negotiation by executing settlement documents or releases if an agreement is reached, or, if no agreement can be reached, by resorting to their "best alternative to a negotiated agreement" (BATNA) such as going to trial.

Even the strongest proponents of the problem-solving approach acknowledge its limitations. As summarized by one scholar:

> Several difficulties may confront the skeptical problem solver. First there is the problem of perceiving resources as finite. In some legal disputes, for example, a case involving a simple transfer of limited dollars or other valued items from one side to the other, it may appear impossible to expand what is available to both parties. A second barrier may be the perceived inequality of power between the negotiating parties. If one side has power in the legal, economic or psychological sense during the negotiation, the weaker party may have insufficient leverage to use problem-solving techniques where the stronger party knows it can gain a great deal by exercising power in a conventional negotiation. Third, an attempt to satisfy needs may itself thwart the problem-solving approach in a situation where, for example, one of the parties has a need for revenge or punishment. Fourth, there may be limited psychological resources. Where one of the parties is used to a competitive style of negotiation, the execution of a problem-solving method may be viewed as impossible unless the other party becomes a problem solver. Finally, a problem-solving model

based on a theory of needs has its own limitations. It will not solve all negotiation dilemmas, but it still offers a potentially more systematic and effective way of thinking about negotiation.[3]

§3.04 Factors Affecting the Utility of the Adversarial and Problem-Solving Models[4]

Many negotiations involve neither a purely adversarial nor a purely problem-solving approach. Thus, negotiators frequently use more than one of these approaches in a single negotiation. For example, the parties might start with an adversarial approach and then move to a problem-solving one, or they may apply different approaches to distinct issues in the case. While it sometimes may be psychologically difficult to shift between approaches, particularly when a highly competitive adversarial approach is taken at the outset and the parties then try to engage in problem solving after egos have been frayed or hurt, the willingness to be flexible in shifting one's approach often makes the difference between reaching and not reaching a satisfactory agreement.

In deciding which negotiating model may be most effective in a particular case, the following factors should be considered:

[1] The Nature of the Dispute or Problem

The nature of the parties' dispute or problem often has a significant impact on the relative effectiveness of the adversarial or problem-solving approach. For example, the adversarial model may be better suited when the parties are bargaining solely over a fixed and finite matter such as money. If the only issue is how much one party will pay the other, and the gain to one party will necessarily be at the expense of the other, this "zero-sum" controversy rarely provides an opportunity or incentive for the parties to collaborate in expanding the resources they might divide or trade to their mutual gain. Thus, if the only issue between a buyer and seller is the price of a single item, or the only

---

3. C. Menkel-Meadow, Toward Another View of Legal Negotiation: The Structure of Problem Solving, 31 U.C.L.A. L. Rev. 829–30 (1984).

4. *See* D. G. Gifford, a context-based theory of strategy selection in legal negotiation, 46 Ohio State L. J. 58-93 (1985). *See generally,* D. Pruitt, *Negotiation Behavior* (1981).

issue between the plaintiff and the defendant is the amount of property damage, the adversarial model is likely to be more appropriate.

On the other hand, the problem-solving model may be more useful when the dispute is more than a zero-sum game. When there are multiple issues, particularly issues the parties value differently, they may benefit from a problem-solving approach. For example, parties in dispute over the issues of child custody, visitation, and support may get a better result and do less damage to their relationship if they work together on options such as joint or split custody, the nature and details of various visitation arrangements and how those arrangements might affect appropriate amounts of child support. Similarly, if the issue between a buyer and seller is not merely price, but involves considerations such as quantity, time of delivery, and manner of payment, the problem-solving approach may be more productive in reaching an agreement addressing these multiple elements. In practice, problem solving is used more frequently in domestic relations, business regulation, and government action cases.

[2] The Other Side's Negotiating Approach

A party's negotiating approach will often be affected by the particular approach taken by the other side. For example, if the other side is unwilling to engage in a problem-solving approach, attempts to employ that model will be largely ineffective because the model presupposes information sharing and collaboration between the parties. This does not mean that a problem-solving negotiator should not try to encourage the other side to use a problem-solving approach. However, if the effort is unsuccessful, it is unlikely the problem solver will be able to make any headway in the negotiation unless he is willing to accommodate the other side's adversarial bargaining.

Sometimes the other side's negotiating approach conforms to some generally accepted convention or norm in a particular geographical area or particular type of case. In simple personal injury cases, for example, most lawyers and insurance adjusters routinely engage in adversarial bargaining; and plaintiffs' lawyers who enter into contingency fee arrangements, whereby their fee is a percentage of the monetary amount received in settlement or at trial, may be less motivated to engage in problem solving if that approach would produce a settlement that is not exclusively resolved by the payment of money.

In addition, the parties may be reluctant to share their true needs or interests. For example, a party might be psychologically or financially distressed as a result of the dispute and not want to reveal these matters out of embarrassment or fear of demonstrating weakness. Similarly, particularly when litigation is contemplated or has already commenced, a party might not want to reveal certain information to give "free discovery" to the other side. In either of these circumstances, the parties may be more likely to resort to adversarial bargaining than problem solving.

[3] Differences in Bargaining Leverage

Negotiating leverage stems from the perception of the negative consequences that a party can inflict on his opponent if an agreement is not reached, or from the benefits that a party can bestow on the other if an agreement is reached. The extent of this leverage is largely dependent upon the alternatives available to each party in the absence of an agreement. Generally, the side that possesses the most viable alternative in the event that an agreement is not reached will have greater power over the other side.

A negotiator who possesses greater bargaining leverage over his opponent may adopt an adversarial approach because his demands will be perceived as more credible, enabling him to extract greater concessions from the other side. Conversely, the negotiator with less bargaining power, *i.e.*, the party with more to lose if there is no deal, will often choose the problem-solving model to offset or neutralize the superior bargaining power he perceives on the other side of the bargaining table. He will appeal to the more powerful negotiator's sense of fairness and justice if the latter believes his leverage makes concessions on his part unwarranted.

When both negotiators have high aspiration levels and possess relatively equal bargaining leverage, rigid adherence to the adversarial model may often result in deadlock. Deadlock may motivate the parties to abandon an adversarial approach and adopt a problem-solving approach.

[4] Future Dealings Between the Parties or Negotiators

The extent to which the parties or their negotiators are likely to have an on-going relationship after the negotiation often affects the incentive for adopting an adversarial or problem-solving approach. The adversarial model sometimes gives rise to distrust and ill will, and thus the problem-solving approach is more frequently used when the parties or their representatives expect to have future dealings with one another. On the other hand, if the parties or their negotiators are merely engaged in a one-shot transaction or encounter, there will be less incentive to avoid the adversarial model with its concomitant risk of impairing future relations.

[5] Pressures to Reach an Agreement

The pressures placed on the parties to reach an agreement may affect their choice of negotiating approach. For example, a party might want to settle quickly because she needs the settlement proceeds immediately, desires to limit legal fees or other expenses, or wants to avoid the psychological stress of protracted controversy. Similarly, court deadlines or heavy caseloads may pressure the negotiators to expedite an agreement.

Generally, the problem-solving model's emphasis on sharing information to identify the interests or needs of the parties and brainstorming to develop possible solutions is more time consuming than the offer-counter-offer and response-counter-response method of adversarial negotiation. Thus, the greater the time pressure placed on the parties, the more likely they are to resort to adversarial bargaining through the swifter device of reciprocal concessions.

§3.05 Negotiating Strategies and Styles

In practice, negotiating strategy is simply a matter of choosing the model or approach in conducting the negotiation—whether adversarial, problem solving, or some combination of the two. Negotiating style, on the other hand, refers to the negotiator's *interpersonal behavior* in the negotiating setting, and often will be affected by the particular strategy chosen. Generally, there are three types of negotiating styles: (1) competitive (hardball), (2) cooperative (softball), or (3) a combination of competitive and cooperative (hardball and softball). Each has its advantages and disadvantages that should be assessed in choosing an appropriate style.

§3.06 Competitive (Hardball) Style

The competitive style is typically characterized by aggressiveness and a confrontational approach. Winning is everything, and personal feelings and interpersonal relationships are viewed as essentially irrelevant. Threats, intimidation, and Machiavellian tactics are sometimes employed.

The advantage of this style is that it tends to pressure the adversary into making concessions, particularly when he is easily intimidated or inexperienced; and extreme demands and hard-nosed positions may sometimes give rise to larger settlements. In addition, the competitive negotiator develops a reputation of strength and toughness that is attractive to many clients. On the other hand, a competitive style frequently alienates the other side and produces mistrust, misunderstanding, and more frequent deadlocks. It often polarizes positions and causes overreaction. Personal relationships may be impaired or destroyed, thus making future negotiations with the same party or negotiator more difficult.

The competitive style may be effective when dealing with an inexperienced negotiator or where the parties and their representatives are involved in a one-time adversarial relationship. On the other hand, if the parties intend to have an ongoing relationship, the competitive style is undesirable because of its propensity to cause mistrust and alienation. For example, this style is generally not well suited for business negotiations.

The negotiator who adopts a highly competitive style can minimize its negative effects by focusing on the subject matter of the negotiation rather than on personalities, and after an agreement is reached, by initiating an effort to repair any damage that has been caused to personal relationships.

§3.07 Cooperative (Softball) Style

The cooperative style is the antithesis of the competitive style. The cooperative negotiator places a premium on interpersonal relations, and strives for common ground, shared interests, and understanding between the parties. The style is typically sincere, accommodating, and low key. While it should not be confused with weakness, it often conveys that image.

The advantage of this style is that it tends to reduce the risk of deadlock and produces more satisfying and longer-lasting agreements. In addition, the parties usually come away from the negotiation with their egos intact and a disposition to continue their relationship in the future. The disadvantage is that the cooperative negotiator may have a tendency to avoid confrontation and make too many concessions. Sometimes a more favorable agreement is forsaken for the mere goal of reaching an agreement.

The effectiveness of a cooperative style depends upon the willingness of both sides to forthrightly exchange information. If the cooperative negotiator is pitted against a competitive opponent, the latter may gain an unfair advantage by obtaining information from the former without reciprocating. In addition, the competitive bargainer may misinterpret the cooperative style as a sign of weakness and escalate her aggressiveness. Thus, the cooperative negotiator should also understand competitive tactics so that she can offset them in appropriate circumstances.

§3.08 Competitive-Cooperative (Hardball and Softball) Style

The competitive-cooperative style represents a middle ground between hardball and softball. Here, many of the advantages of the competitive and cooperative approaches are combined in a style that is professionally amicable, open-minded, but firm. Under this approach, realistic concessions are made to satisfy the objectives of both parties that are consistent or not mutually exclusive. Conflicting objectives are resolved by compromise or by some creative solution that maximizes as many of the parties' remaining objectives as possible.

The advantage of this style is that it preserves personal relationships and facilitates long-term agreements. The disadvantage is that the approach is largely unworkable unless both sides are genuinely willing to "work together" to resolve their differences—an attitude that may be inherently difficult to adopt in the face of a heated dispute. In addition, the approach requires more time and patience.

The competitive-cooperative approach is usually a waste of time if the other side is unrelentingly competitive. However, this approach may be successful if the competitive negotiator has a weak position.

§3.09 Choosing a Negotiating Style and Strategy

The particular negotiating style and strategy you adopt will depend upon your own personality, the nature of the dispute, the style and strategy employed by the other side, and the client's interests and objectives which you have identified in preparing for the negotiation. In choosing an effective style and strategy, it is important to bear in mind that (1) no particular combination of style and strategy is always more effective; (2) you should consider being flexible in your choice of style and strategy throughout the negotiation process; and (3) your choice of style and strategy should always have everything to do with your client's interests in mind and nothing to do with your own ego.

Understanding the differences among negotiating styles and between negotiating strategies is highly useful in choosing a particular style and strategy. In addition, understanding how different styles and strategies tend to operate together is useful in choosing an effective combination for a particular case.

§3.10 Style and Strategy Combinations

[1] Competitive and Adversarial

When a competitive (hardball) style is combined with an adversarial strategy, the negotiation is usually characterized by hard, intense bargaining. The positions of the parties are likely to be extreme at the outset and remain fairly rigid throughout the negotiation. Concessions are hard to come by, and bluffs, threats, and even *ad hominem* attacks may permeate the process. Deadlocks are frequent, and, even if the parties reach agreement, they sometimes leave the negotiation dissatisfied and with their personal relationship impaired or destroyed.

[2] Cooperative (or Competitive-Cooperative) and Adversarial

When a cooperative (softball) or competitive-cooperative (hardball & softball) style is combined with an adversarial strategy, the prospects of reaching an agreement are enhanced. The negotiation is typically cordial and characterized by a reasoned debate about the various offers and counteroffers presented. Concessions made gradually are "in the spirit of compromise." Bluffs and threats may occur from time to time, but not in the sometimes-acerbic manner employed by purely hardball negotiators. If a settlement is reached, it might include the performance of obligations other than the mere payment of money, and the parties usually will conclude the negotiation with their relationship and egos intact.

[3] Competitive and Problem-Solving

A competitive (hardball) style is largely antithetical to a problem-solving strategy. While the competitive problem solver will participate in identifying the needs of the opposing party, he is likely to be less than completely candid about those needs and seek to de-emphasize them in favor of feigning or inflating the needs of his own client. In addition, the competitive bargainer is likely to advance solutions that solely benefit his side, rather than entertain broader solutions that accommodate the interests of the other side. In short, the competitive negotiator is primarily motivated to explore mutually beneficial solutions only to the extent they maximize his own client's interests.

[4] Cooperative (or Competitive-Cooperative) and Problem-Solving

A cooperative (softball) or competitive-cooperative (hardball & softball) style best complements a problem-solving strategy. The cooperative negotiator genuinely seeks to identify the legitimate interests of both parties and is willing to explore mutually beneficial solutions in an open-minded manner. A premium is usually placed on the candid exchange of information. The hallmark of the cooperative problem-solver's style is to emphasize common ground and minimize the parties' differences. Generally, when a cooperative style is combined with a problem-solving strategy, the prospects for reaching a mutually satisfactory agreement are at their greatest.

§3.11 The Overall Importance of Flexibility and Credibility

Regardless of the negotiating style and strategy you choose for a particular case, you should always be flexible in switching or modifying that style or strategy in appropriate circumstances. It is not unusual for a negotiator to use more than one style or strategy in a single negotiation session or during different stages of protracted settlement discussions. In short, if it becomes clear that a particular strategy or style is counterproductive, it may be beneficial to make an adjustment.

Along with flexibility, your choice of style and strategy must be credible. Persuasion depends largely upon believability. If your style or strategy is strained or disingenuous, it is unlikely you will be effective in successfully negotiating the case. A common mistake made by inexperienced negotiators is adopting a style or strategy that is at odds with their own personality. If credibility depends upon using a particular style or strategy that you are uncomfortable with, ask a colleague who is more skilled in using that style or strategy to join you in the negotiation.

§3.12 Summary of Style and Strategy Characteristics, Advantages, and Disadvantages

COMPETITIVE (HARDBALL) STYLE

Characteristics:

1. aggressive and unfriendly
2. confrontational
3. intimidating
4. Machiavellian
5. negotiates by ultimatum
6. makes few concessions

Advantages:

1. pressures inexperienced adversaries into making concessions
2. hard-nosed approach may result in better settlements for one's client
3. establishes reputation for toughness that is attractive to clients
4. may produce one-sided agreements that are advantageous if performed

Disadvantages:

1. causes anger, alienation, and mistrust
2. polarizes positions and causes overreaction or irrationality
3. impairs or destroys personal relationships
4. damages future relations between the parties or negotiators

Continued

Continued

5. may induce the losing party to breach the agreement
6. frequently causes deadlocks

COOPERATIVE (SOFTBALL) STYLE

Characteristics:

1. friendly and mild mannered
2. strives for common ground
3. slow to anger
4. communicates freely
5. prone to make reasonable concessions
6. readily considers alternative solutions

Advantages:

1. reduces the risk of deadlock
2. produces faster, more long-lasting, and creative agreements
3. maintains personal relationships
4. preserves future relations between the parties
5. decisions are made without anger or overreaction

Disadvantages:

1. tends to make concessions too easily
2. may unnecessarily result in a less favorable agreement for one's side
3. conveys a weak negotiating image

COMPETITIVE-COOPERATIVE (HARDBALL AND SOFTBALL) STYLE

Characteristics:

1. friendly but firm
2. open-minded and creative
3. confrontational when necessary
4. strives for common ground and mutually beneficial solutions

5. makes necessary concessions
6. communicates forthrightly
7. analyzes alternative solutions

Advantages:
1. usually results in mutually beneficial solutions
2. produces more long-lasting and creative agreements
3. maintains personal relationships
4. preserves future relations between the parties
5. controls the competitive negotiator
6. encourages concessions from both sides

Disadvantages:
1. unworkable if the adversary is unrelentingly competitive
2. difficult to use when the parties dislike or mistrust each other
3. largely unworkable if the parties refuse to cooperate
4. sometimes sacrifices unilateral gains for joint solutions
5. requires time and patience

ADVERSARIAL STRATEGY

Characteristics:
1. most commonly used negotiation strategy
2. emphasizes maximizing the party's gain (usually in terms of money)
3. constitutes a zero-sum game
4. fact and law rationales are manipulated to advance and defend positions
5. based on a strict cost-benefit analysis

Continued

Advantages:

1. effective when the only matter obtainable is a single objective like money
2. works well when the parties dislike or mistrust each other and are not interested in a cooperative solution
3. negotiation process is less complex and time consuming

Disadvantages:

1. creativity is curtailed in arriving at mutually beneficial solutions
2. the final agreement may not satisfy the parties' true needs or interests
3. parties and negotiators sometimes remain dissatisfied and resentful after agreement

PROBLEM-SOLVING STRATEGY

Characteristics:

1. the people are separated from the problem
2. both parties' needs or interests are identified and acknowledged
3. information is freely exchanged
4. both parties strive for mutually beneficial solutions
5. interests and objectives of both parties are accommodated to the greatest extent possible

Advantages:

1. usually results in greater satisfaction to both parties
2. negotiations are markedly less intense and testy
3. both parties' true needs or interests are often fulfilled
4. preserves personal relationships and future relations between the parties and negotiators

Disadvantages:

1. usually unworkable when only one objective is sought (*e.g.*, money)
2. unworkable if both parties are not committed to finding mutually beneficial solutions
3. negotiations are more complex and time consuming
4. sometimes unnecessarily sacrifices unilateral gains for joint solutions

Chapter Four

Ethical Considerations in Negotiation and Settlement

SYNOPSIS

§4.01 Introduction
§4.02 Attorney's Authority to Settle and Advising the Client
§4.03 Aggregate Settlements
§4.04 Contingent Fees
§4.05 Example of Contingent Fee Contract
§4.06 Truthfulness in Negotiating
§4.07 Civility in Negotiating
§4.08 Threatening Criminal Prosecution in Negotiating

§4.01 Introduction

The American Bar Association's Model Rules of Professional Conduct (Model Rules) contain a number of Rules that are particularly applicable to a lawyer's responsibilities in representing a client in negotiations and settlement. These Rules relate to (1) the authority that an attorney must have from the client to make an agreement or settlement on behalf of the client, and the lawyer's responsibilities in advising the client throughout the negotiating process; (2) the lawyer's responsibilities when entering into an aggregate settlement on behalf of multiple clients; (3) the circumstances under which contingent fees are permissible; (4) the extent to which a lawyer is obligated to make truthful statements to others in connection with negotiations or settlement; (5) a lawyer's duty to behave with civility in negotiations; and (6) whether a lawyer may threaten criminal prosecution in negotiating a civil matter. Although the Model Rules have been modified by many states in various respects, these Rules are instructive about the most important ethical considerations attendant to negotiating and settling a case.

§4.02 Attorney's Authority to Settle and Advising the Client

Rule 1.2(a) of the Model Rules provides, in part, that "a lawyer shall abide by a client's decisions concerning the objectives of representation and... shall consult with the client as to the means by which they are to be pursued." This provision makes a distinction between the client's objectives and the means for achieving them, whereby the lawyer is in charge of "procedural" decisions such as tactics and strategy and the client has the final decision over matters directly affecting the ultimate resolution of the case.[1] Thus, a lawyer generally has no authority to enter into a final agreement or settle a case on behalf of a client merely by virtue of the attorney-client relationship or because she has been given general authority to enter into negotiations.[2] Rather, except in rare emergency situations where prompt action is necessary to protect the client's interests and consultation with the client is impossible,[3] most courts require that the lawyer have *express* authority from the client to enter into a binding agreement or compromise of an action; and Rule 1.2(a) adopts this position by mandating that "[a] lawyer shall abide by a client's decision whether to settle a matter." In many states, the necessity of express authority is also prescribed by statute or local court rule.[4]

Generally, the authority to compromise a client's claim can be given only when a specific settlement is proposed, or when the lawyer has been given

---

1. *See* State v. Debler, 856 S.W.2d 641 (Mo. 1993); State v. Ali, 407 S.E.2d 183 (N.C. 1991); Blanton v. Womancare, Inc., 696 P.2d 645 (Cal. 1985).

2. *See* Faris v. J.C. Penney Co., 2 F. Supp. 2d 695 (E.D. Pa. 1998); Kaiser Foundation v. Doe, 903 P.2d 375 (Or. App. 1995).

3. *See* Sockolof v. Eden Point North Condominium Assoc., 421 So. 2d 716 (Fla. App. 1982); Schumann v. Northtown Ins. Agency, Inc., 452 N.W.2d 482 (Minn. App. 1990); Midwest Federal Savings Bank v. Dickinson Econo-Storage, 450 N.W.2d 418 (N.D. 1990).

4. *See generally*, Annotation, *Authority of Attorney to Compromise Action—Modern Cases*, 90 ALR4th 326 (1991).

prior authority to settle a case within certain limits.[5] This, of course, presupposes appropriate communication between lawyer and client. As Model Rule 1.4 provides, in part:

> (a) A lawyer shall:
>
> (1) promptly inform the client of any decision or circumstance with respect to which the client's informed consent... is required by these Rules;....
>
> (3) keep the client reasonably informed about the status of the matter;
>
> (4) promptly comply with reasonable requests for information;....
>
> (b) A lawyer shall explain a matter to the extent reasonably necessary to permit the client to make informed decisions regarding the representation.

The official Comment to that Rule explains:

> [2] If these Rules require that a particular decision about the representation be made by the client, paragraph (a)(1) requires that the lawyer promptly consult with and secure the client's consent prior to taking action unless prior discussions with the client have resolved what action the client wants the lawyer to take. For example, a lawyer who receives from opposing counsel an offer of settlement in a civil controversy or a proffered plea bargain in a criminal case must promptly inform the client of its substance unless the client has previously indicated that the proposal will be acceptable or unacceptable or has authorized the lawyer to accept or to reject the offer. See Rule 1.2(a)....
>
> [5] The client should have sufficient information to participate intelligently in decisions concerning the objectives of the representation and the means by which they are to be pursued, to the extent the client is willing and able to do so. Adequacy of communication depends in part on the kind of advice or assistance that is involved. For example, when there is time to explain a proposal made in a negotiation, the lawyer should review all important provisions with the client before proceeding to an agreement. In litigation a lawyer should explain the general strategy and prospects of success and ordinarily should consult the client on tactics

5. *See* Lord v. Money Masters, Inc., 435 S.E.2d 247 (Ga. 1993).

> that are likely to result in significant expense or to injure or coerce others. On the other hand, a lawyer ordinarily will not be expected to describe trial or negotiation strategy in detail. The guiding principle is that the lawyer should fulfill reasonable client expectations for information consistent with the duty to act in the client's best interests, and the client's overall requirements as to the character of representation.

Thus, a lawyer is ethically obligated to disclose all good faith settlement offers to the client[6] and to adequately explain all ramifications of a proposed agreement or settlement so that the client can make an informed decision.[7] Settling the case without authority, failing to communicate a settlement offer to the client, or failing to adequately advise the client about a potential settlement, may subject the lawyer to discipline by the bar[8] or liability to the client for malpractice.[9]

§4.03 Aggregate Settlements

An aggregate settlement is one that is made on behalf of two or more clients who are represented by the same lawyer. Rule 1.8(g) of the Model Rules provides, in part:

> A lawyer who represents two or more clients shall not participate in making an aggregate settlement of the claims of or against the clients ... unless each client gives informed consent, in a writing signed by the client.

---

6. *See* In re Cardenas, 791 P.2d 1032 (Ariz. 1990); In re Baehr, 744 P.2d 799 (Kan. 1987).

7. *See* Hartford Accident & Indemnity Co. v. Foster, 528 So. 2d 255 (Miss. 1988); Ramp v. St. Paul Fire & Marine Ins. Co. 269 So. 2d 239 (La. 1972). *See generally*, Perschbacher, Regulating Lawyers Negotiations, 27 Ariz. L. Rev. 76, 115–119 (1985).

8. *See, e.g.*, In re Nugent, 624 A.2d 291 (R.I. 1993) (settling personal injury action without client's consent was grounds for discipline); Comm. On Professional Ethics v. Behnke, 486 N.W.2d 275 (Iowa 1992) (lawyer who handled client's personal injury claim by telephone and settled case without discussion with client violated MRPC Rule 1.4); Culpepper v. Mississippi State Bar, 588 So. 2d 413 (Miss. 1991) (lawyer disciplined for misleading client about true bases of settlement reached with opposing counsel in divorce action, and for failing to advise her that agreement filed was different from her previous agreement). *See generally*, Annotation, *Conduct of Attorney in Connection with Settlement of Client's Case as Ground for Disciplinary Action*, 92 ALR3d 288 (1979).

9. *See, e.g.*, Moores v. Greenberg, 834 F.2d 1105 (1st Cir. 1987) (attorney may be liable for malpractice for failing to inform client of a settlement offer, permitting client to recover damages in the amount of that offer).

> The lawyer's disclosure shall include the existence and nature of all the claims... involved and of the participation of each person in the settlement.

This Rule typically applies where "counsel representing several separate plaintiffs with different claims against a single defendant... settle[s] all of the claims together."[10] While most of the cases discussing the Rule have involved aggregate settlements of only a small number of clients, the Rule is also acutely applicable in mass tort litigation cases where large numbers of plaintiffs are represented by a single lawyer or law firm. The Rule's prohibition against making an aggregate settlement without each client's informed consent (1) aims to prevent lawyers from favoring one client over another in settlement negotiations,[11] (2) empowers clients to prevent lawyers from putting their own economic self-interest ahead of their clients' interest (given the temptation of some lawyers to accept a relatively cheap, comprehensive settlement at an early stage of the representation rather than invest the time and resources that would be necessary to maximize their clients' recoveries),[12] and (3) reflects the mandates of Rule 1.4 that clients have a right to be fully informed about settlement offers and to control the ultimate settlement decision.[13]

When you represent multiple clients[14] against a single adversary and receive an "all or nothing" lump sum settlement offer which conditions settlement upon acceptance of the agreement by all or a particular number of your clients, the initial question will be how the lump sum would be allocated among your clients. If you represent a relatively small number of clients, the simplest approach is to help your clients to agree among themselves as to an appropriate division. However, if you represent a large number of clients, it is likely to be much more difficult to achieve unanimous agreement on the division of a lump

---

10. Kelly v. Johns-Manville Corp., 590 F. Supp. 1089, 1092 n.1 (E.D. Pa. 1984).

11. *See* In re Anonymous Member of South Carolina Bar, 377 S.E.2d 567, 568 (S.C. 1989).

12. *See* Arce v. Burrow, 958 S.W.2d 239 (Tex. App. 1997); Silver & Baker, Mass Lawsuits and the Aggregate Settlement Rule, 32 Wake Forest L. Rev. 733, 751–752 (1997).

13. *See* Hayes v. Eagle-Picher Industries, Inc., 513 F.2d 892 (10th Cir. 1975); Quientero v. Jim Walter Homes, Inc., 709 S.W.2d 225 (Tex. App. 1985).

14. As a threshold matter, the multiple representations must be proper under Model Rule 1.7(b).

sum settlement. In that situation, some lawyers utilize the services of special masters or ask a judge to mediate the division.[15]

After determining the amount that would be received by each client, and before acceptance of the settlement, you should confer directly with each client (rather than communicating with one client and expecting that client to confer with the others),[16] to inform each about (1) the total, lump sum settlement amount, (2) the particular amount the client will receive, (3) every other client's share in the settlement,[17] and (4) all other information necessary to enable the client to make an informed decision whether to accept or reject the settlement. The aggregate settlement cannot be accepted unless *all* clients give informed consent, and this requirement cannot be circumvented by some other agreement, such as a retainer agreement, authorizing settlement by majority vote or by some other method.[18] A violation of Rule 1.8(g) may render the settlement unenforceable against the non-consenting clients[19] and subject the offending attorney to disciplinary action by the bar.[20]

§4.04 Contingent Fees

In many personal injury cases, whether arising out of common law negligence, an intentional tort, or a breach of a duty of care defined by statute, plaintiffs' lawyers are often compensated on a contingent fee basis, whereby the attorney's fee is a percentage of the total monetary amount or interest in property[21] recovered for the client. Contingent fees are common in other types of cases as well. Sometimes the compensation can be a combination of a per-

---

15. *See* Weinstein, Ethical Dilemmas in Mass Tort Litigation, 88 Nw. U. L. Rev. 469, 521 (1994).

16. *See* Gelb, Common Ethical Problems, 79 Mass. L. Rev. 167, 174 (1994).

17. *See* In re Anonymous Member of the South Carolina Bar, 377 S.E.2d 567, 568 (S.C. 1989) (lawyer should provide list showing the names and amounts to be received by other settling clients); *accord* Quintero v. Jim Walker Homes Inc., 709 S.W.2d 225, 229 (Tex. Ct. App. 1985).

18. Hayes v. Eagle-Picher Industries Inc., 513 F.2d 892 (10th Cir. 1975).

19. *See, e.g.*, Knisley v. Jacksonville, 497 N.E.2d 883 (Ill. App. 1986); Quintero v. Jim Walker Homes, Inc., 709 S.W.2d 225 (Tex. Ct. App. 1985).

20. *See, e.g.*, State ex rel. Oklahoma Bar Assoc. v. Watson, 897 P.2d 246 (Okla. 1994); Butler County Bar Assoc. v. Barr, 591 N.E.2d 1200 (Ohio 1992).

21. *See, e.g.*, Beatie v. Delong, 561 N.Y.S.2d 448 (Sup. Ct. App. Div. 1990) (upholding 30% of revenues generated by patents whose rights the lawyer recaptured for the client).

centage of the recovery and an hourly fee.[22] The rationale for contingent fees is that they provide a means by which clients who cannot afford to pay an hourly or fixed fee may employ qualified representation by giving the lawyer a portion of the winning result. The fact that a lawyer might earn a larger sum of money in charging a contingent fee than would otherwise be earned from a fixed fee or at an hourly rate is balanced against the risk that the lawyer will receive no fee at all if no recovery is obtained for the client.

Model Rule 1.5 provides, in pertinent part:

> (c) A fee may be contingent on the outcome of the matter for which the service is rendered, except in a matter in which a contingent fee is prohibited by paragraph (d) or other law. A contingent fee agreement shall be in writing signed by the client and shall state the method by which the fee is to be determined, including the percentage or percentages that shall accrue to the lawyer in the event of settlement, trial or appeal, litigation and other expenses to be deducted from the recovery, and whether such expenses are to be deducted before or after the contingent fee is calculated. The agreement must clearly notify the client of any expenses for which the client will be liable whether or not the client is the prevailing party. Upon conclusion of a contingent fee matter, the lawyer shall provide the client with a written statement stating the outcome of the matter and, if there is a recovery, showing the remittance to the client and the method of its determination.
>
> (d) A lawyer shall not enter into an arrangement for, charge or collect:
>
> (1) any fee in a domestic relations matter, the payment or amount of which is contingent upon the securing of a divorce or upon the amount of alimony or support, or property settlement in lieu thereof;...

Like other types of fees, a contingent fee must be reasonable in terms of the percentage the lawyer will receive of the monetary amount recovered for his or her client, and the courts retain overall supervisory power to monitor the reasonableness of such fees.[23] Even when this percentage falls within the usual range of percentages charged in similar types of cases, a court may find

22. *See, e.g.*, Boston and Maine Corp v. Sheehan, Phinney, Bass & Green P.A., 778 F.2d 890 (1st Cir. 1985) (upholding hourly fee plus reduced contingent fee).

23. Thomton, Sperry & Jensen Ltd. v. Anderson, 352 N.W.2d 467 (Minn. App. 1984); West Virginia State Bar Committee on Legal Ethics v. Taterson, 352 S.E.2d 107 (W. Va. Sup. Ct. App. 1986).

the percentage unreasonable if the risk of no recovery by the client is virtually nonexistent or the lawyer can easily resolve the matter without much effort.[24] For example, the courts have repeatedly warned that contingent fees are usually inappropriate in cases involving the collection of insurance proceeds when the client's right to that money is clear and it will take little effort to collect it.[25] On the other hand, even a 50% contingent fee may be permissible if the case is very complicated, liability is highly questionable, and a favorable outcome of the case will depend upon considerable skill by the lawyer.[26] In addition, by statute or local court rule, some jurisdictions limit the percentages that may be charged in matters such as workers' compensation cases, social security cases, medical malpractice[27] or civil rights actions,[28] or in cases involving the representation of children.[29] These statutory limitations may never be exceeded in a contingent fee contract.

Rule 1.5(c) requires that the contingent fee contract be in writing and signed by the client. The agreement must state the percentage or percentages of the recovery to which you will be entitled if your client's case (1) is settled (making clear whether a different percentage applies if the case is settled during trial, as opposed to prior to trial); (2) goes to trial (or is retried); and (3) is appealed. If a structured settlement is possible, you should state whether the fee will be based on a percentage of the lump sum immediately

---

24. *See, e.g.*, In re Gerard, 548 N.E.2d 1051 (Ill. 1989) (lawyer disciplined for collecting contingent fee of 35.2% to locate and collect client's assets to which no adverse claims were made, where it took the lawyer no more than 160 hours to perform the task and contingent fee amounted to approximately $1000 per hour of work).

25. *See* In re Hanna, 362 S.E.2d 632 (S.C. 1987); West Virginia State Bar Committee on Legal Ethics v. Tatterson, 352 S.E.2d 107 (W. Va. Sup. Ct. App. 1986); Maryland Attorney Grievance Commission v. Kemp, 496 A.2d 672 (Md. App. 1985).

26. *E.g.*, Sweeney v. Athens Regional Medical Center, 917 F.2d 1560 (11th Cir. 1990); Fraidin v. Weitzman, 611 A.2d 1046 (Md. Ct. Spec. App. 1992). *Cf.* West Virginia State Bar Committee on Legal Ethics v. Gallaher, 376 S.E.2d 346 (W. Va. Sup. Ct. App. 1988) (50% contingent fee excessive where lawyer achieved modest settlement of client's case in less than 17 hours; one-third fee would have been more appropriate); Maryland Attorney Grievance Commission v. Korotki, 569 A.2d 1224 (Md. App. 1990) (even though case was complex and involved a trial and two appeals, successive contracts adding up to 75% contingent fee constituted excessive fee).

27. *See generally*, Annotation, *Validity of Statute Establishing Contingent Fee Scale for Attorneys Representing Parties in Medical Malpractice Actions*, 12 ALR4th 23 (1982).

28. *See* Federal Tort Claims Act, 28 USC 2678, limiting contingent fees to 25% (or 20% if the case is settled at the administrative level).

29. *See generally* Annotation, *Court Rules Limiting Amount of Contingent Fees or Otherwise Imposing Conditions on Contingent Fee Contracts*, 77 ALR2d 411 (1961).

received by your client plus the present value of the future payments to which your client is entitled, or on a percentage of each future payment received by your client when it is received. In addition, the agreement must state generally the "litigation and other expenses to be deducted from the recovery," and whether your percentage of the recovery will be taken from the gross amount before deduction of expenses or the net amount after deduction of expenses.[30] The agreement might also contain a clause that, in the event you are discharged from the case without good cause, you will be entitled to a fee amounting to the reasonable value of your services under *quantum meruit*, expressed as either a reduced percentage of the amount recovered by your client or a fee based on an hourly rate.[31]

Rule 1.5(d)(1) states explicitly that you cannot charge a contingent fee if the contingency is your client's obtaining a divorce, or if the amount of the fee is dependent on what your client is awarded as alimony or child support or in a "property settlement" in lieu of alimony or child support. However, in most states you are permitted to charge a contingent fee where your client's right to alimony or child support has *already* been established judicially and the aim of the representation is the collection of past-due payments of alimony or child support. Jurisdictions are divided about whether the Rule's prohibition against contingent fees in "property settlement" matters applies to equitable distribution cases. Some courts have held that a contingent fee in an equitable distribution case is permissible so long as the contract does not simultaneously provide for compensation contingent on securing a divorce, or obtaining alimony or child support.[32]

Finally, Rule 1.5(c) provides that, at the conclusion of the contingent fee representation, you are obligated to provide your client with a written financial accounting of the monies to be disbursed in connection with the case. The disbursement statement must state "the outcome of the matter and, if there is a recovery, [show] the remittance to the client and method of its determination." A failure to abide by this requirement may result in disciplinary action.[33]

30. *See* Louisiana State Bar Assoc. v. St. Romain, 560 So. 2d 820 (La. 1990) (attorney privately reprimanded for using retainer agreement that did not specify how expenses would be deducted).

31. *See generally*, Annotation, *Limitation to Quantum Meruit Recovery, Where Attorney Employed Under Contingent Fee Contract is Discharged Without Cause*, 92 ALR3d 690 (1979); Annotation, *Circumstances Under Which Attorney Retains Right to Compensation Notwithstanding Voluntary Withdrawal from Case*, 88 ALR3d 246 (1978).

32. *See* Williams v. Garrison, 411 S.E.2d 633 (N.C. App. 1992).

33. *See* Florida Bar v. Rood, 633 So. 2d 7 (Fla. 1994).

§4.05 Example of Contingent Fee Contract

Contingent Fee Contract

The law firm of ____________________ (Attorneys) is retained and employed by ____________________ (Client) to represent Client in a claim for damages against ____________________ or any others who may be liable for injuries that Client sustained on ____________________ [Date] ____________________.

1. This is a contingent fee contract and it is agreed that if Attorneys recover no compensation for Client, Client owes Attorneys no fee until a favorable recovery is obtained. If a recovery is obtained on behalf of Client, Attorneys shall receive as attorneys' fees _____% of any recovery obtained, whether by settlement or trial. If an appeal is taken or proceedings are necessary to collect any judgment, the attorneys' fees shall increase to _____%. These percentages shall be calculated and paid based on the gross amount recovered for Client, and before deduction of any costs, litigation expenses, or medical charges and expenses as provided for in paragraphs 3 and 4.

2. If settlement of this case is made by a structured settlement, attorneys' fees shall be based on the present cash value of the settlement as determined by actuarial experts, and such fees shall be paid out of the initial cash lump sum payment.

3. In addition to attorneys' fees, all court costs, expert witness fees, subpoena costs, photographs, depositions, court reporter fees, reports, witness statements, photocopying, telephone, travel, and all other out-of-pocket expenses directly incurred in investigating, preparing, or litigating this claim shall be paid by Client irrespective of the outcome of this case, and Attorneys may deduct those amounts from the Client's share of the proceeds of any recovery.

4. All medical expenses and charges of any nature made by doctors, hospitals, clinics, or Client will pay other health-care providers in connection with the diagnosis or treatment of Client's injuries. In the event that Attorneys recover damages on Client's behalf, Client authorizes Attorneys to pay all such expenses and charges that are unpaid as of that date from Client's share of the recovery.

5. Client agrees not to make any settlement of this case without Attorneys being present and receiving all payments due them under this Contract.

6. Client agrees that Attorneys have made no promises or guarantees about the outcome of this case.

7. Client and Attorneys each have a copy of this Contract, and its terms are acceptable.

This the ____________________ day of ____________________, [year].

______________________ by: ______________________

[Client] [Attorneys]

§4.06 Truthfulness in Negotiating

The Preamble to the Model Rules states that "[a]s negotiator, a lawyer seeks a result advantageous to the client but consistent with the requirements of honest dealing with others." Rule 4.1(a) of the Model Rules provides that "[i]n the course of representing a client a lawyer shall not knowingly: make a false statement of material fact or law to a third person." The Comment to that Rule states, in pertinent part:

> [1] A lawyer is required to be truthful when dealing with others on a client's behalf, but generally has no affirmative duty to inform an opposing party of relevant facts. A misrepresentation can occur if the lawyer incorporates or affirms a statement of another person that the lawyer knows is false. Misrepresentations can also occur by partially true but misleading statements or omissions that are the equivalent of affirmative false statements.
>
> [2] This Rule refers to statements of fact. Whether a particular statement should be regarded as one of fact can depend on the circumstances. Under generally accepted conventions in negotiation, certain types of statements ordinarily are not taken as statements of material fact. Estimates of price or value placed on the subject of a transaction and a party's intentions as to an acceptable settlement of a claim are in this category.

These provisions reflect a tension between the aspiration that lawyers should be honest when negotiating with others and the reality that the parlance of negotiating often includes a certain amount of deception. The failure of Rule 4.1(a) and its Comment to set a bright-line standard of complete truthfulness in negotiating has led one commentator to ruefully remark that these provisions "unambiguously [embrace] 'New York hardball' as the official standard of practice."[34] Thus, some scholars have urged that these provisions should be revised to establish a tighter standard of truthfulness in negotiations,[35] while others recognize that, of necessity, negotiations involve at least some deceptive behavior.[36]

In practice, most experienced lawyers are essentially honest in negotiating. However, they will not mindlessly volunteer or concede weaknesses in their clients' positions and will usually make every effort to portray the facts of the situation in a light most favorable to their clients. Thus, experienced lawyers expect their adversaries will often *characterize* the facts of the case and the reasons their clients are deserving of a more favorable outcome in ways that are less than objectively accurate. Acceptance of this reality, however, should not be interpreted as an endorsement of dishonesty. Rather, it is merely recognition of the fact that part of zealous advocacy involves the ability to tactfully put a favorable "spin" on matters. As the Comment to Model Rule 1.3 provides: "[a] lawyer must also act with commitment and dedication to the interests of the client and with zeal in advocacy upon the client's behalf." Painting one's client's position in the most favorable light is an attribute of lawyer competency that is still consistent with ethical responsibility.

At the same time, most experienced lawyers also expect that their adversaries, if they are also first-rate lawyers, will not conduct themselves in negotiations by engaging in outright prevarication on material matters. This is so because, apart from the prohibition against untruthfulness in Rule 4.1(a), experienced lawyers know that effective client representation depends in large part upon lawyer credibility. Lawyers who lie are usually found out. They are as ineffective in persuading other lawyers as they are ineffective in persuading judges or juries, and persuasion is the lawyer's principal stock in trade, whether

34. G. Lowenthal, The Bar's Failure to Require Truthful Bargaining by Lawyers, 2 Geo. J. Legal Ethics 411, 445 (1988).

35. *See* Rubin, A Causerie on Lawyers' Ethics in Negotiation, 35 La. L. Rev. 577 (1975); Jarvis & Tellam, A Negotiation Ethics Primer for Lawyers, 31 Gonzaga L. Rev. 549 (1995/96); *see also* Steele, Deceptive Negotiating and High-Toned Morality, 39 V and. L. Rev. 1387 (1986).

36. *See* C. Craver, Negotiation Ethics: How to Be Deceptive Without Being Dishonest/How to Be Assertive Without Being Offensive, 38 S. Tex. L. Rev. 713 (1997); *see also* Hazard, The Lawyer's Obligation to Be Trustworthy When Dealing with Opposing Parties, 33 S.C. L. Rev. 181 (1981); James T. White, Machiavelli and the Bar: Limitations on Lying in Negotiation, 1980 Am. Bar Found. Res. J. 927–928 (1980) ("To conceal one's true position, to mislead one's opponent about one's true settling point, is the essence of negotiation.").

in negotiation, litigation, or other aspects of client representation. Moreover, to the extent that actual or perceived "toughness" plays a role in effective representation, experienced lawyers know that the lawyers who have the ability to be truly tough, when necessary, are usually those who also have a strong reputation for credibility through trustworthiness and integrity.

Rule 4.1(a) and its Commentary reflect these realities. Although you generally have no duty to inform an opposing party of relevant facts such as those which would indicate weaknesses in your client's position,[37] and you are not prohibited from zealous advocacy such as by "puffing," giving mere "personal opinions" about the merits of the case, or even embellishing your client's intentions as to what would be an acceptable settlement, you may not go so far as to make any "false statements of material fact or law" to third persons in connection with negotiations. False statements include those that are written as well as oral, statements by you that repeat or affirm false statements made by your client when you know of their falsity,[38] and may include statements of your intent to do something when you actually have no such current intention.[39] A false statement will also violate the Rule if made in response to a third party's question, and such a statement cannot be excused by the duty to protect client confidences because, if the matter is privileged, you have a duty to decline to answer the question altogether.[40] Moreover, if you make a statement that is literally true but is misleading because you purposefully omit material information, the intentionally deceptive nature of the omission may make it equivalent to an affirmative false statement.[41]

---

37. *See* Brown v. County of Genesee, 872 F.2d 169 (6th Cir. 1989) (defense counsel had no general ethical duty to tell counsel for plaintiff during settlement negotiations about the latter's factual error; error was not induced or contributed to by defense counsel).

38. *See, e.g.*, Florida Bar v. Burkich-Burrell, 659 So. 2d 1082 (Fla. 1995) (lawyer notarized false answers to interrogatories on behalf of husband-client, knowing that answers were untrue).

39. *See* In re Graveley, 805 P.2d 1263 (Mont. 1990); ABA Formal Ethics Op. 94-383 (it is unethical to make a false threat to file disciplinary charges against another lawyer).

40. *See* People v. Petsas, 262 Cal. Rptr. 467 (Ct. App. 1989) ("distinct difference [exists] between restricting an attorney from divulging information learned in confidence from a client, and proscribing him from knowingly making affirmative false representations regarding a claim or claims of that client."); ABA Formal Ethics Op. 93-370 (1993) (lawyer may decline to answer improper question by judge regarding settlement authority, but is barred by Rule 4.1 from responding with a deliberate misrepresentation or lie).

41. *See* Florida Bar v. Joy, 679 So. 2d 1165 (Fla. 1996) (lawyer violated Rule 4.1 by making statement that was literally true but intended to mislead opposing counsel); In re Goodsell, 667 So. 2d 7 (La. 1996); Mississippi Bar v. Robb, 684 So. 2d 615 (Miss. 1996); ABA

Rule 4.1(a) only prohibits making false statements of "material" fact or law. Although the Model Rules do not define the term "material," a "[r]epresentation relating to a matter which is so substantial and important as to influence [a] party to whom made is 'material.'"[42] For example, it has been held that information about a personal injury client's alcohol use at the time of the accident, which a lawyer deleted from the client's medical records before submitting them to an insurer, was material.[43] A lawyer was disciplined for stating there was only $200,000 in insurance coverage when documents in the lawyer's possession showed $1 million in coverage.[44] Similarly, a lawyer was disciplined when he failed to disclose the existence of a third insurance policy when the other party mistakenly believed there were only two policies that provided coverage for the accident.[45] And, it has been held that the death of one's client during settlement negotiations is a material fact that must be disclosed to opposing counsel.[46]

Making false statements of law has typically given rise to disciplinary action where the statements were made to non-lawyers. For example, a lawyer was disciplined for falsely telling a debtor that his driver's license would be suspended if he failed to pay a judgment.[47] A lawyer was also held to have violated Rule 4.1(a) for providing false opinion letters to a purchaser regarding title to real property so as to enable his clients to profit from undisclosed double sales of property.[48] On the other hand, rendering a mere "personal opinion" as to the proper interpretation of a statute or case decision would fall outside the scope of the Rule.[49] It has also been said that a lawyer has no ethical duty to inform an opposing party that the statute of limitations has run, so long as the lawyer does not misrepresent the facts or his intent to file suit.[50]

Formal Ethics Op. 93-375 (1993) (attorney representing client in bank examination may not omit information when omission is tantamount to affirmative false statement).

42. *Black's Law Dictionary* 976 (6th ed. 1990).

43. In re Zeiger, 692 A.2d 1351 (D.C. 1997).

44. In re McGrath, 468 N.Y.S.2d 349 (App. Div. 1983).

45. State ex rel. Nebraska State Bar Assoc. v. Addison, 412 N.W.2d 855 (Neb. 1987).

46. Kentucky Bar Assoc. v. Geisler, 938 S.W.2d 578 (Ky. 1997); Virzi v. Grand Trunk Warehouse & Cold Storage Co., 571 F. Supp. 507 (E.D. Mich. 1983); ABA Formal Ethics Op. 95-397 (1995).

47. In re Eliasen, 913 P.2d 1163 (Idaho 1996).

48. In re Duckworth, 914 P.2d 900 (Ariz. 1996).

49. *See* J. Moliterno & J. Levy, *Ethics of the Lawyer's Work* 234 (1993).

50. ABA Formal Ethics Op. 94-387 (1994).

Apart from the disciplinary consequences, making a false statement of material fact or law may result in liability in tort for fraud. For example, it has been held that a lawyer could be sued in tort by the opposing party who alleged that the case was settled for a lower amount in reliance on the lawyer's false representation about applicable insurance policy coverage.[51] A claim for fraudulent misrepresentation was held actionable against a seller's lawyer who allegedly stated to purchasers that they were getting "a lot of property for the money" when the lawyer knew that his client could not convey title.[52] And another court refused to dismiss a complaint for fraud against lawyers who allegedly induced an asbestos manufacturer to settle claims by falsely representing that the claims were valid.[53] Thus, even if misrepresentations of fact or law might not constitute an ethical violation, you should be aware that misrepresentations, or even a failure to disclose in circumstances where the law may impose a duty of disclosure,[54] may give rise to liability in tort.

§4.07 Civility in Negotiating

Rule 4.4(a) of the Model Rules provides, in part, that "[i]n representing a client, a lawyer shall not use means that have no substantial purpose other than to embarrass, delay, or burden a third person." Most of the reported decisions finding a violation of this Rule have involved abusive interpersonal behavior or abusive tactics in the litigation context, whether directed against opposing counsel, opposing parties, witnesses, jurors, or court personnel. For example, numerous cases have found violations of the Rule where lawyers were verbally abusive to third persons or engaged in physical threats or similar types of despicable behavior.[55] In some instances, the courts have found that a violation

51. Fire Insurance Exchange v. Bell, 643 N.E.2d 310 (Ind. 1994).

52. Jeska v. Mulhall, 693 P.2d 1335 (Or. App. 1985).

53. Raymark Industries Inc. v. Stemple, 714 F. Supp. 460 (D. Kan. 1988). *See also* Sainsbury v. Pennsylvania Greyhound Lines, 183 F.2d 548 (4th Cir. 1950) (setting aside release of personal injury claim that was induced by lawyer's false representation that employees in government service could recover only for pain and suffering).

54. *See generally*, Restatement (Second) of Torts, §551 (enumerating circumstances where party has a duty of disclosure in business transactions).

55. *See, e.g.*, Castillo v. St. Paul Fire & Marine Insurance Co. (In re Walker), 828 F. Supp. 594 (C.D. Ill. 1992) (lawyer repeatedly obstructed deposition and engaged in "most egregious example of lawyer incivility that this Court has ever seen," including threatening opposing counsel); In re Ramunno, 625 A.2d 248 (Del. 1993) (lawyer referred to opposing counsel in vulgar terms in office conference before judge and engaged in insolent colloquy

of Rule 4.4 also comes within the prohibitions on "engag[ing] in conduct that is prejudicial to the administration of justice" under Rule 8.4(d).[56]

Rule 4.4 recognizes that a lawyer's means in representing a client may have more than one purpose. The Rule is violated only when the means used have no other "substantial purpose" than to cause embarrassment, delay, or a burden to another person. By requiring that the other permissible purposes be "substantial," the Rule suggests that the lawyer's purportedly legitimate purposes will be closely scrutinized. A good example of this occurred in *State ex rel. Scales v. West Virginia State Bar Committee on Legal Ethics*, 446 S.E.2d 729 (W. Va. Sup. Ct. App. 1994), where Scales was representing a woman in a bitter divorce with her husband, who was a member of the armed forces. Scales contacted the husband's commanding officer to report that the husband was abusing his wife. The Court rejected the State Bar Committee's contention that Scales' sole purpose in contacting the commanding officer was to harass and embarrass the husband. The Court noted that when the wife had contacted the commanding officer to report the abuse, he had told her he could not do anything unless her lawyer contacted army officials. Thus, the Court held that because Scales' intervention had a substantial purpose other than embarrassment and harassment, there was no violation of Rule 4.4.

As in the litigation context, a violation of Rule 4.4 may occur in the context of negotiations. However, because of the overall importance of lawyer credibility as discussed in Section 9.06, in practice, the vast majority of lawyers negotiate with civility. Resort to abusive interpersonal behavior or obnoxious negotiating tactics is relatively rare and, when they do occur, they are usually a product of the lawyer's personal insecurity, professional immaturity, or both.

---

with judge); In re Bechhold, 771 P.2d 563 (Mont. 1988) (lawyer who represented client on a claim submitted to insurance company, contacted claims department employee seven or eight times a day for several days, was rude, and then attempted to serve papers on insurance company by bringing them to the claims office where lawyer engaged in continual profanity).

56. *See, e.g.*, In re Schiff, 599 NYS2d 242 (N.Y. Sup. Ct. App. Div. 1st Dept. 1993) (lawyer's conduct of being unduly intimidating and abusive toward opposing counsel, and directing vulgar, obscene, and sexist epithets toward her in deposition reflected adversely on fitness to practice); In re Holmes, 921 P.2d 44 (Colo. 1996) ("undignified, offensive, threatening, and unprofessional" letters to opponents and court employees); In re Stanley, 507 A.2d 1168 (N.J. 1986) (rude stares at judge, laughing, remarking in undertones, shaking finger at judge).

§4.08 Threatening Criminal Prosecution in Negotiating

One negotiating tactic that could arguably run afoul of Rule 4.4 and has received special attention by the American Bar Association is threatening criminal prosecution in connection with negotiating a civil matter. Before the Model Rules were adopted, Disciplinary Rule (DR) 7-105(A) of the ABA Model Code provided that "[a] lawyer shall not present, participate in presenting, or threaten to present criminal charges solely to obtain an advantage in a civil matter."[57] The Code explained the rationale for this provision in Ethical Consideration 7-21 as follows:

> The civil adjudicative process is primarily designed for the settlement of disputes between parties, while the criminal process is designed for the protection of society as a whole. Threatening to use, or using, the criminal process to coerce adjustment of private civil claims or controversies is a subversion of that process; further, the person against whom the criminal process is misused may be deterred from asserting his legal rights and thus the usefulness of the civil process in settling private disputes is impaired. As in all cases of abuse of judicial process, the improper use of criminal process tends to diminish public confidence in our legal system.

The Model Rules, however, deliberately do not contain a corresponding provision to DR 7-105(A). The ABA Ethics Committee addressed the issue for the first time under the Model Rules in *ABA Ethics Opinion 92-363* (1992). That opinion states that you may use the possibility of presenting criminal charges against an opposing party in a private civil matter to gain relief for your client, provided that the criminal matter is related to the civil claim, both the civil claim and possible criminal charge are warranted by the law and the facts of the situation, and you do not attempt to exert improper influence over the criminal process. In addition, the Committee said you may agree, as part of a settlement, to refrain from presenting criminal charges against an opposing party so long as the agreement does not violate applicable law. The opinion explained that requiring the criminal charges to be related to the civil matter

---

57. *Cf.* West Virginia State Bar Commission on Legal Ethics v. Printz, 416 S.E.2d 720 (W. Va. Sup. Ct. App. 1992) (decided when DR 7-105(A) was still in effect, and holding that the tactic of threatening criminal charges was not prohibited in legitimate negotiations so long as the lawyer did not seek payment beyond restitution in exchange for foregoing criminal prosecution or seek any payment in exchange for not testifying at a criminal trial).

"discourages exploitation of extraneous matters that have nothing to do with evaluating the claim."

Thus, as a general rule, it is not unethical to threaten the initiation of criminal prosecution or to agree to refrain from initiating such process in connection with negotiations in a civil case. However, you should not seek, as part of a settlement, any compensation that is expressly in exchange for not testifying at a criminal trial.[58] In addition, if you make a *direct* threat to initiate criminal prosecution if a settlement is not achieved in a civil case without any present intention of doing so, you may violate the prohibition against "making a false statement of material fact" under Model Rule 4.1(a).[59]

58. *See* West Virginia State Bar Commission on Legal Ethics v. Printz, 416 S.E.2d 720 (W. Va. Sup. Ct. App. 1992).

59. *See* ABA Formal Ethics Op. 94-383 (unethical to make false threat to file disciplinary charge against another lawyer).

Chapter Five

Negotiating Tactics and Techniques

SYNOPSIS

§5.01 Introduction
§5.02 Abdication
§5.03 Adjournment or Caucus
§5.04 Anger/Aggressiveness
§5.05 Asymmetrical Time Pressure
§5.06 Blaming or Fault Finding
§5.07 Bluffing
§5.08 Boulwarism
§5.09 Coalition
§5.10 Company Policy Excuse
§5.11 Deadlines
§5.12 Delay
§5.13 Dodging the Question Through Blocking Techniques
§5.14 Draft Document or Single Negotiating Text
§5.15 Escalating Demands
§5.16 Excessive Initial Demands/Offers
§5.17 Face Saving
§5.18 Fait Accompli
§5.19 False Demands
§5.20 False Emphasis
§5.21 False Multiple Concessions
§5.22 False Scarcity
§5.23 Floating Trial Balloons and Bracketing
§5.24 Good Guy-Bad Guy Routine/Mutt and Jeff

§5.25 Lack of Authority or Limited Authority
§5.26 Little Ol' Country Lawyer
§5.27 Lock-In Positions
§5.28 Low-Balling
§5.29 Misstatement
§5.30 Nibbling
§5.31 Off-the-Record Discussions
§5.32 Personal Attacks
§5.33 Playing Dumb
§5.34 Preconditions or Conditional Proposals
§5.35 Problem Solving
§5.36 Publicity
§5.37 Questions to Facilitate Agreements
§5.38 Questioning by Socratic Method
§5.39 Reversing Position
§5.40 Salami
§5.41 Snow Job/Alleged Expertise
§5.42 Splitting the Difference
§5.43 Surprise
§5.44 Take-It-or-Leave-It
§5.45 Threats
§5.46 Timing
§5.47 Two Against One
§5.48 Walkout
§5.49 Word Smithing
§5.50 Dealing with Disingenuous or Inappropriate Tactics or Techniques
[1] Rule the Tactic or Technique Out of Bounds Before Negotiations Start or When It Arises During the Negotiation
[2] Deflect the Tactic or Technique by Ignoring It
[3] Expressly Expose the Tactic or Technique
[4] Respond to the Tactic or Technique in Kind

§5.01 Introduction

Negotiators routinely employ a variety of tactics and techniques during the negotiating process to advance their clients' interests. These range from subtle games, to overtly obnoxious behavioral ploys, to well-meaning techniques for reaching a reasoned agreement. Some are geared toward adversarial or competitive bargaining, while others are designed to encourage problem solving or cooperative bargaining. Depending upon how they are used, certain tactics or techniques may run afoul of the ethical prescriptions of truthfulness and civility in negotiating discussed in §§4.06 and 4.07.

A glossary of common tactics and techniques variously used in negotiations is provided below in alphabetical order. Further references to them are made throughout this book. This glossary is not provided as an express endorsement of any particular tactic or technique or to encourage their routine use in negotiations generally. Rather, it is provided because understanding these tactics and techniques and how to deal with them are essential to effectively representing your client. Section 5.50 at the end of this Chapter provides a general discussion of how to deal with tactics or techniques used by the other side that are particularly disingenuous or otherwise inappropriate under the circumstances.

You may find some of the tactics or techniques useful to employ in a particular situation. However, before using a special tactic or technique, it is sometimes desirable to advise your client about any advantages or disadvantages of using it so that your client will be able to advise you about any unanticipated reason why the tactic or technique might be inappropriate under the circumstances. Of course, you should never use a tactic or technique that you believe to be unethical, and it is unwise to adopt a tactic or technique that is at odds with your own personality, style, or philosophy. Properly used, tactics and techniques are aids to negotiating a successful agreement in particular circumstances and should not be used for their own sake.

§5.02 Abdication

Abdication is sometimes effective in deadlock situations. It can be used when both sides are close to an agreement and each side has put forward its best arguments as to why the other ought to compromise somewhat more. Then, one negotiator abdicates by telling the other that he is at a loss as to what to do further but will agree to a final proposal if the other side can just come up with a more equitable solution. In effect, the abdicator is putting the entire problem into the hands of the other party but is hinting at the same time that he (the abdicator) will accept a fair solution.

This tactic thus puts pressure on the other side to make one more final concession. Particularly if the abdicator styles his abdication with praise for the other side's creativity and good faith in resolving the impasse, the technique will sometimes produce an additional concession by the other side that is agreeable to both parties.

§5.03 Adjournment or Caucus

Sometimes a negotiator may find it beneficial or necessary to take a temporary recess during the negotiation or to stop it altogether and resume discussions at a later date. Adjournment may be beneficial when momentum has been lost, to evaluate a *Surprise* that has developed, to reflect and relax when you are feeling overly pressured to make an immediate decision, or to change the tone of the negotiation if it has become particularly frustrating, exhausting, or acrimonious. In addition, negotiations might have to be temporarily suspended to consult with your client about a matter. Often the primary objective is simply to buy time to allow for a clearer assessment of the situation.

§5.04 Anger/Aggressiveness

A display of anger, whether real or feigned, is often effective in conveying to the other side the seriousness of one's position and may reduce the other party's expectations. Some negotiators use anger as part of an overall pattern of aggressive and abrasive behavior that is designed to intimidate their adversaries into making concessions. Sometimes a burst of anger is an effective way to conclude an unpleasant interaction. When faced with an angry negotiator, it is often best to let him "blow off steam" rather than try to match the aggressiveness with counter attacks. Remember that most people cannot stay highly angry for very long periods of time. In short, the best counter measure to aggressiveness is to "keep your cool."

A risk of succumbing to anger may be the inadvertent disclosure of information, such as unwittingly revealing your bottom line. For example, if you respond to a settlement demand of $200,000 by angrily responding, "This case can't possibly be worth more than $100,000!" the outburst might well reveal that your bottom line is close to $100,000.

§5.05 Asymmetrical Time Pressure

It is often useful to know whether the other party is under any particular time constraints or deadlines. Do they have other commitments that limit the time they can devote to this negotiation? If an out-of-town opponent has booked a flight home for early in the evening of a negotiation, this information may be used to manipulate the negotiation schedule to reduce the time for discussion before the opponent has to leave. Or it might be used to create the impression that you are willing "stay here all night, if that's what it takes." In either case, the tactic is designed to induce a sense of pressure to make concessions "before the clock runs out" and she has to return home empty-handed. Clearly, constraining the time for negotiation is not always an effective tactic, as it may well backfire. It can also prevent a resolution that might have been had with more time to work together.

§5.06 Blaming or Fault Finding

Another form of *Anger/Aggressiveness* may occur when a negotiator abruptly blames or alleges some fault on the part of the other side for the parties' inability to reach an agreement. Depending upon the relationship between the parties or negotiators, this tactic may result in a further concession induced solely by a sense of guilt or an overriding desire to preserve the relationship. If the accusation of fault has merit, such a concession would not be irrational. On the other hand, if the accusation is unfounded, you should guard against capitulating on an important point merely to placate the accuser or keep the peace.

§5.07 Bluffing

Bluffing usually takes the form of an assertion about what the negotiator is or is not willing to do or staking out a seemingly inflexible position on some matter. A negotiator might bluff about an offer or counteroffer, or in making a threat to walk out. The obvious drawback to bluffing is that the bluffer will lose face and perhaps credibility if the bluff is exposed.

A negotiator might extricate herself from a bluff by claiming that her seemingly unalterable assertion or position warrants modification or retraction based on new or unanticipated information learned during the negotiation, or in light of a misunderstanding about the facts or law. Similarly, the party who exposes a bluff might allow the bluffer to *Save Face* by acknowledging that the seemingly fixed assertion or position was based on incomplete or erroneous information.

§5.08 Boulwarism

Named after Lemuel Boulware, a vice president of General Electric who promoted it, Boulwarism is the practice of offering a "first, last, and best" offer at the beginning of a negotiation and sticking to it. In the context of collective bargaining, Boulwarism has been held to be an unfair labor practice. Legal in other contexts, though of debatable effectiveness, the tactic is also known as *Take-It-or-Leave-It,* discussed below.

§5.09 Coalition

Coalition is the unification of power of two or more parties to increase their leverage in negotiating with a third party. For example, coalition building is often used by consumer groups or in boycott situations. The theory of the tactic is that forming a coalition has the effect of placing more negotiating cards in the hands of its members than would be the case if each member acted independently.

Sometimes the coalition tactic may be effective when the party draws upon or forms an allegiance with a person who may be a key player in the event the negotiation fails. For example, in a domestic custody dispute, having the allegiance of a child psychologist who would testify in court that your client would be the best person to be the primary custodial parent may bring added leverage to a negotiation where custody is the main issue.

§5.10 Company Policy Excuse

Some negotiators attempt to justify their position by the glib assertion that "it's company policy." Usually, such a purported "policy" has nothing to do with the applicable law of remedies or other objective criteria upon which the dispute should be reasonably resolved. Thus, when confronted with a company policy excuse, you should probe the reasons underlying the policy and who has the power to change the policy, while steering the other side toward adopting a more objective standard as the basis for negotiating the dispute.

§5.11 Deadlines

Real or perceived deadlines often exert pressure on the negotiating process. Deadlines may be unavoidable and inflexible (such as the statute of limitations), or they may be unilaterally imposed by one of the parties. Creating a deadline within which to conclude negotiations may be particularly effective if the consequence of not agreeing by the deadline is sufficiently serious or risky. In litigation, for example, one party may create a deadline by filing a motion, giving notice of a hearing, or by refusing to consent to a request by the other party to extend the time within which to meet a deadline imposed by the court.

In setting the length of a deadline, it is important to consider your purpose in exerting pressure on the negotiation process. For example, if your purpose is to induce immediate action, you should set a short deadline, whether an hour, day, or week. Generally, if a deadline exceeds ten days, it will lose its effectiveness for lack of demonstrating urgency. On the other hand, if you are not yet prepared to take immediate action or it is in your best interests to buy extra time to obtain additional information, you should consider a more flexible deadline of a few weeks or months.

Imposing a deadline is most effective when coupled with concrete sanctions for not meeting the deadline. As with the tactic of using a *Threat*, if you are not willing and prepared to follow through with concrete consequences for noncompliance with the deadline, the deadline tactic will be ineffective.

§5.12 Delay

Delaying negotiations until the most advantageous time is a common tactic. Negotiators frequently delay in order to allow a change in position to occur for a more favorable result, or to time the negotiations with an event that puts maximum pressure on the other side to negotiate. Delay is also used to gain time for obtaining more information pertinent to the negotiation, or to preserve the status quo under circumstances where it is temporarily advantageous to preserve the existing situation of the parties.

§5.13 Dodging the Question Through Blocking Techniques

Sharing information between the parties is integral to the negotiating process, particularly when a problem-solving strategy is adopted. On the other hand, negotiators invariably need to protect certain sensitive or damaging information from the other side and thus seek to evade questions that are directed to such information.

This evasion may occur through any one of five methods, sometimes called "blocking" techniques. The first method is to simply ignore the question and change the topic. The second method is to rule the question out of bounds and provide the other side with a reasonable reason for refusing to answer the question. A third technique is to answer the question by asking another question. Fourth, you might attempt to answer the question by answering another question. This might be done by (a) re-framing the initial question so that the answer will not be damaging, (b) simply answering another question as if it had been asked, or (c) by answering another question that has recently been asked. The fifth and final method is to over-answer or under-answer the question by responding broadly to a particular question or narrowly to a general question.

Most of these blocking techniques are, in essence, methods of distraction. The key to avoid succumbing to this distraction is to carefully *listen* to the answer and, when necessary, re-ask the question.

§5.14 Draft Document or Single Negotiating Text

Sometimes a negotiator will bring a draft of a potential agreement to the negotiation to set the agenda and serve as a starting point for discussions. This technique may also be effective in multiparty negotiations, particularly where one of the negotiators or a neutral third party submits the draft in advance of formal discussions to the other parties who are asked to submit suggested changes to the draft. The negotiating text is then revised and resubmitted to the other parties for further suggestions.

The process may involve the preparation of numerous drafts before the parties actually sit down together to hammer out a final accord. By the time they do, the single negotiating text is likely to reflect the most important interests of at least most of the parties and greatly reduce the number of issues that remain to be resolved. The process often creates a powerful momentum to reach a final agreement because the parties will usually be reluctant to unravel what the text has already accomplished, and thus they will be more inclined to make reasonable concessions to close a deal.

§5.15 Escalating Demands

Under this tactic, the negotiator engages in a pattern of raising one of his demands for every concession made on another, or of reopening issues you thought had already been resolved. The effect is to decrease your overall concessions and to induce your side to quickly reach an agreement lest the negotiator escalate one or more of his demands again.

When faced with this tactic, it is usually best not to counter it by engaging in the same conduct. Rather, you should firmly bring the matter to the negotiator's attention and insist that the negotiation proceed in a more principled manner. If the tactic persists, you may be forced to temporarily suspend negotiations or end them altogether.

§5.16 Excessive Initial Demands/Offers

It is generally desirable for a negotiator to make a greater initial demand or offer than a more modest one, so long as some reasonable basis can be provided for the more hardened, initial demand. This approach often has the effect of reducing the other party's initial expectations. However, if the initial demand or offer is extreme in the sense of having absolutely no rational basis, the negotiator is likely to quickly lose credibility with the opposing side.

When confronted with a truly excessive initial demand, the best counter tactic is to expose it by probing the purported justification for the demand. Another approach is to directly point out the disingenuousness of the tactic and indicate that you do not intend to employ the same unproductive technique. Yet another alternative is to refuse to disclose your initial offer until the other side has presented a proposal that is justified with some reasonable rationale.

§5.17 Face Saving

Negotiations frequently reach an impasse not because the particular proposal is unacceptable, but because one party is psychologically unable to accept the proposal for fear of being perceived as having capitulated. Face saving is a technique for allowing a party to change a previously held position in a way that fulfills his needs for self-esteem. In essence, the tactic is designed to make the other party feel that he is really not backing down.

For example, if the other party's change of position involves a concession on a legal or factual point, you might acknowledge that absent the complete facts you also would have taken an initial position similar to that taken by the other side. Another approach is to ask questions about the information relied upon by the other side in support of its proposal, and then point out how that information is incomplete. Oftentimes good-natured humor is also an effective face-saving technique.

§5.18 Fait Accompli

"Fait accompli" is a French phrase meaning "an accomplished fact." As a negotiating tactic, it constitutes some action or inaction by a party to change the status quo and put the other side in a weaker position.

For example, insurance adjusters sometimes create a fait accompli by simply sending a check in an amount deemed appropriate for the injury to the injured party's attorney, thus putting the attorney and her client in the position of having to accept the check or continue with litigation. Filing a lawsuit or obtaining a restraining order during the pendency of negotiations creates the choice of either quickly settling the case or expending money in defense of the legal action. Or, in a breach of contract situation, if the breaching party simply discontinues the acts constituting the alleged breach and sells her business to another company, the injured party may be left with having to deal with a new party or with a remedy limited to damages for a past breach. In both instances, the breaching party has weakened the other side's bargaining leverage and economic justification for bringing suit.

§5.19 False Demands

During the exchange of information between the parties, a negotiator may discover a matter that is particularly important to the other side but of little or no value to his client. In an effort to take advantage of this knowledge, the negotiator may pretend that this matter is also highly important to his client and includes it as an integral part of his client's initial demand or offer. The negotiator then seeks to enhance his client's position by giving up that matter to the other side in exchange for extracting concessions on a matter more valuable to his client. The best way to guard against such false demands is to carefully scrutinize the terms of your opponent's offers to determine whether they contain matters that are of only incidental benefit to your opponent.

§5.20 False Emphasis

Under this tactic, the negotiator temporarily emphasizes matters of lesser importance to her client and de-emphasizes matters of greater importance to her client. The goal is to mislead the other side about the client's true preferences such that the other side is induced to give up the de-emphasized matter (which is actually the more important matter to the client). For example, by creating the impression that an expensive feature on a car is of little importance to her, a buyer may be successful in minimizing the cost she will ultimately have to pay for the car. Conversely, a seller may be able to increase the price that she can obtain for an item by creating the impression that the item is much more valuable to her than it is in reality.

§5.21 False Multiple Concessions

During a negotiation session, one party may make multiple, relatively small concessions in rapid sequence to induce the other party to reciprocate with multiple, larger concessions. For example, in contemplating a move from an initial demand of $800,000 to a new demand of $700,000, instead of making a single, principled concession of $100,000, the party might first move to $780,000, then move to $740,000 after some discussion, and then move to $700,000. Claiming three separate, unanswered concessions, the party then seeks to have the opposing party make a larger counteroffer than would have been produced in response to a single move from $800,000 to $700,000.

When faced with such consecutive concessions, you should focus on the aggregate movement involved rather than the mere number of concessions made. If you then choose to make a single counteroffer to the other party's consecutive concessions, you should make the same counteroffer you would have made had the aggregate movement been made in one concession.

§5.22 False Scarcity

Scarcity adds to a thing's value. People's desire for something and their willingness to pay for it increases if that thing is or is perceived to be rare, or difficult to obtain, or available for only a limited time. Negotiators, like marketers, sometimes attempt to play on this psychological tendency. Thus, a negotiator might seek to extract a better price by creating the impression that there are few similar items available on the market or that others cannot be found without great expense or investments of time.

§5.23 Floating Trial Balloons and Bracketing

This tactic is frequently employed in politics. A politician leaks a particular proposal or contemplated action and waits to see the reaction of his opponent and the public before formally adopting the proposal or implementing the action. The same technique may be used in the negotiating process. The client or a member of his negotiating team privately leaks or "floats" controversial aspects of a potential agreement to test the reaction of the opposing party.

A variant on this tactic, sometimes called "bracketing," might be employed during an actual negotiation session. For example, the negotiator might say, "I know it would be too much for you to pay $50,000, but I also know that no one could get away with paying only $30,000." By presenting these high and low figures, the negotiator tests the opposing party's reaction to each figure to gauge a midpoint range for settlement. In this example, the negotiator may want to negotiate a price between $35,000 and $45,000 even though he knows that the other side desires to pay much less.

§5.24 Good Guy-Bad Guy Routine/Mutt and Jeff

The "good guy-bad guy" (or "Mutt and Jeff") routine is played by a team of two or more negotiators for the same side, one of whom adopts a seemingly reasonable and accommodating approach while the other takes a hard-nosed and intransigent approach. After the good guy heaps praise on the other party for his concessions and it appears that an agreement is close to being reached, the bad guy rejects the proposal as patently unacceptable, and the good guy, in turn, tries to persuade the other party that if only a few additional concessions would be made, the irrational partner may be persuaded to accept the agreement. As a variant on this routine, a single negotiator might play the good guy but insist that greater movement is necessary to satisfy his irrational client.

Law enforcement personnel frequently use the "good guy-bad guy" routine when they are interrogating a suspect. Although not usually described as a "negotiation," the "good guy" interrogator is in effect negotiating with the suspect for additional information (including the names of the other participants in the criminal behavior) in exchange for charging the suspect with a lesser criminal offense. The "bad guy" cop is holding out for more information before agreeing to a negotiated plea to a lesser criminal charge. The suspect often succumbs to the wishes of the "good guy" in order to mollify the "bad guy."

One useful test for determining whether the negotiators for the other side are playing good guy-bad guy, or whether they are genuinely in disagreement with one another, is to watch whether the reasonable negotiator ever assents to an aspect of an agreement without expressing the necessity of obtaining the approval of the unreasonable negotiator. If the reasonable negotiator always seeks the unreasonable negotiator's acquiescence, it is highly probable the game is underway.

When the tactic is employed, it is usually best to simply recognize it rather than openly expose it. If your accusation is wrong, the negotiation may be unnecessarily impaired. If you are right, the opposing negotiators may simply resort to other devious tactics. Thus, place your primary focus on obtaining the assent of the reasonable negotiator. Then, perhaps with the aid of the reasonable negotiator, direct your attention to persuading the unreasonable one.

§5.25 Lack of Authority or Limited Authority

A negotiator may claim that she lacks authority or has limited authority from her client for a number of reasons. First, the tactic may serve as the negotiator's "back door" by giving her an excuse to avoid making a decision in the face of a pushy adversary or to guard against making spontaneous or reactionary decisions. Second, the tactic provides an excuse for the negotiator to stall or temporarily suspend negotiations until there is time to consult with another negotiator or higher authority. Third, the tactic allows the negotiator to insulate the client from the heat of battle of the negotiating process so that a final decision may be made on cool-headed analysis rather than on pure emotion.

The intended effect of claiming lack of authority or limited authority, whether real or feigned, is to obtain psychological commitments from the other side when it is negotiating with complete authority, since most people tend to feel bound by tentative agreements they have reached. The negotiator without complete authority is then able to modify the tentative agreement based on new or unexpected demands from the client. When faced with this tactic, it is often useful to suggest that you also lack final authority over the matter. In this way, it is understood from the outset that any agreement is entirely tentative. If it becomes clear that claims of lack of authority or limited authority are making the negotiation unproductive, recess or suspend the negotiation until the other side obtains the requisite authority to substantively negotiate.

§5.26 Little Ol' Country Lawyer

Some negotiators deliberately adopt a style of seeming inexperience, disorganization, absent-mindedness, meekness, ineptness, or flattery to lure their adversaries into a false sense of security. This tactic is intended to present a "soft target" for the opponent in the hope they will be inclined to take it easy on the "little ol' country lawyer." The best antidote to this tactic is simply to recognize it and maintain a disciplined approach that sticks to your negotiation plan.

§5.27 Lock-In Positions

A tactic particularly common to labor-management negotiations is to have a principal, such as a union president or company executive, give a publicized speech or press conference that "locks in" the party's position in such a way that negotiations cannot effectively proceed until the other side at least acknowledges the party's announced position as a starting point for discussions. For example, a union president might give a speech or call a press conference to proclaim that his membership "will never accept less than a 10% pay increase" to induce management to accept that position as a bottom-line for beginning negotiations. Of course, the representative or chief negotiator for management might also call a press conference and respond with the company's own assertion of a bottom-line.

To counter this tactic, a party's purported lock-in position might simply be ignored, or characterized by the other side as a mere "expectation," "goal," or "discussion point like any other." Alternatively, the party who employed the lock-in tactic might be told that, notwithstanding his public pronouncements, you intend to negotiate the dispute at the bargaining table, not in the press.

§5.28 Low-Balling

Low-balling is a tactic that takes advantage of the psychological tendency to acquiesce to different or additional terms of an agreement once a person has committed themselves to accepting the underlying transaction. It is a form of *Nibbling*, designed persuade a party to agree to a higher price than the once to which she initially agreed.

As one example of this tactic, a car salesman will induce a person to decide to buy a car on what are represented to be particularly favorable terms. The prospective purchaser might even be permitted to try out the car for a few days so as to "hook" her on it. When the time comes to sign a final purchase contract, the salesman claims that there was some mistake or that the manager won't approve the original deal and asks for more money. Since the buyer has become psychologically committed to the idea of owning the car, she may agree to pay the additional money. Of course, the antidote to this tactic is simply to protest the change in terms and threaten to walk away from the deal if the salesman insists on increasing the purchase price.

§5.29 Misstatement

When certain information is difficult to obtain from the other side, a negotiator might make a misstatement of fact to induce the other party to correct the fact and thereby reveal the information sought. For example, if a buyer is negotiating the purchase price of an item, he might say, "We understand that you sold the same machine to X for $35,000." The seller might then correct the misstatement, revealing that the actual sale to X was for $28,000. This may give the buyer leverage to negotiate a price for the same type of machine that is closer to $28,000 than $35,000. The obvious lesson from this tactic is that you must always maintain control over yourself in what you reveal to your adversary.

§5.30 Nibbling

The negotiation has been long and hard, and the deal is ready to close. The other party says, "There's just one more little thing...." The demand they are making now or the new issue they are raising for the first time seems a small thing and unworthy of lengthy debate, and it is certainly not important enough to derail the settlement. So, so you agree. You have just been nibbled, though perhaps it is more accurate to say that your agreement has been nibbled. Nibbling is a common and deliberate tactic.

Acquiescence encourages nibbling. An alternative is to just say no or to demand something in return. If your opponent's last minute or post-agreement request is made in good faith, as is your expectation of reciprocity, she will usually agree to discuss your proposed modification. On the other hand, if your opponent's response is to reject further discussions and to insist upon the terms of the existing agreement, you will know that you have successfully thwarted an attempted at nibbling.

§5.31 Off-the-Record Discussions

Negotiators sometimes find it useful to meet informally with one another, without their clients present, to engage in off-the-record discussions about the dispute. In this way, the negotiators are able "to lay their cards on the table" and freely explore options toward an agreement without making any firm commitments to one another. The tactic is particularly beneficial for exploratory discussions before negotiations begin, or to "separate the people from the problem" in circumstances where negotiations have broken down. This tactic is particularly useful in hotly contested and emotionally laden domestic negotiations.

§5.32 Personal Attacks

Some hardball negotiators deliberately engage in a variety of verbal and non-verbal behavior to insult, belittle, disparage, or otherwise make the opposing party as uncomfortable as possible. The theory is to intimidate the opponent into submission. The best counter measure to this tactic is to tactfully "name the game" and insist that the negotiations proceed on the merits of the parties' respective proposals rather than on personalities.

§5.33 Playing Dumb

A variation on the *Abdication* and *Little Ol' Country Lawyer* tactics occurs when the negotiator "plays dumb" by persistently picking apart the other party's proposals but never makes a proposal of his own out of a feigned inability to come up with any solution. The tactic is designed to induce the opposition to prove that it can formulate a satisfactory settlement. When the negotiator plays dumb, repeatedly ask him what he wants. If he continues to refuse to make a proposal, indicate that you may have to terminate the negotiation unless he can be more forthcoming in making proposals.

§5.34 Preconditions or Conditional Proposals

Some negotiators condition their willingness to negotiate upon the satisfaction of a condition precedent: "We won't negotiate until you do X." The unilaterally imposed precondition is presented as a non-negotiable issue or as a threshold concession that must be made by the other side. The precondition might be "procedural" in the sense of how the negotiation will be conducted, "substantive" in the sense of demanding that the other party agree to a particular term in the agreement, or a combination of both. "We are willing to discuss issue X if agreement is first reached on issue Y."

A precondition is effective if the demanding party has superior bargaining leverage over the other side on the condition being imposed. On the other hand, the danger of imposing a precondition is that the other side may view the tactic as coercive or tantamount to exacting an unfair concession. This may cause the other party to simply ignore the precondition, flatly reject it, or assert a counter precondition.

Closely akin to preconditions are conditional proposals. The latter are offers which are contingent upon receiving a concession on a specific point, resolving a specified issue first, or resolving all of the remaining issues in the negotiation. For example, X is offered for Y so long as the other party gives up Y, does Z, or W is resolved.

§5.35 Problem Solving

Negotiators who adopt a problem-solving approach seek to focus on each party's needs or interests rather than on stated "positions." The people are separated from the problem, and solutions are explored for mutual gain based on objective criteria rather than the naked will of any one party.

In furtherance of this approach, problem-solving negotiators employ the following tactics: (1) they shun any temptation to engage in personal attacks or to react irrationally to the other side; (2) they seek to diffuse anger, fear, and suspicion by listening, acknowledging the other party's points, and agreeing whenever possible; (3) they deflect hardline positions by re-framing them in the form of problem-solving questions that explore the needs and reasons underlying the other party's positions and suggest alternative solutions; (4) they adopt the role of a mediator, trying to identify and satisfy the other side's unmet interests; and (5) instead of employing threats or force, they seek to educate the other party to the costs of not reaching an agreement, and reassure him that the goal of the negotiation is mutual satisfaction, not victory.

§5.36 Publicity

Efforts at using the media to exert pressure on the other side to negotiate or compromise are sometimes used in labor disputes, class actions, or other high-profile cases. Typical examples of these efforts include using press releases, granting newspaper or magazine interviews, and making public pronouncements over the TV or radio. (*See also Lock-In Positions*).

The extent to which a lawyer may make statements to the media is limited by ethical constraints. Rule 3.6 of the ABA Model Rules of Professional Conduct provides, in pertinent part:

> (a) A lawyer who is participating or has participated in the investigation or litigation of a matter shall not make an extrajudicial statement that a reasonable person would expect to be disseminated by means of public communication if the lawyer knows or reasonably should know that it will have a substantial likelihood of materially prejudicing an adjudicative proceeding in the matter.
>
> (b) Notwithstanding paragraph (a), a lawyer may state:
>
> > (1) the claim, offense or defense involved and, except when prohibited by law, the identity of the persons involved;
> >
> > (2) information contained in a public record;
> >
> > (3) that an investigation of a matter is in progress;
> >
> > (4) the scheduling or result of any step in litigation;
> >
> > (5) a request for assistance in obtaining evidence and information necessary thereto;
> >
> > (6) a warning of danger concerning the behavior of a person involved, when there is reason to believe that there exists the likelihood of substantial harm to an individual or to the public interest...
> >
> > ....
>
> (c) Notwithstanding paragraph (a), a lawyer may make a statement that a reasonable lawyer would believe is required to protect a client from the substantial undue prejudicial effect of recent publicity not initiated by the lawyer or the lawyer's client. A statement made pursuant to this paragraph shall be limited to such information as is necessary to mitigate the recent adverse publicity.
>
> (d) No lawyer associated in a firm or government agency with a lawyer subject to paragraph (a) shall make a statement prohibited by paragraph (a).

Lawyers wishing to achieve publicity for their clients without offending Rule 3.6 frequently include extensive details about their clients and the injuries they have suffered in the clients' complaints and answers. Because these pleadings are public records, the details are available to the press. Those lawyers who wish to avoid publicity for their clients should engage in early negotiations to stave off litigation and the creation of a "public record" available to the press.

§5.37 Questions to Facilitate Agreements

Skillful negotiators often use different forms of questions to facilitate an agreement. Examples of these different types of questions include the following:

(1) Questions to get the negotiation started:

- What are the facts of the situation from your perspective?
- What do you consider to be the major issues?
- What are your primary interests and concerns?
- What proposals or solutions are you thinking about?

(2) Questions to obtain specific information:

- Who, what, which, when, where, why, how?
- What do you mean by...?
- Would you explain that further?

(3) Questions to invite clarification:

- How will your proposal work?
- Who will do what, when, where, and how?
- How will this solve the problem?

(4) Questions to reflect understanding:

- Do you mean that...?
- Do I understand you to be saying that...?
- Am I correct in assuming that...?

(5) Questions to explore or suggest alternative solutions:

- What would you think if we tried to...?
- Is it possible to consider...?
- Are there other ways to address that concern?
- What option do you think is better?

(6) Questions to focus on the key issues:

- What does all this lead to?
- Where do we go from here?
- How might we resolve the issue of...?
- Why do you think we are blocked on this issue?

(7) Questions to bring closure to and confirm the agreement:

- So, as I understand it, have we agreed to...?
- Can you think of anything we have left out in our agreement?

§5.38 Questioning by Socratic Method

Some skillful negotiators adopt the "Socratic method" of asking a series of logical questions that are designed to expose the weaknesses in the opposing party's proposals and lead to a particular result. This approach often allows the negotiator to obtain a series of agreements about certain concepts or principles that should underlie a resolution of the dispute. The goal is to induce the other side to participate in the negotiator's reasoning process that leads to a particular result.

This tactic should not be viewed as unfair or illegitimate. If the parties exchange thoughtful questions and answers, they are more apt to understand each other's interests and objectives and develop a solution based on reason rather than naked desire. On the other hand, excessive use of this tactic may come across as patronizing.

§5.39 Reversing Position

The tactic of reversing position may be as effective in breaking a deadlock as in solidifying one. Here, when faced with a stalemate, the negotiator abruptly declares that she has made too many concessions and can no longer live with what she has already offered. She then withdraws some of her concessions. This is intended to serve as a huge blow to the other party who has worked so hard to establish headway but now finds himself "back to square one." The tactic often results in either successfully reducing the other party's aspiration level so that progress resumes, or in solidifying the stalemate unless the negotiator who reversed position reaffirms her previous concessions and offers a new proposal.

§5.40 Salami

If you want to eat the salami on the other person's plate, you should proceed one slice at a time. In a negotiation, it is often easier and more effective if the issues are defined and addressed in smaller, bite-size portions than in their entirety. For example, it may be easier to reach and to justify a total settlement of $600,000 when it comprises separately negotiated amounts for past medical expenses, future medical expenses, past lost wages, reduction in earning capacity, past pain and suffering, future pain and suffering, and the like.

§5.41 Snow Job/Alleged Expertise

In an attempt to gain psychological leverage, some negotiators seek to display their high level of expertise about the subject matter of the negotiation, or to shower their adversaries with a highly detailed presentation of facts and figures in order to dominate and overwhelm the other side. If the other side is relatively unprepared, this factual "snow job" or display of expertise can be effective in conveying the message that the negotiator is prepared to go to trial or to take other alternative action if no agreement is reached.

When faced with this tactic, you should be careful to evaluate whether your opponent's professed expertise is real or illusory, and whether the detailed presentation is really substantive or irrelevant. Often times, slick and detailed presentations are cluttered with meaningless factual and legal minutiae in order to disguise a proposal's true weaknesses. Avoid being hurried into accepting your adversary's data and consider asking him to summarize his position without unnecessary resort to details. In this way, you will be able to keep your focus on the key components of the proposal to evaluate its overall acceptability.

§5.42 Splitting the Difference

Splitting the difference is probably the most common form of concluding an agreement in adversarial bargaining. For example, one party makes concessions down to $20,000, the other party concedes up to $10,000, and the parties agree to split the difference and settle at $15,000. The appropriateness of splitting the difference depends largely on the reasonableness of the parties' respective opening offers and concession behavior. If the negotiation process has effectively negated any extreme initial demand, and the parties have made roughly equal progress toward an agreement, and the remaining gap is relatively small, splitting the difference may save time, appeal to the parties' sense of fairness, and bring the matter to a conclusion.

A risk in making a proposal to split the difference, especially if it is made too early in the process, is that the other side may treat that number as your latest offer and suggest splitting the difference between that point and theirs. For example, suppose X has lowered his demand over the course of the negotiation to $30,000 and Y has come up to $10,000. If Y proposes to split the difference at $20,000, X might treat $20,000 as Y's new position and offer to split the difference between his $30,000 and Y's $20,000 to arrive at a final settlement of $25,000. In response, Y should reject X's deliberate misinterpretation and return to his last legitimate offer of $10,000.

§5.43 Surprise

Regardless of how thorough you are in preparing for the negotiation, from time to time the unexpected occurs and you are suddenly confronted with either a welcome or unwelcome surprise. For example, during the course of negotiations, you may unexpectedly discover some damaging information against the other side or find out about an event or fact that undercuts your position.

If the surprise is welcome news, it is often better to gently use it as an additional tool to reinforce and advance your overall objectives rather than to dramatically spring it upon the other side in an effort to extract an immediate, extraordinary concession. This is because a dramatic and hasty use of the surprise may backfire and eliminate its utility if the other side is unable to save face and recoils by suspending or terminating negotiations. On the other hand, if the surprise is damaging to your side, delaying the negotiations is effective in fending off any short-term advantage that may be gained by the opposition. By buying time, you can usually regroup and analyze the situation to minimize the surprise or neutralize its immediate impact.

§5.44 Take-It-or-Leave-It

A "take-it-or-leave-it" approach, particularly if literally styled that way, often comes across as obnoxious and arrogant, and frequently results in indignant rejection. However, some negotiators who use this tactic genuinely don't intend to create that reaction, but insist upon making a single offer that they deem fair which the other side is simply free to accept or reject. This approach may be particularly effective if the offeror possesses considerable bargaining leverage over his opponent.

When faced with a take-it-or-leave-it offer, you might choose to ignore it, divert it by changing the subject, or try to counter it by pointing out what the offeror stands to lose if no agreement is reached. If the offeror refuses to budge, evaluate the offer dispassionately. After all, you should not automatically assume that a better result could be obtained through ritualistic, give-and-take bargaining.

Because the take-it-or-leave-it approach often results in instinctive rejection, it is usually best not to use it even if you possess far superior bargaining power over your adversary. The more power you have in a negotiation, the more you can afford to engage in its "process." Allowing the other party to participate in protracted bargaining usually has the benefit of leaving him more satisfied after a settlement is reached and more likely to stick by and implement the settlement. Perhaps most importantly, it provides you with a hedge against having misjudged the situation. After all, a settlement reached after protracted negotiations may turn out to be more favorable than your "take-it-or-leave-it" proposal.

§5.45 Threats

A threat is vacuous unless it is credible. To be credible, (1) the threat must be understood; (2) the other side must be convinced that you intend to carry out the threat and possess the capability of doing so without undue cost to your client; and (3) the other side must believe that it would be less costly to comply with your demands than to suffer the consequences that would follow if you carried out the threat. Threats tend to be most effective (a) when styled without hostility but as an unfortunate and unavoidable necessity, (b) when coupled with a deadline and some visible preparatory actions taken by your client to carry out the threat, and (c) when made without anticipation by the other side.

Threats can be countered in a variety of ways. First, you can respond with a threat of your own, but you should recognize that this tactic might cause the negotiation to degenerate into an escalating spiral of additional threats. Second, you can simply ignore the threat. Third, you can act as if the threat were unauthorized or made in the heat of passion. Fourth, you can characterize the threat as something else, such as a purely hypothetical course of action. Fifth, you can attempt to refute the other side's perception of the cost your client will incur if the threat is carried out, or try to convince the other side that it has underestimated its own costs if the threat is carried out. Finally, you can simply dare the other side to carry out the threat to demonstrate its lack of meaning to your client. Of course, the best choice among these options will depend upon the particular circumstances.

§5.46 Timing

Negotiators routinely attempt to conduct or conclude negotiations at times that are most advantageous to their clients. A particular event or particular time pressures placed upon the parties may trigger the most opportune timing. Negotiating at a time when the other party is in the weakest position or your client is in the strongest position will enhance your prospects for a favorable settlement.

Jockeying for the best time to negotiate involves using tactics such as *Asymmetrical Time Pressure, Deadlines, Delay*, or taking preemptive action to create conditions through a *Fait Accompli*. Generally, if a party is operating under a particular time constraint, he should try to withhold that fact from his opponent. If this is not practical, the party may have to communicate a deadline within which negotiations must be completed in order to deprive his adversary of using this time pressure as leverage.

Finally, in a particular case, a negotiator might even consider the best day of the week or time of day to negotiate.

§5.47 Two Against One

Most negotiations are conducted on a one-on-one basis with a single individual representing each side. Sometimes, however, a party may create a negotiating team of two or more representatives to "take on" a single negotiator for the other side. This might be done to permit the team to employ a *Good Guy-Bad Guy Routine* or otherwise to exert psychological pressure upon the opponent. When this occurs, the single negotiator might simply refuse to negotiate with more than one counterpart, or bring in one or more additional negotiators on behalf of her side to counterbalance the opposing party's team.

§5.48 Walkout

Walking out in the middle of a negotiation may appear somewhat dramatic and adolescent, but if done in a genuine and non-hostile manner it may be effective in breaking a deadlock. A walkout is often accompanied by some ultimatum about what will be required to resume negotiations. It is usually best to word such an ultimatum with sufficient ambiguity so that you have the option of walking back into the negotiation if necessary. If the other party is truly committed to on-going negotiations, he will realize that he has simply pushed matters too far and the negotiation may resume after a short recess or at a later time.

§5.49 Word Smithing

Negotiators are wordsmiths. That is, they often couch what they say in language that is designed to subtly signal their intentions or concerns. Thus, you must be sensitive to the verbal cues given by your counterpart's expressions. The following are just a sampling of what certain expressions, depending upon the context, might really mean:

- *Our initial demand is $125,000* = We are prepared to make a lower offer.
- *Our counteroffer is $25,000.... If you have any further information, we will of course consider it* = We need further factual justification to increase our offer.
- *I have no authority to accept less than $85,000 at this time* = I probably can get authority to accept less than $85,000.
- *My client is not inclined to...* = My client doesn't like the idea but might be persuaded otherwise.
- *For the sake of discussion, what would you think about a value of this case in the range of $75,000 to $85,000?* = Is your resistance point $80,000? Mine might be. Let's settle for $80,000.
- *Our final offer is to pay no more than $75,000* = Your resistance point [in the preceding example] is really $75,000, so that's going to be my bottom line.
- *Well, our final counteroffer is that we will accept no less than $77,500* = You might have been correct that our resistance point was $75,000, but you will settle the case for $2,500 more rather than go to the expense of a trial.

§5.50 Dealing with Disingenuous or Inappropriate Tactics or Techniques

A tactic or technique may be inappropriate to a negotiation either because it is disingenuous, counterproductive in the particular circumstances, or even unethical. Generally, there are four ways you can respond when confronted by such tactics or techniques. However, no one method is invariably better than the other, and thus you should simply choose the method or combination of methods you think best in the particular situation.

[1] Rule the Tactic or Technique Out of Bounds Before Negotiations Start or When It Arises During the Negotiation

Ruling the tactic or technique out of bounds before negotiations start may be appropriate if your counterpart has already employed the tactic or technique before formal negotiations begin or you are certain the tactic or technique will be employed when negotiations begin. On the other hand, this method may come across as condescending or patronizing if used when your counterpart never had any intention in the first place of employing the tactic or technique you want to foreclose. Thus, if you are unsure whether the tactic or technique will be used, it is better to rule it out of bounds at the time it first arises during actual negotiations rather than before they start.

Either way, it is important to be *tactful* in ruling a tactic or technique out of bounds. The goal is to foreclose the tactic or technique without unnecessarily foreclosing negotiations by disparaging or insulting your counterpart. For example,

Compare (untactful negotiator):	— *Listen, John, we're not interested in any "Getting to Yes by Getting Past No" problem-solving type of stuff here .... This case is about bucks, only bucks, and nothing but bucks .... So, the only thing I'm interested in knowing is where your bucks stop.* — *George, let me tell you at the outset that if you guys truly want to negotiate this contract, I'm not going to tolerate any "lock-in" tactics in the press .... If you guys want to do that, you and I might just as well get in front of the cameras now and lock horns ....*
with (tactful negotiator):	— *John, I may be wrong, but I really don't think we can "problem solve" this case .... For better or worse, my client's only interest is the amount of money she might receive.*[1] — *George, let me share with you one concern I have before next week's meeting. In these types of cases, I'm always concerned that the press might undermine a deal before we even have a chance to sit down and talk. I can prevent that on my end. Can you give me any help on that from your end?*

1. A tactful problem solver might respond, "I understand. I would just like to explore for a minute the possibility that each side could benefit by ...."

[2] Deflect the Tactic or Technique by Ignoring It

Deflecting a tactic or technique by ignoring it does not mean that you act as if you are naively unaware of it. For example, you might show your awareness of the tactic through subtle body language expressing your irritation, or by making some casual remark indicating that you know the tactic or technique is being employed. Deflecting a tactic or technique by ignoring it simply means that you proceed with the negotiation as if the tactic or technique were not being used. This approach essentially shows the other side that you are not interested in playing his or her game, and that you intend to proceed with your own principled approach to the negotiation.

[3] Expressly Expose the Tactic or Technique

Expressly exposing the tactic or technique involves directly mentioning it to your counterpart when it arises during the negotiation, hoping this will be enough to cause him to abandon the tactic. This approach differs from *[a]* above only in that when you expose the tactic you might not say anything about your unwillingness to proceed with the negotiation if the tactic continues to be used. Again, when expressly exposing the tactic or technique, try to be tactful so that your counterpart will not be unnecessarily embarrassed or lose face. For example, if your counterpart persists in *Dodging the Question* through one or more "blocking techniques," it may be more effective to explain why a candid answer to your question is important to the negotiation rather than to confront your counterpart with, "Why do you always answer my question with a question or with an answer to a question I never asked?"

[4] Respond to the Tactic or Technique in Kind

If you counter a disingenuous tactic or technique by employing the same or similar tactic or technique, the negotiation may rapidly result in deadlock. On the other hand, retaliating in this way may be enough to cause your counterpart to abandon the unproductive behavior. For example, when faced with a *Good Guy-Bad Guy Routine* or a *Two Against One* tactic, you might indicate to your adversaries that you may need to temporarily suspend the negotiation until another colleague can join you in continuing discussions. Similarly, as mentioned previously, a sudden claim of *Lack of Authority or Limited Authority* by your counterpart might be countered with a suggestion that you too may need to confer further with your client before a final agreement can be reached.

Chapter Six

Valuing Cases for Negotiation and Settlement

SYNOPSIS

§6.01 Introduction
§6.02 Target and Resistance Points
§6.03 Intuitive "Case Worth" Analysis
§6.04 Rule-of-Thumb Valuation
§6.05 Computer-Generated Valuation
§6.06 Traditional Economic Analysis
§6.07 Fair Settlement Range Formula
§6.08 Analysis of the Client's Motivations and Aversion to Risk and Motivations
§6.09 Adopting a Holistic Analysis and Advising the Client
§6.10 Example of Holistic Analysis

§6.01 Introduction

The vast majority of cases in the litigation context involve disputes over money, and such cases are usually negotiated through adversarial bargaining. In these negotiations, although the ultimate decision rests with them, clients will look to you for advice as to whether it is in their best interest to settle or take the case to trial. This requires valuing the likely outcome of the case at trial compared with the final settlement offer. It also involves taking into account your client's tolerance for the risk of an uncertain outcome at trial versus the certainty of settlement. Your client may well have other motivations affecting the choice between trial and settlement that must be considered as well. This Chapter discusses a variety of analyses that you might draw upon in valuing a case for negotiation and settlement. In addition, these analyses may help formulate the offers and concessions that your client might make during adversarial negotiations, which is discussed more fully in Chapter 7.

§6.02 Target and Resistance Points

As introduced in §3.02, in adversarial bargaining, the parties prepare for negotiation by establishing "target" and "resistance" points. From the Plaintiff's perspective, his "target point" will be the highest amount of money he realistically believes he could obtain if everything in the case went his way. From the Defendant's perspective, her "target point" will be the lowest amount of money she realistically believes she would have to pay if everything in the case went her way. The Plaintiff's "resistance point" will be the lowest amount of money he will accept in settlement; and if he does not receive at least that sum, he will take his chances at trial. On the other hand, the Defendant's "resistance point" will be the highest amount of money she is willing to pay to settle the case; and if the Plaintiff insists on a settlement that is greater than that amount, she will take her chances at trial.

Target points should not be confused with opening offers made in negotiations. The Plaintiff will usually make an opening offer to settle the case for an amount that is greater than his target point, and the Defendant will make an opening offer for an amount that is lower than her target point. Each party will thereafter make concessions (downwards for the Plaintiff and upwards for the Defendant) to propose settlement amounts that approach their respective target points. Usually, further concessions will be made such that the Plaintiff will end up offering to settle for an amount below his target point and the Defendant will end up offering to settle for an amount above her target point. However, in no event will the Plaintiff settle for an amount that is less than his resistance point, nor will the Defendant settle for an amount that is greater than her resistance point. The significance of the parties' resistance points is that a settlement will occur only if they overlap, where the minimum amount that the Plaintiff will accept is less than or equal to the maximum amount that the Defendant will pay.

For example, assume that the Plaintiff sets his target point at $70,000, resistance point at $30,000, and plans to make an opening offer of $90,000.

The Defendant sets her target point at $20,000, resistance point at $50,000, and plans to make an opening offer of $10,000. As shown in the chart below, Plaintiff's "settlement range" thus falls between $70,000 and $30,000, and Defendant's "settlement range" falls between $20,000 and $50,000. Plaintiff will gradually make concessions downward from his opening offer of $90,000, but never below his resistance point of $30,000; and Defendant will gradually make concessions upward from her opening offer of $10,000, but never above her resistance point of $50,000. The amount overlapping the parties' resistance points ($50,000 to $30,000), constitutes the anticipated "settlement zone"—the range within which the parties are most likely to reach final agreement. If there is no overlap between the parties' resistance points, no settlement can be achieved unless one or both of the parties revise their resistance points to expand the settlement zone.

The foregoing example may be illustrated as follows:

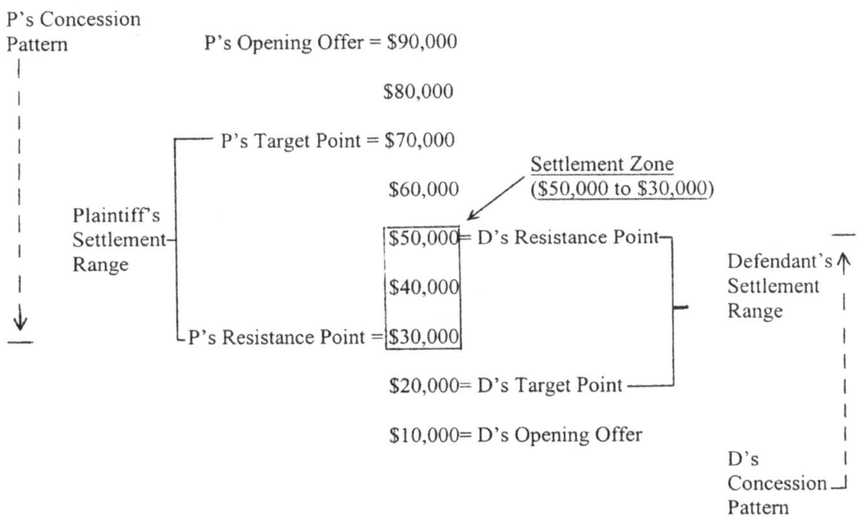

In light of the foregoing, in advising your client about settlement and in preparing for adversarial bargaining, you must be in a position to recommend a "settlement range" represented by a resistance point and target point. Ideally, and from a purely *economic* standpoint, when the only alternative to settling the case is going to trial, an accurate resistance point for the Plaintiff would be an amount that is less than what a jury would award; and an accurate resistance point for the Defendant would be an amount that is greater than what a jury would award. Thus, you must have some analytical method to determine an appropriate resistance point that your client might adopt in connection with negotiations in the litigation context. Once this "bottom line" is established, the goal of bargaining will be to settle the case in an amount that is better than one's resistance point and as close as possible to one's target point.

§6.03 Intuitive "Case Worth" Analysis

In advising clients about an appropriate resistance point, many lawyers engage in an essentially intuitive analysis of "what the case is worth" in terms of the net recovery to the client if the case were tried. This analysis is "intuitive" in the sense that it is largely based on the lawyer's experience and best judgment. It involves predicting what a likely jury verdict would be in light of all the circumstances of the case and then adjusting that verdict expectancy, downward for plaintiffs or upwards for defendants, by the amount that it is likely to cost the client to litigate the case. The resulting figure may serve as the client's resistance point. In making this analysis, lawyers typically consider (1) the cause of action that would be brought and the elements of proof and damages that the substantive law provides for that cause of action; (2) the relative strength of the evidence in support of and in opposition to the client's contentions about liability and damages; (3) the amount of money that could be reasonably argued to a jury in light of the foregoing factors and jury verdicts in similar cases; and (4) the cost of gathering and presenting the evidence in a persuasive manner to a jury.[1]

The particular cause of action and elements of proof and damages involved in the case will affect the accuracy of determining what the case is worth in a variety of ways. For example, in a contract dispute where damages are measured by the financial loss to the plaintiff as a result of the breach, or in a property damage suit where the damages are usually the difference between the fair market value of the property immediately before and after the event

---

1. Some lawyers also consider the relative experience and trial skills of opposing counsel as a factor that may affect the value of the case. However, unless opposing counsel is particularly inexperienced, this factor is usually less important than some lawyers might prefer to think. In any event, when negotiations are conducted prior to the filing of a lawsuit, and the negotiator for the other side is not the person who will represent the opposing party in the event suit is brought, the factor is irrelevant because the opposing litigator is unknown.

causing the damage, the value of the case from a jury-verdict standpoint may be relatively easy to forecast assuming that the essential facts and liability are not in dispute. However, even if there is no question about liability, if the cause of action is for personal injuries in an automobile accident case or for defamation involving damages for injury to reputation and punitive damages, the elements and measure of damage are much more difficult to forecast with any real degree of certainty. Determining what the case is worth becomes increasingly difficult if liability is questionable or the facts relating to damages are in dispute. Moreover, forecasting the likely result at trial is even more difficult if the burden of proof involves "clear, cogent, and convincing evidence" rather than the usual "preponderance of the evidence" standard, or the case involves multiple issues with shifting burdens of persuasion and production, or the existing law is unclear or of uncertain application.

Similarly, trying to determine what a case is worth is complicated by the quantum and quality of the evidence available in the case. For example, factors such as the availability of corroborating witnesses and the extent of their credibility, whether one or both parties have "jury appeal," and whether the particular facts of the case would cause a jury to be more sympathetic to one side or the other all have a bearing on the value of the case, but are not capable of any precise calculation. Similarly, the cost of finding and preparing expert witnesses in a difficult case is hard to calculate in advance.

Nevertheless, under an intuitive "case worth" analysis, a lawyer will take into account all of these factors, notwithstanding their uncertainties, to arrive at a "best judgment" about what a jury would do if the case were tried. Some lawyers consult sources on prior verdicts in similar cases. In addition, lawyers frequently confer with other experienced trial lawyers to solicit their views about what a jury might award in the particular circumstances, even though, when consulted about the same facts, highly experienced lawyers specializing in litigating the same type of case will often have wide differences of opinion.

After the value of the case is estimated from the standpoint of a most likely jury verdict, the lawyer will estimate the costs to the client of achieving that verdict, such as litigation expenses and lawyer's fees. Plaintiffs must subtract these expenses from the estimated jury verdict, while defendants must add them. The resulting figure may become the client's resistance point, and the target point is then set at a higher figure for plaintiffs or a lower figure for defendants based on an estimate of the *best possible* verdict that might be obtained if everything in the case goes the client's way.

§6.04 Rule-of-Thumb Valuation

In personal injury cases, some lawyers and insurance adjusters consider certain crude "rules of thumb" as a starting point in valuing a case. The most common of these is to estimate the settlement value of the case by multiplying the special damages by a factor of three. "Special damages" here means economic or out-of-pocket losses suffered by the plaintiff and will typically include the gross amount[2] of the medical bills and other expenses incurred as a result of the accident. For example, if the Plaintiff's gross doctors' bills are $4,500 and drug expenses are $500, $5,000 × 3 yields a potential settlement figure of $15,000. Although lost wages are part of special damages, insurance adjusters normally do not triple the lost wages, but instead add them after the multiplier is applied to the medical bills and other expenses. Thus, if the Plaintiff also has lost wages in the gross amount of $3,000, the final settlement estimate would be $18,000 ($15,000 ± $3,000).

This crude calculus is most frequently considered when liability is undisputed and the Plaintiff has not suffered any extraordinary pain or significant permanent injury. If the pain and suffering is relatively severe or permanent injury exists, the multiplier applied to the special damages might be increased to five, ten, or more. Generally, however, this multiplier, "rule-of-thumb" approach is only considered in minor personal injury cases.

§6.05 Computer-Generated Valuation

Today, many liability insurance companies utilize a computer software program to aid in the valuation of bodily injury claims. These programs, which contain closely-held proprietary information by their users, aim primarily to compute the general, non-economic damages of a personal injury claim. Adjusters using such a program typically rely upon its dollar valuation of the case in establishing a resistance-point range for settlement.

When the claimant's attorney in a personal injury case is dealing with a claims adjuster who is valuing the case based largely on a software program, the contents of a Settlement Brochure (*see* §§8.05–8.06) must provide the adjuster with all pertinent information that will allow the adjuster to "enter" all appropriate data into the computer program. This means that the claimant

2. This is the total of the medical and other expenses, regardless of whether the plaintiff has been or will be reimbursed for them from his private health insurance carrier or from some other independent source.

attorney's "Summary" of "Medical Treatment," "Lost Earnings," "Pain and Suffering and Permanent Injury" (*see* §8.05[3]–[5]) must be fully and specifically documented by official medical records or additional documentation obtained from relevant health-care providers.

For the attorney hired by an insurance carrier that utilizes a computerized program, effective representation in valuing a case based on that program will require an evaluation as to whether all of the relevant factors affecting the injured party's damages have been properly accounted for by the entries made into the program. Without such an evaluation, the computer valuation will be misleading at best and may result in a jury verdict in an amount far in excess of the computer valuation for the simple reason that factors introduced into evidence at trial were not "entered into" the computer program.

In sum, the use of computer software programs by insurance companies in estimating the value of non-economic damages like pain and suffering and permanent impairment is becoming routine. The effort to provide more "objectivity" to the assessment of general damages may, however, be fraught with gross miscalculation because computerized estimates are only as good as the data entered into the program. If the initial ranges of value plugged into the program for particular injuries and factors are flawed, or if the adjuster enters incomplete data into the program, the resulting valuation will be useless.

Moreover, no computer program can fully account for the often quintessential "personal" factors and dynamics that govern a jury's decision about the amount of general damages—the jury appeal of the claimant, the circumstances surrounding liability and injury, the credibility of witnesses, and the like. Thus, even though an adjuster may be bound by a general "policy" of the insurance carrier to adhere to the computerized valuation, a lawyer hired by the carrier to represent the defendant (and the lawyer for the claimant) should always bear in mind the inherent limitations on the utility of any computerized valuation. This means, at bottom, that, from the lawyers' perspective in terms of advising the client about valuation, the results of a computerized valuation should only be considered as an aid to valuation, rather than as an unyielding resistance point.

§6.06 Traditional Economic Analysis

The traditional economic analysis of valuing cases for settlement involves computing an "expected outcome" by multiplying the gross verdict at trial by the probability that it will occur, and then adjusting for transaction costs that would be incurred in obtaining that outcome. Assuming you represent the Plaintiff, this analysis consists of four calculations:

(1) First, an average verdict expectancy is estimated assuming that the Plaintiff will prevail on liability. For example, if a reasonable verdict range for the particular kind of case is $35,000 to $45,000, the average verdict expectancy would be $40,000.

(2) Second, the $40,000 average verdict expectancy is adjusted by the probability, expressed as a percentage, that the Plaintiff will be successful in obtaining that amount. This results in an "*expected* outcome" for your client. For example, if you estimate that there is a 50% chance on the law and the facts that your client will win $40,000, the "expected outcome" becomes $20,000. This outcome, under probability theory, is "expected" in the sense that if the case were tried 100 times, approximately 50 trials would result in a verdict for your client and 50 would result in a verdict for the defendant; and the average recovery would be 50 Plaintiff's victories multiplied by $40,000 per victory or $2,000,000, plus 50 losses multiplied by $0 per loss, divided by 100 cases for an average recovery of $20,000. When the analysis is conducted for the Defendant, in *theory*[3] she might use the same average verdict expectancy of $40,000 but will adjust it by her own estimate of the probability that the Plaintiff will be successful in obtaining that amount.

(3) Third, an estimate is made of all non-shiftable litigation expenses and hourly lawyer's fees that your client will incur if the case goes to trial, and these costs and hourly fees are also deducted from the average verdict expectancy. Thus, if your client is expected to incur a total of $4,000 in litigation expenses and hourly lawyer fees combined, the bottom-line settlement value of the case becomes $16,000. When the analysis is conducted for the Defendant, the expenses and fees are added.

(4) Fourth, the time value of money is sometimes considered because an amount received now is worth more than the same amount received much later. If your client is not expected to obtain a verdict for a number of years, and the investment yield on a prudent investment is currently X% per year, the amount of money received in a year is worth about X% less than if received now. Thus, for the Plaintiff, this time value of money would also be applied to adjust the $16,000 depending upon how much time is likely to transpire from

---

3. Needless to say, the Defendant's estimate of the average verdict expectancy for the case may be quite different than the Plaintiff's estimate, and disputes about this matter exist in the vast majority of cases.

the point an offer of settlement is made until a judgment would be obtained at a trial. The resulting figure may serve as your client's resistance point.

Setting aside a calculation for the time value of money, the basic formula for establishing the Plaintiff's and Defendant's resistance points may be expressed as follows:

P's Resistance Point	= Average Verdict Expectancy	× P's % Estimate of P's Probability of Winning at Trial	– P's Cost of Going to Trial
or:	(AVE	× PPW)	– PC
D's Resistance Point	= Average Verdict Expectancy	× D's % Estimate of P's Probability of Winning at Trial	+ D's Cost of Going to Trial
or	(AVE	× PPW)	+ DC

Theoretically, a settlement will occur only if Plaintiff's Resistance Point ≤ Defendant's Resistance Point.[4]

Taking the example above, Plaintiff's resistance point of $16,000 was calculated based on $40,000 (the Average Verdict Expectancy) × .50 (P's % Estimate of P's Probability of Winning at Trial) = $20,000 (P's expected outcome) – $4,000 (P's Cost of Going to Trial). Assume that the Defendant calculates her resistance point as follows: $40,000 (the Average Verdict Expectancy) × .40 (D's % Estimate of P's Probability of Winning at Trial) = $16,000 (D's expected outcome) + $5,000 (D's Cost of Going to Trial) = resistance point of $21,000. Since Plaintiff's resistance point of $16,000 is less than Defendant's resistance point of $21,000, a settlement would theoretically occur within the $5,000 zone of overlap.[5]

---

4. Expressed another way, a settlement will occur only if the Average Verdict Expectancy × P's % Estimate of P's Probability of Winning at Trial (P's expected outcome) (the Average Verdict Expectancy × D's % Estimate of P's Probability of Winning at Trial (D's expected outcome) ≥ P's Cost of Going to Trial ± D's Cost of Going to Trial.

5. Under the formula given in the preceding note, a settlement will theoretically occur because Plaintiff's expected outcome of $20,000 ($40,000 × .50) minus Defendant's expected outcome of $16,000 ($40,000 × .40) amounts to $4,000, which is less than the sum of the costs of going to trial for the two sides of $9,000 ($4,000 for Plaintiff + $5,000 for Defendant).

In the parlance of management science, the resistance-point calculation for the Plaintiff or Defendant may be expressed in the form of a "decision-tree" analysis commonly used in business and public-policy decision-making. To illustrate, assume that in the example above the Defendant ultimately makes a settlement offer of $20,500. In deciding whether to accept this offer, Plaintiff's decision tree might look like the following:

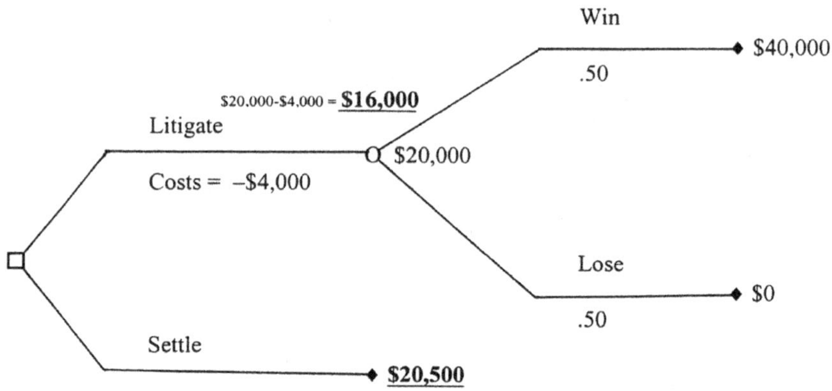

This tree is organized chronologically from left to right. The □ symbol is the "decision node," denoting the point at which the decision-maker must choose between two or more options. The O symbol is the "chance node," denoting the point where the decision maker is faced with an event over which he has no control and to which a probability is assigned that reflects the most likely result of the event. The ◆ symbol is the "terminal node," which denotes the result of an option or particular event.

Here, Plaintiff has two choices—litigate or settle—as shown by the branches stemming from the decision node, □. If Plaintiff accepts Defendant's settlement offer, Plaintiff will receive $20,500 as shown next to the terminal node, ◆, at the end of the branch representing the settlement option. If Plaintiff chooses the litigation option, he is expected to incur $4,000 in non-shiftable trial costs as shown under the branch denominated "Litigate."

The expected outcome of a trial, represented by the "Win" and "Lose" branches stemming from the chance node, O, is calculated with reference to the probabilities of achieving that outcome. That is, Plaintiff estimates he has a 50% (.50) chance of winning an average jury verdict expectancy for the type of case of $40,000, and therefore a 50% (.50) chance of getting $0.[6] The expected outcome of $20,000 shown to the right of the chance node, O, is calculated by: (1) multiplying the 50% probability of winning by the average jury verdict expectancy of $40,000; (2) multiplying the 50% probability of losing by the $0 payoff of defeat; and (3) adding the two together. Thus, .50 × $40,000 ± .50 × $0 = $20,000 as the expected outcome.

Finally, Plaintiff's resistance point of $16,000 (as shown above the "Litigate" option) is calculated by subtracting from the expected outcome of $20,000 the $4,000 in trial costs. Since the option of accepting Defendant's settlement offer of $20,500 yields a greater recovery than the option of going to trial which yields only $16,000, Plaintiff would be best off to accept the settlement offer.

If you were to construct a decision tree for the Defendant using the hypothetical given above, the expected non-shiftable trial costs would be $5,000; the Defendant's estimate of the probability of Plaintiff winning $40,000 at trial would be 40% (.40); and the Defendant's estimate of the probability of Plaintiff getting $0 at trial would be 60% (.60). Thus, .40 × $40,000 ± .60 × $0 = $16,000 as the expected outcome at trial. To this number, the Defendant would then *add* her expected trial costs of $5,000 to arrive at a resistance point of $21,000. If Plaintiff were to make a final settlement offer that is equal to or less than $21,000, Defendant should settle the case.

In short, this decision-tree analysis is substantively the same as Traditional Economic Analysis. However, because the "form" of the analysis is a management tool routinely taught in business schools and continuing education courses in management, it may serve as a more familiar method of presenting the settlement value of a case to a business executive who is making a decision on behalf of a corporate party.

§6.07 Fair Settlement Range Formula

The Fair Settlement Range Formula for valuing cases is essentially a refinement on traditional economic analysis. Under this formula, an over-all fair settlement range for the case is established, after which the Plaintiff might set his initial resistance point at the low end of the range and the Defendant might set her initial resistance point at the high end of the range. The components of the formula are as follows:

---

6. To make the arithmetic work, the sum of the probabilities assigned to the branches stemming from any chance node *must* equal 100%.

AVE = The Average Verdict Expectancy assuming the plaintiff will prevail on liability.

PPW = The Probability the Plaintiff Will Win the Average Verdict Expectancy, considering the law and facts of the particular case.

UPV = The Uncollectible Portion of the Verdict (*e.g.*, where some defendant is uninsured, underinsured, or is partially or completely judgment proof).

PC = The Plaintiff's Cost of going to trial.

DC = The Defendant's Cost of going to trial which the defendant would be willing to contribute to settlement.

SIF = Special Intangible Factors (expressed as a $ amount) that may increase or decrease the verdict (*e.g.*, the particular "jury appeal" of the case for one party or the other).

FSV = The Fair Settlement Value of the case.

FSR = The Fair Settlement Range of the case.

The formula may be expressed as follows:

$$(\text{AVE} \times \text{PPW}) - \text{UPV} - \text{PC} + \text{DC} \pm \text{SIF} = \text{FSV}$$

Then, FSV + (10% of FSV) = FSR (upper end of range)

FSV – (10% of FSV) = FSR (lower end of range)

For example, drawing upon the hypothetical estimates given for the Plaintiff in §6.06, the figures that would be computed in the formula would be:

- AVE = $40,000.
- PPW = 50% (.50).
- UPV = $0 (*i.e.*, assuming the Defendant is not uninsured or underinsured).
- PC = $4,000.
- DC = $3,000 (assuming the Defendant's total cost of going to trial would be $5,000 and it is estimated she would be willing to contribute $3,000 of the costs towards settlement, thereby saving $2,000 in costs).

- SIF = \$5,000 in favor of Plaintiff (*e.g.*, assuming he has much greater jury appeal than does the Defendant).

Applying the foregoing to the formula yields the following:

$$(\text{AVE} \times \text{PPW}) - \text{UPV} - \text{PC} \pm \text{DC} \pm \text{SIF} = \text{FSV}$$

- (\$40,000 × .50) – \$ 0 – \$4,000 ± \$3,000 ± \$5,000 = \$24,000

Then, to establish a Fair Settlement Range, 10% of the Fair Settlement Value is added to and subtracted from that Value to arrive at a range:

FSV ± (.10 × FSV) = FSR (upper end of range)

- \$24,000 ± (.10 × \$24,000) = \$26,400 (upper end of range), and

FSV – (.10 × FSV) = FSR (lower end of range)

- \$24,000 – (.10 × \$24,000) = \$21,600 (lower end of range).

Based on the foregoing, the Plaintiff might set his initial resistance point at \$21,600. He might then set his target point at \$27,000 and opening offer at \$75,000. In the usual case, the Defendant's calculation of the formula is likely to be quite different from the Plaintiff's calculation. However, assuming the Defendant arrives at the same Fair Settlement Range arrived at by the Plaintiff, the Defendant might set her initial resistance point at \$26,400, her target point at \$20,000, and opening offer at \$7,000.

§6.08 Analysis of the Client's Motivations and Aversion to Risk

The foregoing methods of valuation assume a rational actor whose decision to settle or go to trial will be made solely on the basis of economics. However, choosing between settlement and trial is not purely an economic decision. Whether a client will accept a final settlement offer or take his chances at trial also depends his psychological propensity for or aversion to risk—that is, the willingness to gamble on the outcome of a trial versus the certainty of receiving the amount offered in final settlement. Risk aversion varies from individual to individual and will often vary for each individual at different points in time.

Risk aversion helps explain why many settlements occur on the eve of trial and some occur literally on the courthouse steps. When a trial is a year or more away, the consequences of an adverse verdict appear more abstract. On the other hand, those consequences often take on a different reality during the weekend before trial, at which time many clients will suddenly prefer the certainty of a settlement to the risk of an undesirable verdict.

Clients also have various motivations that will affect their decision to settle the case or take it to trial. For example, settlement may be preferred to avoid the emotional strain and time demands of a trial, to preserve the personal or business relationship between the parties, to avoid unwanted publicity, to avoid an adverse legal or factual precedent, or to obtain an immediate source of funds if the client is in financial distress. On the other hand, a client might prefer a trial over settlement out of a desire to inflict punishment on the opposing party, to publicly vindicate a principle by having one side declared the winner and the other the loser, to establish a legal precedent or policy, or to simply delay payment of a claim for lack of sufficient funds to pay it.

Thus, you must always analyze the extent of your client's attitude toward risk and other motivations that may affect the desirability of settling the case or trying it. These factors may be analyzed by (1) identifying the various risks and personal motivations bearing upon the choice between settlement and trial, (2) reducing these to a set of consequences of settling the case on the one hand, and trying it on the other, and (3) asking your client to place a monetary value on the overall consequences in light of his preferences and values to determine how much he is willing to accept or forgo for those consequences. This amount might then be applied to increase or decrease the client's resistance point that was otherwise established based on a purely economic type of analysis.

As a simple example, assume that resistance points of $30,000 for the Plaintiff and $50,000 for the Defendant are arrived at by Intuitive "Case Worth" Analysis, Traditional Economic Analysis, or the Fair Settlement Range Formula. If the Plaintiff does not want to go through the emotional trauma of a bitter trial, he might lower his resistance point by an additional $10,000 to $20,000. If the Defendant is more willing to take the case to trial because she has received adverse publicity from the suit and wants to vindicate herself from any wrongdoing, she might adjust her resistance point such that she will pay no more than $30,000. Now the case that would have had a likely settlement of approximately $40,000 (the midpoint of a $30,000 to $50,000 settlement zone), is now likely to result in a settlement of approximately $25,000, the midpoint of a $20,000 to $30,000 settlement zone.

§6.09 Adopting a Holistic Analysis and Advising the Client

Most lawyers do not employ a standard mathematical formula in valuing cases for negotiation and settlement. Although a strict empirical approach may be tempting and comforting from the standpoint of providing some "objective" analysis, certainty in valuing cases for settlement is almost always illusory. The typical case presents too many factors and unknowns to reconcile through some rote computation. Indeed, if one applies, for example, Traditional Economic Analysis or the Fair Settlement Range Formula to the same case, the resulting computations will likely be very different. Moreover, if there were some foolproof formula for valuing cases, there would be no need for negotiation at all because cases would then simply be settled by applying that formula to the particular facts and arriving at a result.

Thus, most lawyers adopt a "holistic" analysis to valuing cases for settlement that essentially draws upon the various factors considered in Intuitive "Case Worth" Analysis, Traditional Economic Analysis, the Fair Settlement Range Formula, and an analysis of the Client's Aversion to Risk and Motivations. Depending on the particular type of case and the values and preferences of the client, holistic analysis considers the factors variously emphasized in the other approaches, giving those factors more or less weight as the circumstances warrant. In the process of considering and weighing these factors, however, holistic analysis does not attempt to plug them into some standard mathematical formula. Instead, it attempts to arrive at a multi-faceted, reasoned judgment about a reasonable "settlement zone" for the case and a reasonable "settlement range" for each side.

In this process, it is explicitly recognized that the predictions made are uncertain, may well change over time, and may well be revised during actual negotiations. These limitations on the prophetic accuracy of valuing a case are accepted as a reality and reconciled under the assumption that if the lawyer and client engage in an on-going assessment of the advantages and disadvantages of settling the case versus trying it, the final decision—which should always be made by the client—will turn out to be the best decision in the end.

It follows that in advising the client about a reasonable settlement zone and settlement range, most lawyers express their opinions about these matters as a *tentative* predictions or estimates. The reason for this is not, as some might cynically believe, to somehow exonerate the lawyer from making a bad prediction relied upon by the client. Rather, the tentativeness of the prediction or estimate is a candid admission of the inherent complexity and difficulty of valuing cases for settlement. It is consistent with the ethical prescription that a lawyer has a duty to advise his client according to the lawyer's best overall judgment and to place the ultimate decision whether to settle the case with the client. Indeed, a lawyer should explain this to the client in just these terms.

In light of the foregoing, in employing a holistic analysis to case valuation and advising your client about that analysis, you might follow the following 6 steps:

(1) Estimate the "Average Jury Verdict Expectancy" for the type of case, by evaluating:

- The cause of action;
- The burdens of proof for the cause of action;
- The legal elements and measure of damages for the cause of action;
- Jury verdicts in the same type of case, drawn from one's own experience, the experience of other lawyers, or from publications reporting jury verdicts.

(2) Adjust the Average Jury Verdict Expectancy (upwards or downwards) to arrive at an "Estimated Jury Verdict for the Case" that reflects the particular legal and factual circumstances of the case, by evaluating:

- Any uncertainties in the law about whether the case is actionable or damages are recoverable;
- The relative strength of the evidence in support of and in opposition to establishing liability;
- The relative strength of the evidence in support of and in opposition to establishing damages;
- What damages may be calculated as a sum certain (*e.g.*, special damages);
- What damages are amorphous (*e.g.*, pain and suffering, permanent injury, punitive damages);
- The extent to which the case has any special "jury appeal" for one side or the other.

(3) Adjust the Estimated Jury Verdict for the Case (downwards for the Plaintiff and upwards for the Defendant) by the amount of the client's non-shiftable costs of obtaining that verdict to arrive at a "Potential Resistance Point," by evaluating:

- All out-of-pocket expenses the client will likely incur and which the court will not tax against the party who loses at trial (*e.g.*, hourly attorney's fees, and costs associated with case investigation and preparation);
- The time value of money if a trial would not take place for a number of years.

(4) Adjust the "Potential Resistance Point" (upwards or downwards) based on the Client's aversion to risk and personal motivations, by evaluating:

- The client's financial, social, psychological, and other personal circumstances;
- The various risks and personal motivations of the client bearing on the choice between settlement and trial;
- The important consequences to the client of settling the case or trying it;
- Any monetary value that the client would place on settling the case in preference to trial or vice versa.

(5) Adjust the "Potential Resistance Point" further, if appropriate, based on an evaluation of the factors under steps (3) and (4) above from the other party's perspective.

(6) Based on the Potential Resistance Point as adjusted, advise the client about a tentative resistance point and tentative target point, leaving the final decision on these matters to the client.

These steps in holistic analysis are similar to the Fair Settlement Range Formula, but they place a greater premium on the effects that intangible factors play in evaluating whether it is in the client's best interest to settle the case or take it to trial. The analysis also embodies a more fluid reasoning process that better reflects how most clients and lawyers think about case valuation.

This does not mean that the mathematical calculations we have discussed are inappropriate to consider when conducting holistic analysis. For example, many lawyers find it useful to arrive at an "Estimated Jury Verdict for the Case" in Step 2 above by multiplying the "Average Jury Verdict Expectancy" by the probability, expressed as a percentage, that it will occur. Similarly, after arriving at the "Potential Resistance Point" in Step 5 of holistic analysis, it may be useful to consider a fair settlement range by establishing a bracket whose endpoints are 10% on either side of the Potential Resistance Point. In sum, holistic analysis might draw upon or be combined with certain aspects of the Fair Settlement Range Formula or any other valuation method in arriving at a potential resistance point and target point.

§6.10 Example of Holistic Analysis

Assume that a Town has decided to build a water supply reservoir to meet the demands of the Town's growing population. The site chosen for the reservoir is located approximately ten miles outside the Town limits. This is a predominantly rural area consisting mostly of farmland, but some residential subdivision development has occurred in the general area in recent years.

To acquire the land for the reservoir, the Town has given statutory notice to affected landowners that it intends to use its power of eminent domain to condemn eight separate properties, each of which consists of approximately 100 acres of vacant, unsubdivided, and undeveloped land, and each has different owners. However, before filing condemnation actions to officially take each of the eight properties, the Town has decided to negotiate with the affected landowners to purchase their properties at current fair market value. Three of the landowners have already sold their properties to the Town for $7,000 per acre, which is the current fair market value estimated by an independent appraisal firm hired by the Town. The other five landowners remain opposed to the reservoir project, but negotiations with them are still under way.

Ms. Jessica Dalton, a relatively poor, elderly widow, is one of the five landowners who has not yet settled with the Town. Her property also consists of 100 acres of vacant, undeveloped land. However, unlike all the other properties being acquired for the reservoir, Dalton had planned to subdivide her property into 10 contiguous lots of 10 acres apiece for eventual sale to third-party purchasers who would build their homes on the lots. In connection with these plans, last year she spent $50,000, constituting almost all of the proceeds of her late husband's modest life insurance policy, on surveying and various engineering costs to finalize a plat for the subdivision. When she was given formal notice that the Town planned to acquire her property as part of the reservoir project, she ended up not recording the plat with the County Register of Deeds office. Had she done so, her subdivision would have been complete because there were no other local-governmental requirements for its approval. Filing the plat would not have affected the Town's right to condemn her property.

The Town is still waiting for a response to the offers it has made to the four other landowners who were extended purchase offers based on $7,000 per acre. Because of Dalton's frustrated subdivision plans and expenditure of $50,000, the Town Council thinks her situation might be unique and has asked its attorney to estimate the value of Dalton's property for settlement purposes before the Town makes her a purchase offer.

Tracking the 6 steps set out in §6.09, the Town attorney's holistic analysis of the settlement value of Dalton's property might be as follows:

(1) An estimate of the "Average Jury Verdict Expectancy" for the condemnation case:

Although the Town would be the named plaintiff in a condemnation action, for all other litigation purposes it would actually occupy the position of a defendant. The burden of proof is on the landowner to establish, by a preponderance of the evidence, the fair market value of the condemned property as of the date of the taking, which is the date the Complaint is filed. When a lawsuit is filed, the Town must simultaneously deposit with the clerk of court the amount of money the Town estimates to be the current fair market value of the property (which amount is not admissible as evidence at a trial), and the landowner may immediately receive that money from the clerk notwithstanding the pendency of the lawsuit.

At trial, the jury decides the issue of "just compensation," *i.e.*, the fair market value of the property on the date of taking, and the judge decides all other issues. If the verdict exceeds the amount that the Town deposited with the clerk, the Town must pay the landowner the amount awarded in excess of the deposit. If the verdict is for less than the amount deposited, the landowner must pay back to the Town the difference between the amount deposited and the verdict. So long as the verdict is greater than the amount of the deposit, the law requires the Town to pay all litigation expenses of the landowner, such as costs of appraisals, appraisers' expert-witness fees, court-reporter costs for depositions, etc., but not attorney's fees. Landowners are usually represented on a contingent fee basis, whereby the lawyer's fee is a percentage of the amount obtained for the landowner that exceeds the amount the Town deposited with the clerk.

"Fair market value" as the measure of damages is the amount that a willing buyer and willing seller would most likely agree upon for the property, where the buyer is not compelled to buy and the seller is not compelled to sell. Fair market value is also determined based on the "highest and best use" of the property, which means the most economically viable use to which the property may be put, even if that is not how the property was being used at the time of the taking. However, the jury is not permitted to award compensation to the landowner based on a purely speculative use, or for sums such as lost profits from some intended future use. In addition, no compensation may be awarded for specific amounts paid by the landowner to improve her property, such as the $50,000 that Dalton spent, or for general damages such as those stemming from any inconvenience to the landowner, or emotional distress, or the like occasioned by the taking. Thus, the sole measure of compensation is the fair market value of the property on the date of taking, considering its "highest and best use."

Jury verdicts in condemnation cases typically favor the landowner and result in awards that are higher than the fair market value contentions of the condemnor such as a Town. This is usually the case even if the jury essentially rejects the testimony of the landowner's appraisers. Notwithstanding that the burden of proof is on the landowner, juries tend to give the landowner the benefit of the doubt in any valuation, and they are frequently prone to reject the appraisals of both parties altogether, and independently arrive at a determination of fair market value based on the differing "comparable sales" data submitted to them at trial. Apart from this general experience with jury verdicts, there are no reliable statistics that can be drawn upon to predict the average percentage by which verdicts exceed the fair market value contentions of the condemnor.

In the case at hand, because no condemnation suits have yet been filed by the Town, there are no verdicts to draw upon to estimate an "Average Jury Verdict Expectancy" for the per-acre value of the properties being acquired for the reservoir. The best information currently available is that all of the properties being acquired for the reservoir have a fair market value of approximately $7,000 per acre as determined by the appraisal firm hired by the Town. This figure does not appear to be an unreasonable benchmark because three landowners have already accepted this valuation. Thus, an Average Jury Verdict Expectancy for Dalton's 100 acres would be at least $700,000.

(2) Adjustment of the Average Jury Verdict Expectancy to arrive at an "Estimated Jury Verdict for the Case" that reflects the particular legal and factual circumstances of the case:

Estimating what a jury would most likely find to be the fair market value of Dalton's property is complicated by a legal question about the proper appraisal method that may be used in valuing that property. On the one hand, the Town's appraiser is likely to employ the "comparable sales" method of valuation to appraise the fair market value of the property based on actual sales of other approximately 100-acre tracts of undeveloped, unsubdivided land in the general vicinity of the reservoir area. There is no question that an appraisal based on this method would be admissible into evidence. The result would be a value of approximately $7,000 per acre for a total of $700,000.

However, Dalton's appraiser is likely to appraise her property on the assumption that it consisted of a subdivision of 10 lots, and therefore the fair market value should be determined based on the aggregate of the prices that could have been obtained for the 10 lots, less the costs of developing the subdivision and other costs that would have been incurred until all the lots had been sold. The case law in the jurisdiction is arguably conflicting about whether an appraisal based on this "development approach" to valuation would be admissible. On the one hand, the law is clear that a landowner may not value unsubdivided, undeveloped land as if it were subdivided or developed. On the other hand, the law is equally clear that if a final plat has been recorded to subdivide the property, it may be valued as a subdivision. In Dalton's situation, the only reason her plat was not recorded was due to the futility of that act in light of the Town's plans to acquire the property for the reservoir project, and the law would not now permit her to record the plat because she has received formal notice of the Town's condemnation plans.

Notwithstanding Dalton's situation, it is unlikely that the appellate courts in the jurisdiction would hold that a "development approach" to valuation would be admissible in valuing her property. However, because the resolution of this issue remains uncertain in the jurisdiction, there is a 50% chance that a trial judge would permit an appraisal based on that approach to be admitted into evidence in the case. If that were to occur, the jury would be presented with evidence that the fair market value of the property is approximately twice as much as that estimated by the Town's appraiser—*i.e.*, as high as $14,0000 per acre for a total of $1.4 million dollars.[7] Even if Dalton's appraisal based on the "development approach" were not admitted into evidence, she would still be able to introduce the fact that there was one sale of a large tract in the general vicinity of the reservoir area that sold for $8,000 per acre.

Even assuming that Dalton's appraisal of $1.4 million were admitted into evidence, it is highly unlikely that a jury would accept this amount as the fair market value because there is nothing to differentiate Dalton's property from the comparable sales in the $7,000–$8,000 per-acre range, except for the fact that Dalton had prepared a plat to subdivide her property into 10 lots. That is, the mere preparation of the plat (or the recording of it, had that occurred) did not result in any specific physical improvements to the property. Nevertheless, the jury is likely to be highly sympathetic to the fact that Dalton has now essentially lost the $50,000 she expended in surveying and engineering costs to prepare the plat. Although it is unlikely a jury would specifically include this amount in its verdict (given a trial judge's explicit instruction that this element of damage is not compensable), most jurors would have this loss in the back of their minds during deliberations.

From a "jury appeal" standpoint, everything about the case favors Dalton. She is an elderly widow of modest means who is being forced to give up her land. There will be no evidence that she will benefit in any way from the reservoir. Thus, consistent with the typical condemnation case, the jury is likely to give her the benefit of the doubt in any reasonable calculation of fair market value.

In light of the foregoing, even though it is unlikely a jury would give Dalton a "bonus" of $50,000 over and above what it otherwise determines to be the fair market value of her property, it is reasonable to predict that a jury would calculate the fair market value at approximately $7,500 per acre. This would be justified given that $8,000 per acre is the upper end of the available comparable sales data. The "Estimated Jury Verdict for the Case" is thus $750,000.

---

7. In appraisal "theory," at least, an application of the "development approach" and "comparable sales" method should yield the same result, assuming the "highest and best use" is residential development. In reality, however, this is almost never the case in light of the numerous variables considered in a "development approach" which may be manipulated to produce much higher values.

(3) Adjustment of the Estimated Jury Verdict for the Case by the amount of the Town's non-shiftable costs of obtaining that verdict to arrive at a "Potential Resistance Point":

It is expected to cost the Town approximately $35,000 in lawyer's fees, expert-witness fees, and other litigation expenses combined. In addition, it is estimated that the Town will have to pay Dalton approximately $10,000 of Dalton's litigation expenses. This totals $45,000 which, when added to the Estimated Jury Verdict for the Case of $750,000, results in a "Potential Resistance Point" of $795,000.

(4) Adjustment of the "Potential Resistance Point" based on the Town's aversion to risk and motivations:

The Town Council is primarily concerned about the *de facto* precedent that might be established if Dalton were paid much more than $7,000 per acre. This is so not only because three of the landowners have already accepted purchase offers from the Town at $7,000 per acre and might publicly accuse the Council of treating them disparately if Dalton were paid more than $7,000 per acre, but because there are four other remaining landowners who might not agree to accept less than the per-acre value that is given to Dalton. This problem could not be resolved by including a confidentiality clause as part of a settlement with Dalton because the Town is a governmental entity that has a duty to disclose how public funds are expended.

On the other hand, even though Dalton's property has no special characteristics that, from a fair market value standpoint, distinguish it from the tracts of land owned by the other seven landowners, unlike them, she has now lost the $50,000 she spent in preparing the subdivision plat. Out of fairness, the Council is not philosophically opposed to paying her this amount in addition to the reasonable fair market value of her property, even though she would not be legally entitled to recover the $50,000 at trial. Whether in a contract to purchase her property or in a settlement agreement, the Town could denominate the additional $50,000 as an equitable reimbursement for her special loss, thereby distinguishing it from the amount paid to her strictly for the fair market value of her property.

The Town's overriding interest is to settle all cases as close to the $7,000 per acre benchmark as possible because this is the figure that can be justified to the public based on the Town's appraisal. Moreover, the budget is extremely tight. Thus, the Council is not afraid to spend the $45,000 it would cost to try the case in an effort to establish a possible verdict precedent of approximately $7,000 per acre. If a jury awarded Dalton $7,500 per acre, she would receive $50,000 more than she otherwise would receive at $7,000 per acre, and this additional amount could be publicly explained as an equitable result in light of Dalton's loss of the $50,000 she incurred in preparing the subdivision plat. Paying her as much as $750,000 in settlement would be equivalent to the "Estimated Jury Verdict in the Case" and save the Town $45,000 in litigation expenses.

Thus, taking into account the Town Council's motivations, the "Potential Resistance Point" of $795,000 (*i.e.*, $45,000 in non-shiftable costs ∓ a $750,000 "Estimated Jury Verdict for the Case") might be adjusted downward to $750,000. This amount would (a) be consistent with the Council's goal of settling all cases at $7,000 per acre, (b) equitably reimburse Dalton for her special $50,000 loss which she otherwise would not be entitled to recoup at trial, and (c) save the Town $45,000 in litigation expenses that would be incurred in obtaining the "Estimated Jury Verdict for the Case" of $750,000.

(5) Adjustment of the "Potential Resistance Point" further, if appropriate, based on an evaluation of the factors under Steps (3) and (4) above from Dalton's perspective:

Not all of Dalton's litigation expenses are shiftable to the Town in the event of a trial. The trial judge will only award her "reasonable" litigation expenses. For example, if an appraiser charges her a particularly large amount of money to conduct an appraisal or testify at trial, the judge may tax only a portion of that charge against the Town. Moreover, she may incur some litigation-related costs that are not taxable against the Town at all (*e.g.*, the costs of preparing certain illustrative exhibits or preparing a professional video-tape of the property). However, it is unlikely that her non-shiftable costs will be great enough to warrant any adjustment to the Town's "Potential Resistance Point."

Dalton's aversion to risk and personal motivations are not known. However, it is reasonable to assume that given her age she might prefer to settle the case rather than wait out the trial process and an additional number of years if the case is appealed. In addition, it is reasonable to assume that she is aware of the settlements that the Town has reached with three of her neighbors. Regardless of what feelings she might have about their willingness to accept $7,000 per acre, it is also reasonable to assume that she wants to be compensated for her special loss of $50,000 in addition to receiving the fair market value of her property. None of these assumptions, however, warrant any adjustment to the Town's "Potential Resistance Point."

(6) Based on the Potential Resistance Point as adjusted, advise the Town Council about a tentative resistance point and tentative target point, leaving the final decision on these matters to the Council:

Based on the evaluations in Steps (1) through (5) above, a tentative resistance point for the Town would be not to pay Dalton more than $750,000. A tentative target point would be to pay her $700,000 based on $7,000 per acre. Because the Town has extended purchase offers to all of the other landowners based on $7,000 per acre, an initial offer to Dalton should not be less than this amount.

Chapter Seven

Preparing for Negotiation

SYNOPSIS

§7.01 Introduction
§7.02 Information to Obtain
[1] Information from the Client
[2] Information About the Other Party
[3] Information About the Opposing Negotiator
[4] Information About the Law
[5] Other Information
§7.03 Preparing a Negotiation Preparation Outline
[1] Step 1: From the Perspective of Each Party, Make a List of Information to Obtain, Information to Reveal, and Information to Protect
[2] Step 2: Make a List of Each Party's Interests
[3] Step 3: Make a List of Each Party's Primary Objectives, Secondary Objectives, and Incidental Objectives (to Exchange)
[4] Step 4: Make a List of Possible Solutions for Each Party (from most preferred to least preferred)
[5] Step 5: Make a List of Each Party's Best Alternatives to a Negotiated Agreement (BATNA)
[6] Step 6: Make a List of Each Party's Factual and Legal Leverage Points (Strong and Weak)
[7] Step 7: Identify Each Party's Potential Target and Resistance Points
[8] Step 8: Identify Each Party's Negotiating Strategy: Adversarial or Problem-Solving

[9] Step 9: Identify Each Party's Negotiating Style: Competitive (Hardball), Cooperative (Softball), or Competitive-Cooperative (Hardball and Softball)
[10] Step 10: Make a List of Each Party's Offers or Proposals in the Order They May be Presented
[11] Step 11: Consider Each Party's Particular Tactics
[12] Step 12: Revise All of the Foregoing Matters Throughout the Negotiating Process
§7.04 Format for Negotiation Preparation Outline
§7.05 Illustration of Negotiation Preparation Outline (Adversarial Approach)
§7.06 Illustration of Negotiation Preparation Outline (Problem-Solving Approach)
§7.07 The Role of the Client and Advising the Client

§7.01 Introduction

Thorough preparation is indispensable for effective negotiation. Before commencing negotiations, you must (1) obtain all information relevant to understanding what may reasonably be obtained for your client through negotiation, and (2) convert that information into a working outline from which an overall negotiating approach can be developed and employed.

§7.02 Information to Obtain

Generally, you should obtain all information that may be pertinent to the entire negotiation process. This information should serve as the raw material from which you can identify: (1) what further information you need to find out; (2) what information to reveal during the course of negotiating; (3) what information to protect from disclosure; (4) the underlying interests of each party; (5) the primary, secondary, and incidental objectives of each party; (6) possible solutions that may satisfy each party's interests and objectives; (7) each party's best alternatives to a negotiated agreement (BATNA); (8) each party's strongest and weakest factual and legal leverage points; (9) the "target" and "resistance" points for each party; (10) each party's negotiating strategy and style; (11) the specific offers or proposals that may be presented by each party; and (12) the particular tactics each party may employ during the negotiation process. In obtaining this information, consider the following categories.

[1] Information from the Client

Obviously, your client is a critical source of information. You need to know all the facts and circumstances surrounding your client's problem. Carefully probe your client's objectives: what would she want in a final agreement if she could obtain everything she hoped to achieve in the negotiation? And, if everything went against her in the negotiation, what would be the very least she would accept to conclude an agreement? What are her long-term and short-term goals?

Apart from objectives or goals, encourage your client to share her underlying "interests." That is, what are her real needs, desires, concerns, fears, and feelings? Many clients are hesitant to disclose these more deeply rooted matters for fear that revealing them will display some personal weakness or insecurity. However, a candid exploration of these matters may well give rise to alternative and more creative solutions for satisfying your client's objectives.

[2] Information About the Other Party

Just as you need to know all the facts and circumstances surrounding your client's problem from her perspective, it is also essential to understand all the facts and circumstances from the other party's perspective. The latter information will provide a basis for anticipating the other party's objectives and underlying interests. In short, you must be willing to put yourself in the shoes of the opposing party.

In obtaining information about the other party, be sure to obtain information about his personal and financial situation, his emotional or psychological needs, and his disposition. In addition, particularly when the opposing party is a corporation or governmental entity, identify the principal decision-makers who will play the most important roles in fashioning and deciding upon an agreement, and identify the particular pressures and interests that may affect their input into the negotiating process.

When obtaining information about an individual, do not overlook sources such as the Internet, criminal records, records of prior judgments, biographies, *Who's Who* books, clubs, professional societies, trade associations, or other attorneys or parties who have had prior dealings, disputes, or litigation with the individual. In the case of a corporation, useful information might be obtained from sources such as the Internet, the Consumer Protection division or Better Business Bureau of a state, annual and quarterly reports, reports of stockholders meetings, speeches of executives, company press releases, newspapers, or information supplied to governmental entities or public stock exchanges.

[3] Information About the Opposing Negotiator

Obtaining information about the negotiator for the opposing side is particularly important in choosing an appropriate negotiating style and strategy. Find out about the opposing negotiator's personality, style, level of competence, experience as a negotiator, reputation as a trial lawyer, and overall approach to negotiating.

If the opposing negotiator is a lawyer, it is also often useful to consider his likely fee arrangement with his client. For example, if the opposing party is being represented on a contingency fee basis, his lawyer may be primarily interested in a settlement that includes an up-front cash payment rather than a structured settlement with payments made over time. On the other hand, if the fee is based on an hourly rate, you will be able to estimate the pressure that mounting legal costs may impose on the opposing party throughout the negotiation process.

In addition, knowing about opposing counsel's general workload and trial schedule may be useful. For example, if opposing counsel is overworked, consumed by a pressing trial schedule, or is facing crucial deadlines in the case at hand or in other cases, these factors may markedly affect his disposition toward settlement at different times during the negotiation process.

[4] Information About the Law

Thoroughly researching the law applicable to your client's problem is essential. To be effective in negotiating you must not only know the factual strengths and weaknesses of the case, but the legal strengths and weaknesses as well. In addition, when appropriate, you should research any legal issues that may arise from the particular terms of a potential or final agreement.

[5] Other Information

Apart from the foregoing, you should obtain any other information that may be pertinent to the particular negotiation. In this era of information explosion and ever-expanding resources such as the Internet, your ability to obtain information is almost as limitless as your imagination.

§7.03 Preparing a Negotiation Preparation Outline

Once you have obtained as much of the foregoing information as possible, you should evaluate and transpose that information into a Negotiation Preparation Outline like that shown in §7.04. Use your outline to develop an overall negotiating approach. In preparing this outline, use the twelve steps presented below:

[1] Step 1: From the Perspective of Each Party, Make a List of Information to Obtain, Information to Reveal, and Information to Protect

Information to Obtain

An integral aspect of the negotiating process is finding out information from the other side that you have been unable to obtain independently. Having as complete information as possible about the other party's interests, objectives, possible solutions, best alternatives to a negotiated settlement, factual and legal leverage points, target and resistance points, offers or proposals, and particular tactics is essential in shaping your own approach to the negotiation. Thus, based on the information you already possess, make a list of information you need to find out from the other party.

Next, make a list of information you expect the other party will want to find out from you that is not readily obtainable from independent sources. This may or may not include information that you will be willing to reveal to the other side.

Information to Reveal

Make a list of information you want to reveal to the other party (whether or not the other side knows about it already), and a separate list of types of information you expect the other side will gratuitously reveal to you. Information to reveal may consist of each side's strong factual or legal leverage points that will be itemized in Step 6 below, or other important information that each party wants the other to know in order to understand one another's particular interests, objectives, possible solutions, and offers or proposals.

Information to Protect

Finally, make a list of information you want to protect from disclosure to the other side, and a separate list of types of information you expect the other party will not want to reveal to you. Information to protect may include damaging factual or legal points (*see also* Step 6 below), or sensitive information such as trade secrets, work product, or the like.

[2] Step 2: Make a List of Each Party's Interests

Conceptually, a party's "interests" are to be distinguished from her "objectives," even though the two often overlap or end up being the same. A party's objectives are the specific *matters* she wants to obtain from the negotiation, whereas interests are the underlying *reasons* for the party's objectives. There may be multiple interests underlying any one objective, or multiple objectives that are related to a single interest.

To identify the interests of your client or the other party, ask "why" she desires a particular objective. Focus on her underlying *needs, desires, concerns, fears, philosophies*, and *feelings*. What are the personal, psychological, ideological, and emotional motivations behind her goals? Does she have any special needs for power, prestige, acceptance, security, economic well-being, belonging, or control over her life? When listing the interests of your client and the other party, rank those interests from most important to least important, and note which interests may be shared between the parties, as well as those which conflict.

For example, consider the plaintiff in a defamation or wrongful death case. While in both cases the single "legal" objective would be money, the primary interest of the plaintiff in the defamation case might be to restore her reputation, and the primary interest of the plaintiff in the wrongful death case might be to ensure that the accident that killed the decedent would never happen again. These interests may give rise to alternative objectives and solutions apart from the mere payment of money. In the defamation case, the plaintiff's interest in restoring her reputation might be met by obtaining a public retraction and apology. This might not be at odds with the defendant's interests if the retraction and apology are styled in terms of the defendant having made a mistake in making the defamatory statement, and if a payment of a smaller sum is made to the plaintiff in exchange for making the recantation public. Similarly, in the wrongful death case, the interests of the plaintiff and defendant in preventing a future accident will undoubtedly be shared, and this may lead to a possible solution in which the defendant promises to undertake specific steps to correct the product's defect in exchange for paying a smaller sum to the plaintiff.

[3] Step 3: Make a List of Each Party's Primary Objectives, Secondary Objectives, and Incidental Objectives (To Exchange)

As mentioned above, a party's objectives are what she specifically wants out of an agreement, whereas her interests constitute the reasons underlying her objectives. In other words, objectives are the outgrowth of interests. While objectives and interests are conceptually distinct, objectives are quite often nothing more than interests formulated into statements of specific goals.

Based on the interests of both parties identified in Step 2 above, list each party's primary, secondary, and incidental objectives (or objectives to exchange). A "primary" objective is a specific matter that must be obtained if an agreement is to be reached at all. A "secondary" objective is an important but not necessarily vital matter that a party may choose to forgo if the primary objective is resolved in a satisfactory manner. An "incidental" objective is a lower-priority goal that a party would be pleased to obtain, but which will not have a substantial effect on the overall success or failure of the final agreement. In addition, an incidental objective may serve as a matter to trade with the other party for something of greater value. After listing each party's objectives, compare them to note those which are shared, which conflict, and which do not conflict.

[4] Step 4: Make a List of Possible Solutions for Each Party (From Most Preferred to Least Preferred)

In light of the interests and objectives of each party, make a list of possible solutions for each side. In formulating possible solutions, it may be useful to first consider the primary, secondary, and incidental objectives of each party that are shared or do not conflict, and then consider those that do conflict.

Particularly when thinking about solutions to the parties' conflicting objectives, try to develop solutions based on objective criteria that are fair and independent of each party's mere desires. For example, in a property damage dispute, a reasonable solution is more likely to be found if the parties focus on objective criteria such as appraisals or "book values" to establish fair market value, rather than on a sum that one party merely wants to receive or the other is merely willing to pay. Similarly, in a construction contract dispute, a solution might be based on industry-wide standards, rather than on the mere preferences or practices of the particular parties. Depending upon the case, other sources of objective criteria might include what a court might decide, professional standards, moral standards, expert opinions, precedent, costs, efficiency, tradition, and the like.

At this stage, it is particularly important to "brainstorm" and list all possible solutions. These will later be refined into more concrete offers or proposals in Step 10 below.

[5] Step 5: Make a List of Each Party's Best Alternatives to a Negotiated Agreement (BATNA)

The purpose of negotiation is not only to reach an agreement that satisfies your client's objectives and interests, but also to protect your client from an agreement that would be harmful or counterproductive to his interests and objectives. In understanding the dividing line between an acceptable and unacceptable agreement, you must understand your client's Best Alternative to a Negotiated Agreement (BATNA), and whether that "walk-away" option would be better than anything that could be achieved from an agreement.

Knowing your client's BATNA and forecasting the other party's BATNA is essential to understanding the relative negotiating strength of each party. If you know in advance what your client's alternatives are if an agreement is not reached, you will not be negotiating in the dark. Instead, you will have the strength and confidence to walk away from the bargaining table if the best alternative is more attractive than the final agreement. Similarly, the relative negotiating power of the other party will primarily depend on his BATNA.

Understanding the BATNA of both parties also makes it easier to realistically estimate what you can expect from the negotiation. If your BATNA is greater than the other side's BATNA, you will have greater leverage over the terms of any negotiated agreement. Conversely, if the other side's BATNA is greater than yours, you may have to reduce your expectations and modify your objectives accordingly.

[6] Step 6: Make a List of Each Party's Factual and Legal Leverage Points (Strong and Weak)

Factual and legal leverage points are the strong and weak aspects of the case that shape the parties' target and resistance points (see Step 7 below), and the rationales for each party's offers or proposals (*see* Step 10 below). As such, these factual and legal leverage points are used by the parties in arguing for or against various terms of an agreement.

Each party's strong and weak factual and legal leverage points often correspond, respectively, to the information "to reveal" and information "to protect" listed in Step 1 above. In listing these factual and legal leverage points, it is important to maintain an objective perspective. Because you are intimately familiar with your client's situation and may know much less about the other side's situation, it is sometimes tempting to unduly focus on the weaknesses of your own case without recognizing that those weaknesses may not be actually apparent to the other party. Thus, remember that your assessment of the strong and weak points for each party is necessarily limited by the extent of the information possessed by you.

[7] Step 7: Identify Each Party's Potential Target and Resistance Points

As discussed in §6.02, a party's "target point" is the best result she realistically hopes to achieve from the negotiation. It is not to be confused with a party's opening offer (see Step 10 below), which is the point at which a party begins negotiations and thereafter moves, through a series of concessions, toward the target point but not below her "resistance" point. A party's "resistance" point is her "bottom line"—the point below which she would cut off negotiations and resort to her Best Alternative to a Negotiated Agreement (BATNA). In other words, it is the point below which the party is unwilling to make any further concessions or compromises.

Estimating target and resistance points depends upon an overall evaluation of the case in light of all the factors considered in Steps 1 through 6 above. Drawing upon those factors and the valuation methods discussed in Chapter 6, you should establish not only the target and resistance points of your client, but consider and list alternative target and resistance points that may be adopted by the other side so that you can estimate different ranges of potential settlement zones.

[8] Step 8: Identify Each Party's Negotiating Strategy: Adversarial or Problem-Solving

As discussed in Chapter 3, there are generally two types of negotiating strategies: "adversarial" or "problem-solving." Each has its advantages and disadvantages that should be considered in light of the particular case. Taking into account these considerations and the matters developed in Steps 1 through 7 above, identify the particular strategy you intend to adopt in the negotiation and the one you expect will be employed by the other party.

[9] Step 9: Identify Each Party's Negotiating Style: Competitive (Hardball), Cooperative (Softball), or Competitive-Cooperative (Hardball and Softball)

Also as detailed in Chapter 3, there are generally three types of negotiating styles: (1) "competitive" (hardball), (2) "cooperative" (softball), or (3) a combination of "competitive and cooperative" (hardball and softball). Like the different negotiating strategies, the different negotiating styles have their distinct advantages and disadvantages. In addition, there are particular advantages and disadvantages to different style and strategy combinations such as "competitive and adversarial," "cooperative (or competitive-cooperative) and adversarial," "competitive and problem-solving," or "cooperative (or competitive-cooperative) and problem-solving." In light of these considerations and the anticipated negotiating strategy of each side listed in Step 8 above, identify the particular negotiating style you plan to use in the negotiation, and the one you expect will be used by the opposing party.

[10] Step 10: Make a List of Each Party's Offers or Proposals in the Order They May Be Presented

The specific offers or proposals of each party should be formulated in light of all the matters developed in Steps 1 through 9 above. In deciding your opening offer and fallback offers in descending order to your final offer, the target and resistance points and potential concession patterns developed in Step 7 above are particularly important. In addition, for every offer or proposal you make, you should draw upon the factual and legal leverage points listed in Step 6 above to back up each offer or concession with well-reasoned rationales.

In choosing an opening offer, it is important to note that a number of studies have shown that negotiators frequently obtain more satisfactory outcomes when they start with more extreme rather than more moderate demands (*i.e.*, higher initial demands by plaintiffs or lower initial offers by defendants). In this regard, experience has shown that in choosing an initial offer, many successful negotiators first forecast the best result they reasonably expect to achieve in the negotiation, and then deliberately *increase this goal* or target point in setting an opening offer.

On the other hand, if your initial offer or proposal is too extreme and cannot be backed up with sensible reasons, you are likely to quickly lose credibility with the opposing party. In that event, the negotiation may collapse at the outset, or, if it nevertheless proceeds, it will be more difficult for you to justify the meaningfulness of your concessions to the other side. In short, your opening offer and each subsequent offer should be supported by non-frivolous rationales.

In developing your fallback offers and concession pattern, consider (1) the extent of the information possessed by each side and the extent to which the factual and legal aspects of the case have been developed; (2) how protracted the negotiation is likely to be in light of the relative complexity of the case; and (3) the particular negotiating strategy and style (*see* Steps 8 and 9 above) of the opposing party. Generally, the more thoroughly developed the case is in terms of the overall information possessed by each side, the less room you need to leave to maneuver between your opening offer and final offer. Similarly, if the negotiation is not expected to be long or complex, and the opposing party does not take a highly competitive (hardball) approach to the negotiation, it is less important to preserve substantial maneuvering room between your initial proposal and bottom line. On the other hand, if the negotiations start out when the parties possess limited information about each other's interests and objectives, or if the opposing party adopts a highly adversarial strategy and competitive style, you should prepare a concession pattern that leaves ample room within which to maneuver from your opening offer to your final one.

Finally, it is essential to forecast the potential offers and concession pattern of the opposing party. This perspective will help you to anticipate and formulate balanced counter-offers and alternatives to the other side's proposals.

[11] Step 11: Consider Each Party's Particular Tactics

Negotiators invariably employ a variety of particular tactics throughout the negotiating process to advance their clients' objectives. The most common tactics are discussed in Chapter 10. Thus, in preparing for negotiation, you should consider any particular tactics you might employ, and anticipate any tactics that might be used by the other party so that you will be prepared to meet and counter those tactics.

[12] Step 12: Revise All of the Foregoing Matters Throughout the Negotiating Process

The foregoing Steps are designed to systematically develop an overall approach to the particular negotiation. You can then prepare a Negotiation Preparation Outline for use in all stages of the negotiating process. While the outline may serve as a blueprint or road map for the negotiation, you should always be prepared to revise any aspect of it, in whole or in part, as circumstances warrant.

§7.04 Format for Negotiation Preparation Outline

There are many ways to format a Negotiation Preparation Outline. One format is as follows:

	YOUR CLIENT	OTHER PARTY
1. INFORMATION		
To Obtain:	1.	1.
	2.	2.
	3.	3.
	4.	4.
To Reveal:	1.	1.
	2.	2.
	3.	3.
To Protect:	1.	1.
	2.	2.
	3.	3.
2. INTERESTS (from most important to least important)		
	1.	1.
	2.	2.
	3.	3.
	4.	4.

	YOUR CLIENT	OTHER PARTY
3. OBJECTIVES		
Primary:	1.	1.
	2.	2.
Secondary:	1.	1.
	2.	2.
Incidental (to exchange):	1.	1.
	2.	2.
4. POSSIBLE SOLUTIONS (most preferred to least preferred)		
	1.	1.
	2.	2.
	3.	3.
5. BEST ALTERNATIVES TO A NEGOTIATED AGREEMENT (BATNA)		
	1.	1.
	2.	2.
6. FACTUAL AND LEGAL LEVERAGE POINTS		
Strong points:	1.	1.
	2.	2.
	3.	3.
	4.	4.
Weak points:	1.	1.
	2.	2.
	3.	3.
	4.	4.
7. POTENTIAL TARGET AND RESISTANCE POINTS		
Target Points:	1.	1.
	2.	2.

Continued

Continued

	YOUR CLIENT	OTHER PARTY
Resistance Points:	1.	1.
	2.	2.

8. OFFERS OR PROPOSALS

	1st:	1st:
	2nd:	2nd:
	3rd:	3rd:
	4th:	4th:

9. PARTICULAR TACTICS

	1.	1.
	2.	2.
	3.	3.

§7.05 Illustration of Negotiation Preparation Outline (Adversarial Approach)

Assume you represent Polly Pierce, a very attractive nineteen-year-old woman, who lives in Hopeville, a small town in rural North Carolina. Polly's father is a tobacco farmer who has recently been diagnosed with cancer, and her mother is a homemaker.

Polly has just finished her first semester at a small four-year college, the Gordon College of Dance & The Arts in Bakersfield, North Carolina, which is nationally known for training some of the best performing dancers in the country. Although Polly is considered by her instructors to have a promising career and is one of the best dancers the college has seen in the past decade, she is only on a partial scholarship and her parents are struggling to pay the balance of her tuition and other expenses which total approximately $20,000 per year.

On the evening of December 12, Polly went to a party with some of her classmates to celebrate the end of the first semester. At the party, she had four beers during a two-hour period. As she was about to leave and drive back to the college, one of her classmates, Missa Sulick, asked Polly if she was able to drive.

Missa was concerned that Polly had too much to drink. Polly said that she was fine and proceeded to drive back to the college which was approximately 15 miles away. Other classmates at the party would testify that, while they could tell that Polly had been drinking, she was not too intoxicated to drive.

While driving back to the College, Polly was hit head-on by Donald Doan, who lost control of his car while speeding and crossed the centerline into Polly's lane of travel. Polly was not speeding. The accident happened on a lightly traveled road in Bakersville County. There were no independent witnesses to the accident.

Polly was taken by ambulance to Bakersville Memorial Hospital where she was diagnosed with multiple fractures to her right leg and ankle. Her blood alcohol level taken approximately one hour after the accident was 0.07, just below the legal limit. She spent 10 days in the Hospital during which she had surgery and the doctors put a pin in her leg to secure one of the fractures. Her medical and physical therapy bills totaled $30,000. Because Polly had no insurance, the Hospital has asserted a statutory lien in that amount on any personal injury funds she recovers. That is, the $30,000 will have to be paid back to the Hospital out of any personal injury compensation that Polly receives.

Polly was able to attend the spring semester on crutches, and her fractures were healed by the end of April. She has a 25% permanent partial disability rating of her right leg and ankle. She is able to walk without a cane, but she has a permanent limp and a slightly visible four-inch scar on her right leg from the surgery. Her doctors expect that she is at high risk for developing potentially debilitating arthritis later in life, but they have no estimate of what this might mean in terms of future medical costs. Her prospects for any dancing career are now over. She had no medical problems before the accident, except that when she was 18, she was diagnosed with early degenerative disc disease in her back which may or may not have hampered her future dancing career. According to standard mortality tables, she has an average life expectancy of an additional 53 years.

The top dancing graduates from Gordon usually earn between $30,000 and $40,000 per year for the first two to three years, and for the next five to ten years they may earn up to $100,000 or more per year depending upon their success. Polly has now decided to switch her major from dance to art history, and either teach art history in high school or at the college level upon graduating from Gordon.

Doan was miraculously not injured in the accident. He admitted to the police that he had "been going a bit over the speed limit." He was charged with speeding and driving while left of center of the roadway, and he pled guilty to these traffic violations. Doan is a member of the Bakersville County Board of Commissioners, and it is rumored that he might run for Chairman of the Board in the next election that is six months away. To date, there has been no media coverage of the accident. It is also rumored that Doan recently inherited a sizeable sum of money that is believed to be in excess of $500,000.

You have undertaken to represent Polly on her personal injury claim on a contingency fee basis, which is 1/3 of the gross recovery regardless of any medical liens. You have already given notice of your representation to Doan's insurance carrier. The adjuster handling the claim, Arnold Aaron, is based at the carrier's headquarters in Dallas, Texas. Aaron is a senior claims adjuster who is rumored to be an extremely hard-nosed negotiator. Polly's property damage claim for her car has already been resolved.

No lawsuit has yet been filed in the case. If a lawsuit is filed, it will be filed in Bakersville where jury verdicts are significantly lower than in larger cities such as Dallas, Texas. You have found out that at least one recent jury verdict in Dallas on similar facts totaled $600,000.

Polly is still quite angry about the accident and how it has foreclosed her promising career in dance. She plans to finish her college education at Gordon, but she does not want her tuition and expenses for the remaining three years (approximately $60,000) to be a burden on her family, particularly in light of her father's declining health. She is also very concerned about her long-term physical condition in light of the prognosis of early arthritis and because any health insurance she might now obtain would most likely exclude her leg and ankle injury as a pre-existing condition. She is also concerned about how she will pay the $30,000 hospital lien. While Polly is not afraid of a jury trial, she would very much prefer to settle the case and get it over with before beginning her second year at Gordon, which starts in four months. She does not care whether the terms of any settlement are kept confidential, and she also doesn't care if the settlement is "structured" (whereby she would receive payment over a number of years) so long as she receives an initial lump sum that will cover her remaining college education and the hospital lien after attorney's fees are paid.

North Carolina law requires that all motorists carry liability insurance of at least $50,000. You do not know the limits on Doan's policy, but they may be considerably more than $50,000. In addition, North Carolina is a pure contributory negligence jurisdiction, which precludes a claimant from recovering *any* amount on a personal injury claim if she is in any way contributorily negligent.

You estimate that the best monetary result you can realistically obtain for Polly is $479,000 calculated as follows: $30,000 for the medical bills; $25,000 for pain and suffering from December through April; and $424,000 for permanent disability, future pain and suffering, and the loss of her dancing career. You calculated these damages at $8,000 per year for her 53-year life expectancy. Your rough guess is that Aaron will not settle for an amount over $300,000, particularly in light of the potential contributory negligence problem.

It is now early May, five months after the accident. You have told Aaron that in the near future you will provide him with an initial offer along with pertinent documentation about Polly's claim. Aaron already has a copy of the accident report by the police, and a copy of Polly's medical records and bills since December 12 from Bakersville Memorial. You expect that if the case is to be settled in the next three to four months, all of the negotiation is likely to be conducted with Aaron in writing and over the telephone.

Based on the foregoing, your Negotiation Preparation Outline might include the following:

	YOUR CLIENT	OTHER PARTY
1. INFORMATION		
To Obtain:	1. D's insurance policy limit.	1. P's past medical history.
	2. Whether D will run for re-election.	2. Facts about P's drinking at the party.
	3. D's financial situation.	3. P's jury appeal.
To Reveal:	1. P's jury appeal.	1. P's.07 alcohol level.
	2. P's promising dance career.	2. P has recovered from her injuries.
	3. P's disability rating.	
	4. P is uninsured.	
	5. $600,000 Dallas verdict.	
To Protect:	1. P prefers to settle.	1. D's financial situation.
	2. P's prior medical history.	

Continued

Continued

	YOUR CLIENT	OTHER PARTY
2. INTERESTS (from most important to least important)		
	1. Not to burden family with college expenses.	1. Aaron will want to minimize any pay out.
	2. Concerned about future physical problems.	2. D doesn't want publicity.
	3. Pay off hospital lien.	3. D doesn't want a judgment in excess of policy limits.
	4. Settle the case.	4. D probably wants to settle.
3. OBJECTIVES		
Primary:	1. $ to pay remaining college expenses and lien.	1. Aaron wants to pay as little $ as possible.
	2. Future medical insurance.	2. D doesn't want a judgment in excess of policy limits.
Secondary:	1. $ to compensate for future pain and suffering.	1. Settle the case.
		2. Include confidentiality clause in settlement.
Incidental: (to exchange)	1. No confidentiality clause in settlement.	1. --------------------
4. POSSIBLE SOLUTIONS (most preferred to to least preferred)		
	1. Lump-sum settlement.	1. Structured settlement.
	2. Part lump-sum and part structured settlement.	2. Part lump-sum and part structured settlement.
	3. Carrier to provide P with future insurance.	

	YOUR CLIENT	OTHER PARTY
5. BEST ALTERNATIVES TO A NEGOTIATED AGREEMENT (BATNA)		
	1. Binding arbitration or mediation.	1. Jury trial.
	2. Jury trial.	2. Binding arbitration or mediation.
6. FACTUAL AND LEGAL LEVERAGE POINTS		
Strong points:	1. P's jury appeal.	1. P's potential contributory negligence.
	2. Permanent disability.	2. P is fully recovered.
	3. $30,000 in special damages.	3. Speculative future medicals.
	4. Promising career is destroyed.	4. Lower verdict expectancy In Bakersville.
	5. Dallas jury verdict of $600,000.	
Weak points:	1. P's potential contributory negligence.	1. P's jury appeal.
	2. Dancing career speculative.	2. P's permanent disability.
	3. Future medicals speculative.	3. Promising career destroyed.
	4. Lower verdict expectancy in Bakersville.	
7. POTENTIAL TARGET AND RESISTANCE POINTS		
Target Points:	1. $479,000	1. $100,000
Resistance Points:	1. $150,000	1. $300,000
	(Settlement Zone = $150,000 to $300,000)	
8. OFFERS OR PROPOSALS		
	1st: $600,000	1st: $90,000
	2nd: $500,000	2nd: ?
	3rd: ?	3rd: ?
	4th: $350,000 (not lower than $150,000)	4th: $300,000

Continued

Continued

	YOUR CLIENT	OTHER PARTY
	— Consider structured settlement for any amount over $150,000	
	— Trade confidentiality clause for more $	
	— Trade less $ for carrier insuring P for leg and ankle (P to pay premiums)	
9. PARTICULAR TACTICS		
	1. Threaten lawsuit in 30 days if case not settled.	1. Aaron may delay until he gets discovery relevant to contributory negligence.
	2. Send a videotape of P to Aaron.	
	3. Send Aaron affidavits from students who say P was able to drive.	

§7.06 Illustration of Negotiation Preparation Outline (Problem-Solving Approach)

Assume you represent Coble Inc., a small midwestern fertilizer manufacturer. Coble has one plant in the Midwest and has recently developed an improved fertilizer for commercial farming. Coble wants to expand its market for the new fertilizer by establishing new plants throughout the country. While Coble's first plant has been profitable, the company does not have the capital to build new plants on its own and has decided against seeking traditional financing for fear of straining the company's fiscal resources. Moreover, Coble still does not have a well-developed management team with the capability of managing multiple plants in different areas of the country.

Consequently, over the past year Coble has entered into licensing agreements with two other companies, one in the southeast and one in the northeast. Under these agreements, Coble has granted each company an exclusive right to manufacture and sell the new fertilizer and any improvement to the product that is made or acquired by Coble within a 250-mile radius of the licensee's plant. Each company paid Coble an initial fee in the form of a nonrefundable advance against royalties, which provided Coble with immediate cash to expand its own plant and engage in continuing research and development. To prevent the licensees from developing a substitute to Coble's fertilizer and thus avoid payment of additional royalties in the future, the licensees were required to assign all of their improvements in fertilizer substitutes to Coble so that it could remain in control of the business and receive royalties on any improvements to the product that were manufactured and sold by any licensee.

Through these licensing arrangements, Coble's on-going plan is to obtain additional plants throughout the country that are run by management supplied by licensees. The licensees would have the benefit of exclusively manufacturing and selling a top-quality product in their region and generate earnings based on the success of their sales and plant operations.

Although Coble has done well with its Midwestern plant and with the licensees in the southeast and northeast, it has not yet been able to expand its market into the farm belts of the central states such as Nebraska and Kansas. However, Coble has recently been contacted by Baxter, Inc., a manufacturer and seller of pesticides. Baxter owns and operates two plants, one in the southeast and the other in Nebraska, and is interested in entering into a licensing agreement with Coble to manufacture and sell the new fertilizer from both of Baxter's plants.

Representatives of Coble and Baxter have already held preliminary discussions about a potential licensing arrangement. Coble has learned that while Baxter has never been in the fertilizer business, the company has an interest in developing its own line of fertilizers sometime in the near future and would not want to assign those products to Coble and pay royalties on them. Coble has also learned that Baxter has a large share of the pesticide market in the southeast and central states (including Nebraska, Kansas, Oklahoma, and the Dakotas), and virtually all of its customers would be potential buyers of the new fertilizer. Finally, Baxter has made clear that in order to enter into a licensing agreement, Baxter must be permitted to manufacture and sell Coble's new fertilizer from both of Baxter's plants.

Coble is concerned that if Baxter develops new fertilizers in the future and pays no royalties on them, Coble will be in the ironic position of having put Baxter into the fertilizer business, only to lose the ability to earn money from a business initially created by Coble's creative efforts. In addition, while granting Baxter a license in the southeast would not violate Coble's specific territorial agreement with its southeastern licensee, Coble is concerned that competition between two licensees in that region might reduce overall profits.

Notwithstanding the latter concern, Coble has also had some exploratory discussions with Fulton, Inc. of Atlanta, Georgia, which is interested in a licensing agreement on the same terms as those that Coble negotiated with its current southeastern licensee. However, Coble is more interested in making a deal with Baxter because of its broad customer base not only in the southeast but throughout the central states.

Coble's strong preference is to negotiate a licensing agreement with Baxter along the same terms as Coble has negotiated with its other licensees. While Coble intends to be flexible, in no event will it enter into an agreement that does not provide some protection against Baxter's domination of the commercial fertilizer business through the development of its own line of fertilizers. Because Coble's cash flow situation is now much better than it was a year ago, Coble is prepared to be flexible about requiring Baxter to pay a nonrefundable initial fee.

The lead negotiator for Baxter is its in-house attorney, Malcolm Sears. Sears has a reputation for being smart, forthright, and easy going. A meeting has been scheduled between you and Sears in ten days to see if the basic elements of a licensing agreement can be worked out.

Based on the foregoing, your Negotiation Preparation Outline might include the following:

	YOUR CLIENT	OTHER PARTY
1. INFORMATION		
To Obtain:	1. Number of B's potential customers for fertilizer.	1. History of gross sales of fertilizer.
	2. B's ability to convert plants for fertilizer mfg.	2. Other licensees and the terms of their agreements.
To Reveal:	1. C's strong sales.	1. B's broad customer base.
	2. Discussions with Fulton.	2. B's ability to manufacture and sell fertilizer.
To Protect:	--------------------	--------------------

	YOUR CLIENT	OTHER PARTY
2. INTERESTS (from most important to least important)		
	1. Expand market into central states.	1. Expand into fertilizer mfg. and sales at both plants.
	2. Protect control over product and future royalties.	2. Retain all rights to B's own line of fertilizers.
	3. Maintain cash flow for on-going R and D.	3. Pay lowest royalties and initial fee as possible.
3. OBJECTIVES		
Primary:	1. Enter into licensing agreement with B, particularly to expand market into central states.	1. Enter into licensing agreement with C for both of B's plants.
	2. Protect control over product and future royalties.	2. Pay no royalties on any fertilizers developed by B.
Secondary:	1. Require B to pay the same royalties as are being paid by other licensees.	1. Pay lowest royalties and initial fee as possible.
Incidental: (to exchange)	1. Amount of initial fee.	1. -------------------
4. POSSIBLE SOLUTIONS (most preferred to to least preferred)		
	1. Licensing agreement on the same terms as those negotiated with C's other licensees.	1. Licensing agreement without assignment to C of any fertilizers developed by B alone.
	2. Licensing agreement without assignment to C of fertilizers developed by B alone, but B must share any of its improvements/substitutes with C and permit C and its other licensees to use them without cost.	2. Licensing agreement without assignment to C, but B still gets to manufacture and sell any improvements to C's product that are made or acquired by C or its other licensees.

Continued

Continued

	YOUR CLIENT	OTHER PARTY
	3. Licensing agreement without assignment to C, but B only gets to manufacture and sell improvements to product made by C alone and not acquired by C from its other licensees.	3. Reduction in initial fee.
	4. Reduction in initial fee.	
5. BEST ALTERNATIVES TO A NEGOTIATED AGREEMENT (BATNA)		
	1. Grant a license to Fulton.	1. Develop a fertilizer product on B's own.
	2. Find other licensees in the central states.	2. Find another licensor.
6. FACTUAL AND LEGAL LEVERAGE POINTS		
Strong Points:	1. C's strong sales.	1. B's broad market and customers.
	2. Fulton is a potential licensee.	2. B has 2 plants.
	3. C already has a licensee in the southeast.	3. B has ability to manufacture and sell C's product.
	4. B has never been in the fertilizer business.	
Weak Points:	1. C has no market in the central states.	1. C already has a licensee in the southeast.
	2. B has many customers.	2. B has never been in the fertilizer business.
		3. Fulton is a potential licensee.
7. POTENTIAL TARGET AND RESISTANCE POINTS		
Target Points:	1. Licensing agreement on the same terms as those negotiated with C's other licensees.	1. Licensing agreement for both plants.

	YOUR CLIENT	OTHER PARTY
Resistance Points:	1. Licensing agreement with some protection against B dominating the fertilizer market.	1. Licensing agreement without assignment to C of any fertilizers developed by B.

8. OFFERS OR PROPOSALS

	YOUR CLIENT	OTHER PARTY
	1st: Licensing agreement on the same terms as those negotiated with C's other licensees.	1st: Licensing agreement without assignment to C of any fertilizers developed by B alone.
	2nd: Licensing agreement without assignment to C of fertilizers developed by B alone, but B must share all of its improvements/substitutes with C and permit C and its other licensees to use them without cost.	2nd: Same as C's 2nd offer, but B still gets to manufacture and sell any improvements to C's product that are made or acquired by C or its other licensees.
	3rd: Same as B's second offer, but B only gets to manufacture and sell improvements to product made by C alone and not acquired by C from its other licensees.	3rd: Same as C's 3rd offer, but C must reduce its initial fee.
	4th: Same as B's 3rd offer, and initial fee to be 75% of that charged to C's other licensees.	4th: Same as B's 4th offer, but initial fee to be 66% of that charged to C's other licensees.

9. PARTICULAR TACTICS

	YOUR CLIENT	OTHER PARTY
	1. Induce B to make the first offer.	1. --------------------

Continued

§7.07 The Role of the Client and Advising the Client

The client's role in the negotiation is integral to preparation and the overall approach taken to the negotiation. Some studies have indicated that the dollar outcomes of certain settlements are consistently higher when the client is not only regularly informed about the progress of the negotiation, but actively participates in the overall process, even if he is not actually present during the negotiations. Similarly, attorney-client misunderstandings have been found to be the single largest factor resulting in unsuccessful settlements.

Of course, the ultimate decision whether to accept or reject a settlement negotiated by a lawyer rests with the client, and a lawyer generally has a duty to inform his client of all settlement offers. Within this restriction, however, the client may give you broad authority not only over the process of the negotiation, but over what offers or counteroffers to make and what proposals to accept or reject. Thus, it is imperative that there be a clear understanding between you and your client about the extent of your authority throughout the negotiation process.

Generally, in informing and advising the client about the negotiation, you should cover: (1) the procedural and substantive process of the negotiation, including its different phases, the goals of the particular negotiation, and expected time frames; (2) how, when, and to what extent your client may be involved at different stages of the process or during the actual negotiation; (3) when and how your client will receive status reports about the progress of the negotiation; (4) all alternatives to the negotiation process and the relative advantages and disadvantages of those alternatives; and (5) all expenses and attorney fees that are likely to be incurred in negotiating the case or resolving it by other means such as trial. Because negotiation is a dynamic and changing process, it is essential that you regularly advise your client of any reassessments about the foregoing matters as the situation warrants.

In addition, it is imperative that you establish a strong relationship of trust with your client. Never inflate your client's expectations about what may be accomplished through the negotiation, and always inform him that your representation is aimed at achieving the best result consistent with his objectives and interests. A relationship grounded in honesty and trust in your skill and judgment is essential to effective representation.

Chapter Eight

Negotiating in Writing and Over the Telephone

SYNOPSIS

§8.01 Introduction
§8.02 Negotiating in Writing—Advantages and Disadvantages
§8.03 Techniques for Effective Correspondence
[1] Send a Letter by Registered or Certified Mail
[2] Copy the Email or Letter to Other Persons
[3] Identify Your Authority to Represent
[4] Adopt an Appropriate Style and Tone
[5] Highlight the Pertinent Facts and Law
[6] Convey a Specific Proposal or Course of Action
[7] State a Time Frame for Action and Consequences for Inaction
§8.04 Illustration of a Demand Letter
§8.05 Settlement Brochures
[1] Introduction to Brochure/Cover Letter
[2] Statement of Facts and Liability
[3] Summary of Medical Treatment
[4] Summary of Lost Earnings
[5] Summary of Pain and Suffering and Permanent Injury
[6] Damages Summary and Initial Demand
§8.06 Illustration of Settlement Brochure (Personal Injury Case)
§8.07 Negotiating Over the Telephone—Advantages and Disadvantages
§8.08 Techniques for Effective Telephone Negotiations
[1] Do Not Commit Yourself Unless You Are Prepared

[2] Do Not Be Afraid to Be "Unavailable"
[3] Use a Preparation Negotiation Outline
[4] Adjust the Pace and Tone of Your Voice
[5] Do Not Be Afraid to Call Back

§8.01 Introduction

Many negotiations are conducted exclusively in writing, over the telephone, or through a combination of both. This is particularly true for small business deals or disputes, domestic disputes, and non-catastrophic personal injury cases. Typically, one party initiates the negotiation by emailing or mailing a proposal or demand letter, and the other party responds in writing or negotiations proceed over the phone. Particularly in personal injury cases, lawyers usually start negotiations by sending the insurance adjuster a "settlement brochure" that details the client's contentions about liability and damages and provides an initial settlement "demand." There are certain advantages and disadvantages to negotiating in writing and over the telephone. In addition, there are a variety of techniques that can enhance the effectiveness of these methods of negotiation.

§8.02 Negotiating in Writing—Advantages and Disadvantages

The principal advantage of negotiating in writing is that it creates a paper record that leaves less room for misunderstanding and allows the other party to carefully review what is being said and to share it with other persons involved in the negotiation. Also, correspondence is often more articulate. Strong points can be emphasized and weak points carefully downplayed or refuted. Matters that might be difficult to say face to face can be controlled through delicate wording and phrasing. Moreover, writing is an efficient and verifiable way of conveying instructions, sanctions, time frames, and deadlines.

The principal disadvantage of negotiating in writing is that it is impersonal and does not lend itself to interpersonal or emotional appeals. Moreover, a sloppily worded or ambiguous email or letter can create false impressions, confusion, or misunderstandings that may be more difficult to erase later. Preparing the correspondence or other documentation takes time and slows the pace of the negotiation.

§8.03 Techniques for Effective Correspondence

Whether writing an initial business proposal, pre-litigation demand email or letter, or response to either, you should consider the following:

[1] Send a Letter by Registered or Certified Mail

Consider sending a letter by registered or certified mail, return receipt requested. This will inevitably grab the attention of the recipient and foreclose any contention that the letter was not received. If you choose this form of mailing, be sure to designate on the first page of the letter that it was sent by certified mail, return receipt requested. If you fax the letter, be sure to keep the printout showing that the fax went through to the recipient.

[2] Copy the Email or Letter to Other Persons

Particularly if an email or letter is being sent to a business or governmental entity, consider copying the communication to any individual who is likely to be directly or indirectly involved in the negotiation. This is likely to exert pressure on the recipient and increase the chances of getting a corporation or governmental entity to act promptly. However, this tactic should not be employed if it will unnecessarily alienate the addressee or other persons to whom a copy of the communication is sent. Do not send a copy to the opposing party if counsel represents him, because of course you cannot correspond with a represented party.

[3] Identify Your Authority to Represent

In the first paragraph of your communication, clearly identify the subject matter of your representation and authority to represent. This is an essential formality that will require the other side to respond directly to you.

[4] Adopt an Appropriate Style and Tone

Adjust the style and tone of your communication to the particular recipient and anyone else who might read the communication. For example, if you are writing directly to an unrepresented party, you should avoid unnecessary legalese. If the communication is sent to the other side's lawyer, always assume that the communication will be read by his client.

Avoid using language from which any personal attack or insult might be inferred. Although, in an appropriate case, your communication should be firm, your overall style and tone should be identical to that which you would consider professional if you were the recipient of the communication. In this regard, particularly if you are writing to a person you do not know, consider concluding the communication with, "I look forward to hearing from you and working with you on this matter." Similarly, in responding to a communication, you should regulate the tone as well, regardless of the tone used by the other side. For example, you might begin your response with, "This will acknowledge and thank you for your email of..."

[5] Highlight the Pertinent Facts and Law

Be sure to educate the other side to the relevant facts. It is best to state them in an objective tone rather than by editorializing or being argumentative. Because your understanding of the facts is often limited to what your client has told you, leave yourself maneuvering room in the event that your client's version is not totally accurate. This can be accomplished by prefacing your factual recitation with, "According to our client,..." In addition, if you need an immediate response from the other side to verify your understanding of the facts, as where you are contemplating injunctive relief, you might write: "To prevent any misunderstanding about the facts surrounding this matter, please advise us immediately if our understanding is incorrect" [or] "If I do not hear from you on or before..., I will assume that the facts related by my client are accurate."

Educate the other side to your legal position. This might be stated by quoting the particular language of a contract or court order at issue, or by summarizing or citing to specific statutory or case law supporting your legal contention. Also, consider attaching to your communication a copy of any pertinent documentation, legal authority, or even a draft complaint or motion.

Of course, you should highlight the facts and law most favorable to your client. While you should never deliberately misrepresent the facts or law, you have no obligation to disclose weak facts or adverse legal authority in the negotiation context. If your communication cannot summarily deal with weak points, it is often best to deal with them at a later stage of the negotiation. The structure of your communication, word selection, and choice of points to emphasize or omit can help you put the best light on your client's situation.

[6] Convey a Specific Proposal or Course of Action

A business proposal or pre-litigation demand letter is wholly ineffective if it does not specifically convey what you propose or what you are asking the other side to do or not to do. In addition, the terms of your proposal or demand should not be vague or ambiguous unless you have a deliberate reason for leaving matters open ended or imprecise. Thus, in stating a particular proposal or demand, make sure that it appropriately answers who, what, when, where, why, and how.

[7] State a Time Frame for Action and Consequences for Inaction

Consider including in your communication a time frame or deadline within which you expect the other side to act. Imposing a time constraint on the other party will exert pressure on the negotiating process. In choosing a time frame or length of a deadline, you must bear in mind whether your purpose is to induce immediate action or to bide time (*see Deadlines* in Chapter 5).

Setting a time frame for action is most effective when coupled with an indication or specific statement of the consequences that could occur or sanctions that could be imposed if the other side is unresponsive. Thus, it is often desirable to educate the other side to these consequences or what you will be forced to do in the event that no timely agreement is reached (*see Threats* in Chapter 5). For example, a pre-litigation demand letter or email might say: "If we do not hear from you by... p.m. on..., we will have no alternative but to immediately institute appropriate legal proceedings. If that should become necessary, in addition to the principal amount of $______________________, we will request that the court award reasonable attorneys' fees, interest, and all court costs pursuant to [cite statute]."

§8.04 Illustration of a Demand Letter

June 7, [year]

Mr. Franklin Sinclair, Esq.
Suite 300, Bartlett Building
210 N. Jones Street
Raleigh, North Carolina 27602

CERTIFIED MAIL
RETURN RECEIPT
REQUESTED[1]

RE: Unauthorized Sale of Marital Home of Ida L. Doe and Austin T. Doe

Dear Mr. Sinclair:

Our law firm represents Ms. Ida. L. Doe in connection with her recent separation from her husband, Austin T. Doe, who I understand you represent. Ms. Doe has authorized me to contact you regarding your client's apparent plans to sell the parties' marital home and potentially defeat Ms. Doe's interest in it as distributable marital property under G.S. 50-20 *et. seq.*[2]

As you may know, the parties separated on May 17, [year], and since then Mr. Doe has been in possession of the marital home at 3629 Briarwood Court in Raleigh, and Ms. Doe has been living with her mother in Charlotte. The marital home was purchased for $106,000 on March 6, [year] during the marriage of the parties, but for some unexplained reason title was placed solely in Mr. Doe's name. (*See* Attachment 1). There is currently no mortgage or other indebtedness on the home, and, according to Ms. Doe, each of the parties paid one-half of the $15,000 down payment from their separate, premarital funds. Accordingly, the home constitutes distributable marital property under G.S. 50-20, notwithstanding that title is in Mr. Doe's name alone. *See Smith v. Smith,* 314 N.C. 80, 331 S.E.2d 682 (1985) (equal division of marital property is generally mandatory even though title to marital assets may be listed in the name of only one spouse during the course of the marriage).[3]

Ms. Doe has informed me that on June 6, [year] at approximately 7:30 p.m., Mr. Doe telephoned my client from Canada where he is currently on a two-week business trip. During the conversation, the parties appar-

1. *See* §8.03 at [1]. A letter such as this might be emailed.
2. *See* Id. at [3].
3. *See* Id. at [5].

ently had an argument, and Mr. Doe said he intends to put the marital home up for sale immediately upon his return to Raleigh on June 22. Ms. Doe reports that Mr. Doe also said he wants to sell the home by no later than August 1, [year] does not care if the home is sold at a depressed price, and that he will "fix it" so that Ms. Doe will not get any of the proceeds from the sale. According to Ms. Doe, your client indicated further that he intends to list the house for only $180,000 even though the latest tax value alone is $200,000. (*See* Attachment 2).[4]

This letter serves as formal notice of Ms. Doe's objection to any listing or sale of the marital home at 3629 Briarwood Court without her consent. Any unauthorized sale of the home by Mr. Doe (or anyone on his behalf) will be considered unlawful conversion and waste of a marital asset in which Ms. Doe has at least a one-half interest. Ms. Doe is requesting that the parties immediately execute a written agreement that prohibits the listing or sale of the marital home without the consent of both parties and which acknowledges Ms. Doe's interest in the home as distributable marital property under G.S. 50-20. (*See* draft of proposed Agreement at Attachment 3).[5]

If I do not hear from you by 4:00 p.m. on or before June 19, [year], I will assume that the facts set forth in this letter are accurate and that Mr. Doe has no intention of entering into an agreement like that proposed above. If a satisfactory agreement cannot be reached on or before that date and time, we will be forced to seek immediate injunctive and other relief under G.S. 50-20 (i); G.S. 1A-1, Rule 65; G.S. 1-485; and G.S. 1-116 *et. seq.*[6]

Notwithstanding the circumstances giving rise to the parties' separation, Ms. Doe wishes to resolve all matters respecting the parties' rights as cooperatively and amicably as possible. I look forward to hearing from you and working with you on this case.[7]

Sincerely, ______________________

4. *See* Id.
5. *See* Id. at [6].
6. *See* Id. at [5] and [7].
7. *See* Id. at [4].

§8.05 Settlement Brochures

A settlement brochure is a document that sets out the legal and factual basis for a claimant's claim and details her damages. The brochure may be in the form of an email, letter, or a more formal, bound document that contains extensive exhibits. Brochures are often used by plaintiffs' lawyers in personal injury cases to establish the basis for initial settlement demands and to define the issues for ensuing negotiations.

The brochure is often sent to the adjuster for the defendant's liability insurance carrier before any lawsuit is filed. The adjuster then responds to the claimant's initial offer in writing or over the telephone. After an exchange of one or more counteroffers, the case is often settled without the parties or their representatives having engaged in any face-to-face negotiations. If in-person negotiations do occur, the plaintiff's lawyer often uses the brochure to structure the negotiation agenda.

Effective brochures usually contain extensive documentary and illustrative exhibits to back up the claimant's assertions about the facts, liability, and damages. Broad disclosure is justified on the theory that the materials contained in the brochure would otherwise be revealed through discovery, and meaningful settlement discussions cannot occur without substantiating the claim. If these exhibits are voluminous, the brochure might contain an index of them. Such documentation lends credibility to the brochure and shows the opposing side that the claimant is prepared to litigate the case if necessary. Supporting documentation also serves to "paper" the defense representative's file to justify the amount of a final settlement.

While much of the documentation in a brochure will consist of materials that would be admissible at trial, you should not limit yourself to revealing strictly admissible evidence. So long as the information is pertinent to the claim, it should be included regardless of technical rules of evidence. Although, in the event of litigation, formal discovery will require you to reveal certain information that may be damaging to your client's case, weak aspects of your client's claim may usually be omitted from the brochure unless the opposing side already knows about these weak points and they can be effectively countered in the brochure. On the other hand, you should never make a false statement of material fact in the brochure.

The format and content of a brochure are limited only by your imagination. Most brochures take the form of a written summary or narrative that makes reference to the documents or exhibits collected at the end of the brochure.

However, some brochures are organized in a sequence of documents, photographs, and other materials that are arranged under captions and interspersed with commentary to provide a dramatic, pictorial presentation of the client's case. In addition, some attorneys will include a videotape that reenacts the accident or displays the client's injuries and physical limitations. Occasionally, video footage from television news stations or from the highway patrol might be included. Regardless of the particular format chosen for the brochure, you should usually include within it the following elements:

[1] Introduction to Brochure/Cover Letter

Your brochure should contain an introduction or be accompanied by a prefatory letter that provides a general introduction to the case and specifies any restrictions or limitations on the use of the brochure. These might include: (1) a statement that the brochure is being provided for settlement purposes only (*see* Fed. R. Evid. 408); (2) a statement that the brochure is the property of your client, may not be copied without permission, and must be returned upon demand; (3) a date specified for a reply, after which the settlement offer will expire or be withdrawn; (4) an expression of willingness to settle the case reasonably; and (5) an offer to discuss the case further or to meet for future negotiations.

[2] Statement of Facts and Liability

The brochure should detail the facts giving rise to your client's claim and the basis for the defendant's liability. This statement of facts and liability should be written as a narrative, and refer, whenever possible, to exhibits such as police or accident reports, private investigative reports, witness statements (whether by affidavit or recorded interview), diagrams or photos of the accident scene or instrumentality causing the injury, or newspaper articles, etc. In addition, it is important to humanize your client and provide appropriate information about his background, such as age, marital status, family, education, military service, avocational interests, awards, commendations, financial status, work history, and the like.

When liability is clear, it is unnecessary to discuss the applicable law. Even when liability is disputed, many attorneys avoid any specific discussion of the law because the representative for the defendant is usually aware of the applicable legal principles and might be offended or feel patronized by counsel's citation to legal authority. On the other hand, if the recipient of the brochure is unlikely to be familiar with the applicable law, or if a discussion of the law otherwise seems appropriate, the legal grounds for liability should be set out and supported by accurate citations to case law and statutory authority. In this regard, some attorneys also include a copy of the plaintiff's proposed complaint.

[3] Summary of Medical Treatment

The brochure should contain a chronological summary of your client's pertinent medical treatment. This might be written in narrative form or by quoting verbatim the most important portions of the medical records. A copy of all relevant medical records (including test results and x-rays) should be included as an exhibit and indexed if the records are voluminous. Any emails or letters from physicians that are not part of the formal medical records and that discuss the extent and nature of your client's future medical treatment, future medical costs, prognosis, and extent of disability should also be summarized and included as an exhibit. If the medical records contain references to a medical condition or course of treatment that is wholly unrelated to the accident, the summary should omit those matters.

[4] Summary of Lost Earnings

If your client has incurred lost wages due to her injury or will incur future lost wages or a reduction in earning capacity, these elements of damage should be described with particularity. In the case of past lost wages, the brochure should include a statement from your client's employer showing your client's gross wage rate, time out of work due to the accident, and total lost wages. In the event of future lost earnings or a reduction in earning capacity, the brochure might include a report prepared by an economist that calculates the future lost wages and fringe benefits, reduced to present value.

[5] Summary of Pain and Suffering and Permanent Injury

Your client's general damages for past, present, and future pain and suffering and permanent injury should be vividly described in narrative form. The description should cover all pertinent aspects of your client's life, including physical, psychological, social, and economic effects. Whenever possible, this description should be accompanied by photographs of your client before and after the accident and during different stages of recovery. Particularly in catastrophic injury cases, a day-in-the-life video of your client may be highly effective. If permanent injury is involved, your client's life expectancy should be stated based on standard mortuary tables.

[6] Damages Summary and Initial Demand

The conclusion of the brochure should provide an itemized summary of your client's damages along with an initial demand or first offer. Each item of damage, whether special or general, should be separately enumerated and supported by available statements, bills, receipts, or other documentation. Special damages might include: (1) medical expenses, (2) future medical expenses, (3) lost wages, (4) future lost earnings and benefits, and (5) miscellaneous expenses (past and future).

Items of general damage should also be separately enumerated when appropriate. These might include: (1) past pain and suffering, including humiliation and emotional distress, (2) future pain and suffering, and (3) loss of life's pleasures or other damage resulting from permanent disfigurement or disability. In an appropriate case, some attorneys also set out the amount that would be sought at trial for punitive damages.

At the conclusion of the brochure, the special and general damages should be combined to produce a single figure representing an initial settlement demand or first offer.

§8.06 Illustration of Settlement Brochure (Personal Injury Case)

SETTLEMENT BROCHURE
Prepared on behalf of
JANE R. POOLE
June 14, [year]
By: John W. Doe, Jr.
DOE & DOE
Suite 344, 30 Columbia Avenue
Charlotte, North Carolina 28212
Telephone: (704) 333-2868
E-Mail: jwdoe@lightspeed.com

June 14, [year]
Mr. Donald Delaney
Senior Claims Adjuster
All-Care Insurance Company
629 Bellview Road
West Newton, Massachusetts 02165

RE: My Client: Ms. Jane R. Poole Our File No.: JWD-2392 #1 Your Insured: Winslow S. Hall Date of Collision: January 4, [year]

Dear Mr. Delaney:

As I mentioned to you in my letter of January 10, [year], I represent Ms. Jane R. Poole in her personal injury claim arising out of an automobile collision on January 4, [year] in Charlotte, North Carolina caused by your insured, Mr. Winslow S. Hall. This settlement brochure summarizes Ms. Poole's personal injury claim, and all information provided herein is intended for settlement purposes only. You are free to copy the brochure if you wish, but it is the property of Ms. Poole and DOE & DOE law firm and is returnable to us on demand.[8]

---

8. Here, there is no reason to prohibit copying of the brochure because all of the materials contained in it would be discoverable in the event of litigation and there is no reason to suppose that the adjuster will inappropriately disseminate the contents of the brochure. Thus, the requirement that the brochure be returned to the claimant's lawyer upon demand is, in this case, a purely *pro forma* safeguard.

FACTS AND LIABILITY

There is no question about liability in this case. On Monday, January 4, [year], at approximately 8:30 a.m., Ms. Poole was on her way to work, traveling east on Harnette Avenue in Charlotte, North Carolina. She stopped at a stoplight at the intersection of Harnette Avenue and St. Mary's Street. Mr. Hall, who was also traveling east on Harnette Avenue, lost control of his vehicle and crashed into the rear of Ms. Poole's car at an estimated speed of 45 miles per hour in a 35 mile per hour zone. (*See* Charlotte Police Accident Report at Exhibit 1).

Mr. Milton Reeves, who was traveling in a car behind Mr. Hall, witnessed the accident and will testify that Mr. Hall was "speeding," driving "erratically," and "weaving" in the road just before the impact. (*See* statement of Milton Reeves at Exhibit 2). Officer T. L. Fennell, who responded to the accident scene and prepared the police report, charged Mr. Hall with "Failure to Reduce Speed to Avoid an Accident" to which Mr. Hall entered a plea of guilty on March 6, [year]. (*See* Citation at Exhibit 3). Although the accident report also notes that the rear brake lights on Ms. Poole's car were not working at the time of the accident, under the circumstances of this case no jury would find that this fact was a contributing or proximate cause of the accident.[9]

Upon impact, even though Ms. Poole was wearing her seatbelt, she was thrown violently forward and backward in her seat, and her left knee slammed into the dashboard. The force of the impact broke the driver's seat. Her car was nearly totaled. (*See* photographs at Exhibit 4).[10]

MEDICAL TREATMENT

Ms. Poole was taken by ambulance to the emergency room at Hopeview Memorial Hospital in Charlotte. The following are the most pertinent, verbatim portions of her medical records during her five-month course of treatment (*See* medical records at Exhibit 5):[11]

---

9. If there was any real doubt about this proposition, the attorney might cite an appropriate appellate decision.

10. For purposes of effect, the attorney might put the photographs immediately following this paragraph rather than including them in an attached exhibit.

11. This approach would not be practical if the medical records were particularly voluminous. In that event, the attorney might summarize the course of treatment in a narrative and make specific reference to key medical records such as surgical procedures or discharge summaries.

1/4/yr: **Emergency Room, Hopeview Memorial Hospital.**

Chief complaints: low back pain and stiffness; numbness; soreness in neck; left knee pain from impact with dashboard. Thorough examination.

Small contusion, bruising to medial left knee.

DIAGNOSIS: Musculoskeletal pain.

DISCHARGE INSTRUCTIONS:

1. Expect to be sore.
2. Advil for pain.
3. Heating pad for pain.
4. No strenuous activity for next 2–3 days, then advance as tolerated.
5. Return immediately if problems develop or symptoms worsen.

1/8/yr: **Dr. Bruce Cooper, MD, Charlotte Family Medicine Center, P.A.** New patient.

Chief complaints: development of increased lower back pain and left upper back pain; persistent pain in right lower rib cage; difficulty in sleeping.

EXAM: Neck reveals some mild left trapezial tightness; tenderness; mild to moderate paralumbosacral tenderness over both iliac crests; point moderate to severe tenderness over mid-thorzic right rib cage and around T7–8.

ASSESSMENT: Neck and back strain; probable fractured rib.

PLAN: Will obtain rib x-rays. Sent to Spellman Radiology for x-rays. Recommend local ice packs to rib cage; gentle flexible exercises, avoiding any activities that exacerbate any of her pain;

avoid high impact activities. Prescribed: Advil for pain; Ambien 10 mg for sleep. Follow-up recheck in one week.

1/9/yr: **Spellman Radiology, Dereck S. Spellman, MD.**
X-rays taken of right ribs: reveal nondisplaced fracture of right 10th rib.

1/14/yr: **Dr. Bruce Cooper, MD, Charlotte Family Medicine Center, P.A.**
Follow-up examination.

Slight "clicking" left hip; some occasional discomfort on that side with walking. Slight pressure lower back.
Examination of lower back reveals some mild paralumbosacral tenderness over left superior anterior iliac crest. Mild-moderate tenderness over right lateral rib cage.

ASSESSMENT: Mild left hip, low back strain; rib fracture.

PLAN: Encourage patient to get back into normal exercise program at 50% level and slowly increase. Recommend hot packs and stretching. Recheck in 3 weeks. Consider physical therapy. Advise patient to expect several weeks to heal but she should have complete resolution of symptoms.

2/16/yr: **Dr. Bruce Cooper, MD, Charlotte Family Medicine Center, P.A.**
Follow-up examination.

No longer has pain in rib cage; now has most of pain in neck: right side greater than left. Neck gets tired upon flexion or leaning forward. Occasional blurring of vision, but no apparent visual field defects. Examination of neck reveals some mild-moderate tenderness on right paracervical ridge.
Noted that patient saw her gynecologist for pregnancy test: positive a week ago, but negative serum test four days ago. Apparently since accident she has also had galactorrhea which is being monitored by her GYN.

ASSESSMENT: Neck strain secondary to motor vehicle accident.

PLAN: Get baseline cervical spine x-rays; send to physical therapy with follow-up in one month.

ASSESSMENT: Galactorrhea; possible spontaneous abortion.

PLAN: Follow-up with GYN. Galactorrhea could be due to emotional trauma of motor vehicle accident causing patient's hormone imbalance.

<u>2/20/yr</u>: **Spellman Radiology, Dereck S. Spellman, MD**
Cervical Spine x-rays: minor straightening of cervical spine which could represent muscle spasm.

<u>3/16/yr</u>: **Dr. Bruce Cooper, MD, Charlotte Family Medicine, P.A.**
Follow-up. Gets occasional sharp pain in head and neck; some stiffness in lower back. Will be starting on regular exercise aerobic program soon and will be seeing Ian Tersky, Physical Therapist for strengthening and flexibility exercises. Galactorrhea apparently resolved. No new symptoms.
Low back reveals some slight limitation in forward flexion.

ASSESSMENT: Resolving neck and back strain.

PLAN: Physical therapy to get patient back on road to recovery and help get back to normal full-time activity and exercise. Cervical spine x-rays unremarkable except for slight straightening consistent with spasm. Advised to follow-up when ready to come to closure on this.

<u>3/28/yr</u>: **Ian Tersky, P.T., Charlotte Comprehensive Physical Therapy Center.**
Initial evaluation.

Chief complaints: neck/back pain; headaches. Symptoms aching in nature and intermittent. Discomfort caused by symptoms severe in intensity, affecting her most in afternoon and evening.

ASSESSMENT: Diagnosis: Cervicolumbar strain.

Problem list: Limited cervical range of motion; limited lumbar range of motion; increased density right levator and lumbar myofasia.

GOALS:
Short term: Decrease inflexibility and inflammation; increase cervical range of motion to full.
Long term: Increase lumbar ROM to full; decrease headache frequency and intensity.

PLAN:
Treatment: Ice; facet stretching; massage; and flexibility exercises. Treatment to be followed 2 times per week for approx. 3 weeks.

4/2/yr: **Charlotte Comprehensive Physical Therapy Center.**
Physical therapy.

4/5/yr: **Charlotte Comprehensive Physical Therapy Center.**
Physical therapy.

4/10/yr: **Charlotte Comprehensive Physical Therapy Center.**
Physical therapy.

4/13/yr: **Charlotte Comprehensive Physical Therapy Center.**
Physical therapy.

4/17/yr: **Charlotte Comprehensive Physical Therapy Center.**
Physical therapy.

5/10/yr: **Dr. Bruce Cooper, MD, Charlotte Family Medicine, P.A.**

Patient here to achieve some closure on her motor vehicle accident. Gets occasional mild tightness in lower back with rotation. Finds physical therapy helpful.

Examined.

ASSESSMENT: Resolved back and neck strain.

PLAN: Patient to continue as she has been doing. No need for further physical therapy at this point. Continue with home exercise program.[12]

MEDICAL EXPENSES

Listed below are Ms. Poole's medical and miscellaneous, pharmaceutical expenses to date (*See* Exhibit 6):

MECKLENBURG COUNTY AMBULANCE SERVICE	$250.00
HOPEVIEW MEMORIAL HOSPITAL	$200.00
CHARLOTTE FAMILY MEDICINE CENTER, P.A.	$350.00
SPELLMAN RADIOLOGY	$250.00
CHARLOTTE COMPREHENSIVE PHYSICAL THERAPY CENTER	$500.00
MISCELLANEOUS PHARMACEUTICAL EXPENSES	$80.00
	$1,630.00

LOST WAGES[13]

Ms. Poole is employed as an Account Technician I at the University of North Carolina at Charlotte. Due to the accident, she missed 52 hours of work at a gross wage of $35.00 per hour. (*See* Letter from UNC Personnel and Benefits Office at Exhibit 7).

TOTAL LOST WAGES **$1,820.00**

12. If the claimant sustained an injury that required future medical treatment, the next section of the brochure would summarize that on-going treatment under a heading styled, "FUTURE MEDICAL TREATMENT."

13. If the client will sustain future lost wages or a reduction in earning capacity, these matters would also be detailed here.

PAIN AND SUFFERING[14]

Prior to the collision, Ms. Poole was a healthy 43-year-old woman. She had no prior history of medical problems like those sustained in this collision. Given the tremendous force of the collision (*see* photos at Exhibit 4), Ms. Poole was fortunate that she was not more seriously injured and that she was able to recover in five months.

As the medical records show, Ms. Poole sustained at least 116 days of continuous pain of varying intensity from January 4, [year] through the end of April [year]. As the physical therapy record of March 28 [year] states, her "discomfort [is] caused by symptoms severe in intensity, affecting her most in [the] afternoon and evening." Accordingly, the jury would be permitted to compensate approximately 80% of Ms. Poole's pain and suffering through a *per diem* calculation.

The medical records objectively show that the elements of her pain and suffering include (1) "a fracture of her right 10th rib," (2) "bruising to medial left knee," (3) "lower back pain,"(4) "upper back pain," (5) "difficulty in sleeping," (6) "avoiding any activities that exacerbate any of her pain," (7) "left hip pain," (8) "neck strain and pain," (9) "blurring of vision," (10) "muscle spasms," (11) "sharp pain in head," (12) "limitation in forward flexion," (13) "headaches," (14) "limited cervical range of motion," and (15) "galactorrhea due to emotional trauma of motor vehicle accident."

Ms. Poole's injuries markedly affected her daily activities. Her sleeplessness, headaches, and blurred vision left her lethargic and at times disoriented. Her rib fracture and cervical and paralumbosacral pain limited her movement. Routine household chores, grocery shopping, and even driving were difficult. Prolonged sitting at work exacerbated her pain in the afternoons and into the evenings. She was forced to markedly limit her social activities. She canceled her aerobics classes, and was forced to restrict other recreational activities. She was under Advil for pain, Ambien for sleeplessness, and variously used heating pads, ice packs, and hot packs to relieve her condition. The prolonged emotional trauma of the collision even manifested itself in a physical hormone imbalance.

---

14. If the claimant has permanent injury or will sustain future pain and suffering, these matters would also be detailed here under a heading such as "PAIN AND SUFFERING AND PERMANENT INJURY."

DAMAGES SUMMARY

MEDICAL EXPENSES	$1,630.00
LOST WAGES	$1,820.00
PAIN AND SUFFERING	$________
TOTAL DEMAND	$________

Based on the foregoing, we propose that $____________________ would be a reasonable sum to settle this case. After you have had an opportunity to review this brochure, I look forward to hearing from you and working with you on this case.

Sincerely,

____

John W. Doe, Jr.

§8.07 Negotiating Over the Telephone—Advantages And Disadvantages

When negotiations are conducted over the telephone, communication is enhanced and misunderstandings or misperceptions can be addressed and reduced. Questions can be asked to clarify ambiguous proposals, and the interests and reasons underlying a party's proposals can be fully explored. The negotiators are able to share each other's views firsthand and focus on the particular matters they consider important. Moreover, even though the negotiators are not meeting face to face, they can usually get a sense of each other's true intentions by discerning changes in tone and voice inflection.

Telephone negotiations also give the parties a greater sense of freedom and security than they might feel when negotiating face to face. The negotiator is free to choose the time when he is willing to talk, and the pressure to make an on-the-spot response can be simply eliminated with a promise to phone the other party back after his proposal has been reviewed. Moreover, it is easier to say no to the other party over the phone, and discussions can be more gracefully terminated than would be the case if they were being conducted face to face.

On the other hand, because telephone negotiations are less personal than face-to-face interactions, they are almost always more abbreviated than personal meetings. Consequently, it is usually more difficult to create a concerted, psychological commitment to resolve the case over the phone. For the same reason that it is easier to say no over the phone, it is also easier for a party to engage in overtly competitive and deceptive tactics. In addition, some individuals feel psychologically pressured to negotiate once they are on the phone even though they may be distracted or unprepared. This may lead to hasty concessions and uninformed decisions.

§8.08 Techniques for Effective Telephone Negotiations

Many of the bargaining techniques that are effective in face-to-face negotiations (*see* Chapter 9) apply to telephone negotiations as well. In addition, you should keep the following in mind:

[1] Do Not Commit Yourself Unless You Are Prepared

The negotiator who makes the telephone call often has an advantage over the recipient because the former will be prepared, and the latter may be caught unawares. This may allow the phoning party to be more persuasive and exact greater concessions than would be possible if the negotiation had been formally scheduled. Thus, the recipient of the phone call should never hesitate to postpone making a response or decision until she is fully prepared to do so. In addition, the recipient should use the call as an opportunity to listen, ask questions, and obtain as much information from the other side as possible. After this information has been fully evaluated, the recipient can always call the other side back to give a response.

[2] Do Not Be Afraid to Be "Unavailable"

Of course, the recipient of a call may simply use the excuse that she is "unavailable" to take the call at the time. This is the best choice to make if you are so hurried or distracted that you cannot even use the call for the limited purpose of obtaining information from the other side. Moreover, if your objective is to delay negotiations, you can always have your secretary or assistant tell the other side that you will return the call at a later time.

[3] Use a Preparation Negotiation Outline

To negotiate effectively over the phone, you should prepare for it as you would for a face-to-face meeting. Thus, it may be useful to use a Preparation Negotiation Outline like that shown at §7.04. It is also useful to prepare a checklist of items to be discussed to ensure that you present your points in a logical order and that important matters are not overlooked.

In addition, take careful notes of the conversation so that you have a record of what was said. Concessions, promises, or other important points can often be forgotten during a protracted discussion. Throughout the conversation, confirm in your own words your understanding of the proposals or points being made by the other side. If an agreement is reached, promptly confirm its terms by email or a follow-up letter to avoid any misunderstanding.

[4] Adjust the Pace and Tone of Your Voice

Unless you are negotiating on a televised conference call, telephone conversations do not, of course, allow the negotiators to observe one another. Thus, to enhance comprehension, you should consciously try to talk more slowly during a telephone negotiation. In addition, try to "put a face" in your voice. Even though the listener cannot see your expressions, if you talk as if he were sitting across the table from you, your tone of voice will convey greater feeling behind your words and enhance the persuasiveness of your presentation.

[5] Do Not Be Afraid to Call Back

After a telephone conversation is over, never hesitate to promptly call back if you discover an error or suspect a possible misunderstanding. The more abbreviated nature of telephone negotiations may sometimes cause the parties to overlook important matters or fail to clear up ambiguities in a final settlement offer. Thus, if you have any doubt about a proposal or agreement made over the phone, it is best to immediately call back and clarify the issue in lieu of having to reopen negotiations after a written agreement has been prepared for the parties to execute.

Chapter Nine

Negotiating Face to Face

SYNOPSIS

§9.01 Introduction
§9.02 With Whom to Negotiate
§9.03 When to Negotiate
§9.04 Where to Negotiate
§9.05 Who Should Attend the Negotiation
§9.06 Setting the Tone
§9.07 Setting the Agenda
§9.08 Reading Body Language
§9.09 Exchanging Information
§9.10 Obtaining Information
[1] Ask Broad, Open-Ended Questions When Seeking Maximum Information
[2] Use Silence, Encouragement, and Questions that Call for Elaboration
[3] Listen Intently and Patiently
[4] Ask Specific Questions to Clarify, Pin Down, and Confirm Information
[5] Insist upon the Necessity of Receiving Crucial Information
§9.11 Protecting Information
[1] Ignore the Question and Change the Topic
[2] Answer the Question by Asking Another Question
[3] Answer the Question by Answering Another Question
[4] Over-Answer or Under-Answer the Question
[5] Rule the Question Out of Bounds
§9.12 Revealing Information
§9.13 Adversarial Bargaining
[1] Making Offers

[a] Who Should Make the First Offer
[b] When to Make the First Offer
[c] The Amount of the First Offer
[d] Communicating Offers
[2] Making Counteroffers
[3] Making Concessions
[a] When to Make Concessions
[b] Concession Strategy
[c] Communicating Concessions
[4] Forms of Persuasion
[a] Argument
[b] Exhibits
[c] Emotional Appeals
[d] Threats and Promises
§9.14 Problem-Solving Bargaining
[1] Identifying and Sharing Interests or Needs
[2] Brainstorming for Solutions
[3] Making Problem-Solving Offers, Counteroffers, and Concessions
§9.15 Combining Adversarial and Problem-Solving Bargaining
§9.16 Concluding the Negotiation

§9.01 Introduction

Negotiating face to face is a highly complex form of human behavior. Indeed, to negotiate effectively in person is much more of an art than a science. This effectiveness can be enhanced by understanding (1) how to set the stage for a face-to-face negotiation (*i.e.*, with whom, when, and where to negotiate, and who should attend the negotiation); (2) how to set the tone and agenda for the negotiation (*i.e.*, the negotiating atmosphere and the issues to be discussed); (3) the importance of reading body language during the negotiation; (4) how information is exchanged during the negotiation (*i.e.*, techniques for obtaining, protecting, and revealing information); (5) the process and techniques associated with traditional, adversarial bargaining (*i.e.*, the making of offers, counteroffers, and concessions, and using different forms of persuasion); (6) the process and techniques associated with problem-solving bargaining (*i.e.*, identifying the parties' interests or needs, and brainstorming for mutually beneficial solutions); (7) how to combine adversarial and problem-solving bargaining when appropriate; and (8) how to conclude the negotiation.

§9.02 With Whom to Negotiate

In most circumstances, you will have no control over choosing the person with whom you will negotiate. Once the opposing negotiator has been identified, you will want to discover his style and strategy toward the negotiation. Sometimes it is desirable to arrange a pre-negotiation get-together to become acquainted with your counterpart and establish rapport. This initial meeting may also be used to find out preliminary information about others who may be involved in the negotiation, and the general attitude of the other side toward the negotiation.

In the early stage of negotiations, it sometimes may become apparent that the negotiator for the other side has little authority to bind his principal. This is an undesirable situation because the success of a negotiation depends far more upon negotiating with a person who can make binding decisions than on negotiating with someone with whom you might feel more comfortable. If it is clear the other side's agent has little authority, consider suggesting that the negotiation might be expedited by involving the principal or other decision-maker directly in the negotiation. This must be done tactfully so as not to offend the agent, and preferably should be arranged with the cooperation of the agent. If the agent is not agreeable to your suggestion, at the very least try to arrange a meeting or conference call with the agent and his principal.

Either at the outset of negotiations or as they progress, it may become apparent that you and your counterpart simply cannot get along with one another. In this situation, you might also suggest that the principals be directly included in the negotiation. Alternatively, you might suggest that additional negotiators participate in the discussions, or even that it would be in the best interests of both sides that each call upon some other representatives to continue the negotiation.

When the negotiation involves more than two parties, it is necessary to decide with which party you should start negotiations. While there may be myriad factors to consider in making this selection, generally it is desirable to start negotiations with the party who (1) is most likely to accept your position, (2) is most likely to establish a precedent during the negotiations, or (3) possesses the weakest bargaining power.

§9.03 When to Negotiate

Although it is rare to have a choice about the person with whom you will negotiate, you will often have greater control over the timing of negotiations. Generally, you should initiate negotiations when the other party is in the weakest position or your client is in the strongest position. The optimal time for negotiating may be influenced by tactics such as *Asymmetrical Time Pressure*, setting *Deadlines, Delaying,* taking some action to create a *Fait Accompli*, or the development of a *Surprise* (*see* Chapter 5). In addition, you should consider the most optimal day of the week or time of day to negotiate, which should usually be a time when the parties are most apt to be alert or when the opposing side is under a pressing time constraint.

§9.04 Where to Negotiate

Whenever possible, you should seize the opportunity to choose the site of the negotiation—usually your own office. The negotiator who negotiates on her "home court" is apt to be more relaxed, confident, and assertive. In contrast, the visiting negotiator occupies the subordinate status of a guest and is more likely to feel constrained and distracted in unfamiliar surroundings. Because familiar surroundings tend to reduce tension and anxiety, arranging the negotiation on your home turf may be particularly important if your client will attend the negotiation. One circumstance in which you might deliberately choose to hold the negotiation at the opposing party's office is if you believe that you may have to use a *Walkout* tactic (see Chapter 5) in the event the negotiation deadlocks.

If you are unable to arrange the negotiation at your office and have a strong reason for not negotiating at your opponent's office, propose that the meeting take place at a neutral location. If you make the arrangements for the neutral site and pay the expenses for its use and refreshments, you will effectively make it an extension of your own office. In addition, gratuitously making these arrangements shows respect for the other side and the importance you attach to the negotiation.

When you can control where the negotiation will take place, it is also important to give attention to the overall environment and available seating arrangements. Generally, the negotiating room should create a relaxed, noncompetitive environment. There should be a conference table if documents are to be reviewed, and if there will be groups of participants, it is desirable to have adjacent rooms available for private caucuses. Refreshments should be made available, and the room should be quiet and free from outside distractions and interruptions, particularly the telephone.

Seating arrangements can also affect the initial tone of the negotiation. For example, a more adversarial atmosphere may be created when participants are seated opposite one another at a rectangular or round table, whereas a more cooperative atmosphere may exist when the participants sit together in an L-shaped configuration at a rectangular table, or together in a semicircle at a round table.

§9.05 Who Should Attend the Negotiation

If a negotiator intends to employ a *Good Guy-Bad Guy Routine/Mutt and Jeff* approach or a *Two Against One* strategy (*see* Chapter 5), it is necessary to have a colleague join in the negotiation. A negotiator might choose to have a colleague or assistant join him to serve as an observer, or to assist in note taking, or locating and presenting documentation or other materials during the discussion. An assistant may also provide psychological support and give the lead negotiator the benefit of a detached perspective as the negotiation progresses.

Having your client attend the negotiation presents certain drawbacks. When your client is present: (1) it may be more difficult for you to control the negotiation and prevent inappropriate argumentation between your client and the other side; (2) the emotional aspects of the dispute may be more likely to pervade the negotiation; (3) candor may be inhibited; (4) the other side may not be able to engage in emotional venting as a prerequisite to serious discussions; (5) you may create the impression that your client does not have complete confidence in you; (6) you will be deprived of the convenient excuse of having to *Adjourn or Caucus* with your client; (7) a *Good Guy-Bad Guy Routine/Mutt and Jeff* or *Lack of Authority or Limited Authority* tactic cannot be employed; and (8) it may be difficult to engage in any *Off-the-Record Discussions* with the opposing negotiator (*see* Chapter 5).

On the other hand, having your client and the other side's client present during the negotiation may be useful (1) if the parties expect to have a continuing relationship; (2) if substantive or emotional misunderstandings can be smoothed over in a face-to-face meeting; (3) if the client's presence is necessary to provide technical expertise, clarification of the facts, or input about an unforeseen issue; (4) if it would be beneficial to demonstrate the client's sincerity or jury appeal; or (5) if having the client present will muzzle an obstreperous or irrational negotiator. If your client will attend the negotiation, he must be fully advised about what to expect in terms of his role and your role, the agenda of the negotiation, potential tactics, and the importance of carefully monitoring nonverbal behavior.

If you represent an institution, labor union, or large corporate client, it may be necessary to have client officials present during the negotiation for "political" reasons or to authorize a settlement. In these circumstances, it also is sometimes psychologically desirable to have your audience outnumber the other side's audience. In the absence of an actual audience at the negotiation, the effect of an audience might otherwise exist when a party establishes a *Coalition*, publicly pronounces a *Lock-In Position*, or engages in other *Publicity* by utilizing press releases or news leaks (*see* Chapter 5).

Even if your client attends the negotiation, generally you will take the lead. Your client's role should be carefully restricted to the reasons for his attendance. For example, if it is to demonstrate his jury appeal or to smooth over a misunderstanding, at some point during the negotiation, you might have your client describe the events surrounding the controversy or permit the other side to ask him questions about those events. Apart from your client's pre-planned role, it is generally unwise for him to speak during the negotiation, and you might decide to continue the negotiation with the opposing side without your client present. Finally, in lieu of having your client present at the negotiation, you might choose to have him on telephone standby in the event you need to confer with him while the negotiation is underway.

§9.06 Setting the Tone

Once the stage has been set for the negotiation, the initial phase of the actual face-to-face meeting is a crucial opportunity to set the tone for the ensuing negotiation. The atmosphere should be established from the time the opposing side walks in the door. A host negotiator who greets the other side with a smile, a handshake, and on a first name basis exudes warmth and trust. Greeting the visiting negotiator promptly and personally escorting her to the office or conference room show equality and respect. If the negotiators choose seats next to or adjacent to one another, as opposed to separating themselves by a wide distance or across from one another with a table in between, they will create a more cooperative atmosphere. On the other hand, addressing the other side more formally, a reserved demeanor, and seating that is designed to create spatial separation, distance, or dominance may achieve the opposite effect.

Whatever the initial greeting, a congenial tone may be created by engaging in a bit of "small talk" to establish rapport before "getting down to business." This preliminary conversation is useful to humanize the setting, to relax the participants, and to allow them to get to know one another if they have never met before. A genuine expression of empathy regarding the circumstances of the case, even an apology, made at this time can have a dramatic effect on the entire tone and ultimate success of the negotiation. This is so, in part, because it is not commonly done. A direct expression of a non-adversarial attitude toward the negotiation can be uniquely powerful precisely because of the instinctive, competitive style and adversarial strategy that characterize most legal negotiations.

§9.07 Setting the Agenda

The issues to be resolved and the order in which they will be addressed constitute the agenda for the negotiation. The agenda might be tacit, *ad hoc*, expressly agreed upon before the negotiation begins, or established through discussion or debate at the negotiation session. Whether the agenda is prearranged or established during the negotiation, you should have a specific agenda in mind before the face-to-face meeting.

The agenda should be prepared from your "Negotiation Preparation Outline." If you are able to define the issues to be resolved and the order in which they will be addressed, you will sometimes have an advantage over your opponent, particularly in complex adversarial bargaining. This is because the negotiator who controls how the issues are defined and when they will be discussed is in a better position to dictate the focus of the negotiation by framing the issues in the light most favorable to his client, emphasizing those topics or points of most importance to his client, and de-emphasizing the matters of most importance to the other side.

Most negotiations involve two types of issues: (1) those which center around the parties' "primary objectives" (*i.e.*, those matters which must be obtained to reach an agreement), and (2) those which constitute the parties' "incidental objectives" (*i.e.*, those matters which are of lesser importance and might be traded in order to obtain a primary objective) (*see* §7.03[3]). The outcome of a negotiation may largely depend upon the order in which these different types of issues are presented and discussed.

There are distinct advantages and disadvantages to starting the negotiation with the "primary" issues on the one hand, or "incidental" issues on the other. Adversarial negotiators who put their primary objectives at the forefront of the agenda do so on the theory that it may be easier to resolve these difficult matters at the outset when the negotiators may have a more conciliatory attitude. Putting off the tough issues until the end may make them more difficult to resolve when the parties are tired and have already used up most, if not all, of their "bargaining chips." Moreover, dealing with the hard issues first creates a challenge that tests the parties' initial willingness to be flexible, and places pressure on them to determine more quickly whether a settlement can be reached or deadlock is inevitable. When problem-solving negotiators take this approach, they are sending the message that it is essential to first address the parties' most important needs or interests in order to reach an accord that accommodates as many of those needs or interests as possible.

The obvious disadvantage of starting with the primary issues is that the negotiation may result in premature deadlock. The haste associated with "cutting to the chase" may cause the negotiators to become discouraged and abandon the negotiation before giving it a chance to work its course. In addition, if the primary issues are resolved first, the bargainers may not have a chance to use their "bargaining chips" to optimal advantage because they have traded them for a more favorable resolution of a primary issue.

Adversarial negotiators who put the incidental issues at the top of the agenda theorize that resolving these easier matters at the outset builds an atmosphere of trust, cooperation, and conciliation between the parties, and establishes a positive momentum for subsequently tackling the tougher, primary issues. Similarly, problem-solving negotiators may start with the less difficult issues to demonstrate to the other side how a mutual effort to accommodate the parties' varying needs or interests may be effectively employed in resolving the remaining harder issues.

The principal disadvantage to this approach is that it may create the false impression that the party initiating the resolution of the easier issues at first instance is being flexible, accommodating, and eager to reach agreement because of weakness. This misperception may cause the opposing side to take a more hardened, demanding, and unrealistic approach to the primary issues and push the negotiation into unnecessarily deadlock. Moreover, if both parties have exhausted their "bargaining chips" at the outset, neither side may be left with any matters to trade once the bargaining turns to the toughest issues.

In light of the relative advantages and disadvantages of starting the negotiation with either the primary or incidental issues, many negotiators strive to balance the discussion of these different matters throughout the negotiation. In this way, the risks associated with the "all or nothing" approach of starting with the primary issues, or the "easy does it" approach of beginning with the incidental issues are minimized. The adversarial negotiator's technique of controlling the agenda is thus tempered with a willingness to be flexible in discussing the various issues in whatever order best promotes progress in the negotiation.

From the problem solver's standpoint, so long as the parties are focusing on their real needs or interests, it matters less whether those interests involve primary or incidental issues at any particular stage in the negotiation. Indeed, many problem-solving negotiators allow the other side to dictate the agenda to find out what interests are most important to the opposing party and may be compatible with their own. It is only when the opposing party deviates from focusing on the joint needs or interests of the parties and becomes entrenched in positional bargaining that the problem solver becomes more concerned about controlling the agenda. In that event, the problem solver will strive to refocus the parties' attention back to their respective needs or interests, by trying to "separate the people from the problem," and using "brainstorming" to arrive at mutually beneficial solutions based on objective criteria (*see* §9.14[2]).

Setting the agenda at the negotiation usually takes the form of one party suggesting that the discussion begin with a particular issue. Alternatively, a party might simply begin discussing some issue without expressly stating the issue as a starting point. The advantage of the subtlety of the latter approach is that it disguises the party's attempt at agenda control and obviates a mini-negotiation over what will be negotiated and how. Sometimes, particularly in complex business or labor negotiations involving numerous participants, the agenda will have been pre-negotiated and reduced to writing such as through a *Draft Document or Single Negotiating Text* (*see* Chapter 5).

§9.08 Reading Body Language

To be a skilled negotiator you must be attentive to what is being said, careful to "read between the lines" of what is being said, and alert to what is not being said. Additionally, you must be sensitive to the other party's nonverbal thoughts and feelings expressed through body language. Some negotiators become so consumed with the ritualistic aspects of making and meeting offers and concessions that they unwittingly ignore what they can learn intuitively from the nonverbal reactions of the other side. It is essential to keep in mind that what the other party "feels" during the negotiation is often integral to the bottom-line outcome.

Reading body language is much more instinctive than scientific. It is essentially grounded in experienced intuition. That experience cautions that many people react differently under different circumstances, and the mannerisms displayed by one person may mean something quite different when displayed by another. Thus, reading body language accurately must be done contextually and holistically.

§9.09 Exchanging Information

After the "small talk" has set the tone for the negotiation and the agenda has been explicitly or implicitly established, the substantive portion of the negotiation usually begins with the parties exchanging information that is relevant to their ensuing bargaining. This "information stage" (sometimes called the "assessment stage") is, from a conceptual standpoint, often viewed as a distinct component of the negotiation process that is followed by the so-called "persuasion" and "exchange" stages during which the parties make their offers, counteroffers, and concessions toward a final agreement. While these stages provide a useful analytical framework for understanding the negotiation process, it is important to emphasize that they are invariably intertwined and permeate the entire negotiation process.

In general, the parties exchange information during the negotiation in order to (1) predict what each one will do, (2) understand what each is proposing, (3) determine the accuracy or truthfulness of what is being said, and (4) evaluate what matters are of greater or lesser importance to each party. In addition, information is used to persuade in that it forms the basis for the reasons underlying the parties' offers, counteroffers, concessions, needs or interests, and proposed solutions. Where competitive, adversarial bargaining is involved, the ability to control critical information about the strengths and weaknesses of the parties' respective positions is integral to the successful outcome of the negotiation. For cooperative problem solvers, exchanging information is essential to identifying the parties' varying needs or interests and in fashioning mutually beneficial solutions.

§9.10 Obtaining Information

As detailed in Chapter 7, prior to commencing the negotiation, you should obtain as much information as possible from your client, the other party, and the opposing negotiator that is pertinent to (1) the underlying needs or interests of each party; (2) the primary, secondary, and incidental objectives of each party; (3) the possible solutions that may satisfy each party's interests and objectives; (4) each party's best alternatives to a negotiated agreement (BATNA); (5) each party's strongest and weakest factual and legal leverage points; (6) the target and resistance points of each party; (7) each party's negotiating strategy and style; (8) the specific offers or proposals that may be presented by each party; and (9) the particular tactics each party may employ during the negotiation. This information may be contained in a Negotiation Preparation Outline for use during the face-to-face negotiation. The Outline will also contain an "Information" category that lists information "to obtain" from the other side, information "to reveal" to the other side, and information "to protect" from the other side (*see* §7.04).

During the face-to-face negotiation, you will need to confirm and obtain information from the other side about one or more of the nine categories listed above. Thus, these categories serve as a useful checklist of information that is relevant to both adversarial and problem-solving bargaining.

In obtaining information from the other side during the negotiation, in addition to the technique of using *Questions to Facilitate Agreements* in Chapter 5, it is useful to keep the following matters in mind:

[1] Ask Broad, Open-Ended Questions When Seeking Maximum Information

The best technique for obtaining maximum information is to ask broad, open-ended questions, as opposed to directed or leading questions that call for a "yes" or "no" answer. Open-ended questions invite the other negotiator to talk, and the more she talks, the more information you are likely to obtain.

Consider the difference between likely responses to the following questions. "Can you tell me how the contract came about?" "You proposed $20,000 as the purchase price, is that right?"

[2] Use Silence, Encouragement, and Questions That Call for Elaboration

Using silence and not interrupting the speaker are also effective in obtaining maximum information. In addition, you can encourage the speaker to elaborate by using responses such as "I see," "hmmm," "uh huh," or by asking open-ended follow-up questions that call for elaboration, such as "Could you explain that?" or "What happened next?" You may also find that reflecting feelings encourages the speaker to continue talking. Phrases such as, "That must have upset you," or "I understand," convey your focus on the listener and facilitate the continued exchange of information.

[3] Listen Intently and Patiently

Part of the art of information gathering and effective questioning is listening. While this point is obvious, many negotiators are prone to talk more than to listen. Effective listening requires patience. So long as the other side is talking, even if what is being said is repetitive or rambling, patience may yield additional relevant information. Moreover, it is difficult to listen effectively if you are distracted by excessive note taking or preoccupied with preparing your response to what is being said.

[4] Ask Specific Questions to Clarify, Pin Down, and Confirm Information

Specific or leading questions are most useful to clarify information, pin down ambiguous responses, or to confirm the accuracy of information you already possess. When taking a deposition, for example, many lawyers use a so-called "funnel" technique whereby the examiner begins with open-ended questions that elicit a plethora of information metaphorically represented by the wide mouth of the funnel, and then asks a series of more specific questions to clarify and pin down the details of what is being said which is represented by the bottom tip of the funnel. Information can also be clarified or confirmed by recapitulating what has been said and asking for confirmation. For example, "So, if I understand your point, it is .... Is that right?"

[5] Insist upon the Necessity of Receiving Crucial Information

If the other side is being evasive or refuses to reveal information that is essential to the negotiation, do not hesitate to point out why the requested information is important and why the failure to supply it will make further negotiation unproductive or impossible. An appeal to fairness and reciprocity is often successful. Alternatively, if the other negotiator is being unreasonably secretive, you might explain to him that his evasiveness has forced you to assume the facts in the light least favorable to his client. Notwithstanding the risks associated with this confrontational approach, it may be enough to cause the other side to be more forthcoming.

§9.11 Protecting Information

Although sharing information is integral to the negotiating process, lawyer negotiators must protect privileged information, and they invariably avoid revealing other sensitive or damaging information whenever possible. This occurs even in the most cooperative, problem-solving negotiations.

When protecting privileged information or avoiding the disclosure of damaging information, a negotiator should never engage in outright misrepresentation. As discussed previously (*see* §4.06), it is unethical to make false statements of material fact, and if a misrepresentation is exposed, the negotiator's credibility will be severely if not irreparably impaired. To avoid revealing information without misrepresentation, negotiators sometimes employ one or more of the *Blocking Techniques* introduced in Chapter 5. The most common blocking techniques are as follows:

[1] Ignore the Question and Change the Topic

If you are faced with a question that asks for information you do not want to reveal, it is often effective to simply ignore the question and continue the conversation on a different topic. The effectiveness of this technique is enhanced if your response relates to a matter of importance to the other side, notwithstanding its unresponsiveness to the particular question asked.

[2] Answer the Question by Asking Another Question

Sometimes asking a question in response can deflect a question. For example, suppose your opponent asks, "What tax returns do you have to support your client's claim for lost wages?" If you want to avoid revealing your client's tax returns, you might respond: "Don't you think that my client's W-2 statement accurately shows his earnings before the accident?"

[3] Answer the Question by Answering Another Question

If you are asked a compound question (*e.g.*, "How has the boycott affected local sales and your last year's contract with Corporation X?") you can choose which part of the question to answer and ignore the other part. Alternatively, you might attempt to answer the question by answering another question. This may be done by re-framing the question in a way that the answer will not be damaging, by answering another question that has recently been asked, or by simply answering another question as if it had been asked (*e.g.*, "If you're asking about the nationwide effect on our business, I can tell you it has been devastating... over a dozen suppliers have canceled their contracts with us.").

[4] Over-Answer or Under-Answer the Question

Giving broad, general responses can often deflect specific questions. Similarly, giving narrow responses can often deflect general questions. This technique of over-answering a specific question or under-answering a general question is a variation of the technique in [3] above.

[5] Rule the Question Out of Bounds

If a question is asked that calls for revealing privileged information, such as confidential attorney-client communications or work-product material, explain that you are not at liberty to reveal such information and why. However, be careful to be consistent about the types of information you claim to be privileged. Revealing certain portions of information claimed to be privileged but declining to reveal other information on the same subject will be construed as disingenuous.

§9.12 Revealing Information

Exchanging relevant information is, of course, essential to the negotiating process. Generally, there are five categories of information you will want to reveal: (1) your client's interests or needs; (2) your client's objectives; (3) possible solutions to the dispute or problem at hand; (4) your strongest factual and legal leverage points; and (5) your specific offers or proposals. All of this information should be contained in your "Negotiation Preparation Outline." In short, these types of information are necessary to educate and persuade the other side to the result you hope to obtain through the negotiation.

Revealing information is a dynamic process that occurs throughout the negotiation. Information is most effectively revealed through a dialogue rather than a monologue. While some negotiators prefer to start the substantive phase of a face-to-face negotiation with an "opening statement" that essentially "lays all of the cards on the table," this is usually undesirable. Notwithstanding the directness of this approach, opponents are often suspicious of wholesale voluntary disclosures and sometimes view them as patronizing, disingenuous, self-serving, and even manipulative.

Thus, it is usually best to divulge important information gradually. Allow the other side to extract information through her questions. In this way, the other side is more likely to listen to your information. When appropriate, you can always emphasize or reveal additional information in responding to particular questions.

The effective exchange of information occurs in a fluid, mutual, and cooperative process. It is conversational and sharing in nature, not a structured presentation of alternating opening speeches or a staid question-and-answer session. In sum, it is most effective when conducted in an open, free-flowing discussion.

§9.13 Adversarial Bargaining

In adversarial bargaining, after the parties have set the tone and agenda and exchanged pertinent information, the negotiation proceeds into the so-called "persuasion" and "exchange" stages whereby the parties make offers, counter-offers, and concessions in an effort to reach a final agreement. The process and techniques associated with these aspects of the negotiation are discussed below.

[1] Making Offers

[a] Who Should Make the First Offer

Often, one party will simply decide to "get the ball rolling" by making a first offer. Out of custom, the party who filed the claim or initiated the negotiation is often expected to make the first offer.

Many negotiators try to avoid making the first offer. Those who would avoid going first usually cite one or more of the following reasons. First, making the first offer may be taken as a sign of weakness, of being overly eager to reach an agreement. This reason for not making the first offer is unpersuasive. After all, no negotiation can proceed unless someone makes the first offer, and negotiators understand this.

If the other side makes the first offer, the negotiator can adjust his initial counteroffer to control the mid-point, which some negotiators value. For example, if one's goal is to obtain $50,000 and the other side makes a first offer of $10,000, an initial counteroffer of $90,000 will keep the target point of $50,000 in the middle.

Inducing the other party to make the first offer will normally require that they make the first concession to the other party's initial counteroffer. There is some statistical evidence to suggest that the party who makes the first concession does less well in the negotiation, perhaps because an initial concession provides the first forecast of the conceding party's concession strategy and potential target and resistance points.

There is one circumstance in which making the first offer carries real risk. A lawyer who has seriously underestimated the value of his case or the other side's resistance point may well have "left money on the table" if his initial offer falls close to the other party's bottom line. For example, assume the plaintiff's lawyer has valued the case and has targeted $50,000 for settlement and set his bottom line at $40,000. He makes a first offer of $75,000. The defendant has valued the case much higher and has targeted $85,000 for settlement and has set his bottom line at $75,000. One can confidently predict the case will settle. It also may be that the plaintiff will be pleased with the result, so long as he does not learn what might have been.

In the final analysis, with the exception of the situation where you are unsure about the value of the case, it makes little difference which party makes the first offer. Indeed, the party making the first offer will have the advantage of observing the other party's initial reaction to the proposal and thus may learn something about his potential settlement range.

Nevertheless, if you have a good reason to induce the other party to make the first offer, you should try to do so. If your opponent steadfastly declines to make the first offer, you can always protect yourself against a miscalculation by (1) making an opening offer that is more extreme than the one you originally planned to make, or (2) expressing your first offer in the form of a dollar range (*e.g.*, "I would estimate that this case is worth anywhere from $100,000 to $200,000."). If you discover that your first offer was a gross miscalculation and it is the only way to avoid a bad agreement for your client, you should consider making a revised offer and giving an explanation for your original miscalculation. Doing so is not only embarrassing; it will likely damage your credibility.

[b] When to Make the First Offer

Before making a first offer, you should be sure you have obtained as much information as possible from the other party about (1) his underlying needs or interests; (2) his primary, secondary, and incidental objectives; (3) possible solutions that may satisfy his interests and objectives; (4) his best alternatives to a negotiated agreement (BATNA); (5) his strongest and weakest factual and legal leverage points; (6) his potential target and resistance points; and (7) his potential offers or proposals (*see* §7.03). While, prior to the face-to-face meeting, you will have forecast these matters in your Negotiation Preparation Outline, you must appropriately revise the information in your Outline based on what you have learned first-hand at the meeting. Once you have taken into account any revisions to your Outline, you will be in a position to make your first offer.

[c] The Amount of the First Offer

Setting the amount of your first offer, or your first responsive counteroffer, depends upon the estimate you have made in your Negotiation Preparation Outline of both parties' target and resistance points. As mentioned previously, studies have shown that a negotiator might obtain a better outcome if her first offer represents a goal that is greater than her estimated target point (*see* §7.03[10]). Thus, in a damages case, if the plaintiff's target point is $70,000 and her resistance point is $30,000, and the defendant's target is to pay only $20,000 and his resistance point is $50,000, the plaintiff might make a first offer of $90,000, and the defendant might make an initial counteroffer of $10,000 (*see* diagram at §6.02). Generally, for the purpose of making first offers, it would be disadvantageous for either party to make an opening offer that falls within the parties' "settlement zone" of $50,000 to $30,000 (*i.e.*, the range between the parties' respective resistance points).

However, it is also unwise for a party to make an opening offer that is extreme, one that cannot be justified on any rational basis. An outrageous opening offer may result in premature deadlock and loss of credibility. If you are confronted with an outrageous opening offer, it is usually best to summarily reject it and resume preliminary discussions or the exchange of further information. After your opponent is given some time to save face, you can either induce him to make another first offer or make your own first offer.

[d] Communicating Offers

The cardinal rule of making any offer is to make it succinct, specific, and justifiable. Brevity is important for clarity. It also prevents unnecessary elaboration that might reveal information you would rather keep to yourself.

Second, the offer should be specific rather than vague. All essential terms about timing and performance should be spelled out. Specificity avoids misunderstandings and demonstrates the negotiator's commitment to the offer.

Third, every offer must be justifiable. You must be prepared to provide precise and persuasive reasons for your offer based on the strongest factual and legal leverage points contained in your Negotiation Preparation Outline. When communicating your offer, provide the other side with specific reasons for your proposal. For example, "Our $11,668 offer is based on $5,000 in lost wages, $2,668 in medical expenses, and $4,000 for four months of pain and suffering during which Mr. Smith was undergoing regular treatment." Avoid giving a lecture about your reasons. You can always amplify your reasons in response to questions from the other side. (*See also* §9.13[4][a].)

[2] Making Counteroffers

Like opening offers, counteroffers should be made with brevity, specificity, and justifiable reasons. However, before making a counteroffer, you should carefully evaluate the other side's offer in terms of understanding (1) exactly what is being offered, and (2) the other party's reasoning behind his offer. Do not hesitate to ask follow-up questions about any specifics of the offer and why the other party considers his proposal reasonable before making a counteroffer.

When probing the rationale for an offer, you will often recognize fallacies or weaknesses in the other party's position or analysis. This will provide you with an opportunity to expose and discuss those weaknesses to (1) lower your opponent's aspiration level, and (2) formulate and justify your counteroffer. It is important to re-emphasize that although you will have prepared one or more counteroffers in your Negotiation Preparation Outline, you should revise any counteroffers in light of the additional information you have learned about your opponent's offers and emerging concession strategy.

[3] Making Concessions

[a] When to Make Concessions

Concessions are an integral part of negotiation. They may be triggered by any number of the tactics or techniques discussed in Chapter 5 such as *Abdication, Asymmetrical Time Pressure, Boulwarism*, the formation of a *Coalition, Deadlines* or other time pressures, *Escalating Demands*, a *Fait Accompli, False Demands, False Emphasis, False Multiple Concessions, Lock-In Positions, Low-Balling, Nibbling, Preconditions or Conditional Proposals, Reversing Position, Splitting the Difference, Surprise*, a *Take-It-or-Leave-It* approach, *Threats*, or a *Walkout*. In addition, a party's desire to put an end to the dispute, to preserve good will, or to accede to the advice of a third party such as a judge or mediator often results in a concession.

Generally, concessions are appropriate when your use of argument, persuasion, threats, promises, or other tactics have been unsuccessful, and you still have some distance between your latest offer or counteroffer and your resistance point. Concessions are necessary to further movement toward an agreement. Thus, you should be willing to make concessions so long as you believe that the outcome of the negotiation will be better than your best alternative to a negotiated agreement.

Whether to make the first concession or wait for the other party to do so is a controversial issue. As mentioned in §9.13[1][a], there is some statistical evidence suggesting that the party who makes the first concession does less well in the negotiation. However, if you make one or more minor concessions at the outset without losing bargaining leverage, you may have greater success later on in extracting more important concessions from the other party who has been psychologically induced to reciprocate out of a sense of fairness.

[b] Concession Strategy

Effective negotiators tentatively plan out their concession strategy in advance of the face-to-face negotiation. This strategy should be reflected in the 1st, 2nd, 3rd, and 4th "Offers or Proposals" contained in your Negotiation Preparation Outline. Each successive offer will reflect one or more additional concessions. Your planned concession pattern will also be based on the successive offers or proposals that you anticipate will be made by the other party.

Some research suggests that when one party's concessions are few and small, the opposing party is more likely to reduce her aspirations and make both greater and more frequent concessions. Thus, as a general rule, negotiators tend to be more successful if they make both fewer and smaller concessions than their adversaries. As summarized by one authority:

> The research data suggest you can construct an effective concession pattern as an adversarial negotiator by doing the following: Be sure your rate of concession is not too rapid, nor the size of the concessions too great, nor the number too many. Consistent with the research, taking a strong stand on a moderately high or low opening offer with one or, at most, a few concessions to your resistance level will produce the most effective results. Finally you should attempt to accurately identify the minimum your opponent will accept to settle the matter [*i.e.*, his resistance point] and then position yourself just outside that point, resisting a further concession for as long as possible.[1]

Consider the following example:

1. R. M. Bastress & J. D. Harbaugh, *Interviewing, Counseling, and Negotiating* 520 (1990). *See also*, M. Saks & R. Hastie, *Social Psychology in Court* 124 (1978) (advocating "extreme initial offers, well above (or below) one's resistance point, making concessions few, small, reciprocal, and each one rationalized, explained, justified on some basis other than mere pursuit of agreement.").

Example 1

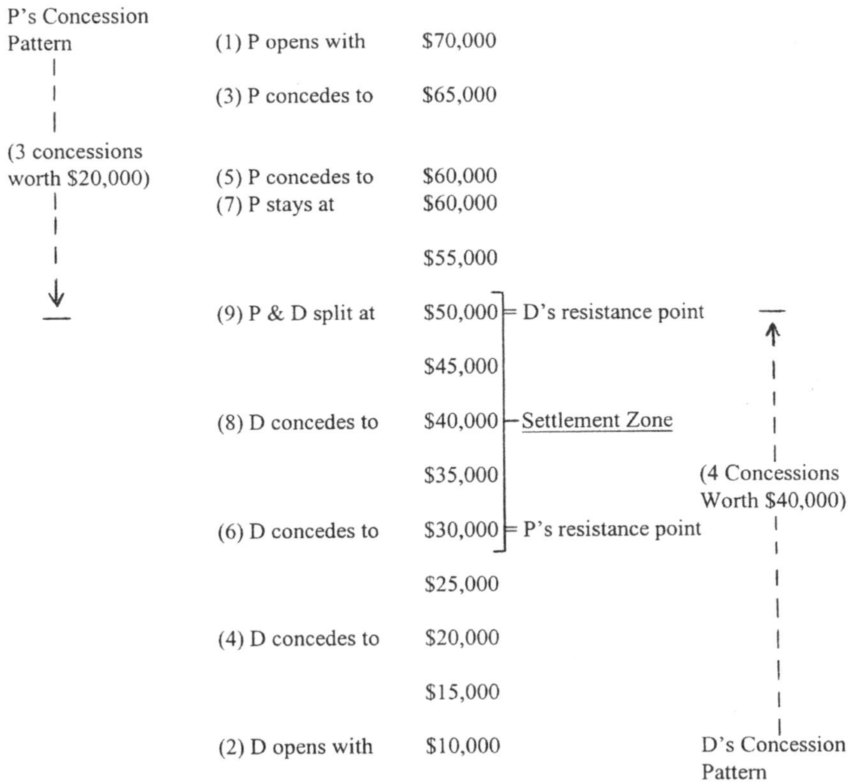

In this example, the settlement zone is $30,000 to $50,000, with P's resistance point at $30,000 and D's resistance point at $50,000. The following exchange steps occur: (1) P makes an opening offer of $70,000; (2) D makes an opening offer of $10,000; (3) P makes a first concession to $65,000; (4) D makes a first concession to $20,000; (5) P makes a second concession to $60,000; (6) D makes a second concession to $30,000; (7) P refuses to move from his latest offer of $60,000; (8) D grudgingly makes a third concession to $40,000; and (9) P proposes to split the difference by conceding to $50,000 and D agrees by conceding to $50,000. The net result is that P has made slower, smaller, and fewer concessions than D. That is, P has made a total of 3 concessions worth $20,000 (while holding out at $60,000 for a time), and D has made 4 concessions worth $40,000 (while never resisting a concession). Although the mid-point of the settlement zone is $40,000, P managed to achieve a settlement of $50,000 that constituted D's resistance point, as compared with P's resistance point of $30,000.

Consider, however, another example:

Example 2

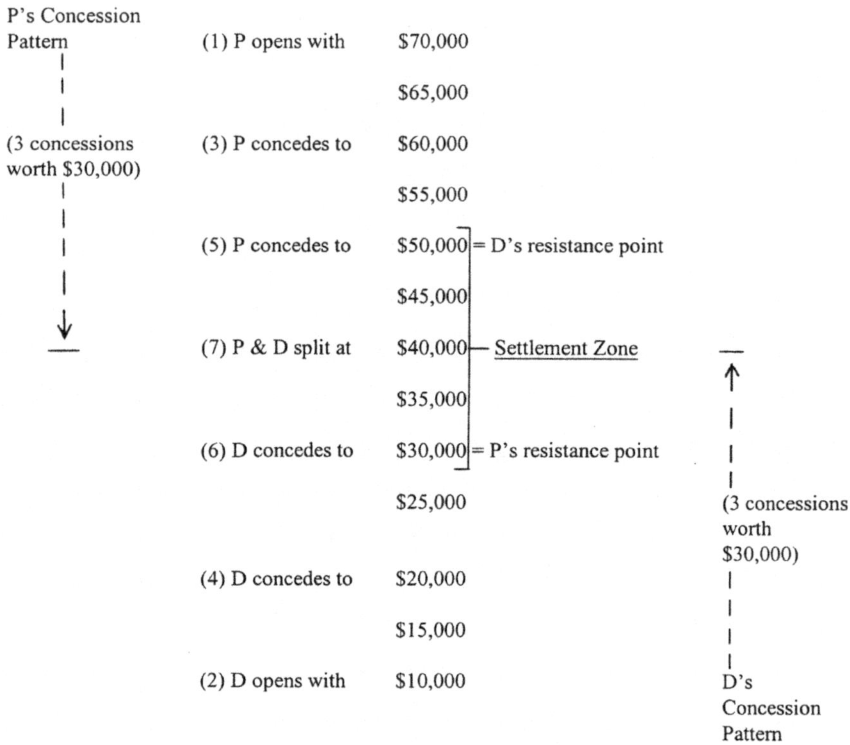

In this example, the settlement zone is still $30,000 to $50,000, with P's resistance point at $30,000 and D's resistance point at $50,000. The following exchange steps occur: (1) P makes an opening offer of $70,000; (2) D makes an opening offer of $10,000; (3) P makes a first concession to $60,000; (4) D makes a first concession to $20,000; (5) P makes a second concession to $50,000; (6) D makes a second concession to $30,000; and (7) P and D split the difference by each conceding an additional $10,000 to settle at $40,000. The net result is that neither party has made slower, smaller, or fewer concessions than the other. That is, each party has made 3 concessions worth $30,000 and settled at the mid-point of the settlement zone ($40,000), which is the mid-point of their respective resistance points.

The foregoing examples teach that you can generally prevent the other side from having an undue advantage by (1) keeping careful track of the number and value of the other side's concessions, (2) seeking to extract reciprocal concessions in number and value, and (3) modifying your planned concession strategy in light of the particular concessions made by the other side. Monitoring the other side's concession behavior will also gradually reveal how close that side is coming to its resistance level and the relative impact that one's efforts at persuasion and use of various tactics are having upon the other side's concession pattern.

Patience is important because many position changes tend to occur during the last stages of the negotiation. Being too hasty in making concessions may thus cause you to make a greater, aggregate compromise at the end of the negotiation than you would have made had your earlier concessions been fewer in number and value. Impatience with the negotiating process may cause you to become frustrated and angry with your more cautious and grudging adversary. This can lead to becoming psychologically entrapped by the negotiation "game" so that you feel compelled to reach an agreement regardless of the cost. This entrapment can be avoided by keeping your resistance point and best alternative to a negotiated agreement (BATNA) in mind, regardless of the time, effort, and energy expended in attempting to reach an accord. There is nothing wrong with failing to reach an agreement, but it is poor advocacy to acquiesce to an agreement on behalf of your client simply for the sake of reaching an agreement.

This does not mean you should never reevaluate or change your bottom line. If the negotiation process reveals that you have misjudged your planned bargaining limits or that the consequences of non-settlement are more onerous than a negotiated result, you should be flexible in reassessing your resistance point. On the other hand, if it becomes apparent that a negotiated agreement would be more costly than your best alternative to negotiation, do not hesitate to tell the other side that you cannot make any further concessions. If negotiations deadlock at that point and thereafter do not resume, you can resort to your best alternative option.

[c] Communicating Concessions

Because concessions are almost always embodied in counteroffers, your concessions should be communicated with brevity, specificity, and justifiable reasons (*see* §9.13[1][d]). Providing one or more reasons for your concessions demonstrates to the other party that you are not simply engaging in a ritualistic offer, counteroffer, response, counter-response march along the bargaining scale toward your ultimate resistance point. Rather, you want to demonstrate that your concessions are based on a rational assessment of the dispute or the problem at hand.

Your reason for making a concession might stem from a persuasive point made by the other side, an effort to accommodate a particular need or interest of the other side, new information, or a willingness to engage "in the spirit of compromise." Be succinct in giving your reasons and avoid being defensive.

Sometimes, particularly when there are multiple issues in the negotiation, it may be useful to forecast your willingness to make a possible concession in exchange for a specific concession from the other side. For example, "We might agree to make a larger lump sum payment if you are willing to accept our non-compete clause." Using flexible language in communicating a concession makes it easier to retract your position and resurrect the concession later. However, the excessive use of ambiguity in suggesting concessions may lead to misunderstandings and undermine your credibility for lack of committing yourself to making firm concessions.

[4] Forms of Persuasion

[a] Argument

Argument as a form of persuasion permeates the making of offers, counter-offers, and concessions. Effective arguments contain six elements.

First, the argument should be based on some normative standard or objective criterion that is independent of the naked will of either side. Thus, the argument might be based on applicable law, the facts of the dispute or problem at hand, economic considerations, custom, ethical norms, expertise, analogy, or rule. These should be included as part of the "Factual & Legal Leverage Points" in your Negotiation Preparation Outline (*see* §7.03[6]). The most effective arguments are based on as many of these normative standards or objective criteria as possible.

Second, the argument must show how the normative standard or objective criterion chosen applies to the parties' situation. That is, the legal, factual, or other reason asserted must be rationally related to the case at hand.

Third, the normative standard or objective criterion chosen must be credible or authoritative in the sense of being supported by appropriate evidence or other proof. Such evidence or proof might be based on indisputable or verifiable facts, logical presumptions, or so-called "customary proofs" such as generally accepted assumptions, beliefs, or values.

Fourth, the argument must be "balanced" in the sense of taking into account the other party's legitimate contentions. If you fail to be evenhanded or distort the merits of the other side's arguments, your own arguments will be unpersuasive. When possible, you must be prepared to distinguish away the strongest points advanced by the other party, or persuasively show how his standards or criteria are inappropriate, inapplicable to the situation at hand, or based on inadequate evidence or proof.

Fifth, when appropriate, your argument should be emphasized by highlighting and amplifying upon key points, without muddling the force of your argument with minutiae or ancillary matters. In addition, arguments should be emphasized by repeating them in different forms, and they should be expressed with tact and controlled emotion that takes into account the legitimate feelings of the parties.

Sixth, although it is usually best to be relatively brief when communicating an offer, your justification for it will have more persuasive force if you give multiple reasons for your proposal. That is, if you can show that no matter which way one looks at the problem the best solution always seems to be the same, your proposal will be much more convincing. This also means that you should be prepared to provide detailed factual information that supports the multi-dimensional reasoning behind your proposal.

[b] Exhibits

Exhibits, such as models, diagrams, charts, photos, slides, or videos may be highly effective in presenting arguments or proposals. Of course, proper attention to considerations such as format, placement, layout, size, and style is essential. Similarly, careful attention should be given to the use of color schemes in exhibits to make them easy to read and understand.

[c] Emotional Appeals

In contrast to rational argumentation, emotional appeals are directed to the other party's psychological needs and motivations. People need and are often motivated by (1) sensory rewards such as feeling good or free from anger, fear, tension, and anxiety; (2) social rewards such as prestige, acceptance, and love; and (3) ego-supporting rewards such as self-esteem and meaning in life. Cooperative negotiators frequently appeal to these psychological rewards through positive behaviors such as altruism, good will, friendship, humor, flattery, and the like. Conversely, some highly competitive negotiators employ a variety of negative behaviors or tactics, such as *Anger/Aggressiveness, Blaming or Fault-Finding, Escalating Demands, Reversing Position,* or *Threats* (*see* Chapter 5), that are designed to create frustration, guilt, embarrassment, discomfort, indebtedness, or other unpleasant pressures upon their adversaries. Whether emotional appeals are made through deliberately positive or negative behavior, the ultimate goal is the same—to induce the other party to enter into an agreement more favorable to one's own terms, either under circumstances where the other party will feel good about himself in reaching an agreement, or under circumstances where he would prefer to conclude an agreement in lieu of having to further endure the unpleasant encounter.

[d] Threats and Promises

Threats and promises, whether express or implied, are commonly used forms of persuasion. A threat is intended to induce the other party to believe that the cost of disagreement outweighs the cost of reaching a particular agreement. Threats are negative in the sense that they forecast preplanned negative consequences if carried out. As such, threats tend to elicit greater feelings of hostility and competitiveness.

An affirmative promise, on the other hand, is a proposal to act in a beneficial way toward another if she takes certain action (*e.g.,* "We would be willing to do X if you would be willing to accommodate us on Y."). Promises imply reciprocal cooperation. Accordingly, in contrast to threats, positive promises tend to elicit greater feelings of conciliation and cooperativeness. Thus, it is not surprising that the prospects for reaching a mutually satisfactory agreement are greater when affirmative promises are employed in lieu of negative threats.

The elements of a credible threat and techniques for responding to threats are set out in §5.45. In addition, whenever possible, negotiators should consider using a "warning" in lieu of an express threat. A warning might take the form of a strong word of caution, argument, or an appeal to the other side about the consequences that might result in the event an agreement is not reached. In contrast to a formal threat, such a warning does not presage specific, adverse action on the part of the declarant, but forecasts undesirable consequences that will independently occur in the absence of an accord.

§9.14 Problem-Solving Bargaining

The substantive stages of problem-solving bargaining involve the identification and sharing of the interests or needs of both parties and brainstorming to develop solutions to satisfy those needs and maximize the parties' mutual gain. The making of offers, counteroffers, and concessions is deliberately tied to this objective. The process and techniques of this problem-solving approach are given below.

[1] Identifying and Sharing Interests or Needs

Because the aim of problem solving is to reach an agreement that is mutually satisfactory to both parties, this approach to negotiation is predicated upon a cooperative effort between the parties to identify and share each other's underlying interests or needs. A party's "interests" are akin to his "objectives" in that the former constitute the *reasons* underlying his specific negotiation goals. Identifying interests involves asking why one desires a particular objective. The focus is on the *needs*, *desires*, *concerns*, *fears*, *philosophies*, and *feelings* that shape a party's personal, psychological, ideological, or emotional motivations underlying his negotiation goals. For example, consider the following potential interests:

- <u>Ego or psychological interests</u>: recognition, status, personal satisfaction, career satisfaction, sense of power or authority, self-esteem and self-respect, freedom from anxiety or stress
- <u>Moral or ideological interests</u>: reputation, good will, integrity, fairness, religious or political beliefs
- <u>Economic or efficiency interests</u>: financial security, short-term or long-term profits, reducing costs or inefficiency, developing new business opportunities, establishing or avoiding certain precedents
- <u>Relationship interests</u>: fostering better interpersonal relationships, working with others, ending detrimental relationships, developing new relationships or contacts

The interests (and objectives) of both parties should be listed in your Negotiation Preparation Outline, ranked from most important to least important, and evaluated to determine which are shared between the parties, which are independent of each other but do not conflict, and which conflict. When the parties exchange information during problem-solving negotiation, they (1) consciously strive to "separate the people from the problem" through a mindset that attacks the problem, not each other; and (2) focus on each other's interests, as against the mere "wants" reflected in each side's stated "positions."

If one side is resistant to these efforts, the other party will (1) shun any temptation to participate in personal attacks or react irrationally to the other side; (2) seek to diffuse anger, fear, and suspicion by listening and acknowledging the other side's points and concerns; (3) deflect hard-line positions by re-framing them in the form of problem-solving "why" and "what if" questions; (4) adopt the role of a mediator, trying to identify and satisfy the other side's unmet interests; and (5) instead of employing threats or force, seek to educate the other side to the costs of not reaching an agreement and emphasize that the overriding goal of the negotiation is mutual satisfaction, not victory.

[2] Brainstorming for Solutions

After the parties identify and share their interests or needs, they jointly brainstorm for as many solutions as possible that may satisfy their mutual needs. These potential solutions should be drawn and developed from the "Possible Solutions" listed in your Negotiation Preparation Outline.

In brainstorming for possible solutions, it has been suggested that the parties employ the following techniques:[2]

1. They should initially spend time thinking of all possible solutions by promoting broad discussion and agreeing to outlaw negative criticism of any kind. (These potential solutions might be outlined on a chart for all to see).
2. They should clarify at the outset that each party's mere listing of solutions is not an expression of an official position. The point is to generate as expansive a list as possible, which can later be refined for detailed discussion.
3. They should strive to broaden the potential options that might be considered, rather than look for a single answer.

---

2. *See* R. Fisher & W. Ury, *Getting to Yes* (1981); W. Ury, *Getting Past No* (1991).

4. Multiple options might be generated by identifying (i) the overall problem at hand, (ii) potential causes of or barriers to solving the problem, (iii) theoretical solutions, (iv) solutions that might be proposed by experts or persons from the perspective of different professions or disciplines, and (v) specific steps that might be taken to deal with the problem.
5. The parties should consider which options might be more desirable or workable than others, distinguishing among those that are substantive versus procedural, comprehensive versus partial, and unconditional versus contingent.
6. Options for mutual gain should be explored based on shared interests and the possibility that the parties' divergent interests can be mutually satisfied without undue cost to any particular party.
7. Each party should consciously consider potential options from the other side's point of view.
8. The parties should be particularly advertent to possible solutions that are based on normative standards or objective criteria, such as the facts at hand, applicable law, economic considerations, custom, industry standards, ethical norms, expertise, analogy, or rule, rather than the naked will of any one party.

[3] Making Problem-Solving Offers, Counteroffers, and Concessions

After developing a broad list of potential solutions, the parties will have to decide which solution or combination of solutions to formally propose or adopt. In contrast to negotiators engaged in strictly adversarial bargaining, problem solvers are much less hesitant to initiate first offers, and they are less inclined to view subsequent offers as incremental steps in a pre-established concession strategy toward a defined resistance point. This is because the problem solver often uses the making of offers to encourage joint problem solving by analyzing what the other party's responses to those offers mean about the other party's underlying interests or needs. Therefore, it is not unusual for problem solvers to make multiple offers at the same time. By gauging the other party's reaction to these offers and engaging in a discussion about them, more specific proposals can be fashioned to maximize mutual gain.

Unlike adversarial bargainers, problem solvers tend to make offers, counteroffers, and concessions that are more general and expansive. Specificity is replaced with generality (at least at the outset), and brevity is replaced with a willingness to expansively share explanations and rationales for what is being proposed. In this way the problem solver is able to reveal and reinforce the needs of her own client and simultaneously demonstrate a willingness to recognize the legitimate interests or needs of the other side. Purely singular solutions are shunned, and fervent commitment to any particular proposal is avoided in order to invite open, honest, and legitimate criticism. The goal is that, through joint sharing, exploring, and discussion, a concrete proposal will emerge that best satisfies as many of the interests or needs of both parties as possible.

In freely making offers, counteroffers, and appropriate concessions, the problem solver, like the adversarial bargainer, buttresses them with justifiable reasons. Thus, arguments are based on normative standards or objective criteria that are rationally related to the case at hand, are credible or authoritative in the sense of being supported by appropriate evidence or other proof, and are "balanced" in light of the legitimate points made by each side. Notwithstanding the problem solver's disposition to seek solutions that maximize the mutual gain of the parties, she still guards against becoming entrapped by the negotiation process and keeps in mind her best alternatives to a negotiated agreement (BATNA).

§9.15 Combining Adversarial and Problem-Solving Bargaining

Few negotiations are either purely adversarial or purely problem solving. Many negotiators combine the two approaches to different aspects of a single negotiation, where the salient features of each strategy best complement the dispute or the problem at hand or otherwise enhance the prospects for a favorable agreement. In addition, some negotiators might start with a wholly adversarial approach and, when it becomes plain that the negotiation is stalling or near deadlock, pursue a largely problem-solving approach. That the adversarial and problem-solving models are analytically and conceptually distinct is not a reason to employ one to the exclusion of the other. Negotiation is a complex and dynamic form of human interaction that often requires flexibility to achieve a successful outcome.

As a practical matter, in most negotiations there is an on-going tension between "win-win" cooperative efforts to create solutions for an agreement and "win-lose" competitive efforts to claim the best solutions for one's own side. In this sense, problem solving "giveth" and adversarial bargaining "taketh." The tension can be counterproductive and subject to abuse because win-lose tactics often impede the creation of desirable solutions. Win-win tactics—while tending to promote creative solutions—may be exploited by a disingenuous problem solver who changes his approach in midstream, adopting an adversarial posture to reap the fruits of cooperatively created solutions for his unilateral benefit. From the perspective of a "zealous advocate," this type of giving with the right hand and taking with the left may seem clever (and arguably creative) negotiating—*i.e.*, problem solve to create and then compete to take.

To effectively deal with this tension and create cooperative solutions without being vulnerable to exploitation, a so-called TIT-FOR-TAT or "conditionally open" approach has been suggested. Under this approach, problem-solving and adversarial bargaining are combined. The negotiator (1) warily seeks mutual cooperation at first instance; (2) engages in competitive tactics when the other party does so; (3) resorts back to cooperative behavior when the other side appears so inclined; and (4) attempts to induce an overall problem-solving approach by developing a reputation for being a consistently "principled" negotiator, but one who is not a push-over and will meet highly competitive tactics in kind when necessary. This "conditionally open" approach is a form of "tough love," whereby the negotiator genuinely exemplifies cooperation and fairness when it is reciprocated, but will respond with firmness to disingenuous or exploitive conduct, and still is willing to forgive and move forward in cooperation when the opponent has demonstrated a return to problem solving.

Alternatively, the parties might agree in advance to a problem-solving approach toward certain issues in the case or during certain phases of the negotiation, and to an adversarial approach toward other issues or during other phases. For example, problem solving would be used for those issues where the parties are capable of exchanging or trading things other than money, but adversarial bargaining would be employed where the issue is merely how much money one party receives and the other pays. Or the parties choose to engage in problem-solving to understand each other's underlying interests or needs and the issues at hand, and thereafter engage in adversarial bargaining when it comes time to constructing a specific agreement. There is nothing wrong with or undesirable about bifurcating and then recombining adversarial and problem-solving bargaining in these ways, so long as each party is aware which playing field is being used for any particular issue or at any particular time during the negotiation.

§9.16 Concluding the Negotiation

In every negotiation there comes a time when it becomes apparent to the parties either that an agreement is likely to be reached or that the negotiation will conclude in an impasse or final deadlock. If an impasse occurs, or even if a deadlock seems inevitable, it is usually best to indicate that you are willing to "keep the door open" for future negotiations. In addition, you should close the stalled or deadlocked negotiation with civility.

If it appears that the parties are close to reaching an agreement, it is essential to avoid being caught up in the anticipation of the moment. As mentioned previously, the most significant concessions tend to be made toward the end of the negotiation (*see* §9.13[3][b]), and thus it is not uncommon for a negotiator to become overly anxious to conclude an agreement by forfeiting at the last moment much of what she had gained by patience throughout the balance of the negotiation session. Accordingly, effective negotiators tend to be particularly patient, cautious, and persistent when making final offers, counteroffers, or concessions toward the end of the bargaining session. This means always keeping in mind one's resistance point and best alternative to a negotiated agreement.

In light of the psychological tendency of many negotiators to accelerate and increase their concessions toward the end of the negotiation, you might be able to capitalize on this tendency by (1) applauding the other party for the movement or position changes he has made thus far, (2) encouraging him to continue his conciliatory behavior for the sake of reaching a final agreement, or (3) providing him with convincing reasons for making one or more additional concessions. Even in problem-solving bargaining, the most successful negotiators tend to be more competitive than cooperative during the closing phase of the negotiation.

Sometimes negotiators seek to accelerate the closing phase of a negotiation through tactics discussed in Chapter 5 such as *Abdication*, *Asymmetrical Time Pressure*, creating *Deadlines*, using other *Timing* pressures, *Escalating Demands*, creating a *Fait Accompli*, *Reversing Position*, offering to *Split the Difference*, announcing a *Take-It-or-Leave-It* position, or engaging in a *Walkout*. In general, to protect yourself against such tactics you should (1) not allow the other side to press for a closing until you are ready to close, (2) not press for a closing yourself until you are ready to close, and (3) not press for a closing when the other side is likely to view your pressure with mistrust or suspicion.

After you have reached an agreement, and before you leave the face-to-face meeting, it is desirable to repeat the major terms of the transaction or, better yet, to reduce them to a memorandum of understanding. If there is any confusion or misunderstanding at this point in the process, it should be dealt with on the spot so as not to lose the momentum toward closure. In addition, you should be careful to clarify any details attendant to the execution of the agreement. These matters might include (1) time frames for performing the agreement; (2) any follow-up action to be taken by the parties; (3) what information or documents are needed to effectuate the agreement; (4) whether any third parties need to be notified of the agreement; (5) details regarding the preparation and submission of appropriate releases, pleadings, or other documents; (6) contingency plans in the event either client rejects the agreement (assuming final client approval is necessary); and (7) who will bear any applicable expenses such as court costs, legal fees, and expenses.

If the agreement is to be formalized in writing, and particularly if its terms are complex, you should volunteer to draft the final documentation. This reduces the risk that the other party will insert new terms or provisions into the agreement that were not discussed or agreed upon during the negotiation. In addition, if you are the draftsman, you will be in a better position to exact some reciprocal concessions if the other party requests any significant changes, additions, or deletions to your draft. If you do not prepare the final documentation, you must carefully review it to ensure that it accurately and completely reflects the agreement reached at the face-to-face meeting. If it does not, firmly insist upon appropriate changes to the draft, and, if the other side repeatedly resists your modifications, volunteer to take over the final drafting process yourself.

Finally, conclude the face-to-face meeting with appropriate parting salutations and professionalism. If you have achieved a particularly advantageous agreement for your client, do not gloat; and if the final agreement was less desirable than you hoped for, do not pout. In either case, by graciously commending your counterpart for her efforts in handling the negotiation, you will bolster your reputation for integrity and professionalism in any future dealings.

Chapter Ten

Negotiating During Civil Litigation

SYNOPSIS

§10.01 Introduction
§10.02 General Considerations About Preparation
§10.03 General Considerations About Pretrial Strategy and Style
§10.04 Filing the Complaint and Answer
§10.05 Using Discovery
§10.06 Making Offers of Judgment
§10.07 Using Timing and Deadlines
§10.08 Using Pretrial Settlement Conferences
§10.09 Settling at the Last Minute
§10.10 High-Low Agreements
§10.11 Collaborative Law Agreements

§10.01 Introduction

Approximately 90% of all lawsuits are settled, and it is likely that this percentage will increase with court-annexed mediation and the growth of other forms of alternative dispute resolution. Litigation is expensive, risky, and time consuming, and the economic and emotional drain on the parties is usually considerable. Because settlement is so prevalent during litigation, lawyers should not hesitate to initiate settlement discussions as a rule rather than as an exception.

Much of the discussion in the preceding chapters is relevant to negotiating during litigation. Given below are some additional considerations when negotiating a settlement of a litigated case, whether before, during, or after trial.

§10.02 General Considerations About Preparation

As in any negotiation context, to effectively prepare for a lawsuit settlement you should develop a Negotiation Preparation Outline like that discussed in Chapter 7. In addition, in developing an overall approach to settlement, it is particularly important to obtain information about the opposing lawyer, not only as a negotiator, but also as a trial advocate. After all, in the litigation context, the parties' best alternative to a negotiated agreement will usually be trial, and the outcome of a trial may have much to do with the relative trial skills of the parties' lawyers.

Particularly when settlement discussions are initiated before the filing of a lawsuit, it is important to obtain information about the settlement attitudes and practices of any insurance carrier or other entity that will be involved in the negotiation. For example, if you represent the plaintiff and the particular carrier has a reputation for taking a hardline position in response to initial settlement overtures, you may prefer to file a lawsuit before initiating any discussion of settlement. On the other hand, if you represent the defendant under circumstances where liability seems clear and the plaintiff's lawyer has a reputation of being reluctant to try cases and settling quickly, you might choose to be more active in initiating or responding to settlement proposals. In either case, the simplest way to find out about the general settlement attitudes of the other side is to ask lawyers or other people who have had prior dealings with your counterpart.

§10.03 General Considerations About Pretrial Strategy and Style

As mentioned previously, lawsuit negotiations are usually adversarial and competitive. This is because, in many instances, once lawyers have become involved and litigation is contemplated or underway, the parties' relationship has become badly strained or even destroyed. In addition, both sides are aware that, regardless of who prevails in the lawsuit, each is still a potential loser. A victory for the plaintiff may be offset by the costs of time and money in pursuing his claim, and a victory for the defendant in preserving the status quo may be offset by substantial legal fees and other costs. Perhaps most importantly, both sides have already begun to pay the emotional cost of the stress, pressure, anxiety, and animosity that comes with litigation.

The litigation process itself aggravates this adversarial and competitive atmosphere. After initial settlement discussions have broken down, the plaintiff and defendant often engage in the following series of actions and counteractions: (1) the plaintiff files his complaint; (2) the defendant takes as long as permissible to answer, and interposes a counterclaim if possible; (3) the plaintiff initiates discovery by taking depositions, submitting interrogatories and requests to produce documents, etc.; (4) the defendant responds in kind and often initiates even more discovery; (5) the plaintiff files dispositive motions; (6) the defendant responds or counters with her own dispositive motions; (7) one side or the other calendars the case for trial; (8) the other side sometimes seeks to delay the trial; and (9) after trial, the losing party appeals and, if she loses on the initial appeal, an appeal is taken to the jurisdiction's highest court. In sum, each party seeks to wear down the other through pressure, counter-pressure, action, counter-action, delay, and spiraling expense.

Against this background, settlement discussions tend to occur when one or both parties begin to realize (1) that it may be more advantageous to substitute the certainty of a settlement for the uncertainty of a trial outcome, or (2) that the time and expense associated with the litigation process is becoming unbearable. Of course, there is no standard point in the litigation process when either of these realizations will be triggered. However, in general, the strategy often employed by the plaintiff is to exert maximum pressure on the defendant through the litigation process until the latter realizes that the plaintiff is prepared to go the distance. Conversely, an often-used strategy for the defendant is to erect as many barriers as possible to the plaintiff's pursuit of his claims with the hope that he will significantly reduce his expectations and settle the case cheaply, or even abandon his case altogether due to the financial costs of continuing to pursue the case. In the end, the party who possesses the greatest persistence, patience, and economic and emotional wherewithal is most likely to effectuate the most advantageous settlement.

This description of the effects of the litigation process on settlement should not be interpreted as an endorsement of engaging in such a highly competitive and adversarial approach as a matter of course. A more cooperative approach is often instrumental in blunting the adversarial instincts inherent in the litigation setting, and a problem-solving strategy is neither conceptually nor practically inappropriate after a lawsuit has been filed. Particularly when the parties' dispute involves multiple issues, may be resolved through a variety of solutions other than the mere payment of money, or requires ongoing dealings between the parties, a problem-solving approach is often the best means for settling litigation.

§10.04 Filing the Complaint and Answer

As discussed in Chapter 8, many lawyers initially try to resolve disputes through a demand letter, settlement brochure, or negotiations by email or over the telephone. A lawsuit is typically not filed until negotiations break down or unless initiating them would be fruitless at the outset. On the other hand, a number of experienced litigators advocate filing a lawsuit at first instance, or, at the least, sending the other side a draft of the complaint when initiating settlement discussions. The rationale for this approach is that it demonstrates the plaintiff's preparedness and seriousness about his claims.

Once the decision has been made to file a lawsuit, there are a number of considerations to take into account for settlement purposes. First, when possible, the plaintiff's lawyer should bring the suit in the most convenient place for his client and most inconvenient place for the defendant. For example, if the defendant lives in Wyoming but the transaction took place in New York where your client lives, the forum of choice would be New York. The inconvenience and expense to the defendant of having to litigate the case away from home may exert significant settlement pressure.

Second, despite the bare requirements of notice pleading, for settlement purposes, it is sometimes desirable to draft a complaint that sets forth one's factual allegations and the calculation of damages in extra detail. This has the benefit of beginning to educate defense counsel to the merits of your case at the outset, rather than gradually revealing them later on through a drawn-out discovery process. Additional specificity in your complaint also shows the other side that you are not bluffing about the bases for your causes of action, which are often otherwise expressed in rather conclusory terms. However, you should always bear in mind that filing a complaint for an improper purpose or with frivolous factual or legal allegations is unethical and may expose you or your client to potential sanctions by the court.[1]

1. *See* Fed. R. Civ. P. 11(b) and (c).

Third, causes of action ancillary to the main claim should be included in the complaint. For example, if the defendant's negligence was accompanied by extreme and outrageous conduct resulting in severe emotional distress, additional causes of action for intentional infliction of emotional distress should be included. Similarly, if such outrageous behavior involved willful, wanton, reckless, or malicious conduct, a claim for punitive damages should be added even if the applicable insurance would not cover exemplary damages. In short, the greater the number of causes of action and claims for damages, the greater the defendant's potential exposure becomes.

Fourth, in an appropriate case, seeking a temporary restraining order or preliminary injunction might increase bargaining leverage. Even if an *ex parte* TRO is not granted, the climate for settlement might be enhanced pending a hearing on the motion for a preliminary injunction. If injunctive relief is granted, the plaintiff will have scored a *Fait Accompli* (*see* Chapter 10) by changing the status quo to require the defendant to refrain from certain action or take certain action to protect the plaintiff.

Fifth, including a demand for a jury trial in the complaint may increase bargaining leverage because jury verdicts and awards are much less predictable than decisions and awards rendered by judges. From the plaintiff's standpoint, a jury trial is particularly important when the defendant is a so-called "target defendant," such as a large corporation or governmental entity for whom the jury may have little sympathy.

Sixth, even the choice of how to effect service of the complaint upon the defendant may exert psychological pressure toward settlement. For example, serving a defendant by sheriff at the defendant's home or office will generate greater stress and anxiety than serving her by registered or certified mail, return receipt requested.

In answering the complaint, the defendant should, when permissible, first consider moving for an extension of time within which to answer. This is important not only to gain time to conduct an adequate investigation into the plaintiff's allegations, but it may be desirable as part of an overall strategy to preserve the status quo as long as possible.

Second, when applicable, the defendant's answer should detail all available counterclaims against the plaintiff. Apart from compulsory counterclaims which must be raised to avoid waiver,[2] it is often desirable for settlement purposes to plead all permissive counterclaims[3] in order to reduce the plaintiff's

2. *See* Fed. R. Civ. P. 13(a).

3. *See* Fed. R. Civ. P. 13(b).

expectation of recovery. In addition, any appropriate cross-claims or third-party impleader or interpleader should be raised.[4]

Third, just as the plaintiff should consider including in his complaint all potential causes of action, the defendant should consider raising all affirmative defenses and allege factual bases for those defenses in extra detail. In this regard, instead of making mere general denials of the plaintiff's allegations, the defendant should consider, when permissible, expanding upon her denials by stating the relevant facts that contradict the plaintiff's averments.

Fourth, the defendant should raise in the answer (or by motion, when appropriate) any pertinent defenses such as lack of jurisdiction, improper venue, insufficiency of process or service of process, failure to state a claim on which relief can be granted, or failure to join a party.[5] In addition, if the plaintiff's complaint contains any redundant, immaterial, impertinent, or scandalous matter, a motion to strike should be made;[6] and if the allegations are vague or ambiguous, a motion for a more definite statement should be filed.[7]

Filing the complaint and answer usually puts a temporary hold on settlement discussions. Thereafter, the attorneys usually allow the discovery process to proceed at least for a while before negotiations resume. Once the parties have a clearer understanding of the factual and legal issues in the case and begin to feel the effects of time pressures and expense, there is a heightened incentive to discuss settlement possibilities.

§10.05 Using Discovery

Discovery may be effectively used formally or informally to induce settlement. Informal discovery occurs when the plaintiff details his claims, along with supporting documentation, in a demand letter or settlement brochure. Sometimes, as in negotiations with an insurance adjuster, the plaintiff's lawyer might allow his client to be interviewed by the other side to demonstrate the plaintiff's jury appeal. Alternatively, both sides might agree to freely exchange information and documentation that would otherwise be discoverable in order to evaluate the prospects for settlement. Given the breadth of information that is discoverable under the formal discovery rules, exchanging information

4. *See* Fed. R. Civ. P. 13(g), 14, and 22.
5. *See* Fed. R. Civ. P. 12(b).
6. *See* Fed. R. Civ. P. 12(f).
7. *See* Fed. R. Civ. P. 12(e).

informally is usually a desirable method for educating the parties about settlement possibilities.

Promptly taking depositions is another effective method for moving a case toward settlement. The deposition is the most useful discovery device for obtaining information, testing legal theories, evaluating a witness's demeanor, gathering impeachment material, setting up the case for possible summary judgment, and asking about facts not directly related to the lawsuit but which may lead to discovery of admissible evidence. A videotape deposition may be particularly effective for revealing the extent of the plaintiff's injuries or her jury appeal.

The usual goal of a deposition is to obtain information for use at trial, not to provide the witness with a rehearsal for trial. However, for settlement purposes, it is sometimes useful to depose the opposing party with the specific intention of giving her a taste of what it will be like when she is cross-examined or called as an adverse witness before the jury. The rigorous cross-examination of a party-opponent during a deposition may cause her to seriously rethink the desirability of settling the case in light of the embarrassment and discomfort she will incur when taking the witness stand. A similar approach might be used when deposing a key witness for the other side.

Submitting interrogatories, requests for admissions, or requests for production of documents not only demonstrates a commitment to prepare for trial, it may reveal information that will induce the parties to settle. For example, obtaining information about applicable insurance policy limits or requesting extensive financial records from a party against whom punitive damages are sought may dramatically change the prospects for settlement.

Litigants often engage in extensive "paper" discovery and various obstructionist tactics to thwart discovery requests in an effort to wear down the opposition. Motions to compel and motions for protective orders are still commonplace. However, this is changing in many jurisdictions in light of revisions to discovery rules and the growing intolerance of judges to discovery abuses. For example, the requirements under the federal rules to provide "initial disclosures" and "pretrial disclosures," along with limitations on the number of interrogatories that may be submitted and depositions that may be taken,[8] have tended to curtail abuses and the use of the discovery process to overwhelm less wealthy litigants.

---

8. *See* Fed. R. Civ. P. 26, 30, and 33.

§10.06 Making Offers of Judgment

Rule 68 of the Federal Rules of Civil Procedure provides:

> (a) Making an Offer; Judgment on an Accepted Offer. At least 14 days before the date set for trial, a party defending against a claim may serve on an opposing party an offer to allow judgment on specified terms, with the costs then accrued. If, within 14 days after being served, the opposing party serves written notice accepting the offer, either party may then file the offer and notice of acceptance, plus proof of service. The clerk must then enter judgment.
>
> (b) Unaccepted Offer. An unaccepted offer is considered withdrawn, but it does not preclude a later offer. Evidence of an unaccepted offer is not admissible except in a proceeding to determine costs.
>
> (c) Offer After Liability Is Determined. When one party's liability to another has been determined but the extent of liability remains to be determined by further proceedings, the party held liable may make an offer of judgment. It must be served within a reasonable time—but at least 14 days—before the date set for a hearing to determine the extent of liability.
>
> (d) Paying Costs After an Unaccepted Offer. If the judgment that the offeree finally obtains is not more favorable than the unaccepted offer, the offeree must pay the costs incurred after the offer was made.

A number of states have similar rules, and some states even permit plaintiffs to make offers of judgment. However, under Fed. R. Civ. P. 68, only a defendant or a plaintiff defending a counterclaim[9] may make an offer of judgment. The offer must be in writing and served upon the adverse party (usually the plaintiff). The rule is not satisfied by a mere oral offer made in settlement negotiations or an offer made before suit is filed.[10]

Federal Rule 68 is generally applicable to any civil action in district court involving a claim for money or property, and an offer of judgment must be for a specific dollar amount or specified property. Settlement offers are not offers under the Rule.

---

9. Simon v. Intercontinental Transport (ICT) B.V., 882 F.2d 1435 (9th Cir. 1989).

10. Clark v. Sims, 28 F.3d 420 (4th Cir. 1994); Cox v. Brookshire Grocery Co., 919 F.2d 354 (5th Cir. 1990).

The essential effect of the Rule is that, once a final judgment is entered, if the party that did not accept the offer has won a judgment more favorable than the amount of the offer of judgment, the refusal of the offer has no consequence; but, if the nonaccepting party receives a final judgment that is less favorable than the amount in the offer, the nonaccepting party must pay the offering party's costs incurred after the offer was made.[11] Although the Rule does not define the scope of "costs," it is settled that the law underlying the cause of action determines whether costs can include attorneys' fees.[12]

Rule 68 was designed to encourage settlements. If you represent the defendant, making an offer of judgment may cause the plaintiff "to 'think very hard' about whether continued litigation is worthwhile"[13] An offer of judgment may exert significant pressure on a plaintiff to settle if liability is clear, the costs of the litigation will be high, but the plaintiff's damages will be difficult to prove or are very uncertain. It is also effective when the plaintiff is in need of immediate funds or is not disposed to bear the time and stress of lengthy litigation.

§10.07 Using Timing and Deadlines

The most opportune times for engaging in pretrial negotiations are influenced by numerous factors and circumstances. Among them are the following:

1. If the parties are attempting to avoid litigation and the statute of limitations on the plaintiff's claim is drawing near, negotiation efforts may be accelerated.
2. Sometimes negotiations will be triggered merely by the filing of the complaint, or when the defendant aggressively asserts a counterclaim, cross-claim, or seeks to add additional parties to the lawsuit.

---

11. Brown v. Cox, 286 F.3d 1040, 1047 (8th Cir. 2002); Stanczyk v. City of New York, 752 F.3d 273, 280 (2d Cir. 2014).

12. Marek v. Chesny, 473 U.S. 1, 8-9 (1985).

13. Marek v. Chesny, 473 U.S. 1, 11 (1985).

3. Parties may be motivated to pursue settlement when discovery reveals particular strengths or weaknesses in the case or when continuing discovery becomes cost prohibitive for one or both of the parties.
4. If the trial judge denies the defendant's motion for summary judgment but otherwise indicates that the plaintiff's case is tenuous, the prospect for settlement is likely to increase.
5. The extent to which the trial judge encourages the parties to settle or pushes the case to trial will often influence the parties' disposition toward settlement.
6. If the plaintiff is in need of money, he is more likely to settle for a smaller sum now than gamble on recovering a larger sum later at trial.

If a party is receiving adverse publicity about the case or her litigation position, she may be induced to negotiate a settlement.

The outcome of another lawsuit or appellate decision on issues similar to those being litigated between the parties may induce settlement.

Corporate parties may be more receptive to settlement toward the end of the calendar or fiscal year, either for tax purposes or because the resolution of the case can be announced in the corporation's annual report.

The arrival of the holiday season toward the end of the year may cause the parties to be more inclined to discuss settlement, and an indigent plaintiff might accept a lesser sum than he might otherwise in order to buy Christmas or Chanukah presents.

The unexpected postponement of a trial after the parties have strenuously prepared for trial may cause them to consider settlement possibilities.

Settlement prospects may be affected by factors such as the illness of a party or her attorney, the extent to which a party is really prepared to go to trial, whether the party is being represented on an hourly or contingent fee basis, or whether a party's witnesses have become unavailable or difficult to secure for trial.

Establishing deadlines can also exert pressure on the parties toward settlement. For example, a party might notify the other side that numerous depositions will have to be noticed by a certain date if no settlement is reached by that date. Similarly, they might obtain a court order for a deadline within which discovery must be completed, make a calendar request to schedule the case for trial, obtain a court order that peremptorily sets the case for trial, or file a motion for a pretrial conference with the judge.

§10.08 Using Pretrial Settlement Conferences

A pretrial settlement conference with the trial judge or magistrate is frequently an appropriate time to advance the settlement of a case. Many jurisdictions require pretrial settlement conferences or make them available upon motion of a party.[14] Sometimes clients are required to attend along with the lawyers. In cases where a conference is not required, requesting one is particularly useful when the other party is being recalcitrant. After all, a judge is not likely to look with favor upon a party who refuses to discuss settlement.

Judges vary in their approaches to pretrial settlement conferences. Many simply encourage the parties to seriously consider settlement possibilities. Others take a more active role by asking the parties to explain their most recent offers, probing the factual and legal contentions of each side, and even giving an assessment of the case or suggesting a possible compromise.

The local rules of some jurisdictions require the parties to submit written settlement conference statements to the court in aid of the conference. These rules vary in terms of what should be included in the statements, whether they are to be filed with the court or only "lodged" with it (*i.e.*, submitted solely to the judge without becoming part of the official record of the case), and whether they are to be served on opposing counsel. In general, these written statements should (1) be brief and to the point, (2) reflect candor by appropriately acknowledging the weaknesses in your case, (3) clearly state the *reasons* for your settlement contentions, and (4) avoid emotionalism. Except as the applicable local rule might otherwise prescribe, your written statement should include:

- A brief summary of the facts giving rise to the lawsuit, including an itemization of damages, and the anticipated trial evidence in support of those facts;
- A summary of your legal contentions about liability and damages in light of the facts and anticipated evidence;
- A summary of the procedural status of the litigation (*i.e.*, the extent of discovery conducted in the case and the pendency of any pretrial motions);
- A summary of any settlement offers or counteroffers that have already been made in the case; and

---

14. *See* Fed. R. Civ. P. 16.

A summary of your client's current settlement position in terms of a specific settlement amount or settlement range, and your specific reasons justifying that amount or range.

How to best conduct yourself at the pretrial settlement conference will, of course, largely depend upon the style of the presiding judge. In general, however, with or without a written settlement conference statement, you should be prepared to (1) summarize the past and current offers of the parties; (2) explain your strongest factual and legal points, while appropriately acknowledging your weaker ones; (3) show the judge any admissible documentation or key exhibits that substantiate your claims or defenses; (4) provide rational reasons for your offer or propose a modification of your latest offer; (5) downplay any emotionalism or acrimonious history of the litigation; and (6) avoid using any deceptive tactics.

If you demonstrate some willingness to compromise, it is likely that the judge will look to the other side to reciprocate. However, as in the closing phase of a face-to-face negotiation, it is best to be patient and cautious in making final concessions. If you appear overly eager to compromise, the judge may end up exerting more pressure on your side to effectuate a final settlement.

Finally, unless you know in advance that the judge would flatly decline to do so, you should not hesitate to ask her for her general assessment of the case for settlement purposes. While most judges are reluctant to give a direct opinion on this subject, some will at least indicate their instincts about the general settlement value of the controversy, or they will use your question as a springboard to actively encourage settlement. Of course, this does not mean that you should be bound by any assessment the judge might make, but the opinion of a trial judge who has seen hundreds of verdicts and awards is worth careful consideration.

§10.09 Settling at the Last Minute

Last minute settlements—whether at the courthouse steps, during trial, or while an appeal is being contemplated or pending—are not unusual. No matter how thoroughly prepared you are for trial, unexpected events invariably occur. A party might be induced to settle (1) the night before or minutes before the trial starts, (2) after the judge has ruled on a critical pretrial motion such as a motion *in limine*, (3) after an unfavorable jury has been empaneled, (4) after one or more key witnesses fails to show up for trial, (5) after a particularly destructive cross-examination, (6) after a witness gives unexpected or surprise testimony, (7) after the plaintiff has rested his case and before the defendant makes a motion for a directed verdict, (8) during or after the defendant's evidence, (9) after the judge has made his rulings at the jury instruction conference, or (10) after the closing arguments and before the jury returns from the jury room to announce its verdict and award. In short, nearly every trial has its own pressure points that may cause the parties to settle.

If the trial has not gone well and you have been unable to reach a settlement, you might still be able to force a last-minute agreement. For example, as the jury is returning from the jury room to render a verdict, you might inform the judge of your final settlement offer. The judge is likely to give the other side a few minutes to accept the settlement or hear the verdict. The pressure of this "last ditch" effort, coupled with the certainty of a reasonable settlement, may induce the other party to accept.

Alternatively, after the closing arguments and while the jury is deliberating, the parties might consult with the judge about a last-minute settlement. Obtaining the judge's perception about the presentation of the evidence and the risks to each party in gambling on the jury's verdict may facilitate a final agreement.

Even after the jury verdict, a settlement might be reached while the losing party contemplates filing an appeal or while an appeal is pending. The appellate process is likely to take years, and the parties may choose to forgo the time, expense, and uncertainty of the outcome on appeal. This is so even for the party who prevailed at trial. If an objective assessment of the outcome on appeal indicates that a reversal and remand for a new trial is likely, serious consideration should be given to renewing settlement discussions.

§10.10 High-Low Agreements

The parties will sometimes enter into a so-called "high-low" agreement that provides for a floor and a ceiling on a settlement amount that is tied to the jury's verdict or award. For example, if the plaintiff believes that his case is worth $250,000, and the defendant thinks that she might prevail at trial but is concerned about being faced with a large verdict by a run-away jury, the parties might agree that if the jury finds liability, the plaintiff will receive $150,000; and if no liability is found, the plaintiff will receive $50,000. Alternatively, it might be agreed that if the jury returns an award of $100,000 or more, the plaintiff will get $150,000, but if the jury renders any verdict below $100,000, the plaintiff will receive $50,000. This type of agreement guarantees the plaintiff a reasonable award but protects the defendant from an excessive verdict.

§10.11 Collaborative Law Agreements

Collaborative Law is a model of dispute resolution sometimes employed in the family law arena. In this model, a couple contemplating separation or divorce and their respective attorneys enter into a pledge or agreement at the outset of the case promising to participate in the settlement process in good faith with full disclosure. They also agree that if the settlement process breaks down prior to resolution, the attorneys cannot continue their representation in any future legal proceedings.

During the Collaborative Law process, both clients and their respective attorneys meet in several "four-way conferences" to exchange documents and discuss resolution of the parties' issues. As a rule, prior to each four-way conference, the attorneys meet to discuss areas of conflict that may act as "triggers" for their clients. They then develop an agenda for each meeting as well as an overall plan that will give the clients a sense of accomplishment early in the process so that movement towards a settlement will not stop when the difficult issues must be tackled.

The attorneys also meet with their respective clients to train them in various communication techniques that will allow them to better understand one another's needs. According to one commentator: "Collaborative communication is critical throughout the process. How language is used is very important in this negotiation model. Using words such as 'we', 'let's', 'and', 'our', and 'together' create a sense of cooperation and teamwork and decrease the feelings of competition."[15] The attorneys work with their respective clients to get them to express their concerns about the future and to focus on long-lasting practical solutions. If the parties need expert advice during their negotiations, the parties jointly choose and retain the experts.

The attorneys who practice Collaborative Law do not see themselves as "negotiators" for their clients, but instead as "facilitators" of the needs-based

15. Angela L. Haas, "The Difference Between Practicing Law Collaboratively and Practicing Collaborative Law", CLE Manuscript for "Getting to Equal Protection," LGBT Legal Issues in N.C., Apr. 22, 2005, RTP, N.C. p. V-4.

discussions that will allow "clients to negotiate in a respectful, non-competitive environment."[16]

A few state legislatures have enacted statutes and rules of practice delineating the parameters of Collaborative Law for attorneys practicing in the domestic area.[17] The American Bar Association has also described the Collaborative Law process in its Handbook for Clients:

> Collaborative Law: Each person retains his or her own trained collaborative lawyer to advise and assist in negotiating an agreement on all issues. All negotiations take place in "four-way" settlement meetings that both clients and both lawyers attend. The lawyers cannot go to court or threaten to go to court. Settlement is the only agenda. If either client goes to court, both collaborative lawyers are disqualified from further participation. Each client has built-in legal advice and advocacy during negotiations, and each lawyer's job includes guiding the client toward reasonable resolutions. The legal advice is an integral part of the process, but all the decisions are made by the clients. The lawyers generally prepare and process all papers required for the divorce.[18]

Although the concept of Collaborative Law originated in the family law arena, Pauline Tesler in her article, *Collaborative Law: What It Is and Why Family Law Attorneys Need to Know about It*, recommends its use "in any situation where preservation of an ongoing relationship between the parties is an important objective."[19]

---

16. Angela L. Haas, "The Difference Between Practicing Law Collaboratively and Practicing Collaborative Law", CLE Manuscript for "Getting to Equal Protection," LGBT Legal Issues in N.C., April 22, 2005, RTP, N.C. p. V-4.

17. *See* N.C.G.S. §50–70 *et seq.*; Tex. Fam. Code §6.603; and Minn. Gen. R. Prac. §111.05 (2008).

18. American Bar Association, Handbook for Clients.

19. Pauline H. Tessler, "Collaborative Law: What It Is and Why Family Attorneys Need to Know about It" (2001, www.collaborativefamilylawofUtah.com).

Part II

Mediation

Chapter Eleven

The Mediation Process and Mediator Styles and Strategies

SYNOPSIS

§11.01 Introduction
§11.02 The Mediation Process, in General
§11.03 Facilitative v. Evaluative Mediation
§11.04 Mediator Styles and Strategies

§11.01 Introduction

Mediation is an informal, non-adversarial alternative dispute resolution process, whereby a neutral third party, who is either selected by the parties or is appointed from an approved list of mediators eligible to mediate the type of case at hand, encourages and facilitates the parties to voluntarily resolve their dispute. The mediator does not decide what the outcome should be. The process is different from arbitration, in which a neutral third party hears evidence and arguments from the parties and makes a binding or non-binding decision about how the parties' dispute should be resolved. In mediation, the parties themselves make the decision; and if they do not voluntarily resolve their dispute, they may resolve it through some other alternative dispute resolution process or, if the case is actionable, litigate it.

Virtually all jurisdictions—by statute, agency rule, or court rule—either mandate mediation or otherwise formally make it available in certain types of cases. Illustrative are family-law disputes, collective bargaining and other labor-law disputes, personal injury cases, medical malpractice actions, products liability cases, civil rights actions, contract cases, wrongful discharge cases and other employment-related disputes, landlord-tenant cases, small claims actions, toxic tort cases, consumer complaints, environmental disputes, professional conduct and licensing cases, neighborhood or community disputes, farm mortgage disputes, housing disputes, agricultural producer-distributor bargaining, geothermal energy development disputes, criminal misdemeanor cases, and rule-making disputes. Many jurisdictions mandate mediation in a broad range of civil cases as a prerequisite to taking the case to trial. These "court-annexed" mediation programs have burgeoned as a means of easing the backlog of cases and reducing the time and expense of litigation. In short, a "mediation explosion" has permeated our society in the both the public and private sector.

Mediation has several advantages over traditional inter-party or lawyer-to-lawyer negotiations. First, mediation provides a structured opportunity to bring the parties together, not just to exchange demands and positions, but to discuss and explain their interests, needs, and emotions in a setting where the parties can feel that another person, the mediator, has heard their side of the story and given them a "fair shake." Second, mediation structures the negotiating process in ways that increase more reliable information sharing and better understanding between the parties so that they can better decide how to resolve their dispute. Third, skilled mediators can help facilitate an agreement by breaking down cognitive and emotional barriers for the parties through a variety of tactics and techniques that help to diffuse suspicion and irrationality. Mediators also promote reality testing and face saving. Fourth, mediation gives the parties a greater sense of participation and control over their case through a process in which they can address the issues they themselves feel are most important. In sum, the advantages of mediation are consistent with the well-established fact that clients are often as concerned with how they are treated in dispute resolution as they are with its results.

Often mediation will occur after traditional negotiations have failed to produce an agreement. Sometimes, however, the parties will choose mediation as a means of first resort in trying to resolve their dispute. This chapter describes the mediation process and different mediator approaches, styles and strategies.

§11.02 The Mediation Process, in General[1]

Mediation typically occurs in a conference room at a neutral location or at a lawyer's office agreed upon by the parties and the mediator. Present are the mediator, the individual parties, or a designated representative of a party if it is a corporation or governmental entity, and their lawyers. If there is insurance coverage in the case, an insurance adjuster will usually also attend. In many court-annexed mediations, all of the foregoing persons are required to attend. Sometimes, by agreement between the parties, other support persons might attend all or part of the mediation or be on telephone standby for consultation. These might include, for example, a spouse of a party, a person who has some special expertise, or someone otherwise integrally involved in the case. Because the mediation process is usually confidential, stenographers, court personnel, news reporters, or other observers are usually excluded from the process.

Typically, the mediator begins the mediation in a joint session in the presence of all participants. After introductions, she will make brief introductory remarks that explain her role and the over-all mediation process. Typically, these remarks will explain that:

1. Mediation is an informal process in which the rules of evidence and other formal rules of procedure do not apply;
2. The mediator is neutral and impartial in the case and has no conflict of interest;
3. The mediator has reviewed any pre-mediation submissions that the parties may have sent to her in advance of the mediation;
4. The mediator's role is to assist the parties in reaching a voluntary agreement, not to serve as a judge or jury in the case;
5. Generally, most things said or done during the mediation are confidential, in that they cannot later be used by one side against the other in litigation;
6. If a party privately shares anything with the mediator that the party expressly states he wants kept confidential, the mediator is prohibited from disclosing that information to the other side or to anyone else, unless required by law;

---

1. *See also* "General Suggestions to Mediators for How to Mediate a Case" in Appendix B of this book.

7. The mediator is prohibited from giving any legal advice during the mediation;
8. Each side will be given an opportunity at the outset to make an opening statement about the case;
9. Each side might then wish to ask some clarifying questions of the other to bring as much non-confidential information to the table as early as possible in the mediation process;
10. After the case is discussed in joint session, the mediator typically will hold multiple private caucuses, meeting separately with each party to clarify information and to discuss underlying interests, feelings, objectives, and possible solutions to the dispute;
11. If a settlement is reached, the mediator will have all participants reconvene in a joint session at which she will summarize the terms of the agreement and make sure the parties understand what steps will be taken to prepare and execute any settlement documents;
12. If no agreement is reached, it is the mediator's duty to declare an impasse; and
13. The fees for the mediation will be borne equally between the parties unless they have otherwise agreed about how those fees will be paid.

After the mediator has made her introductory remarks and answered any questions about her role or the overall mediation process, each side will make an opening statement, usually beginning with the claimant. The lawyers typically give these opening statements, which generally set forth the parties' factual and legal contentions. Sometimes, however, the clients will participate in the opening statements. After the opening statements, the mediator might ask some clarifying questions, might allow the parties to share further information between one another, or might let the parties engage in a free-flowing discussion of the dispute. If there are multiple issues in the case, the mediator might devote part of the joint session to establishing an appropriate agenda.

When it becomes apparent that discussions in a joint session are no longer productive, the mediator will begin private caucusing through separate meetings with each side. Usually, she will hold the first private meeting with the claimant and his attorney or the side that is in the position to respond to the latest offer or proposal, and then caucus with the opposing side. In most cases, private caucusing will begin shortly after the parties have given their opening statements, and the mediator will hold numerous private meetings with each side. Indeed, in the mediation of legal disputes, it is common for the balance of the time to be spent in a kind of "shuttle diplomacy," with the mediator meeting alternately with the opposing sides. Sometimes, after holding a number of private caucuses with each side, the mediator will bring the parties back together in a joint session if, for example, they express a desire to do so, or if exchanging certain information or discussing a particular proposal would be more efficient in a joint meeting.

During the private caucuses, the mediator will engage in five overlapping functions or stages:

1. Obtaining information about the facts, the law, the issues, the parties' underlying feelings, interests or needs (*e.g.*, emotional, psychological, economic, physical, or social), the parties' primary, secondary, and incidental objectives, potential solutions or proposals and the reasons supporting them;
2. Generating and discussing potential solutions or proposals in light of the parties' interests and objectives;
3. Assessing, selecting, and communicating specific proposals, offers, and counteroffers of the parties;
4. Creating movement in the negotiations by encouraging the parties to compromise and consider the risks, costs, and alternatives to not reaching an agreement; and
5. Forging and finalizing the terms of an agreement.

Throughout these stages, the mediator will engage in a variety of tactics and techniques to encourage the parties to be cooperative and realistic in the bargaining process.

Mediation can be done in a matter of hours or it may take several days, depending on the case. Some mediators schedule two cases a day, such as workers' compensations claims or relatively minor personal injury cases, though most will not schedule more than one a day. Family law cases often involve several meetings spread out over weeks or even months. Complex business disputes and mass tort cases can go on for several days in a row.

§11.03 Facilitative v. Evaluative Mediation

An important distinction is drawn between "facilitative" and "evaluative" mediation. In facilitative mediation, the mediator's role is limited to assisting the parties to arrive at their own decision about whether and on what terms to resolve their dispute. The mediator facilitates communication between the parties. The facilitative mediator does not express opinions on the strength of an argument, the reasonableness of a proposal, or the value of the case. He does not push for a particular settlement. The case belongs to the parties, as do all decisions with respect to it. He sees the parties' right to self-determination is mediation's highest value, and it is not for the mediator to interfere in that right.

In contrast, an evaluative mediator may well do those very things. An evaluative mediator will use tactics and strategies to move the parties toward settlement that a facilitative mediator might shun as being "directive." She might give an opinion or recommendation about the settlement value of the case or suggest how the case could be resolved. In a combined facilitative-evaluative mediation, the mediator will usually first try to achieve a resolution through pure facilitation, and if that is unsuccessful, will then offer an opinion or recommendation about how the case should settle. In selecting a mediator, the parties are usually free to choose which type of mediation they prefer for their case. Some jurisdictions permit only "facilitative" mediation in court-annexed mediation programs.

It is important to emphasize that even in strictly "facilitative" mediations, the mediator still engages in important evaluative functions throughout the mediation. For example, mediators constantly evaluate the body language of the parties, the relative importance of their feelings, needs, interests and objectives, the reasons behind their offers and counteroffers, the costs and risks associated with not reaching an agreement, and the extent to which the parties' negotiating positions are realistic. This is because an on-going evaluation of these matters is critical to the mediator in deciding what styles, strategies, and tactics and techniques to employ in helping the parties reach an agreement. Thus, although the strictly "facilitative" mediator will never *directly* render an opinion about the settlement value of the case or how the case should be resolved, she will inevitably indicate her views or sense about these matters by *indirection*—through the questions she asks the parties, the information she shares between one side and the other, and the various matters she emphasizes as she encourages the parties toward their goal of achieving a mutually satisfactory agreement.

§11.04 Mediator Styles and Strategies

Mediators may engage in styles of interpersonal behavior that range from fairly passive to quite aggressive. In mediation training programs, mediators are typically taught to act in a mild-mannered and low-key way, to keep their emotions under control, and to be sensitive to the feelings and concerns of the parties through focused questioning, active listening, and empathetic understanding.

In pursuit of the overall goal of trying to bring the parties together to reach an agreement, mediators employ different strategies or methodologies that, in turn, may affect their interpersonal style. These different strategies or conceptual approaches to mediating have been usefully described as "trashing," "bashing," or "hashing it out."[2]

Under the "trashing" approach, the mediator uses the private caucuses to "tear apart" each side's case by asking pointed questions about its strengths and weaknesses. In this way, the parties are forced to take a hard look at the merits of the case from a more objective factual and legal standpoint. Despite the bombastic-sounding term "trashing," this strategy of facilitating honest case assessment is employed by mild-mannered and aggressive mediators alike. After each side's case has been "torn down," the mediator proceeds to press both sides to put more realistic proposals or settlement figures on the table. The mediator then continues to shuttle back and forth between the parties in private caucuses to help forge an agreement out of their more reasonable proposals or positions.

Many lawyers appreciate this sometimes blunt, no-nonsense approach to mediating. This is especially so in adversarial cases where money is the sole or primary issue and the lawyers, or their clients, have unrealistic assessments of the value of the case. The effectiveness of the strategy, however, largely depends upon the litigation experience of the mediator and her ability to accurately point out the strengths and weaknesses of the case from a trial standpoint. Although the approach may also be used in problem-solving situations, it is likely to be less effective when the parties are driven by concerns such as establishing precedent or obtaining vindication.

Under the "bashing" strategy, the mediator, who might, for example, be a retired judge, spends much less time discussing the relative strengths and

2. James J. Alfini, Trashing, Bashing, and Hashing it Out: Is this the End of "Good Mediation"? 19 Fla. St. Univ. L. Rev. 47 (1991).

weaknesses of the parties' positions, and instead "bashes away" at the initial settlement offers to try to get the parties to settle somewhere in between. The basher draws upon her trial experience to emphasize the risks and costs of litigation, and then aggressively exhorts the parties to compromise. The ensuing mediation becomes a sort of "mad dash for the middle." As explained by one basher:

> The plaintiff wanted $75,000. The defendant told me he would pay $40,000. I went to the plaintiff and said to him, "They're not going to pay $75,000. What will you take?" He said, "I'll take $60,000." I told him I wasn't sure I could get $60,000 and asked if he would take $50,000 if I could get it. He agreed. I then went back to the defendant and told him I [sic] couldn't settle for $40,000, but "you might get the plaintiff to take $50,000" and asked if he would pay it. The answer was yes. Neither of them were bidding against themselves. I was the guy who was doing it, and that's the role of the mediator.[3]

Some lawyers welcome this highly aggressive approach because it tends to expeditiously "hammer sense" into the parties.

Under the "hashing it out" approach, the mediator places greater importance on direct communication between the parties and takes a less directive role in pressing them toward an agreement. The preference is for the parties to communicate freely and hash out an agreement on their own accord. If they have difficulty communicating with one another, the mediator will facilitate communications. The mediator variously plays the roles of "facilitator, orchestrator, referee, sounding board, [and] scapegoat."[4] Unlike the trashers and bashers, hashers are more flexible within the mediation process, varying their style and their tactics as best fits the circumstances of the case. If the parties are not making headway toward an agreement and wish to terminate the mediation, the hasher will usually accede and declare an impasse without pressing the parties to reach an agreement.

Hashers thus tend to take a somewhat more passive role in the mediation process. The strategy is well suited for problem-solving and works particularly well when the parties are willing to engage in non-adversarial and cooperative bargaining.

3. Id. at 70.
4. Id. at 71.

These different mediator strategies are not necessarily mutually exclusive. That is, in a particular mediation, a mediator might first hash, then trash, and finally bash. Similarly, a mediator might adopt a more passive style at the outset of the mediation and then employ a more aggressive style later if the parties appear able to reach an agreement but are having difficulty achieving closure. In short, different strategies and styles have their own advantages and disadvantages depending on the particular case, the parties involved, and where the parties are in the mediation.

Chapter Twelve

When to Mediate, Choosing a Mediator, and Mediator Tactics and Techniques

SYNOPSIS

§12.01 What Cases to Mediate and When to Mediate
[1] Factors That Favor Mediation
[2] Factors Unfavorable to Mediation
§12.02 Choosing a Mediator
§12.03 Mediator Tactics and Techniques
[1] Tactics and Techniques Drawn from Traditional Negotiating
[2] Tactics and Techniques for Obtaining Information
[3] Tactics and Techniques for Generating and Discussing Potential Solutions
[4] Tactics and Techniques for Assessing, Selecting, and Communicating Specific Proposals
[5] Tactics and Techniques for Creating Movement in the Negotiations
[6] Tactics and Techniques for Forging and Finalizing the Terms of an Agreement

§12.01 What Cases to Mediate and When to Mediate

Many jurisdictions now require mediation as a predicate to maintaining a lawsuit. In some, the mediation can be waived by mutual agreement of the parties or by the judge for good cause shown. Even if mediation is not mandated, it is often a wise choice. Voluntarily mediation may be pursued in lieu of traditional negotiation or after negotiations have failed.

Mediation is typically not considered until after there has been at least minimal settlement discussion between the parties or until full scale traditional negotiations have broken down. However, if the parties or their lawyers have a particularly strained relationship, if there are multiple parties involved, or if there are numerous or complex issues in dispute, it may be beneficial to mediate the case from the outset. What follow are just a few of the factors to consider in deciding whether a case is suitable for mediation.

[1] Factors That Favor Mediation

- The parties or their lawyers are finding it difficult to engage in negotiations, or negotiations are deadlocked.
- The parties want to settle the case confidentially.
- The parties want to avoid establishing judicial precedent.
- Communication between the parties is poor, or their emotional involvement in the case is preventing settlement.
- The parties want to minimize litigation costs.
- The interests or needs of the parties are interdependent, and they would benefit from each other's cooperation in satisfying those interests or needs.
- The parties want or will have to maintain a relationship after the dispute is resolved.
- The parties have different perceptions about the facts of the case, or they disagree about what data or other information is needed to resolve it.
- The parties are divided over different values or interests.
- There are multiple parties in the case, or there are a number of other persons whose input is necessary or desirable for resolving the dispute.
- There are multiple issues in the case and the parties disagree about the order in which the issues should be addressed.

- The parties are seeking a non-monetary remedy or some other remedy that a court cannot provide.
- The parties are unable to agree on an acceptable forum or structure for negotiations.
- Stereotyping, prejudices, misunderstandings, or other misperceptions are preventing the parties from resolving their dispute.
- The parties are having difficulty evaluating the factual or legal merits of the case or its value, or they have unrealistic views about those matters.
- The parties desire to resolve at least some, if not all, issues in the case.
- The parties wish to engage in informal discovery, or they want to evaluate each other's credibility or jury appeal.

[2] Factors Unfavorable to Mediation

- The parties have a need for formal discovery that has not yet been completed, and they are unable to provide necessary information to one another through the mediation process.
- The parties want a judicial resolution of the dispute because they want to establish a precedent, they want a court to resolve ambiguous or conflicting law, or they want vindication.
- The sole issues dividing the parties are ones of principle.
- Punitive damages are an indispensable issue in the case.
- The events giving rise to the parties' dispute were so traumatic that the parties are not yet psychologically able to discuss a possible resolution of their dispute.
- Negotiations have been so acrimonious or unproductive that the parties have essentially decided to take the case to trial.
- The parties stand to gain from a strategy of delay.
- There are numerous parties involved in the dispute and one or more of them is unwilling to mediate.
- The parties' dispute affects the public interest, and the government is not represented.

§12.02 Choosing a Mediator

In jurisdictions that mandate mediation in civil litigation, the parties are usually free to select their mediator by mutual agreement. If they cannot agree, a mediator will usually be appointed from a list of mediators eligible to mediate the particular type of case. Typically, these mediators have been certified to mediate cases after completing a mandatory mediation training course.

One scholar has summarized the qualities and abilities of a good mediator as a person who is "capable of appreciating the dynamics of the environment in which the dispute is occurring, intelligent, effective listener, articulate, patient, non-judgmental, flexible, forceful and persuasive, imaginative, resourceful, a person of professional standing or reputation, reliable, capable of gaining access to necessary resources, non-defensive, person of integrity, humble, objective, and neutral with regard to the outcome."[1] When choosing a mediator, in addition to these qualities and abilities, you should consider whether the prospects for settling the case would be enhanced by a "facilitative" or "evaluative" mediator, and whether the particular mediator has a style and strategy that would complement the case.

For many lawyers, the most sought-after mediators are those who are "willing and able to 'push' the parties, not in an antagonistic or hostile sense, but in the positive sense of inviting, supporting, encouraging, motivating, and urging the parties to work [toward an agreement]."[2] This involves pushing each side (1) to obtain, disclose, and consider all information relevant to resolving the dispute; (2) to carefully assess the importance of any missing pieces of information in deciding whether and how to proceed in the absence of complete information; (3) to identify and consider all possible options for resolving the issues before focusing on specific options and making actual decisions; (4) to consider and fully understand the consequences of reaching an agreement or not reaching an agreement; (5) to articulate clearly their positions and the reasons behind them; and (6) to hear and understand each other's positions and the reasons underlying them.[3] In sum, many lawyers appreciate mediators who are willing to be persistent in the mediation process by engaging in a dil-

---

1. Joseph B. Stulberg, The Theory and Practice of Mediation: A Reply to Professor Susskind, 6 Vt. L. Rev. 94 (1981).

2. Robert A. Baruch Bush, Efficiency and Protection, or Empowerment and Recognition? The Mediator's Role and Ethical Standards in Mediation, 41 Fla. L. Rev. 277 (1989).

3. Id. at 278–281.

igent effort to push *for* the parties to reach an agreement and push *with* them toward that end.

Finally, in unusually complex cases or where there are numerous parties and issues, it may be desirable to have co-mediators conduct the mediation. In selecting co-mediators, you might consider whether gender, racial, or ethnic balance would enhance the mediation. In addition, you might select one mediator for her skills as an effective mediator and the other for his special expertise in the subject matter of the case to be mediated.

§12.03 Mediator Tactics and Techniques

[1] Tactics and Techniques Drawn from Traditional Negotiating

It is often said that good mediators are good negotiators. Accordingly, mediators routinely employ a variety of tactics and techniques that are like those employed in inter-party negotiations. Thus, mediators may use several of the "Negotiating Tactics and Techniques" discussed in Chapter 5. However, good mediators will not use tactics and techniques designed to mislead or exert undue pressure upon a party, nor any that are disingenuous or unethical.

Based on the list of Negotiating Tactics and Techniques given in Chapter 5, the following chart (next page) separates the tactics and techniques that mediators will not use in mediation from those they might use in mediation:

Negotiating Tactics and Techniques Mediators Will Not Use:

Anger/Aggressiveness
Blaming or Fault Finding
Bluffing
Boulwarism
Coalition
Company Policy Excuse
Dodging the Question
Escalating Demands
Excessive Initial Demands/Offers
Fait Accompli
False Demands
False Multiple Concessions
False Scarcity
Good Guy-Bad Guy Routine/Mutt and Jeff
Lack of Authority or Limited Authority
Little Ol' Country Lawyer
Lock-in Positions
Low-Balling
Misstatement
Nibbling
Personal Attacks
Playing Dumb
Publicity
Reversing Position
Snow Job/Alleged Expertise
Take-it-or-Leave-it
Threats
Two Against One
Walkout

Negotiating Tactics and Techniques Mediators Might Use:

Abdication
Adjournment or Caucus
Deadlines
Delay (in a constructive application)
Draft Document or Single Negotiating Text
Face Saving
Floating Trial Balloons and Bracketing
Off-the-Record Discussions
Preconditions or Conditional Proposals
Problem-Solving
Questioning by Socratic Method
Questions to Facilitate Agreements
Salami
Splitting the Difference
Surprise
Timing
Word Smithing

In addition to the foregoing, there are a number of other tactics and techniques that mediators commonly use and that are important to understand as you prepare for mediation. We will summarize these tactics and techniques in the context of five overlapping functions or stages of the mediation process itself: (1) Obtaining Information; (2) Generating and Discussing Potential Solutions; (3) Assessing, Selecting, and Communicating Specific Proposals; (4) Creating Movement in the Negotiations; and (5) Forging and Finalizing the Terms of an Agreement.

[2] Tactics and Techniques for Obtaining Information

Mediators consider it essential to obtain complete information from both parties about the facts; the law; the issues; the parties' underlying feelings, interests or needs; the parties' primary, secondary, and incidental objectives; potential solutions or proposals; and the reasons supporting particular proposals, offers and counteroffers. This information serves as the raw material from which the mediator can understand the issues in the case, and then proceed to explore potential solutions, discuss specific proposals, create movement in the negotiations, and hopefully forge and finalize an agreement.

Sometimes this information is discussed openly in a joint session, but more often than not, the mediator will seek to obtain this information during private caucusing. In doing so, the mediator might:

- Ask direct questions about the facts, law, issues, and the parties' interests, objectives, and possible solutions (*see also* §5.37);
- Ask why the parties have the particular interests and objectives that they do;
- Ask the parties to rank, from most important to least important, their interests, objectives, the issues in the case;
- Explore the extent to which the interests and objectives of the parties are mutually exclusive, competing, compatible, or shared;
- Allow the parties to vent their emotions;
- Ask for counsels' analysis of the merits of the case and what might resolve it.

In this information gathering stage, the mediator is primarily concerned with building rapport with the parties, understanding all factors underlying the dispute, and identifying the key issues in the case. At this point, the mediator will also begin to assist the parties in building an agenda for the mediation. If the parties cannot agree, the mediator might (a) ask the parties to take turns choosing the issues to be discussed, (b) pick one or two issues that both parties consider of greatest importance and place them at the top of the agenda, (c) identify the easier issues and place them at the top of the agenda, (d) negotiate first those issues that are a necessary or logical predicate to resolving other issues, or (e) negotiate a number of issues simultaneously through packaged proposals containing multiple-issue solutions.

[3] Tactics and Techniques for Generating and Discussing Potential Solutions

Mediators often encourage the parties to consider as many potential solutions to the dispute as possible before making a specific proposal or offer. (*See also* §9.14[2].) The objective is to encourage the parties to consider solutions that may satisfy their mutual interests or needs, and to discourage them from engaging solely in positional bargaining. Consistent with this objective, mediators often do not care to know the parties' bottom lines until late in the mediation process, if ever. This is to keep the parties open to modifying their bottom lines in light of the information they learn during the mediation process.

In helping the parties generate and discuss a broad range of potential solutions, the mediator might:

- Encourage the parties to explore non-monetary as well as monetary solutions to the case;
- Engage in "brainstorming for solutions" (*see* §9.14[2]) either in a joint session or during the private caucuses;
- Ask each party to consider the opposing party's interests and views about the dispute;
- Pose hypothetical solutions to the parties to test their reaction to alternative ways of resolving the dispute;
- Ask the parties what elements of an agreement they might be willing to trade in exchange for obtaining certain other commitments in an agreement;
- If the parties have an ongoing or past relationship, ask which aspects of their relationship have worked well and whether any of those aspects might be incorporated into an agreement;

- Encourage the parties to consider objective standards such as custom, industry standards, ethical norms, or expertise in generating possible solutions;
- Suggest that the parties consider modeling their resolution on agreements that others have used to resolve similar disputes.

[4] Tactics and Techniques for Assessing, Selecting, and Communicating Specific Proposals

After the parties have generated and discussed potential solutions, they will begin the bargaining phase of the mediation by making specific proposals, offers, and counteroffers, which the mediator will communicate to the parties, usually by shuttling between them in private caucuses. Sometimes this will occur in a joint session when, for example, a party's proposal contains multi-faceted elements that require detailed explanation or discussion.

In assisting the parties to assess and select specific proposals, the mediator might:

- Help the parties value the case through any of the valuation methods discussed in Chapter 6;
- Encourage the parties to make reasonable first offers and counteroffers;
- Ask the parties to articulate specific reasons for their particular proposals or offers;
- Suggest that the parties work from a *Draft Document or Single Negotiating Text* (*see* §5.14);
- Ask that the parties consider incorporating into a proposal, as might be appropriate:
    - instead of in money, a payment in kind, a transfer of goods or property, or performance of services;
    - a structured settlement or payment in installments;
    - payment of a portion of the settlement to a mutually acceptable charity or other public interest organization;
    - a future business arrangement or relationship, for example, in a contract dispute;

  - in an employment dispute, a change in an employee's title or work status in exchange for a smaller pay increase;
  - a promise to take certain corrective action to prevent the recurrence of the type of accident that occurred;
  - a substitution of goods (*e.g.*, in a dispute involving a purchase or lease of goods);
  - an apology;
  - a confidentiality clause in the agreement;
  - a provision to abide by the recommendation of a third-party expert, such as the recommendation of a child psychologist in a custody or visitation dispute.

In communicating specific proposals being made by one party to the other, the mediator might:

- Present the proposal as if it were the mediator's own idea so as to keep the party to whom the proposal is made from rejecting it out of hand due to "reactive devaluation" (*see* §2.06[4]);
- Make a proposal conditional without communicating a commitment on the part of the offering party (*e.g.*, "If I can get the other side to do X, will you do Y?");
- Time the communication of a particular proposal to coincide with that point in the process when presentation of the proposal will have the greatest impact;
- Act as translator by explaining the parties' reasons for their particular offers, or their reasons for rejecting or modifying particular proposals.

[5] Tactics and Techniques for Creating Movement in the Negotiations

Creating movement is often the mediator's most difficult task. To this end, as discussed in §11.04, a mediator might employ a "trashing," "bashing," or "hashing it out" strategy, or a combination of these strategies. As specific tactics and techniques for bringing the parties closer together and reducing their commitment to unreasonable or unrealistic positions, the mediator might:

- Directly or indirectly indicate the mediator's views about the merit or lack of merit of a particular proposal or position;
- Engage in *Questioning by Socratic Method* (*see* §5.38) by asking a series of logical questions that are designed to expose the weaknesses in a party's proposals or positions;
- Suggest that counsel for the parties phone another lawyer or a law professor they respect to render an opinion about the relative merits of a novel or controversial legal theory advanced in the case;
- Ask what evidence would be introduced at trial in support of a particular factual or legal theory in the case;
- Inquire about the parties' willingness to take the case to trial (*see* §2.06[1]);
- Help the parties think about the economic and emotional costs of taking the case to trial or the consequences of impasse;
- Help the parties resist the influence of "sunk costs" (*see* §2.06[3]);
- Engage in an off-the-record, private discussion solely with the parties' lawyers to discuss the barriers that are preventing settlement;
- Suggest that the mediation be temporarily adjourned so that the parties might reconsider their positions or try to come up with new proposals;
- Ask a variety of questions designed to moderate the parties' positions, such as:
    - If you were in the other party's situation, would you accept the proposals that you are making now, or would you expect that more should be offered in exchange for an agreement?
    - Is your offer fair? Will those whom you respect, the community or the public, perceive it as such?
    - Is your offer in line with community, legal, or other norms?
    - Is the demand that you are making in line with other negotiated settlements or court decisions on similar issues under similar conditions?
    - Do you have the power to force the issue?
    - What are the benefits to you of pursuing your present course? Are there any risks?

- How certain are you that you can win in court? Ninety percent? Seventy-five percent? Fifty percent?
- What if you lose in court? What will your life be like then?
- What impact do you think your victory in court will have on your on-going relationship with the other party? Will you ever be able to work together again? Who else might be affected?

[6] Tactics and Techniques for Forging and Finalizing the Terms of an Agreement

When the parties are close of reaching an agreement, mediators often become somewhat more aggressive in helping to forge the terms of a final settlement. For example, the mediator might press harder in applying the tactics and techniques set forth in subsection [5] above. In addition, the mediator might:

- *Abdicate* by pressing one or more of the parties to come up with a final concession (*see also* §5.02);
- Provide one or more of the parties with a rationale for changing position that allows the party to save face in making a final concession;
- Make a "mediator's proposal," which must be accepted or rejected without amendment, in confidential communications by each party with the mediator;
- Suggest that the parties split the difference.

If the parties reach an agreement, the mediator will usually reconvene in a joint session to summarize the terms of the agreement and seek clarification about any loose ends. At this time, arrangements for preparing and executing final settlement documents are made. In many court-annexed mediation programs, the mediator is required to have the parties sign a memorandum of understanding about the terms of the settlement before leaving the mediation session.

Chapter Thirteen

Preparing for Mediation

SYNOPSIS

§13.01 Preparing a Mediation Preparation Outline
§13.02 Holding a Pre-Mediation Conference with the Mediator or Between Counsel
§13.03 Who Should Attend the Mediation
§13.04 Preparing the Client for Mediation

Preparing for mediation is much like preparing for negotiation. You need to (1) prepare a Mediation Preparation Outline from which an overall negotiating approach can be developed and employed during the mediation; (2) decide whether to hold a pre-mediation conference with the mediator or opposing counsel; (3) decide who should attend the mediation for your side and what roles those participants will play; and (4) prepare the client for the mediation session.

§13.01 Preparing a Mediation Preparation Outline

In preparing a Mediation Preparation Outline, you should follow the same twelve steps and format used for preparing a Negotiation Preparation Outline as set forth in §§7.03 and 7.04. These steps, with a few additional considerations pertinent to the mediation process, are as follows:

Step 1: *From the Perspective of Each Party, Make a List of Information to Obtain, Information to Reveal, and Information to Protect.* Any special information you decide "to reveal" to the other side would presumably be information you would want to reveal to the mediator as well. Under "information to protect," list any information that you do not want to disclose to the mediator, even in confidence, and any information that can be disclosed to the mediator but not to the other side.

Step 2: *Make a List of Each Party's interests.*

Step 3: *Make a List of Each Party's Primary Objectives, Secondary Objectives, and Incidental Objectives (to Exchange).*

Step 4: *Make a List of Possible Solutions for Each Party (from most preferred to least preferred).*

Step 5: *Make a List of Each Party's Best Alternatives to a Negotiated Agreement (BATNA).*

Step 6: *Make a List of Each Party's Factual and Legal Leverage Points (Strong and Weak).*

Step 7: *Identify Each Party's Potential Target and Resistance Points.*

Step 8: *Identify Each Party's Negotiating Strategy: Adversarial or Problem Solving.*

Step 9: *Identify Each Party's Negotiating Style: Competitive (Hardball), Cooperative (Softball), or Competitive-Cooperative (Hardball and Softball).* Also identify the mediator's most likely style and strategy during the mediation. Is she facilitative or evaluative, passive or aggressive, a "trasher," "basher," or "hasher"?

Step 10: *Make a List of Each Party's Offers or Proposals in the Order They May Be Presented.*

Step 11: *Consider Each Party's Particular Tactics.* Also consider any special tactics and techniques that might be effectively used by the mediator during the mediation.

Step 12: *Revise All of the Foregoing Matters Throughout the Mediation Process.*

Because mediation often occurs after the parties have already engaged in negotiations and filed a lawsuit, it is particularly important to review the case file when preparing your Mediation Preparation Outline. This means reviewing all pleadings, formal admissions, responses to interrogatories and requests for production of documents, transcripts of depositions, correspondence setting forth the history of prior settlement discussions and any instructions from your client about your settlement authority, and any other important documents in the case, including medical reports, medical bills, statements showing lost earnings, reports of expert witnesses or investigators, documents that might be introduced at trial, etc. If your review of the case file shows that documentation is incomplete or that you need additional information to support your client's case, this information should be obtained in advance of the mediation.

§13.02 Holding a Pre-Mediation Conference with the Mediator or Between Counsel

It is sometimes desirable to hold a pre-mediation conference, either by telephone or an in-person meeting with the mediator or opposing counsel. Such a conference may be useful:

- To work out the agenda, format, or logistics of the mediation;
- To brief the mediator about the issues in the case, prior settlement discussions, the status of the litigation, and the basic positions of the parties;
- To determine whether there is any essential information that the parties need to obtain or submit to the mediator in advance of the mediation;
- To forewarn the mediator about any delicate aspects of the controversy that may impede a resolution of the case;
- To provide the mediator with insights about any special ways in which the mediation session might be structured or conducted to best facilitate a resolution of the dispute;
- To discuss the need for having any third persons attend the mediation or be on telephone standby for consultation on questions of settlement authority or to provide certain expertise during the mediation;

- To apprise the mediator of any technical, legal, or sensitive information so as to save time or awkwardness in discussing these matters at the mediation session;
- To suggest that the mediator meet in advance with one or more persons who have information relevant to the dispute but who will not be able to attend the mediation;
- To suggest that, where numerous parties are involved or the parties are particularly emotional about the dispute, the mediator meet privately with each party in advance of the mediation to understand the issues and, as appropriate, calm the parties; or
- To discuss any other matters that may enhance the overall efficiency of the mediation session and the prospects for resolving the case.

In most situations, you will find that an informal pre-mediation discussion with opposing counsel will be sufficient to pave the way for an effective mediation session and that it is not necessary to hold a formal pre-mediation conference with the mediator. And most mediators will not engage in *ex parte* pre-mediation conversations about substantive issues without disclosing the fact of the conversation to opposing counsel, though the information discussed may be kept confidential.

§13.03 Who Should Attend the Mediation

Court-annexed mediation programs usually set out who must attend the mediation session. Typically, all individual parties, or a designated representative if the party is a corporate or governmental entity, are required to attend, as are insurance company representative if there is insurance coverage in the case, and the parties' lawyers. Most require that lienholders be notified, but rules vary as to whether they must or may participate. The goal is to ensure that all persons who are necessary to reaching a workable and binding settlement be present. Even in jurisdictions that prescribe who must attend, parties are usually permitted, by mutual agreement and consent of the mediator, to excuse a person otherwise required to attend. For example, in automobile personal injury cases where liability is not in issue, the parties will often agree that the defendant driver need not be present, given that the defendant's insurance carrier will be represented at the mediation by a claims adjuster and defense counsel hired by the carrier.

In nearly every case, you will want your client to attend the mediation even if it is not required. Active client participation in the mediation, particularly during the private caucuses, is in most cases instrumental to reaching a satisfactory settlement. Recall that participation in the process is gratifying to the parties in dispute. Moreover, your client's attendance at the mediation gives effect to the ethical prescription that he alone must make the final decision about whether and on what terms to settle the case and makes it easier for you to fulfill your ethical responsibility to ensure he is reasonably informed about all matters essential to making that decision. His attendance may be an opportunity to display his credibility and likeability to the opposing side. This is important because many mediations occur before the lawyers have deposed any of the parties. In the rare case of a client whose personality or behavior would be seriously detrimental to the process, you might suggest requesting an excuse from attendance or, more likely, that the mediation be done entirely by private caucus. If, however, despite your best advice, the client insists on attending the mediation and participating fully, you must honor that choice.

Sometimes a client will want a family member or close friend to be physically present during the mediation session as a support person. This may be permitted with the consent of the opposing party and the mediator, but it is not common in practice. More often, the support person will be permitted to come to the office where the mediation is being held to confer privately with the client when breaks are taken or when the mediator is holding private caucuses with the other side.

Parties sometimes also find it useful to have an expert attend the mediation or, more commonly, be on telephone standby for consultation. Examples include structured settlement experts, accountants or tax lawyers, medical experts, psychologists, or economists. If one side has an expert attending the mediation, mediators will typically suggest that the other side also have an expert present. That is, mediators are particularly sensitive to maintaining a "level playing field" for both parties.

Lastly, counsel and the mediator should take care to ensure that anyone necessary to a full resolution of the dispute attends the mediation session. If an essential person is cannot attend physically, the parties might agree to have that person on telephone standby during the session. Though it is sometimes necessary, this arrangement is less than ideal. Phone calls may go unanswered, or the person may be unavailable at a particular moment, often a rather long, even interminable moment. If the person on standby is a critical decision maker, they will not have heard the presentations, or the exchange of information, or the arguments and discussion that has gone on during the session. They will not have the same sense of the people involved or the situational sense that comes from participating in the process. As a result, they may exercise their power to decide without the benefits, and without the insight, that mediation has been developed to confer.

§13.04 Preparing the Client for Mediation

In preparing your client for mediation (or any other person who will attend the mediation for your side), you should explain the mediation process (*see* §11.02); whether the mediation will be "facilitative" or "evaluative" (*see* §11.03); and the general style and strategy of the particular mediator (*see* §11.04), including her background and qualifications. In particular, emphasize that:

- The process is not a trial and will be conducted in an informal atmosphere that is designed to make all parties feel comfortable;
- The offers and counteroffers or proposals discussed at the mediation are not admissible as evidence at a trial;
- The mediator, even in evaluative mediation, does not have the power to decide the case, but is trained to assist both sides to consider each other's perspectives about the controversy to make an informed and voluntary decision about whether to settle the case, and if so, how to settle it;
- The ultimate decision whether to settle the case is your client's, but that you will be providing advice to your client throughout the mediation to help him make that decision;
- In the private caucuses with each side, the mediator is likely to play the devil's advocate—not to criticize your client's interests or positions, but to encourage a realistic assessment of the case and discussion of all possible solutions;
- Particularly in the private caucuses, the mediation process is designed to encourage free-flowing discussion and open information sharing;
- Many mediations last for the better part of the day, or even longer, and experience has shown that patience and open-mindedness in the process often leads to a satisfactory settlement of the case; and

- During the mediation session there will be ample opportunity for you and your client to confer privately.

Irrational or inflated client expectations about the value or outcome of the case are common problems that lawyers face when representing a client in mediation. If you have these problems with your client, stress the knowledge and experience of the mediator, and that the mediation process provides a unique opportunity to listen to the mediator and draw upon her special skills and experience as you and your client assess the case and the prospects for a reasonable settlement. In short, point out that the input of an impartial and neutral mediator is worth careful consideration when one is trying to make a decision about settlement.

After explaining the process and the role of the mediator, you should review and discuss your Mediation Preparation Outline with your client. As appropriate, make any changes or additions to it. Be sure to emphasize to your client that the Outline is only a general game plan for the mediation. It is not an inflexible blueprint of unalterable interests, objectives, positions, and bottom lines. Explain that it is typical to discover new information or perspectives about the case during the mediation process that may cause one or both parties to reconsider their earlier assessment of what would be a reasonable settlement of the dispute. Emphasize the importance of keeping an open mind, of being flexible and willing to learn.

Next, discuss with your client the specific role he will play during the mediation. In the joint session, this role may range from saying nothing to making pre-planned remarks as part of the opening statement or answering questions of the other side. If your client is articulate, credible, likeable, and persuasive, you might have him participate in the opening statement by explaining certain facts or events in connection with the case, explaining how he has been affected by those events, or sharing his general perspectives or feelings about the dispute. Conversely, if your client's personality or emotional involvement in the case would make it inappropriate or uncomfortable for him to participate in the presentation of the opening statement or respond to questions of the other side, he should be advised to let you do all of the talking in the joint session.

Similar considerations apply in determining the extent to which your client should speak during the private caucuses. In this setting, however, your client's active participation carries less risk because what he says, and how he says it, is known only to the mediator and can be shielded from the other side. Therefore, it is generally a good idea to encourage your client to speak freely during the private caucuses, particularly in responding to questions asked directly to him by the mediator. Remember that you can always take a recess from a private caucus if your client is engaging in counterproductive or other inappropriate behavior.

Notwithstanding the desirability of your client speaking freely in the private caucuses, you should specifically advise your client:

- Not to reveal any information that both of you have agreed to keep confidential from the mediator;
- Not to reveal any attorney-client privileged information, such as your negotiating strategy;
- Not to get into an argument with the mediator or anyone else at the mediation session;
- Not to engage in exaggeration, hyperbole, speculation, or misrepresentation;
- Not to interrupt when another person is speaking; and
- Not to react to any settlement proposals in a way that may reveal or undermine your negotiating strategy.

These cautionary instructions also apply, of course, to any joint session during the mediation.

As for your role during the mediation, explain that your responsibility is to take the lead for your client's side. Make clear that your role as an advocate during mediation is quite different from your advocacy role at a trial or in an arbitration. That is, during mediation, you will not be engaging in the formal presentation of evidence, cross-examining any witnesses, or delivering a closing argument. Rather you will be engaging in a respectful dialogue with the other side and the mediator, where you will be doing at least as much listening as talking. Moreover, explain that you will be using the mediation process as part of an on-going assessment of the case, so that you can give him your best judgment and advice from which he can make an informed decision about settlement.

Chapter Fourteen

Effective Advocacy During Mediation

SYNOPSIS

§14.01 Introduction
§14.02 Preparing a Pre-Mediation Submission
§14.03 Making the Opening Statement
§14.04 Using the Private Caucuses
- [1] Assist the Mediator in Obtaining Information
- [2] Discuss the Strengths and Weaknesses of the Case
- [3] Invite the Mediator's Perspectives About the Case
- [4] Listen to the Mediator's Cues and Clues
- [5] Specify Confidential Information
- [6] Make Reasonable Settlement Offers Supported by Sound Reasons
- [7] Do Not Disclose Your Bottom Line Up Front
- [8] Confer Alone with the Mediator and Opposing Counsel, If Necessary
- [9] Be Patient with the Process and Take Time to Confer Privately with Your Client

§14.05 Concluding the Mediation

§14.01 Introduction

To be an effective advocate during the mediation process, it is important to understand (1) how to prepare a pre-mediation submission to the mediator; (2) how to present your opening statement; and (3) what to do during the private caucuses. Also, you must use the mediation process to *actively negotiate* with the other side. Do not rely on the mediator to do this work for you. While a good mediator is one who is also a good negotiator, her role is not to resolve the parties' dispute. Rather, her negotiating skills are used to facilitate *your* negotiations with the other side and vice versa. Therefore, it is essential that you draw upon and apply all of the concepts, skills, and techniques of effective negotiating discussed in the preceding chapters of this book when representing your client during mediation.

§14.02 Preparing a Pre-Mediation Submission

The primary purposes of a pre-mediation submission are to educate the mediator about the general nature of the dispute, to identify the issues to be addressed, and to set out the basic contentions of the parties. It is essentially an introductory preview of the case that gives the mediator a general idea of what the dispute is about before the mediation takes place. The submission is often useful in helping the mediator to move more quickly in assisting the parties to reach a resolution during the mediation.

Some mediators invite or even require a pre-mediation submission. Other mediators expressly prohibit or prefer not to receive any pre-mediation materials out of a fear that such submissions might taint their impartiality in the case. Still others have no standard practice about the matter and will review any pre-mediation materials sent to them. Therefore, as a threshold matter, it is important to find out your mediator's preferences about pre-mediation submissions and whether the applicable jurisdiction has any rules governing them.

If you are not prohibited from making a pre-mediation submission, it is often a good idea to send one to the mediator, bearing in mind the limited purposes of a submission mentioned above. Clarify whether the communication will be held in confidence by the mediator. Mediators will keep information confidential when asked to do so, but they may reveal the fact of the communication to the other side. Ordinarily, the submission should be very brief—no more than a two- or three-page synopsis of the case.

1. It may take the form of a letter, succinctly setting out in a non-argumentative style:
2. The basic facts of the case or events giving rise to the dispute, including the amount of any special damages;
3. If a lawsuit has been filed, the basic legal claims and defenses involved;
4. If no lawsuit has been filed, the basic contentions of your client;

5. The nature of the issues to be addressed, if they are not apparent from the foregoing;
6. The status of any prior negotiations and the latest settlement offers of the parties, if that information would be instructive to the mediator in understanding the dispute;
7. A reference to any documents attached to the letter, for example, a copy of the contract involved, an accident report, a governing statute if the law is not generally known, or a copy of the pleadings if reading them is essential to understanding the case, etc.; and
8. A concluding sentence that confirms the time and place of the upcoming mediation, along with an expression of your hope that the mediation might be successful in resolving the case.

It cannot be overemphasized that, in the routine case, brevity is the hallmark of an appropriate submission. Mediators do not want to read (and rarely will read) prolix or voluminous pre-mediation materials. Accordingly, do not send the mediator packages or boxes of medical records, medical bills, or documentary trial exhibits, etc. If, before the mediation, it is absolutely necessary for the mediator to understand certain matters contained in voluminous records, summarize that information in a short attachment to your letter submission. Remember that at the mediation you will have your complete file in the case, from which you can show the mediator any pertinent document or set of documents that may become the focal point of discussion.

In extremely complex cases or multi-party cases, however, your pre-mediation submission may have to be more detailed. In these situations, your pre-mediation submission might include, for example, an indexed notebook containing important documentary evidence, portions of discovery, court orders, legal memoranda, or even copies of appellate decisions. If the case being mediated is on appeal, it may be necessary for the mediator to read such matters as the final judgment and any Memorandum Opinion, the jury instructions, any special verdicts, rulings on any post-trial motion, portions of the trial transcript, and the appellate briefs and record on appeal if they have been filed.

Unless it contains confidential information, you may choose to send a copy of your pre-mediation submission to opposing counsel. If you do, it is important to be objective in your summary of the facts and contentions, and to draft your submission in a way that does not unnecessarily escalate the dispute or impair the prospects for constructive mediation. Even if submitted *ex parte*, be mindful of the context and the mediator's role. She is not going to decide the case, so there is no need to take the tone you might in a brief to the court.

Finally, if you discover any new documents or additional information that are pertinent to the dispute and have not yet been furnished to the other side, such as updated medical records or year-end financial statements, share this information with opposing counsel before the mediation. In addition, it is often desirable to phone opposing counsel to ask if there is any further information he needs from you to evaluate settlement prospects in the case. This saves time during the mediation. The idea is to ensure that the parties have exchanged as much pertinent information as possible before the mediation takes place and are, thus, in good position to discuss settlement.

§14.03 Making the Opening Statement

Mediation is not a trial. In mediation, there is no judge or jury, no burden of proof, no restrictions on the admissibility of evidence, and no verdict. At trial, the opening statement is a forecast of what will be proven, and the closing argument is a summary of what has been proven. Both speeches are designed to convince the fact finder that one side must win and the other must lose. In mediation, however, there is no fact finder to decide the case. Thus, in mediation, it is not helpful to think in terms of winning or losing your case.

Many lawyers who are inexperienced in mediation unwittingly equate mediation with a trial. They will, for instance, deliver an opening statement that sounds much like a trial opening statement and closing argument wrapped into one: the facts are meticulously set out; the key points of law are explained; the facts are applied to the law; the other side's proof is attacked; and the presentation is concluded with an argument that the only logical conclusion is that the lawyer's client is the winner. The advocate then turns and looks at the mediator, as if looking at a jury to say, "Please render a verdict in our favor." It is futile to ask the mediator to do the one thing she cannot do—decide the case and declare a winner and a loser. Such an opening statement is entirely at odds with the mediator's role as an impartial facilitator of an agreement. Unlike a trial, where the objective is an all-or-nothing decision on the merits, in mediation, the only all-or-nothing question is whether there will be an agreement or not. If no agreement is reached, neither side leaves the mediation with a verdict that pronounces victory or defeat.

Therefore, lawyers who are experienced in mediation know that the primary objective of an effective opening statement is not to convince the mediator which side has the better case; it is instead to convince the opposing party that a satisfactory resolution is possible and to motivate them to work together to achieve it.

This means that an opening should present the facts, law, and themes of the controversy in a way that points to a possible resolution. The tone and content of an effective opening statement in mediation should treat the other party with respect; convey a willingness to fairly consider the other side's points of view and the expectation that they will fairly consider yours; and explains your client's real needs and interests, so that the other party might better understand why your client has taken a particular position or why a particular resolution is important to him. You may also in the opening statement speak to the costs and risk that will attend the failure to settle the case. Remember, however, in addressing these matters, the target audience is the opposing side, not the mediator. Only your opponent can agree to settle the case. So, if the opening statement is presented in a way that is aimed solely at advancing the righteousness of your cause and disparaging the other side (as is the intention in an opening statement at trial), you may end up "losing" in the mediation process by making it impossible to obtain the only thing mediation can give you—a final settlement offer from the other party that is better than what you are likely to obtain at trial or through some other means.

Each opening statement will usually last between fifteen and thirty minutes. In an unusually complex case, an opening statement may take an hour or more. In a routine case, such as a non-catastrophic personal injury case, the opening statement by plaintiff's counsel will usually consist of the following:

1. A brief summary of how the accident occurred;
2. An explanation of the plaintiff's theory of liability, if liability is in issue;
3. A brief summary of the plaintiff's course of medical treatment;
4. A summary of the diagnosis and prognosis for the plaintiff's injuries, including the extent of any permanent injury;
5. A summary of how the plaintiff's injuries have affected his life;
6. An itemization of the plaintiff's special damages, such as medical expenses and lost wages; and

7. An expression of willingness to fairly consider all aspects of the case from the perspectives of both sides, with the goal of mutually satisfactory settlement.

If the plaintiff participates in the opening statement, counsel might call upon his client to explain, for example, how the accident occurred or how the plaintiff's injuries have affected his life.

Defense counsel's opening statement will then usually consist of the following:

1. An explanation of any additional facts about how the accident occurred;
2. An explanation of the defendant's theory of liability, if liability is in issue;
3. Questions they may have with respect to the plaintiff's medical treatment, such as time gaps or treatment that appears to have been unnecessary;
4. Any references in the medical reports to a pre-existing medical condition, or any ambiguities in the reports about diagnoses, the plaintiff's prognosis, or extent of permanent injury;
5. An itemization of any special damages that seem unwarranted in the case;
6. An expression of apology to the plaintiff or similar expression of regret about how the accident has affected the plaintiff; and
7. Like that of plaintiff's counsel, an expression of willingness to fairly consider all circumstances of the case with the hope that it might be resolved by agreement.

When delivering the opening statement, most advocates use a low-key, non-argumentative style. In addition, most advocates will primarily make eye contact with the mediator, even though they are consciously addressing their remarks to the opposing side. There are two reasons for this. First, part of the function of an opening statement is to educate the mediator about the case. Second, and most importantly, advocates correctly intuit that an opening statement directed at opposing counsel or her client may feel confrontational or come across as a lecture. To avoid reactive devaluation (*see* §2.06[4]) or other negative responses, the opening statement is directed at the mediator. This way, the opposing party can better hear what is being said and, perhaps, be more receptive to it.

Deciding exactly what to say and how best to present the opening statement varies with the case. Consider whether any of the following tactics and techniques will contribute to fruitful settlement discussions.

- Using audiovisual aids such as models, charts, diagrams, photos, a video, a chalkboard, a power point slide presentation, a tape recording, or a computerized simulation;
- Showing potential trial exhibits, such as a day-in-the-life video of the injured plaintiff or other demonstrative evidence;
- Providing all participants with a notebook containing pertinent documents for reference during the opening statement;
- Suggesting an agenda, or outlining the parameters of a potential settlement or other proposal that may resolve the dispute;
- Acknowledging at the outset certain strengths in the case for the opposing party, but pointing out that there are two sides to the story and that the risks and costs of litigation for both sides warrant a reasoned effort to try to resolve the case by agreement;
- Making an initial offer or concrete proposal and explaining the reasons behind the offer or proposal;
- Declining to make an initial offer or proposal at the outset until after there has been an opportunity for private caucusing;
- Suggesting that at the conclusion of the opening statements, both sides engage in a free-flowing, uninhibited discussion about the dispute and possible ways to resolve it;
- Extending a sincere apology for the events giving rise to the dispute;
- Establishing a deadline for completing the mediation session by mentioning that you or your client will have to leave the mediation by a certain time to meet another commitment.

§14.04 Using the Private Caucuses

In the vast majority of cases, with the exception of family-law disputes, the private caucuses are the most important part of the mediation process. It is here that the mediator works his craft: obtaining and sharing information; generating and discussing potential solutions; assessing, selecting, and communicating specific proposals; creating movement in the negotiations; and helping to forge and finalize the terms of an agreement. Effective advocacy during the private caucuses demands that you try to *assist* the mediator in these tasks, rather than manipulate him by using some of the negotiating tactics previously discussed.

Trying to manipulate the mediator is a bad idea for three reasons. First, it doesn't work. The mediator will know immediately what you are up to. Mediators are typically experienced and effective negotiators themselves. Second, it alienates the mediator. He will not like it and, perhaps as a result, he will not like you. You need the mediator's help, so make him want to help you. Third, it undermines the process. The mediator needs your help to make the process work, so give it to him. He will appreciate it; perhaps he will appreciate you. One final note. It is futile to call upon the mediator to threaten the other side or to demand that he play hardball with them on your behalf. You can fairly expect the mediator to request any information you seek or to deliver precisely the message you want to send. But how they ask for that information or how they deliver that message, in other words, how they practice their craft, is their business, not yours.

This is not to say that you should be weak or irresolute in your analysis of the case and your representation of your client. Mediators appreciate firmness in well-considered and well-grounded positions and proposals. Nor does it mean you should accept settlement for its own sake. Agreement is the best way to resolve a dispute only when it is better than the best alternative to a negotiated agreement. Mediators understand that as well. If a final offer is not acceptable to your client or not better than your best alternative, you should walk away.

In using the private caucuses to negotiate with the other side and assist the mediator, consider the approaches and techniques provided below.

[1] Assist the Mediator in Obtaining Information

Because private caucusing is more a discussion than a question-and-answer session, you should be willing to share any information that may help the mediator understand the dispute. Remember that the mediator will often want to know why your client has taken a particular position he has or why he thinks that a particular objective is important, so expect the mediator to ask. These "why" questions are usually designed to assess the possibility of non-monetary solutions to the dispute, and the answers may be important even in a case that appears to be solely about money. A mediator might ask a plaintiff, "How would your life be different if you could settle for $X?" After listening, he might follow up with, "And how different from that would your life be if you settled for $X–Y?" Sometimes people want money for concrete reasons, and knowing what they are may point the way toward a resolution.

If your client is articulate, credible, likeable, and persuasive, allow him to freely respond to the mediator's questions and actively participate in the private caucuses. Even if your client is angry about the events giving rise to the dispute, the mediator will better understand your client's feelings and views about the case if you permit him to appropriately vent his feelings. Your client's likeability will often have a favorable psychological effect on the mediator. Also, if your client is credible and persuasive, the mediator is likely to mention those qualities in private caucus with the other side. Of course, if your client is reticent or uncomfortable in the private caucuses, you should intercede in responding to the mediator's requests for information.

You should also point out to the mediator any important information that you need from the other side. Explain why you need that information, how it will help you in the negotiation, and ask the mediator if he will help you get that information from other side. In sum, use the private caucuses not only to share information but to obtain it as well.

[2] Discuss the Strengths and Weaknesses of the Case

The private caucus is a safe opportunity to realistically discuss the strengths and weaknesses of your case. Understanding both is critical to making a sound decision about settling the case or taking it to trial. Therefore, it is only sensible to acknowledge the weaknesses in your case as well as its strengths.

It is useful to discuss weaknesses for three reasons. First, the mediator is likely to play the devil's advocate at some point during the private caucuses, and acknowledging weaknesses and problems you might face at trial enhances your credibility with the mediator. Second, a candid, private discussion with the mediator may reveal that you either underestimated or overestimated a particular facet of the case, which may require you to adjust your negotiating strategy. Third, and perhaps most important, your client might be led to a more realistic understanding by a fair and frank acknowledgment of the problems in the case.

When the weaknesses in your case are not readily apparent to the other side, you have no obligation point them out. It is usually best to wait until the subject is prompted by the mediator's questions to you or her comments about the other side's views of the case. In this way, you can hedge against unnecessarily revealing weaknesses that are unknown to the other side.

[3] Invite the Mediator's Perspectives About the Case

Except in evaluative mediation, mediators will not *directly* express their views about any aspect of the case, particularly of its value or how it should be resolved. This is true of some facilitative mediators even when you specifically ask them to do so. A disciplined refusal to give a direct response to a party's question about the value of the case or how to settle it is consistent with the role of the mediator as a neutral and impartial facilitator of an agreement that should be fashioned and owned by the parties, not the mediator. However, as discussed below, the mediator's views are sometimes suggested by the way they frame their questions, by their casual comments or remarks, and by their body language.

Short of precisely evaluating the claim or proposing a concrete solution, the mediator will be responsive to your requests for assistance in resolving the case. It is entirely legitimate for you to invite the mediator's *general* perspectives any matters in dispute. After all, the whole mediation process involves the interplay between differing perspectives and analyses of the dispute. The mediator's perspective—precisely because she is neutral and impartial—is often useful in helping the parties reach an agreement.

The mediator's willingness to reveal her general perspectives about these matters may well depend on whether she perceives you as asking for her assistance in doing your own work or as asking for her personal opinion about the merits of your positions or how to resolve the case. You are not likely to get a useful response to question like "What do you think a jury would do in this case?" or "How do you think we can settle this case?" On the other hand, if you ask her to help you "think through" an evaluation of the case using the Fair Settlement Range Formula calculation (*see* §6.07) or constructing a Decision Tree (*see* §6.06), she will likely be eager to assist. She will be more inclined to engage when asked, "Is there something I'm missing about this aspect of the dispute?" or "What might we do to accommodate the other side about X?" or "I wonder if there is anything more we should be thinking about to resolve this matter?" And her responses are likely to reveal more about her perspective.

When inviting the mediator's perspectives about the case, bear in mind that she must not be made to feel as if she is being asked to take sides in the case.

The aim is to encourage her to see that you are earnestly willing to be educated about the relative strengths and weaknesses of the overall case and possible ways to resolve it.

[4] Listen to the Mediator's Cues and Clues

Mediators may communicate indirectly through their questions, their demeanor and reaction and through their body language. That is, mediators often give you cues and clues about their views of the case and, more importantly, what might be acceptable to the other side in resolving it. These usually subtle (and sometimes not so subtle) hints are routinely given by mediators, even by those who profess to engage in strictly "facilitative" mediation.

For example, consider a mediator who asks: (1) "Are you aware of any six-figure jury verdicts for this type of case?" (2) "Do you think the other side would perceive your offer as being fair?" (3) "What would you say if the other side offered to do X?" On the one hand, these questions might be asked strictly for the purpose of obtaining information, without intending to suggest anything about the mediator's views or what she knows from the other side. On the other hand, depending upon the context of the discussion in which the questions are asked, they may actually mean: (1) "The value you have placed on the case is way out of line"; (2) "Your offer is unreasonable and unrealistic"; and (3) "The other side has told me that they are willing to do X, but you must give them something in return."

Thus, it is essential to carefully consider the context in which the mediator asks her questions and to listen carefully to her comments during the private caucuses. Asking rhetorical questions is the primary device that mediators use to indicate their assessment of the case, the viability of your settlement proposals, and what is going on in the mind of the other side. Needless to say, an ability to accurately read between the lines of what the mediator is asking or saying may be of significant strategic assistance in negotiating with the other side.

[5] Specify Confidential Information

You should assume that it is fair game for the mediator to share with the other side anything you or your client have said to her during the private caucuses, unless you have specified it as confidential. This is not to say that mediators invariably share everything said and done in caucus. Instead, they tend to be quite selective about what information they share between one side and the other, doing so only when they believe that the particular information will advance the prospects of reaching an agreement.

However, because of the mediator's general license to share with one side what she has learned from the other, you must make clear to her what information you want kept in confidence. Accordingly, before the mediator leaves a caucusing session with you to meet with the other side, remind her of what information you wish to keep confidential.

[6] Make Reasonable Settlement Offers Supported by Sound Reasons

As in traditional face-to-face negotiations, making an extreme initial offer is likely to insult the other side, impair your credibility, and may cause the mediation to unnecessarily end in impasse. Whenever you make a settlement offer or a concession through a counteroffer, provide the mediator with specific reasons for your proposal so that these may be conveyed to the other side. If you can, try to incorporate into your proposals something that the other side wants, or provide reasons why your proposal would have some benefit for them. In these ways, you will assist the mediator in explaining to the other side that your proposals are principled and rationally based.

[7] Do Not Disclose Your Bottom Line Up Front

If you represent the plaintiff, it is unwise in the initial caucuses to tell the mediator the minimum amount you would accept to settle the case; and if you represent the defendant, it is unwise to reveal up front the maximum amount you would be willing to pay. There are four reasons for this.

First, the opposing party might have evaluated the case much differently from what you had thought, and therefore, might be willing to settle the case on terms much more favorable than you had anticipated. Second, during the caucusing process, you might learn critical information that will cause you to change your bottom line. Third, the mediator does not need to know your bottom line at the outset. It is not helpful information at this stage of the process. And fourth, the mediator often does not want to know your bottom line, especially early in the negotiation, because that information can put the mediator in an awkward position, even a troubling ethical dilemma.

Likewise, if your client has decided that in no event will they take the case to trial, that is another bit of information that would be unwise to disclose to the mediator. It is hard to see how knowing that fact could help the mediator help you. For example, in many relatively minor automobile personal injury cases, the plaintiff will decide that he does not want to go through the delay, expense, and inconvenience of litigation, but simply wants to use the mediation to get as much money from the insurance carrier as it might be willing to pay on the claim. If the mediator knows that is the plaintiff's sole goal, the mediator may be much less likely to "push" the defendant to consider making higher settlement offers.

[8] Confer Alone with the Mediator and Opposing Counsel, If Necessary

Though not typical, there may be situations that call for meeting with the mediator without your client present or for meeting with opposing counsel and the mediator. For example, a client who is difficult to control or who is emotionally distraught may have derailed the process. Or, the negotiation has become bogged down in the minutiae of complex technical details or fine distinctions being made regarding the facts of the case. In the latter type of case, it is often better for the lawyers to talk directly to each other rather than through the mediator. In the former, simply sharing the difficulties the lawyers may be having with their clients is enough to get the negotiation back on track and the mediation progressing toward settlement.

Such a meeting must be arranged with care. It is best to make this suggestion to the mediator outside the presence of your client, for example, during a break in the session. If you and opposing counsel agree to meet privately with the mediator, explain to your client (or preferably have the mediator explain) that the mediator has asked for the private meeting because they believe it will be helpful to the process. Assure your client that nothing will be decided without his full knowledge and consent, and that he will be briefed about the meeting after it is over. When the meeting is over, either you or the mediator can summarize for your client what was discussed and any suggestions that arose about how to resume more constructive negotiations.

[9] Be Patient with the Process and Take Time to Confer Privately with Your Client

As mentioned in §11.01, the principal advantage of mediation over traditional inter-lawyer negotiations is that it provides a "process" in which the clients are directly involved in resolving their dispute. Working through this process takes time, and therefore you must be patient with it even though hours may pass before the mediation begins to get to the point of addressing specific terms of a potential agreement. Clients, for whom this may be their one and only mediation, are apt to become impatient. Prepare them to be patient by explaining in advance how the process works and how long it may take.

In addition, after each private caucus with the mediator, take the time to talk with your client. Discuss the matters raised during the caucus and consider your next move. If during a caucusing session you or your client wants to speak privately, simply tell the mediator you would like time to do so. Above all, remember that even though you have established a game plan for the mediation through your Mediation Preparation Outline, you should modify that plan based on what you learn as the circumstances warrant.

§14.05 Concluding the Mediation

If an agreement is reached during the mediation, the mediator will typically bring the parties back together in a joint session to summarize the terms of the settlement and to discuss arrangements for the preparation of final settlement documents. At the joint session, be sure that the mediator's summary of the terms of the agreement is accurate. This is also the time to clarify any ambiguities or tie up loose ends with opposing counsel.

If no agreement is reached, leave the mediation with civility toward the other side. In an appropriate case, indicate to opposing counsel your willingness to resume the mediation or further lawyer-to-lawyer negotiations at some later time. Always bear in mind that in many cases where mediation has failed to produce an agreement, the parties still end up settling the case.

Appendix A

Negotiation & Mediation Role Plays

SYNOPSIS

(1) Bloch & McDonald (Premarital Agreement)
(2) Bloch v. Bloch (Separation Agreement)
(3) Daye v. City of Rexford (Employment Discrimination)
(4) French v. Goff (Automobile Personal Injury)
(5) Hillsborough v. Hughes (Condemnation Case on Appeal)
(6) Joseph v. Peters (Medical Malpractice)
(7) Kegnim v. Drake (Automobile Personal Injury)
(8) Lowe v. Interstate Feed Cooperative, Inc. (Wrongful Employment Discharge)
(9) Mann v. Parsons University Medical Center (Nursing Malpractice)
(10) Martel v. Simba (Unfair Debt Collection)
(11) Monolith v. Sat-Lith (Breach of Covenant Not to Compete)
(12) Seaver v. Excellent Pet Foods Co. (Breach of Distributorship Agreement)
(13) Solomon Clinic v. Carr (Breach of Employment Contract)

Note on Dates: YR-0 means the present year; YR-1 means last year; YR-2 means the year before last, etc.

Note to Mediators: If you are asked to serve as a mediator in a case, see the "General Suggestions to Mediators for How to Mediate a Case" in Appendix B.

Your professor will provide you with any confidential facts for the role you are assigned to play in a particular case.

(1) Bloch & McDonald (Premarital Agreement)

Henry Bloch and Jane McDonald plan to marry February 1, YR+1. They have been dating for four years. Henry is three-fourth's owner of Cape Fear Textiles and Jane has been his secretary for the last four years. Henry has been married before and wishes to have a premarital agreement prepared so that he is protected in case the marriage ends. Jane has agreed to sign the agreement so long as she agrees with its contents. Jane has never been married before and currently lives with her elderly mother.

The State of Jefferson has adopted the provisions of the Uniform Premarital Act given below. The parties seek to negotiate a premarital agreement.

§1 Definitions.

As used in this Act:

(1) "Premarital agreement" means an agreement between prospective spouses made in contemplation of marriage and to be effective upon marriage.

(2) "Property" means an interest, present or future, legal or equitable, vested or contingent, in real or personal property, including income and earnings.

§2 Formalities.

A premarital agreement must be in writing and signed by both parties. It is enforceable without consideration.

§3 Content.

(a) Parties to a premarital agreement may contract with respect to:

(1) the rights and obligations of each of the parties in any of the property of either or both of them whenever and wherever acquired or located;

(2) the right to buy, sell, use, transfer, exchange, abandon, lease, consume, expend, assign, create a security interest in, mortgage, encumber, dispose of, or otherwise manage and control property;

(3) the disposition of property upon separation, marital dissolution, death, or the occurrence or nonoccurrence of any other event;

(4) the modification or elimination of spousal support;

(5) the making of a will, trust, or other arrangement to carry out the provisions of the agreement;

(6) the ownership rights in and disposition of the death benefit from a life insurance policy;

(7) the choice of law governing the construction of the agreement; and

(8) any other matter, including their personal rights and obligations, not in violation of public policy or a statute imposing a criminal penalty.

(b) The right of a child to support may not be adversely affected by a premarital agreement.

§4 Amendment, Revocation.

After marriage, a premarital agreement may be amended or revoked only by a written agreement signed by the parties. The amended agreement or the revocation is enforceable without consideration.

§5 Enforcement.

(a) A premarital agreement is not enforceable if the party against whom enforcement is sought proves that:

(1) that party did not execute the agreement voluntarily; or

(2) the agreement was unconscionable when it was executed and, before execution of the agreement, that party:

(i) was not provided a fair and reasonable disclosure of the property or financial obligations of the other party;

(ii) did not voluntarily and expressly waive, in writing, any right to disclosure of the property or financial obligations of the other party beyond the disclosure provided; and

(iii) did not have, or reasonably could not have had, an adequate knowledge of the property or financial obligations of the other party.

(b) If a provision of a premarital agreement modifies or eliminates spousal support and that modification or elimination causes one party to the agreement to be eligible for support under a program of public assistance at the time of separation or marital dissolution, a Court, notwithstanding the terms of the agreement, may require the other party to provide support to the extent necessary to avoid that eligibility.

(c) An issue of unconscionability of a premarital agreement shall be decided by the court as a matter of law.

* * *

(2) Bloch v. Bloch (Separation Agreement)

Henry and Jane Bloch, who consulted you about a premarital agreement ten years ago (*see* (1) Block & McDonald—Premarital Agreement) have run into hard times, and are anticipating a separation. When Henry and Jane first contemplated marriage, they asked you to draft a Premarital Agreement. However, because things were going so well and they had stars in their eyes, they decided they didn't need one. They never signed a Premarital Agreement. They have been married ten years. (Assume they married on February 1, YR-10.)

When Henry and Jane first consulted you about the Premarital Agreement eleven years ago, Henry owned three-fourths of Cape Fear Textiles. Henry bought out his sister-in-law's one-quarter interest in Cape Fear Textiles on March 1, YR-10. Jane was Henry's secretary at Cape Fear Textiles at the time of their marriage.

Jane and Henry have never been able to conceive a child, but they adopted one child, Katherine (Kathy) McDonald Bloch, who was born on January 1, YR-8. A final Order of Adoption was entered on September 1, YR-8.

After Kathy came to live with them, Jane stopped working as Henry's secretary at Cape Fear Textiles. At first, she planned to return to work after six months. However, Jane found that it was too hard to leave Kathy with a babysitter. Henry agreed that Jane should try staying home from work. His business had picked up, and he was able to pay another secretary a good salary.

Both of Henry's children from his first marriage, Daniel and John Bloch, are now adults. On March 1, YR-2, Henry transferred one-third interest in Cape Fear Textiles to Daniel and one third to John. Henry continues to own one-third of Cape Fear Textiles.

Henry continues to pay alimony of $1000 a month to his first wife. Although old alimony orders continue in force in our state of Jefferson, the Jefferson legislature has enacted a new statute to replace alimony. It is called Post-Separation Support. Because it is a new statute, there is no case law interpreting it. The statute is provided below.

Henry and Jane's joint tax return for YR-1 shows Henry's gross salary from Cape Fear Textiles was $75,000 and Jane's income from her inheritance from her father was $20,000. Henry and Jane also have $25,000 in a money market account.

The State of Jefferson has adopted child support guidelines, which a court uses to determine how much should be paid in child support by a non-custodial parent to the custodial parent. Jefferson's guidelines are based on the "Income Shares Model," in which each parent's income is added to the income of the other parent and then adjusted for health insurance obligations and work related childcare costs. The amount of the child support obligation is then derived from a chart showing the amount of child support the child support enforcement agency has determined will be necessary for the number of children in the family with parents whose adjusted combined income is of a certain amount. That child support obligation is then divided between the two parents based on the percentage of the total income each earns.

Based on Jefferson's child support guidelines, and based on the parties' reported income for YR-1 and the fact that Henry currently pays $300 a month for health insurance for the family ($100 per person), Henry would be expected to pay $676 in child support if Jane has custody of Kathy for more than 243 days per year. Jane would be expected to pay $260 to Henry if he has custody of Kathy for more than 243 days per year. However, a judge may deviate from these amounts for "good cause." Some Jefferson judges have deviated from the guidelines if the non-custodial parent has an outstanding spousal support order. The amount of the deviation is within the judge's discretion. Judges may also deviate from the guideline amount for other "good cause." Under the Jefferson child support guidelines, child support terminates when the child reaches eighteen years of age. However, the parties may extend support beyond that age in their Separation Agreement.

If the parties work out a child support agreement and do not litigate the issue, they of course can agree to any child support amount for any length of time. However, a court will not enforce an agreement that is not in the child's best interest. If the parties include child support in their Separation Agreement and ask the court to incorporate the agreement into their divorce decree, the agreement will be a court order enforceable by contempt. The judge who has been asked to incorporate the separation agreement into the divorce decree has the authority to reject the child support amount reached by the parties if he determines that it is not in the best interests of the child. He can then substitute the state guideline amount into the child support portion of the agreement.

The State of Jefferson has also adopted Equitable Distribution. The relevant statute regarding equitable distribution is also given below. The parties seek to negotiate a comprehensive separation agreement.

SPOUSAL SUPPORT AT DIVORCE

§50-16.1A Definitions.

As used in this Chapter, unless the context clearly requires otherwise, the following definitions apply:

(1) "Dependent spouse" means a spouse, whether husband or wife, who is actually substantially dependent upon the other spouse for his or her maintenance and support or is substantially in need of maintenance and support from the other spouse.

(2) "Marital misconduct" means any of the following acts that occur during the marriage and prior to or on the date of separation:

(i) Illicit sexual behavior. For the purpose of this section, illicit sexual behavior means acts of sexual or deviate sexual intercourse, deviate sexual acts, voluntarily engaged in by a spouse with someone other than the other spouse;

(ii) Involuntary separation of the spouses in consequence of a criminal act committed prior to the proceeding in which alimony is sought;

(iii) Abandonment of the other spouse;

(iv) Malicious turning out-of-doors of the other spouse;

(v) Cruel or barbarous treatment endangering the life of the other spouse;

(vi) Indignities rendering the condition of the other spouse intolerable and life burdensome;

(vii) Reckless spending of the income of either party, or the destruction, waste, diversion, or concealment of assets;

(viii) Excessive use of alcohol or drugs so as to render the condition of the other spouse intolerable and life burdensome;

(ix) Willful failure to provide necessary subsistence according to one's means and condition so as to render the condition of the other spouse intolerable and life burdensome.

(3) "Post-separation support" means spousal support to be paid until the earlier of either the date specified in the order of post-separation support, or an order awarding or denying alimony. Post-separation support may be ordered in an action for divorce, whether absolute or from bed and board, for annulment, or for alimony without divorce.

(4) "Supporting spouse" means a spouse, whether husband or wife, upon whom the other spouse is actually substantially dependent for maintenance and support or from whom such spouse is substantially in need of maintenance and support.

§50-16.2A Post-separation support.

(a) In an action brought pursuant to this Chapter, either party may move for post-separation support. The verified pleading, verified motion, or affidavit of the moving party shall set forth the factual basis for the relief requested.

(b) In ordering post-separation support, the court shall base its award on the financial needs of the parties, considering the parties accustomed standard of living, the present employment income and other recurring earnings of each party from any source, their income-earning abilities, the separate and marital debt service obligations, those expenses reasonably necessary to support each of the parties, and each party's respective legal obligations to support any other persons.

(c) Except when subsection (d) of this section applies, a dependent spouse is entitled to an award of post-separation support if, based on consideration of the factors specified in subsection (b) of this section, the court finds that the resources of the dependent spouse are not adequate to meet his or her reasonable needs and the supporting spouse has the ability to pay.

(d) At a hearing on post-separation support, the judge shall consider marital misconduct by the dependent spouse occurring prior to or on the date of separation in deciding whether to award post-separation support and in deciding the amount of post-separation support. When the judge considers these acts by the dependent spouse, the judge shall also consider any marital misconduct by the supporting spouse in deciding whether to award post-separation support and in deciding the amount of post-separation support.

(e) Nothing herein shall prevent a court from considering incidents of post date-of-separation marital misconduct as corroborating evidence supporting other evidence that marital misconduct occurred during the marriage and prior to the date of separation.

PROPERTY DIVISION AT DIVORCE

§50-20 Distribution by court of marital property upon divorce.

(a) Upon application of a party, the court shall determine what is the marital property and shall provide for an equitable distribution of the martial property between the parties in accordance with the provisions of this section.

(b) For purposes of this section:

(1) "Marital property" means all real and personal property acquired by either spouse or both spouses during the course of the marriage and before the date of the separation of the parties, and presently owned, except property determined to be separate property in accordance with subdivision (2) of this subsection. Marital property includes all vested and non-vested pension, retirement, and other deferred compensation rights, and vested and non-vested military pensions eligible under the federal Uniformed Services Former Spouses' Protection Act. It is presumed that all property acquired after the date of marriage and before the date of separation is marital property except property which is separate property under subdivision (2) of this subsection. This presumption may be rebutted by the greater weight of the evidence.

(2) "Separate property" means all real and personal property acquired by a spouse before marriage or acquired by a spouse by bequest, devise, descent, or gift during the course of marriage. However, property acquired by gift from the other spouse during the course of the marriage

shall be considered separate property only if such an intention is stated in the conveyance. Property acquired in exchange for separate property shall remain separate property regardless of whether the title is in the name of the husband or wife or both and shall not be considered to be marital property unless a contrary intention is expressly stated in the conveyance. The increase in value of separate property and the income derived from separate property shall be considered separate property. All professional licenses and business licenses which would terminate on transfer shall be considered separate property.

(3) "Distributive award" means payments that are payable either in a lump sum or over a period of time in fixed amount, but shall not include alimony payments or other similar payments for support and maintenance which are treated as ordinary income to the recipient under the Internal Revenue Code.

(c) The difficulty of evaluating any component asset or any interest in a business, corporation or profession, and the economic desirability of retaining such asset or interest, intact and free from any claim or interference by the other party;

(d) Before, during or after marriage the parties may by written agreement, duly executed and acknowledged, or by a written agreement valid in the jurisdiction where executed, provide for distribution of the marital property in a manner deemed by the parties to be equitable and the agreement shall be binding on the parties.

(e) Subject to the presumption of subsection (c) of this section that an equal division is equitable, it shall be presumed in every action that an in-kind distribution of marital or divisible property is equitable. This presumption may be rebutted by the greater weight of the evidence, or by evidence that the property is a closely held business entity or is otherwise not susceptible of division in-kind. In any action in which the presumption is rebutted, the court in lieu of an in-kind distribution shall provide for a distributive award in order to achieve equity between the parties. The court may provide for a distributive award to facilitate, effectuate or supplement a distribution of marital or divisible property. The court may provide that any distributive award payable over a period of time be secured by a lien on specific property.

(f) Unless good cause is shown that there should not be an interim distribution, the court may, at any time after an action for equitable distribution has been filed and prior to the final judgment of equitable distribution, enter orders declaring what is separate property and may also enter orders dividing part of the marital property, or debt, or marital debt between the parties. The partial distribution may provide for a distributive award and may also provide for a distribution of marital property and marital debt. Any such orders entered shall be taken into consideration at trial and proper credit given.

(g) In any order for the distribution of property made pursuant to this section, the court shall make written findings of fact that support the determination that the marital property has been equitably divided.

* * *

(3) Daye v. City of Rexford (Employment Discrimination)

On July 31, YR-2, at approximately 1:30 a.m., Marsha Woods, who worked as a cleaning lady for a small office complex, was walking home from work in the City of Rexford, State of Rexford. As she walked by the unfenced parking lot of the Rexford Police Department, she saw two males who had somehow managed to break into one of the police cars parked in the lot and who were rummaging through the contents of the car. The lighting in the parking lot was poor and it was difficult for her to see the two men. However, she heard one of them, who was African-American and later identified as Max Stimpson, refer to the other as "Joey." Although she wasn't at all positive, she thought that "Joey" (who was white) looked like "Joey Smith" who some months ago had worked one night with her and her co-workers cleaning the office complex.

Upon seeing what the two men were doing, she hurried across the street and called 911 from a phone booth. The police operator told her that officers would be dispatched to the scene right away, and asked her to stay in the phone booth until the officers arrived.

Within two minutes, Officers Blake Bowes and Donald Crews arrived in their squad car. Upon seeing the officers, the two suspects ran. Officer Crews gave chase on foot and tackled Stimpson on the street about 25 yards away from where Ms. Woods remained in the phone booth. According to Ms. Woods, she saw Officer Crews beat Stimpson four times with a flashlight while Stimpson was on the ground and was not offering any resistance. Officer Crews, who is white, claims that he subdued Stimpson with the flashlight by hitting him with it two times because Stimpson was struggling and resisting arrest. "Joey," who had also run when the officers arrived, was never caught.

Officer Bowes interviewed Ms. Woods about what she had seen in the parking lot and from the phone booth. In his police report, Bowes wrote that Ms. Woods had described the suspect called "Joey" as being "white; blue eyes; dark hair; about medium height & build; and 25-30 years old." The report noted that Ms. Woods thought the suspect "looked like one, Joey Smith, but witness couldn't see suspect very well."

Stimpson, who was bleeding from his head and face from the flashlight blows, was arrested for "resisting arrest" and "felony breaking and entering into a police vehicle." Officer Crews took Stimpson in handcuffs to the local hospital to be treated. However, when the handcuffs were removed at the hospital and Stimpson was being treated by a physician's assistant, Stimpson somehow managed to escape through a fire-door exit and has not been apprehended since.

On August 3, YR-2, the case was turned over to Detective Kyle Daye, the only African-American detective in the Rexford Police Department and one of four African-Americans on the force out of a total of 40 officers. Daye is 38 years old and has been with the police department for ten years. He began as a patrol officer, and worked his way up to the rank of detective which he has held since January, YR-3. Like other detectives on the force, Daye's primary job is to investigate unsolved felony cases.

When Daye was assigned the instant case to apprehend Stimpson and "Joey," he was well aware of the significant media criticism that had been brought against the police department for its failure to adequately secure the unfenced parking lot area at the police station, and its failure to prevent the escape of Stimpson. The Chief of Police, Harold Burns, expressly told Daye to "solve this case quickly and at all costs."

On August 4, YR-2, Daye reviewed Bowes' report and interviewed Ms. Woods. She told him the same things she had told Bowes about what she saw in the parking lot and how Crews subdued Stimpson. The next day, Daye presented Ms. Woods' account of what she saw in the parking lot to the local magistrate, Richard Larson, and obtained a warrant for the arrest of a defendant (who was named in the warrant as "Joey Smith") for felony breaking and entering into a police vehicle. The warrant was a standard, pre-printed form that contained designated spaces to enter the defendant's address, telephone number, race, sex, date of birth, age, social security number, drivers license number and State, and name of defendant's employer. As a matter of proper practice, an officer who swears out an arrest warrant will include as much of this information on the warrant as is known to the officer. However, none of the foregoing information was filled in on the warrant when it was signed and issued by Magistrate Larson on August 5, YR-2. Magistrate Larson, who was 72 years old at the time, is now deceased.

On August 6, YR-2, Daye contacted Ms. Woods' employer who told him that a "Joey Smith" had worked only one night for the cleaning company some months ago, and that the only information the company had on Smith was that his last known address was 1211 Mineral Springs Drive in Rexford City. Daye went to that address, but no "Joey Smith" was living there, and the current residents said they knew nothing about a "Joey Smith."

On August 7, YR-2, Daye asked Assistant Detective, Fran Payton, to provide him with a computer printout of all the "Joey Smith's" in the State of Rexford's drivers license data bank. The printout listed six persons under the name of "Joey Smith," one of which was a "Joey Lee Smith," born March 7, YR-29, with an address at 1211 Mineral Springs Drive, Rexford City. Payton is white and is the only female officer on the Rexford City Police force. She had no formal responsibilities in connection with Daye's investigation.

On August 8, YR-2, Daye ran a criminal record check on "Joey Lee Smith," which showed that this individual had two convictions for misdemeanor larceny in the State of Rexford in the past five years. Thus concluding that "Joey Lee Smith" was the proper suspect in the case, on August 8 Daye wrote in the address of 1211 Mineral Springs Drive onto the arrest warrant that had been issued by Magistrate Larson on August 5, YR-2. Daye says that when Magistrate Larson had signed the warrant, Daye had told Larson that Daye would add to the warrant the proper address for "Joey Smith" when Daye ascertained it, and that Larson said, "Ok." Daye made no other additions or changes to the warrant.

On August 9, YR-2, Daye took the computer printout from the State of Rexford's drivers license data bank to Assistant Detective Payton and told her to enter the name of "Joey Lee Smith, DOB 3/7/YR-29" into the National Crime Information Center (NCIC) database as being wanted on a Rexford City warrant for felony breaking and entering into a police vehicle. This NCIC computer database contains the names of and other pertinent information on all persons in the country for whom there are outstanding arrest warrants, and all police departments throughout the country can access the database. Payton, however, emphatically says that Daye told her to enter the name of "Joey Allen Smith, DOB 3/7/YR-39" (who was one of the other six names listed on the State of Rexford's drivers license data bank printout) into the NCIC database; and this was the name that she entered into that database.

After entering "Joey Allen Smith, DOB 3/7/YR-39... wanted on Rexford City warrant for Felony B & E of a Police Vehicle" into the NCIC computer database, Payton handed Daye a hard copy of the computer entry, which Daye admits he did not review but simply put in his file. There is nothing in the Rexford City Police Department Officers Manual that either expressly required Payton to give Daye a hard copy of the NCIC database entry or expressly required Daye to review it for accuracy.

On September 1, YR-1, the "Joey Allen Smith" who had been entered into the NCIC database was in the Town of Tarville, some 150 miles from the City of Rexford. When he went to the local Department of Motor Vehicle's Drivers License Office to renew his driver's license, the DMV officer checked the NCIC database and saw that Mr. Smith was wanted on the unserved felony warrant for breaking and entering into a police vehicle. Accordingly, the Tarville police promptly arrested Mr. Smith and took him into custody, where he remained in jail for 48 hours until the Tarville Chief of Police and the City of Rexford Chief of Police (Harold Burns) figured out the mistaken entry into the NCIC database and that Mr. Smith was in fact not the proper suspect wanted on the warrant.

Mr. Joey Allen Smith is a prominent citizen and certified public accountant in the small Town of Tarville. He is married, has two young children, and has no criminal record. His arrest received extensive coverage in the local media.

On September 4, YR-1, The Rexford City Manager, pursuant to the recommendation of Chief Burns, placed Daye on temporary suspension without pay as permitted by the City's Personnel Policy. This suspension lasted until October 5, YR-1 when, after Burns had completed an investigation, the City Manager decided to demote Daye to Patrol Officer. As a detective, Daye was making $48,000 per year; but effective October 5, YR-1, his demotion resulted in his making $36,000 per year. Although Chief Burns also investigated Payton's involvement in what had happened, she was not suspended or disciplined in any way. There was extensive media coverage in the City of Rexford about Daye's demotion and the mistaken arrest of Joey Allen Smith.

The parties agree that the City Manager followed all proper procedural due process requirements under the Personnel Policy in disciplining Daye. However, Daye's attorney has advised counsel for the City that Daye intends to pursue a claim against the City for race discrimination in violation of Title VII of the Federal Civil Rights Act, but is willing to try to resolve the matter before initiating procedures under Title VII. Daye's attorney contends that there were no grounds for disciplining Daye at all. And, to the extent there were any valid grounds for disciplining Daye, he was the victim of disparate treatment because Payton, who is white and who Daye contends was solely responsible for entering the wrong "Joey Smith" into the NCIC database, was not disciplined at all.

Counsel for the City of Rexford has advised Daye's lawyer that the City Manager's decision was based on Chief Burns' opinion (1) that Daye had no "probable cause" under the Fourth Amendment to the U.S. Constitution and State law to support a warrant for the arrest of anyone in the case (*i.e.*, that Daye had no reasonably trustworthy information that would lead an officer of reasonable caution to believe that Joey Lee Smith committed the breaking and entering of the police vehicle); (2) that the arrest warrant did not "particularly describe" the person to be arrested as required by the Fourth Amendment and State law; (3) that Payton was not disciplined because it could not be conclusively determined which "Joey Smith" Daye told Payton to enter into the NCIC database, and Payton otherwise had no responsibilities in the investigation of Daye's case; and (4) that Daye nevertheless should have reviewed the hard copy of the NCIC computer entry given him by Payton to ensure the accuracy of the information entered into the database. However, counsel for the City of Rexford is also agreeable to exploring a resolution of Daye's race discrimination claims without litigation.

The parties are in agreement about the basic legal principles pertaining to proof and damages in a Title VII case. Title VII prohibits discrimination (*i.e.*, treating individuals differently) in connection with employment based on race, color, sex, national origin, and religion. The burden of persuasion in such a case remains throughout on the plaintiff. The plaintiff must first establish a prima facie case that he was disciplined when another employee of a different race should have been disciplined and was not. The defendant then bears the burden of production to show some specific and legitimate non-discriminatory reason for the employment action.

The plaintiff must then show that the defendant's reason for the employment action was either (a) false or (b) a mere pretext for discrimination (*i.e.*, that the defendant's proffered reason was not the true reason for the employment action but was, at least in part, motivated by discriminatory animus).

A showing of *either* of these things is, by itself, sufficient to permit a jury to infer that the employment action was motivated by discriminatory animus. The State of Rexford allows the plaintiff to prevail in so-called "mixed motive" cases, where the employment action was motivated by both lawful and unlawful considerations. A prevailing plaintiff is entitled to backpay; reinstatement to former position; if reinstatement is not practical or available, to "front pay" (*i.e.* lost wages likely to be incurred until the employee obtains new employment at a wage that is comparable to what he was previously earning); damages for emotional distress and medical expenses for such distress upon a showing of "some specific discernible injury to the plaintiff's emotional state;" and reasonable attorney's fees and litigation expenses.

* * *

(4) French v. Goff (Automobile Personal Injury)

Counsel for Sandy French has sent the following settlement brochure letter to the adjuster for Pat Goff's automobile liability insurance carrier:

Ms. Rose A. Braves
Claim Specialist
Auto Mutual Insurance Co.

Re:	My Client:	Sandy French
	Your Insured:	Pat Goff
	Your Claim No.:	33-1795-262
	Date of Accident:	August 11, YR-2

Dear Ms. Braves:

As you know, I represent Ms. Sandy French in connection with the personal injuries she sustained in an automobile accident on August 11, YR-2 when your insured's car rear-ended Ms. French's van on Weaver Dairy Road. This letter and its enclosures are provided for settlement discussions only. After you have had the opportunity to review this claim, I look forward to hearing from you and hope we can resolve this matter without the necessity of litigation.

LIABILITY

On August 11, YR-2, at approximately 10:30 a.m., Ms. French was driving south on Weaver Dairy Road, a two-lane road in rural, Orange County. She had not driven this road before and was on her way to the town of Pittsborough. The speed limit on Weaver Dairy is 55 m.p.h.

Pittsborough Road intersects Weaver Dairy approximately five miles from the Orange County and Caswell County line. As Ms. French was driving south on Weaver Dairy, she realized that she had inadvertently passed the turn-off from Weaver Dairy to Pittsborough Road. Accordingly, she pulled over to the right-hand, paved shoulder of Weaver Dairy; and, after seeing no cars behind her or any traveling north in the opposite lane of Weaver Dairy, she executed a three-point turn or U-turn to travel north on Weaver Dairy and back towards the intersection of Weaver Dairy and Pittsborough Road.

Approximately one-tenth of a mile south of the point where Ms. French executed her U-turn on Weaver Dairy, there is a moderately sharp curve in the road. (The speed limit for the curve is 45 m.p.h.) Mr. Goff, who was traveling north on Weaver Dairy, rounded that curve at a high rate of speed, and crashed into the rear of Ms. French's van just as she had completed her U-turn and was about to proceed north on Weaver Dairy. The police officer who investigated the accident gave no citation to either driver, apparently because he was unable to determine fault in the accident. (*See* Accident Report enclosed).

It is our contention that your insured was negligent in that he was driving in excess of the speed limit, was otherwise driving at a speed that was in excess of what was reasonable when rounding the curve on Weaver Dairy, or failed to properly reduce his speed to avoid the collision. As you know, this State recognizes the doctrine of "comparative negligence" whereby, in any action to recover damages for personal injury, the contributory negligence of the claimant does not bar recovery, but the amount of damages otherwise recoverable will be diminished in the proportion which the contributory negligence of the claimant bears to the negligent conduct which caused the damages. The doctrine of last clear chance is not recognized in our jurisdiction. Of course, we contend that Ms. French was not contributorily negligent in causing the accident; but, if she was, her damages are merely to be reduced by the extent of any such negligence.

MEDICAL TREATMENT

The following summarizes Ms. French's medical treatment with verbatim excerpts from the pertinent records. (*See* enclosed medical records).

Orange County Emergency Medical Services

8/11/YR-2: Taken by ambulance to Rolland Hospital. Patient was spinally immobilized. Patient had neck pain, and lower outside left leg pain. Has trouble remembering events of motor vehicle accident, either events leading up to the accident or after the accident.

Rolland Hospital Emergency Room:

8/11/YR-2: Pain at base of neck. Soreness above left ankle. Pain in shoulder blades, wincing with pain. C-spine films show possible ligamentous injury. Advised to take warm soaks and showers. Given analgesics, Ibuprofen 800 mg.

Midtown Family Medicine:

9/4/YR-2: Persistent stiffness in lower back, especially after sitting for long periods of time. Also, pain in left calf, and pain in dorsiflexion of left ankle. Diagnosis of flexion extension injury; low back; contusion left leg. Physical therapy recommended.

Comprehensive Physical Therapy Center:

9/8/YR-2 to 2/24/YR-1: (Patient had 14 physical therapy sessions to treat left foot pain, and thoracic and lumbar back pain.)

Midtown Family Medicine:

9/25/YR-2: Occasional pain and stiffness above the left iliac crest. Still some limitation of dorsiflexion in ankle. Advised to continue physical therapy.

Midtown Family Medicine:

2/12/YR-1: Patient has persistent back pain from MVA 6 months ago. Pain is poorly localized, felt diffusely in upper and lower back, dull in quality and most bothersome at night. Diagnosis of back pain and referred to Spine Center for further therapy.

Spine Center:

2/13/YR-1 to 4/9/YR-1: Patient has persistent back pain from MVA 6 months ago. Pain is poorly localized, felt diffusely in upper and lower back, dull in quality and most bothersome at night. Diagnosis of back pain and referred to Spine Center for further therapy.

Norville Chiropractic Center:

2/16/YR-1 to 4/13/YR-1: (Patient underwent 14 therapy sessions, consisting of electrical muscle stimulation, manipulation, and ultrasound.)

Midtown Family Medicine:

10/28/YR-1 Patient's back pain has resolved, but she has continued to have discomfort in her left foot and ankle that becomes aggravated with activity as well as decreased dorsiflexion in the left ankle.... It is my impression that the persistent symptoms are related to the initial accident on 8/11/YR-2. If she continues to have persistent pain, I believe she will need further evaluation with left foot and ankle x-rays and would strongly recommend further evaluation by an orthopedist.

SPECIAL DAMAGES

A. Medical Expenses

Orange County EMS	$ 400
Rolland Hospital	$1,500
Midtown Family Medicine	$ 400
Spine Center	$1,000
Comprehensive PT Center	$1,400
Norville Chiropractic Center	$1,300
Total Medical Bills:	$6,000

B. Lost Income

Ms. French is self-employed as the sole instructor in "French's Aerobic Dance & Fitness Studio," which she has owned and operated for the past eight years. She is married, and her husband is a lieutenant in the Oxford Police Department. At the time of the collision, she was 38 years old.

From August 12, YR-2 to September 12, YR-2, she was forced to cancel all of her aerobics classes. These are group classes with approximately 10 students in each group. She has two group classes a day (one hour each session) four days a week. Each student pays a $20 fee per one-hour session. Thus, in the four weeks from August 12 to September 12, YR-2, Ms. French's gross lost income totaled $6,400 (*i.e.*, 10 students per group/session × 2 groups/sessions per day = 20 students per day × $20 per student = $400 per day × 4 days per week = $1,600 per week × 4 weeks = $6,400). In addition, from September 13, YR-2 to October 28, YR-1, she missed an additional 30 one-hour sessions for gross income lost of $6,000 (*i.e.*, 10 students per session × $20 per student = $200 per session × 30 sessions = $6,000).

Total lost income: $12,400
TOTAL SPECIAL DAMAGES = $18,400

The foregoing shows that Ms. French's course of treatment spanned a period of eight months. Although her cervical and lumbar problems have resolved, she still continues to have periodic pain in her left ankle.

I am authorized to extend an offer to settle this case for $40,000. Again, I look forward to hearing from you after you have had an opportunity to review this claim.

Sincerely,
Counsel for Ms. French

* * *

(5) Hillsborough v. Hughes (Condemnation Case on Appeal)

On April 25, YR-3, the Town of Hillsborough filed a lawsuit condemning 79.767 acres of land owned by George Hughes for the purpose of building a reservoir for the Town's future water supply. The case was tried before a jury which, on December 30, YR-1, rendered a verdict for $323,073 as just compensation for the taking. On December 31, YR-1, the trial court entered a final Judgment in accordance with the jury verdict and, as authorized by statute, taxed an additional $9,500 against the Town for Hughes' expenses for expert witnesses and other costs. The Town has timely filed a notice of appeal to the State Court of Appeals, but the parties are interested in exploring a settlement of the case to avoid the delay and expense of an appeal and a possible retrial of the case.

The property condemned by the Town consisted of 79.767 acres of a 93.112-acre tract of vacant, undeveloped land located in rural, Cedar Grove Township. Hughes retained 13.345 acres of the entire tract after the taking. Where, as in this case, less than the entire tract is condemned, the applicable measure of just compensation is the greater of (a) the fair market value of the tract taken (the 79.767 acres), or (b) the difference between the fair market value of the entire tract (the 93.112 acres) and the fair market value of the remainder retained by the landowner (the 13.345 acres). Fair market value must be established as of the time of the taking which is the date of the filing of the condemnation action—in this case, April 25, YR-3. The jury's verdict of just compensation in the instant case represented the difference between the fair market value of the entire tract and the fair market value of the remainder.

At trial, Hughes called Charles Moody as an expert in real estate and timber appraisal. Moody testified that, at the time of the taking, the fair market value of the entire tract (93.112 acres) was $358,500, the fair market value of the parcel taken (79.767 acres) was $307,120, and the fair market value of the remainder (13.345 acres) was $33,500. In arriving at his opinion about the value of the entire tract and parcel taken, he employed a three-step analysis.

First, based on twelve comparable sales, he concluded that the average fair market value of properties similar to the Hughes' property was $2,500 per acre. These comparable sales included properties that had timber, and he assumed that the highest and best use of the Hughes' property was for residential development. Second, based on a "Forest Inventory Data Summary Appraisal Report" dated June 21 and September 25, YR-4 that he had received from a timber expert, Richard Bernard, Moody estimated that the separate value of the timber on the entire tract and parcel taken was $1,350 per acre and that an astute seller could obtain this per acre amount by selling the timber before putting the property on the market for sale. Third, he then added the separate $1,350 per acre timber value—a calculation that he characterized as "a lump sum adjustment for the timber contribution value"—to arrive at $3,850 per acre which, in turn, he multiplied by the 93.112 acres of the entire tract for a total value of $358,500 (rounded), and by the 79.767 acres of the parcel taken for a total value of $307,120 (rounded).

Stated another way, as he explained on cross-examination, Moody's $358,500 (rounded) total fair market value for the entire tract was calculated as the sum of $232,780 based on the average per acre price of the twelve comparable sales ($2500 per acre × 93.112 acres) and $125,701 based on the average per acre timber value ($1,350 per acre timber value × 93.112 acres). Similarly, the $307,120 (rounded) total value for the parcel taken was calculated as the sum of $199,418 ($2,500 per acre × 79.767 acres) and $107,685 ($1,350 per acre timber value × 79.767 acres). Because Moody did not attribute any merchantable timber value to the 13.345-acre remainder, he based its fair market value of $33,500 (rounded) solely on $2,500 per acre figure derived from his twelve comparable sales.

Hughes also called Richard Bernard, an expert in timber valuation, to testify about his June 21 and September 25, YR-4 appraisals of the timber on the Hughes' property that were relied upon by Moody. Bernard testified that, as of June, YR-4, the clear-cut value of the timber was $98,500, and as of September, YR-4, the clear-cut value was $160,000. If only a "selective cut" were done (*i.e.*, only 51 trees per acre were removed and 70 trees per acre remained), the value of the timber on the 79.767 acres taken was $131,360 in YR-4. Bernard admitted that his valuations, inasmuch as they were made in YR-4, were not based on the time of the taking of April 25, YR-3, and none of his valuations were "to a reasonable degree of professional certainty or probability."

The trial judge overruled the Town's timely objections to all of the foregoing testimony by Moody and Bernard.

The Town's expert appraiser, Frank Leatherman, drew upon twenty-four comparable sales to appraise the Hughes' property. His opinion about the per acre fair market value was similar to the $2,500 per acre "base" value used by Moody, except that Leatherman valued the property as a whole and did not add on a separate, additional amount for the timber on the property. Leatherman concluded that the fair market value of the entire tract was $232,780 ($2,500 per acre × 93.112 acres), the fair market value of the parcel taken was $183,464 ($2,300 per acre × 79.767 acres), and the fair market value of the remainder was $49,376 ($3,700 per acre × 13.345 acres).

Notwithstanding the trial court's decision to admit the testimony of Moody and Bernard, the Court ultimately provided the jury with a legally correct jury instruction proposed by the Town as follows:

> The testimony suggests the existence of a certain amount of timber on the Hughes property on the date of the taking, and that this timber had some value. In determining the fair market value of the property, you may take into consideration all the factors you conclude affected the fair market value of this property on the date of the taking consistent with my other instructions. If you are persuaded that the existence of the timber on this property affected the market value, you may take this into consideration in your determination of the fair market value of the property. However, you may not add to the fair market value of this property the sales value of the timber that might have been or could have been removed from the property.

The jury's verdict of $323,073 was within $2000 of Moody's just compensation calculation of $325,000 (*i.e.*, $358,500 for the entire tract less $33,500 for the remainder). In contrast, the verdict was $139,609 greater than Leatherman's just compensation calculation. His just compensation calculation was $183,464 for the tract taken, which is greater than his calculation of the difference between the value of the entire tract and the value of the remainder at $183,404 (*i.e.*, $232,780 for the entire tract less $49,376 for the remainder).

On appeal, the Town would contend that Moody's and Bernard's testimony about the separate value of the timber on Hughes' property violated the so-called "unit rule" of valuation, which thus far has not been addressed in any appellate decision in the instant jurisdiction but has been recognized in the majority of other jurisdictions. Under this rule, in a condemnation case, an expert may not testify to the fair market value of timber or any other substance or commodity on the land and then add that value to the fair market value of the land itself as additional compensation for the taking. That is, the land must be valued as a whole, and not as the sum total of the values of different components or features of the land. Numerous cases in other jurisdictions have held that the admission of testimony that violates the rule constitutes reversible error and mandates a new trial. Moreover, Bernard's valuation of the timber was neither based on the time of the taking nor based on "a reasonable degree of professional certainty" as is required by the rules of evidence.

The Town contends that had Moody (and Bernard) not been permitted to testify to the separate value of the timber on the property in arriving at the property's value, Moody's ultimate just compensation calculation would have been based on $2,500 per acre. This would have established a value for the tract taken at $199,418 ($2,500 × 79.767 acres), a value for the entire tract at $232,780 ($2,500 × 93.112), and a value for the remainder at $33,362 ($2,500 × 13.345). Just compensation would then have been $199,418, or only about $16,000 more than Leatherman's just compensation calculation of $183,464.

On the other hand, Hughes would argue on appeal that (1) the unit rule of valuation has not been recognized in the instant jurisdiction; (2) even if the State Court of Appeals were to recognize that rule, Moody's consideration of the value of the timber on the property was limited to merely making an upward "adjustment" to the value of Hughes' property in light of the fact that it contained merchantable timber and therefore was more valuable than any of the twelve comparable sales Moody relied upon; (3) even though Bernard's appraisals of the timber were conducted in YR-4 and were not to "a reasonable degree of professional certainty," his testimony was not in admissible *per se* and the judge had broad discretion to admit it and allow the jury to accord it whatever weight the jury chose to give it; and (4) even if the trial judge erred in admitting Moody's and Bernard's testimony about the separate value of the timber, the error was harmless and thus "probably did not influence the verdict" under the applicable harmless error standard in light of the correct jury instruction that the judge gave to the jury about the extent to which the value of the timber could be considered in determining the fair market value of the property for just compensation purposes.

(Other general legal considerations about condemnation cases are found at §6.10 of the main text.)

* * *

(6) Joseph v. Peters (Medical Malpractice)

Matthew Joseph, 23 years old, filed a medical malpractice action against his podiatric physician, Dr. Andrew Peters, alleging medical negligence and an additional cause of action for battery. Prior to treatment, Joseph was an avid amateur triathlete who showed considerable promise in his sport. As a triathlete, he competed in events that combine swimming, bicycling, and running.

Joseph sought medical care from Dr. Peters on two occasions for treatment of acute pain at the insertion of the achilles tendon on the back of the right heel. Initial conservative treatment prescribed by Dr. Peters provided Joseph little, if any, relief. Treatment at Joseph's second office visit consisted of a steroid injection adjacent to the tendon insertion at the back of Joseph's right heel, and the application of an ambulatory, below the knee, fiberglass cast.

Feeling better one week after this treatment, Joseph removed the cast at home in order to resume his triathlon-training program. During the first training session after removing the cast, Joseph sustained a rupture of the achilles tendon that required surgical repair and several months of physical therapy and rehabilitation. Despite the surgery and subsequent physical therapy, Joseph continues to experience pain and limitation in his right leg. Physicians that have recently evaluated Joseph agree that he has a 15% permanent disability of the right leg and, as such, he will be unable to competitively compete in future triathlons.

Injection of steroid near the achilles tendon is a controversial treatment. In his complaint, Joseph seeks $20,000 for the cost of surgery and therapy following tendon rupture, $10,000 for lost income, $400,000 for past, present and future pain and suffering, and $250,000 in punitive damages. Dr. Peters' medical malpractice limits are $1,000,000.

* * *

(7) Kegnim v. Drake (Automobile Personal Injury)

Paul Kegnim, 28 years old, and Mary Kegnim, 26 years old, were married shortly after they graduated from high school. Both are intelligent but pursued no further schooling after high school. They have no children and live in a modest apartment. Throughout their marriage, they have made just enough money to make ends meet.

On June 1 YR-4, at dusk, Mary was driving Paul home from his work in their old pick-up truck. As Mary was driving north on Highway 54 (a two-lane road) and came upon the intersection of Highway 54 and Elm Street, she saw two cars that had apparently been involved in an accident and were partially blocking the intersection. She slowed her truck and, as the light at the intersection was green for the cars traveling on Highway 54, began to slowly turn to the right with the intention of going around the two cars in the intersection and continuing to proceed north on Highway 54. However, just as she turned to the right, her pick-up truck was struck from behind at approximately 15 m.p.h. by a sport utility vehicle owned and operated by Don Drake who was driving home on Highway 54 after work. The rear brake lights and turn-signal lights on Mary's truck were not working at the time, but these defects do not constitute negligence *per se* in the applicable jurisdiction. The impact broke the tailgate on Mary's truck and moderately damaged the front bumper on Don's vehicle.

Mary, Paul, and Don were all wearing their seatbelts. Although each of them was somewhat "shaken up" at the time of impact, none of them sought medical treatment that evening. The police officer who investigated the accident issued a citation to Mary for "improper vehicle equipment" for the non-working rear brake lights and turn-signal lights, and a citation to Don for "failure to reduce speed to avoid an accident" when he failed to slow down and rear-ended Mary's truck. Mary and Don paid off the fines for these traffic violations without having to make any court appearance.

Since YR-8, and continuing through the time of the accident, Paul was employed in the maintenance department at a local manufacturing plant, where he had health insurance for himself and his wife that essentially covered all medical bills except for chiropractic bills and nonprescription medications. He also had a life insurance policy through his employer that would pay Mary $150,000 upon his death. Paul's gross salary in YR-4 was $36,000 per year. Mary was not working at the time of the accident, but she had periodically worked as a cashier in a grocery store and had been actively looking for a full-time job as a cashier at which she could earn about $24,000 gross per year.

In YR-6, Paul had a kidney transplant. As a result, he has monthly checkups and takes medications to prevent kidney rejection at a total cost of $200 per month. These checkups and the monthly medical expenses are ongoing. Mary's only relevant medical history is that she severely dislocated her left knee about one year before the accident. She underwent physical therapy for that knee injury and says that, just before the automobile accident, her knee was "basically back to normal."

On the morning after the accident, Mary and Paul went to Rex Hospital because both were experiencing significant soreness. In addition, Mary's left knee was aching to the point that it was difficult for her to walk. Both were initially diagnosed with "cervical lumbar strain and sprain" and referred to physical therapy. Mary's medical record from Rex Hospital on the day after the accident also noted that she had pain in her left knee.

Thereafter, from June 1, YR-4 to the end of YR-1, Mary and Paul received extensive and fairly regular medical treatment from a variety of health-care providers. Both are still currently receiving periodic treatment, but medical records and bills after the end of YR-1 have not yet been obtained. A summary of the existing medical bills for Mary and Paul are as follows:

Health-care Provider	Mary	Paul
Rex Hospital	$6,000	$7,500
Orient Acupuncture Clinic	$400	$400
Dix Hospital	$700	$1,500
Tri-County Orthopedics, P.A.	$500	$800
Physical Therapy, Inc.	$2,000	$3,000
Rogers Chiropractic	$2,200	$2,200
	$11,800	**$15,400**

Mary's medical reports variously describe her as having anxiety; depression; muscle tension; muscle spasms of her back, shoulder, and neck; muscle strain; myofacial pain; chronic fatigue; chronic back syndrome; long-term headaches; left arm pain; and chronic left knee pain. Dr. Wu at Rex Hospital has given her a 5% permanent partial impairment rating to her back, and Dr. Jones at Dix Hospital has given her a 20% permanent partial impairment rating to her left knee. All x-rays and MRI tests were negative. Both doctors have also diagnosed Mary as suffering from "fibromyalgia"—a condition represented by chronic pains, spasms, stiffness, and fatigue in the back, neck, shoulder region, arms, hands, knees, hips, legs, and feet, also accompanied by anxiety, headaches, and sleep disturbance. One of Dr. Jones' medical reports expressly states that all of Mary's medical problems are directly attributable to the trauma of the automobile accident.

Paul's medical reports variously describe him as having chronic back pain; myofacial pain syndrome; muscle spasms in the back and neck; rib pain; shoulder pain; swelling and pain in the left ankle; constant aching; limited spinal mobility; and significant lumbar facet pain. Drs. Wu and Jones have also diagnosed Paul with "fibromylagia related to auto accident and not in any way related to kidney transplant or renal disease." One of Dr. Jones' medical reports states that "I feel the patient is 100% disabled from his occupation due to accident, and this is permanent." All x-rays were negative, but an MRI showed "minimal disc protrusion central and slightly to the left, T8–9 and T9–10 level."

Paul worked half time for one week after the accident, and he took off the remaining three weeks in June YR-4 by using up his accumulated vacation and sick-leave time. He had hoped that he could return to full-time work on July 1, YR-4, but his persistent neck and back pain prevented him from doing so. Consequently, he was placed on temporary leave from his work (without pay) from July 1, YR-4 to the end of December, YR-4, and ultimately was terminated from his job effective January 1, YR-3. By March 1, YR-3, Paul's health insurance coverage had lapsed and his life insurance policy was cancelled because he was unable to afford the monthly payments. Since that time, he and Mary have had no health insurance and he has had no life insurance. Mary has not worked since the accident. From April 1, YR-3 to the present, Mary and Paul have been living on monthly social security disability payments.

On May 1, YR-1, Mary and Paul filed a personal injury action against Don. Don's answer to the Complaint denied any negligence on his part and alleged that Mary was contributorily negligent. (The applicable jurisdiction is a "pure contributory negligence" state, which means that contributory negligence on the part of a claimant—however slight—bars any recovery for the claimant as a matter of law). In addition, Don filed a counterclaim against Mary, alleging that her negligence in the accident proximately caused him to incur medical expenses in the amount of $200 and pain and suffering.

Mary, Paul, and Don have each been deposed, and the parties have engaged in other discovery. Don has received a copy of all of Mary's and Paul's medical records and bills through the end of YR-1, along with pertinent lost-wages information regarding Paul. Mary and Paul have received a synopsis of a report from Dr. Joel Smith who Don intends to call as a medical expert at trial. In this report, Dr. Smith opines that after reviewing the medical reports and bills for Mary and Paul: (1) Mary was not injured in the accident except for minor aches and pains that should have resolved within one week and for which reasonable medical expenses should not have exceeded $500; (2) Paul sustained only a relatively minor whiplash injury for which reasonable medical expenses should not have exceeded $2,000; and (3) fibromyalgia is essentially a fictitious medical condition which, to the extent it exists at all, exists "only in a patient's mind."

Discovery also revealed that Don had one doctor's visit on the day after the accident for which he paid $200, and his whiplash injury resolved in a few days. Don incurred no lost wages through his full-time employment as an Emergency Medical Technician and ambulance driver. His automobile liability insurance policy limits are $50,000 for each person, and $100,000 total for each accident. He has no personal assets to pay a judgment in excess of $100,000. The same automobile liability insurance carrier insures Mary, Paul, and Don. Property damage is not an issue.

* * *

(8) Lowe v. Interstate Feed Cooperative, Inc. (Wrongful Employment Discharge)

Les Lowe is now 29 years old. After completing high school at age 18, he took a job with Interstate Feed Cooperative, Inc., where he worked until he was terminated on January 14, YR-1. By all accounts, he was a "satisfactory" employee throughout his approximately 10 years of employment with Interstate Feed.

Interstate Feed is a manufacturer and supplier of feed and fertilizer for commercial farmers. It has approximately 30 plants throughout the country, including the plant where Lowe worked in the State of Caldonia. As a "Cooperative," the company is owned by the thousands of commercial farmers nationwide who regularly buy their feed and fertilizer from it. The company is run by a Board of Directors which is elected by the farmers, and none of the employees of the company (except for the Chairman of the Board of Directors) is under a written contract of employment for a specified term. That is, all employees of the company are "employees at will"—which means that they may be terminated with or without cause and at any time, except that no employee may be terminated in violation of certain public policies declared by the State of Caldonia.

In Caldonia, it is a violation of public policy for any employer to discharge or terminate any employee in retaliation for that employee's testimony at a judicial or quasi-judicial proceeding, such as a proceeding to determine whether another worker who is terminated from his job or otherwise leaves his job is entitled to State unemployment benefits. For example, even in the case of an "at will" employee, if an employer fires such an employee in retaliation for his testimony against the employer at a Caldonia Employment Security Commission (ESC) hearing to determine whether another employee of the employer is entitled to unemployment benefits, the employee who is terminated in retaliation for his testimony is accorded a cause of action for "wrongful discharge." Under this cause of action (1) the employee claiming wrongful discharge bears the burden of proving that his testimony at the Employment Security Commission hearing was "a substantial factor" in the employer's decision to terminate him; (2) the employer bears the burden of proving (as a complete defense) that the employer would have terminated the employee even if the employee had not testified at the hearing; and (3) only if the jury finds in favor of the employee on both issues (1) and (2), may the jury award to the employee "actual damages" he sustained (*i.e.*, that amount of money necessary to place him in the same economic position in which he would have been had the wrongful discharge not occurred).

When Lowe first began working for Interstate Feed, he worked in the Feed Manufacturing Department of the plant. In September of YR-3, he was transferred to a newly created department called the Feed Bin Repair (FBR) Department in which he held the title of Supervisor. This Department, which did not exist at any other plants owned by Interstate Feed, was an experimental project. Employees in the FBR Department installed, maintained, and repaired large metal feed bins at no cost to farmers who purchased the bins from Interstate Feed to store feed for their livestock. According to Lowe, Russ Reese who was the Plant Manager for Interstate Feed in Caldonia in YR-3, told Lowe that if the project was unsuccessful, Lowe would be transferred back to the Feed Manufacturing Department.

In January of YR-2, Gary Huttle, who had not previously worked at the Caldonia Plant, replaced Reese as the Plant's new manager. At that time there were, in addition to Lowe, two other employees in the FBR Department. These employees were Thad Archer (an elderly gentleman who essentially did odd jobs in the Department and was not actively engaged in the rigorous labor involved in installing and repairing feed bins), and Henry Sowler. On at least three occasions between January and November, YR-2, Huttle told all three employees that the FBR Department would have to be shut down if it did not become profitable.

In late November, YR-2, Randy Barker, a long-time employee in the Feed Manufacturing Department at the plant, tendered his resignation from Interstate Feed. Shortly thereafter, he filed a claim for unemployment benefits with the Caldonia ESC. To be eligible for unemployment benefits, Barker had to prove to the ESC that he did not voluntarily resign, but was essentially forced to resign due to unfair or intolerable working conditions imposed upon him by Interstate Feed.

In connection with his hearing before the ESC, Barker subpoenaed Lowe and two other employees at the Plant, Wayne Dolely and Tom Teeter, to testify on Barker's behalf. Barker's hearing with the ESC was scheduled for January 7, YR-1. The day before (January 6, YR-1), Huttle summoned Lowe to Huttle's office and said to Lowe in a brief, private conversation: "Don't let Randy Barker get you into any trouble." Lowe interpreted this remark as an effort on Huttle's part to induce Lowe to ignore the subpoena and not attend the hearing, or otherwise to testify in favor of Interstate Feed at the hearing. However, Lowe said nothing to Huttle or anyone else about Lowe's interpretation of Huttle's remark, and Lowe simply left Huttle's office after the remark was made.

The next day (January 7, YR-1), Lowe, along with Dolely and Teeter, showed up at the ESC hearing as commanded by Barker's subpoena. Lowe testified that Barker was a "first-rate employee," and that in Lowe's opinion Barker was forced to resign because Huttle imposed various excessive and unreasonable working conditions and demands upon Barker. Lowe left the hearing immediately after his testimony and did not hear the testimony of any other witnesses. The other witnesses who testified were Dolely, Teeter, and Huttle. At the conclusion of the hearing, the ESC Judge ruled that Barker was ineligible for unemployment benefits because he had voluntarily resigned and had not carried his burden of proof to show that Interstate Feed had essentially forced him to resign.

On January 10, YR-1, Henry Sowler abruptly resigned from the FBR Department. On January 14, YR-1, Huttle told Lowe and Thad Archer that in light of Sowler's resignation and the lack of profitability of the FBR Department, "higher management" at Interstate Feed had decided to close down the Department, and both Lowe's and Archer's jobs would be terminated effective the next day (January 15, YR-1). Lowe asked Huttle whether Lowe could be transferred back to the Feed Manufacturing Department (as Reese had promised), but Huttle told Lowe that there were no other current openings at the Plant. Lowe and Archer were given two-weeks severance pay. Archer did not ask for any transfer and decided to retire.

On March 15, YR-1, Lowe filed an administrative complaint with the Caldonia Department of Labor's Workplace Retaliatory Discrimination Division (WRDD), alleging that he was wrongfully discharged by Interstate Feed in retaliation for his testimony for Barker at the ESC hearing. The WRDD conducted an investigation but took no action in the case in light of Interstate Feed's claim that Lowe's job was terminated when the FBR Department was closed down for lack of profitability. On November 1, YR-1, as required by statute, the WRDD issued Lowe a "right to sue letter" which permitted him to file, if he wished, a lawsuit against Interstate Feed for wrongful discharge. This "right to sue letter" neither expressly nor impliedly indicated any opinion by the WRDD about the merits of Lowe's claim.

On December 1, YR-1, Lowe's attorney wrote to counsel for Interstate Feed, offering to discuss the possibility of resolving the case without litigation. The letter pointed out that (1) at the time Lowe was terminated, he was making $48,000 gross per year with Interstate Feed; (2) from January 15, YR-1 to the end of March, YR-1, Lowe had no income (other than the two-weeks severance pay which totaled approximately $2,000); (3) from April 1, YR-1 to the end of September, YR-1, Lowe received unemployment benefits of $1000 per month; and (4) since October 1, YR-1, Lowe has been working for a construction company at an approximate gross salary of $2,000 per month. The letter included appropriate documentation verifying these factual assertions.

* * *

(9) Mann v. Parsons University Medical Center (Nursing Malpractice)

Amy Mann is a 76-year-old widow of modest means. She is a retired elementary school teacher and spends most of her time engaged in various civic and charitable organizations.

Parsons University Medical Center is a renowned medical research institution at Parsons University. Nearly all of the medical research conducted at the Center is federally funded through grants given out by the National Institutes of Health (NIH). As a condition to receiving federal grants from NIH, the Center must comply with various safety and reporting procedures established by the Office for Protection from Research Risks (OPRR) of NIH. The purpose of these safety and reporting procedures is to ensure that persons who participate in clinical research trials are not negligently exposed to dangers that may harm them. Participants in clinical research trials at the Center are either patients at the Center's Hospital or volunteers who are paid a modest fee for participating in a research study.

On July 2, YR-2, Ms. Mann volunteered to participate in a research study conducted by the Mental Health Clinical Research Section for Late Life Depression at Parsons University Medical Center. She was not a patient at the Center and was in excellent physical and mental health. On the same day, in connection with the study, she underwent an MRI, which she had never had before. A young nurse inserted earplugs into Ms. Mann's ears; and even though Ms. Mann told the nurse that the ear plugs were not blocking out any sound, the nurse took no steps to ensure that the plugs were properly inserted to protect against the noise from the MRI. The MRI lasted one hour.

During the MRI, Ms. Mann experienced extreme noise from the machine, but she assumed that the procedure was safe. Within hours after the procedure, she began experiencing a continuous high-pitched ringing and humming sound in her ears, a symptom she had never experienced before. During the next few days, the ringing did not go away, and she therefore reported her symptoms and what had happened to Mr. Bobby Barnes, the research-study coordinator. Mr. Barnes told her that he had been concerned about the competence of the nurse on several occasions, and Ms. Mann later learned that Ms. Simone Poole, another volunteer in the study, had also complained to Barnes that the nurse apparently did not know how to properly insert the earplugs.

On July 9, YR-2, Ms. Mann consulted Drs. Steve Gatch and Harold Tofler at Tryon Hospital. They diagnosed her with "tinnitus secondary to noise exposure during [the] MRI at Parsons Medical Center." (Tinnitus is a persistent ringing, whistling, or humming sound in the ears). Follow-up examinations by Dr. Wendell York on July 24, YR-2 and Dr. Harold Pointer on September 21, YR-2 revealed that her tinnitus had not improved.

In March, YR-1, Ms. Mann consulted three physicians to obtain a final diagnosis and prognosis about her chronic tinnitus. Dr. Paula Mosley, Dr. Wendell York, and Dr. Carrie Jones all now confirm that her tinnitus is permanent. Each of them is of the opinion that the cause of Ms. Mann's condition stems solely from the MRI she received at the Center when she was provided inadequate hearing protection during the procedure.

Ms. Mann's medical bills total $900.00. According to standard mortality statistics, Ms. Mann has a remaining life expectancy of 10.6 years. The Center paid her a total of $100 for the four hours during which she participated in the clinical study.

* * *

(10) Martel v. Simba (Unfair Debt Collection)

This case involves a dispute between the Martel family and the Simba Rental Corporation. Although no complaint has been filed yet, the attorneys for the opposing sides have already discussed the case and are familiar with each other's positions.

On July 9, YR-2, Cindy and Mark Martel went to Simba Rental to rent a television. They signed one of Simba's standard "rental with option to buy" contracts for a 19" color T.V. The contract required weekly payments of $16.00 for 78 weeks. If the Martels wanted to purchase this T.V. at the end of the rental period, they could do so for a final payment of $55.00. Thus, total payments to purchase were $1,303.00. The contract had a blank for Simba to fill in the "cash price," but this was not completed. The T.V. the Martels acquired from Simba regularly costs about $350.00 at national retail stores. At furniture stores that cater to low-income customers who purchase by installment sales contracts, similar sets frequently cost about $600.00.

Things proceeded smoothly for almost a year, during which the Martels made a total of 50 payments at $16.00 each. Then, Simba did not receive two $16.00 payments from the Martels. Simba sent out one of its employees, Richard Johnson, to confer with the Martels. Johnson, who is 6'5" tall and weighs 240 lbs., went to the Martels' home on a Monday afternoon. Mr. Martel was not home. Ms. Martel, who is 5 feet tall and weighs 100 lbs., told Johnson that she was sure her husband had sent the payments, but if he hadn't, they would send them at once.

On Thursday, after the mail revealed no payment from the Martels, Johnson went back to the Martels' home. What exactly happened then is in dispute, but everyone agrees that Johnson entered the house and took the T.V.

Ms. Martel says that on the Monday afternoon when Johnson first went to the Martels' home, Johnson told her that if the Martels didn't pay, he would be back to take the television. She told him that her husband left for work at 3:00

p.m., and that if Johnson came back, he would have to come before 3:00 p.m. so he could talk to her husband. She said Johnson ended the conversation by repeating that if he had to come back, he wouldn't leave without the T.V. She says Johnson came back to her house after 3:00 p.m. on Thursday. She was there with her three-year-old son and a neighbor's child. Johnson knocked on the door, and her son went to the door and told her who was there. She says that the knocking then continued for at least five minutes before she opened the door and told Johnson to leave. He refused to leave. She closed the door and he started banging on the door again. Finally, she opened the door a little to tell him to leave. She then backed away from the door because she thought he was going to push her out of the way. She kept telling him to leave. He came in and unplugged the television and took it with him.

Ms. Martel was so upset that she called her husband to come home from work. When Mr. Martel got home, he discovered that the door had come away from the hinges in two places. The Martels called the police. The investigating officer, after talking to the Martels, went to the Simba office to talk to Johnson.

Johnson told the officer that when Johnson went to the Martels' house on Thursday, he knocked on the door just two or three times before a child came to the door. When a minute passed with nothing else happening, he knocked once more, waited, then knocked steadily for three or four minutes. When Ms. Martel finally opened the door, he told her that he had to take the T.V. She told him to come back when her husband was home, but he told her he couldn't wait. After a few minutes of discussion in this vein, she stepped away from the door, leaving it open. Johnson took this to mean that it was okay with her for him to enter. He went in, she again told him to leave, and he picked up the T.V. and left.

The police officer arrested Johnson and charged him with misdemeanor trespass, felony larceny, and misdemeanor malicious destruction of property. A criminal trespass is the entering upon the premises of another by one who knows that he is not authorized to do so, as where he enters in defiance of an order not to enter the premises. Felony larceny is the trespassory taking and carrying away of the personal property of another (where the property has a fair market value in excess of $1,000) with the intent to permanently deprive the possessor of the property. The offense occurs so long as the trespassory taking of the personal property is from the *possession* of another; ownership is not the key. The charges have come up for trial on three occasions but have been postponed each time at the defendant's request.

The Martels are considering suing for:

1. Intentional infliction of emotional distress
2. Damage to their door
3. Trespass
4. Unfair debt collection
5. Violation of Chapter 25A of the Retail Installment Sales Act (RISA).

The elements of the tort of intentional infliction of emotional distress are (1) extreme and outrageous conduct, (2) which is intended to cause and does cause (3) severe emotional distress. The term "severe emotional distress" means "any emotional or nervous disorder such as, for example, neurosis, psychosis, chronic depression, phobia, or any other type of severe and disabling emotional or mental condition which may be generally recognized and diagnosed by professionals trained to do so."

Unfair Debt Collection: If the Martels can show that in collecting the debt Mr. Johnson "used or threatened to use violence or any illegal means to cause harm to the person, reputation or property of any person" in violation of the Unfair Debt Collection Act, they would be entitled to (1) an automatic civil penalty of $2,000, (2) actual damages (*e.g.*, for damage to the door), (3) compensatory damages (*e.g.* for any intentional infliction of emotional distress), (4) at least nominal damages (*e.g.*, for any trespass), and (5) reasonable attorney's fees.

Violation of Chapter 25A of the Retail Installment Sales Act (RISA): If the contract between Simba and the Martels is found to be a "consumer credit sale" contract as opposed to a mere "rental" contract, RISA would apply to the contract. *See* General Statute Sec. 25A-2 below. Under the Retail Installment Sales Act (RISA), "[t]he finance charge for a consumer credit installment sales contract may not exceed: (1) Twenty-four percent (24%) per annum where the amount financed is less than one thousand five hundred dollars ($1,500)." In this case, if RISA applies, the "amount financed" for the Martels' television set would be $600.00 given that, at stores that cater to low-income customers who purchase by installment sales contracts, similar sets cost approximately $600.00. According to interest tables, if the contract is in fact a "consumer credit sale" of a television, and the cost of the item was $600.00, the finance charge for 18 months was well over the 24% permitted under the statute. That is, a 24% finance charge on a $600.00 item for 18 months is $120.38, but the

Martels were paying a finance charge of $648.00 (*i.e.*, $16.00 × 78 weeks = $1,248 ($1248-$600 = $648). The statutory penalty permitted for a violation of the Retail Installment Sales Act is given in Section 25A-44 below. As stated earlier, the Martels have made a total of 50 payments of $16.00 each.

§25A-2 "Consumer credit sale" defined.

A "consumer credit sale" is a sale of goods or services in which:

(1) The seller is one who in the ordinary course of business regularly extends or arranges for the extension of consumer credit, or offers to extend or arrange for the extension of such credit,

(2) The buyer is a natural person,

(3) The goods or services are purchased primarily for a personal, family, household or agricultural purpose,

(4) Either the debt representing the price of the goods or services is payable in installments or a finance charge is imposed, and

(5) The amount financed does not exceed twenty-five thousand dollars ($25,000).

"Sale" includes but is not limited to any contract in the form of a bailment or lease if the bailee or lessee contracts to pay as compensation for use a sum substantially equivalent to or in excess of the aggregate value of the goods and services involved, and it is agreed that the bailee or lessee will become, or for no other or for a nominal consideration, has the option to become, the owner of the goods and services upon compliance with his obligations under such contract.

§25A-44 Remedies and penalties.

The following remedies shall apply to consumer credit sales:

(1) In the event that a consumer credit sale contract requires the payment of a finance charge not more than two times in excess of that permitted by this Chapter, the seller or an assignee of the seller shall not be permitted to recover any finance charge under that contract and, in addition, the seller shall be liable to the buyer in an amount that is two times the amount of any finance charge that has been re-

ceived by the seller, plus reasonable attorney's fees incurred by the buyer as determined by the court. However, if the requirement of an excess charge results from an accidental or good faith error, the seller shall be liable only for the amount by which the finance charge exceeds the rates permitted by this Chapter.

(2) In the event that a consumer credit sale contract requires the payment of a finance charge more than two times that permitted by this Chapter, the contract shall be void. The buyer may, at his option, retain without any liability any goods delivered under such a contract and the seller or an assignee of the rights shall not be entitled to recover anything under such contract.

(3) Any buyer injured by any violation of this Act may bring an action for recovery of damages, including reasonable attorney's fees.

* * *

(11) Monolith v. Sat-Lith[1] (Breach of Covenant Not to Compete)

Monolith, Inc. is a New York-based corporation with headquarters in White Plains, New York. Monolith is engaged in the manufacture, sale, and servicing of sophisticated, high technology lithographic/printing equipment, including computer-controlled laser printing for books, newspapers and magazines. C. Icon started the company in YR-30. It became a publicly held corporation in YR-20, but Icon has remained as President and CEO. Monolith has shown phenomenal growth since YR-20 and now has assets exceeding $750 million.

B. Clubb, a Texan, joined Monolith as an assistant design engineer in Monolith's RTP (Research Triangle Park, North Carolina) office in YR-25. Clubb demonstrated outstanding design expertise and an adroit ability to learn the finest details about the printing and lithographic business. Clubb designed Monolith's new plant that opened in Mebane, North Carolina in YR-19 and was made plant manager.

1. This role play was developed by Professors Neil Vidmar and Diane Dimont of Duke Law School and Professor David Cohen of the University of Texas (Austin) School of Law, and is reproduced in this book with their permission.

In YR-15, Monolith's research staff produced a technological breakthrough that permitted the use of long-distance phone lines that allowed point-source lithography printing from any location in the country. The process is unique and has a number of speed and cost benefits that promised to move Monolith to the forefront of U.S. companies in the field. Projections were that the new technology might eventually be responsible for more than fifty-percent of Monolith's profits. However, the process needed further development and application before it could bear fruit.

In YR-13, Clubb moved back to Texas to a new Monolith plant where the still-secret process could be further developed, tested, and marketed. Icon considered the project his/her personal project and Monolith has spent millions of dollars on the research and development of technology, marketing, and materials that will allow efficient trouble shooting and maintenance of production equipment.

However, Clubb recently tendered his/her resignation and gave Monolith two weeks notice. In a phone call to Icon, Clubb said s/he had just started an independent lithographic/printing company, Sat-Lith, that will use a newly developed process that relies on satellites rather than long-distance phone lines. Clubb developed the idea for the satellite technology after meeting N. Mallott, a design engineer. Clubb expressed regrets to Icon over leaving Monolith but said that s/he felt constrained at Monolith, particularly over Icon's commitment to the phone line technology. Clubb told Icon that s/he believed satellites are the technology of the future and that once the process is fully developed it will propel Sat-Lith to the front of the field.

Icon became very angry during the conversation and threatened Clubb with a lawsuit. Icon reminded Clubb that Clubb's contract of employment with Monolith contained a "non- competition" clause, a covenant forbidding Clubb to utilize the proprietary materials of Monolith gained through employment with Monolith and forbidding employment with a competing business for two years after termination of employment with Monolith. Angry words on the part of both Clubb and Icon were exchanged before Clubb hung up.

Icon then learned through an informant that about six-weeks ago, Clubb made copies of what Clubb claims are "personal papers", including training and service manuals, technical specifications, and design and marketing materials. In fact, all of the materials came from Monolith's files. An independent company copied fifteen boxes of files of original documents. The originals were returned to the Texas Monolith plant. The copies were shipped to the Sat-Lith office outside Houston. Upon learning this information, Icon placed a call to Clubb and threatened a legal injunction to make Clubb return the copies.

Both Icon and Clubb have retained legal counsel on the matter but no lawsuit has been filed. Sat-Lith's attorney, Auston, called Monolith's attorney, Wrangle, to see if the dispute can be settled without a lawsuit. Icon reluctantly agreed. A meeting has been set up between Icon and Clubb.

The relevant parts of the Contract of Employment signed by Clubb in YR-12 (after s/he had re-established domicile in Texas) are as follows:

> (1) Whereas, Employee, in consideration of the agreements herein contained and the compensation to be paid to Employee, expressly agrees that Employee will not, for a period of twenty-four (24) months after termination of employment hereunder for any reason whatsoever, directly or indirectly as Employer, Employee, Stockholder or in any other capacity whatsoever, solicit, serve or cater to or engage in, assist, be interested in or be connected with any other form of corporation in the same or similar business of Employer soliciting, serving or catering to any of the customers served by Employee or by any other employee of Employer during the term of Employee's employment.
>
> (2) Employee's employment is subject to termination at any time by Employer Monolith, Inc.
>
> (3) Employee... expressly agrees upon employment to maintain as confidential and proprietary all material—service manuals, diagrams, schematics, and other compilations—specifically designated as confidential and proprietary. Upon termination of employment with Monolith, Employee expressly agrees to return to Monolith all property then in Employee's possession... [and] not retain any copies or reproductions of materials entrusted to Employee during period of employment.
>
> (4) New York law shall govern the interpretation and enforcement of this contract.

[The contract also included provisions giving Clubb a promotion and raise in salary].

Decisions in the following cases are relevant to consider: Travel Masters, Inc., et. al. v. Star Tours, Inc., 827 S.W.2d 830 (Tex. 1991); Picker International, Inc. v. Blanton, 756 F. Supp 971 (D. 1990); Desantis, et. al. v. Wackenhut Corp., 793 S.W.2d 670 (Tex. 1990); Light v. Centel Cellular Co. of Texas, 883 S.W.2d 642 (Tex. 1994).

* * *

(12) Seaver v. Excellent Pet Foods Co.[2] (Breach of Distributorship Agreement)

Excellent Pet Foods Co. is a privately owned company run by its owner and president, Bill Clowson from its headquarters in Atlanta, Georgia. The company manufactures pet foods for dogs, cats, fish, birds, and other domestic animals. It sells its dog food under the brand name Happy Pet.

Excellent has been successfully selling its Happy Pet dog foods throughout the southeastern United States for many years. Happy Pet is distributed directly by the Company through a series of regional and district warehouses.

Happy Pet is a premium dog food whose price tends toward the higher end of the range of dog food prices. Competition for shelf space in the dog food business is fierce. As a product, Happy Pet differentiates itself from its competitors on the basis that its ingredients and formula provide a dog food that is more easily digested, especially good for dogs with food allergies, and breeds that tend to have flatulence. Happy Pet dog foods include specially blended foods for puppies, adults, and older dogs, as well as dogs with sensitive skin.

Bill has decided to expand sales of Happy Pet north into all of the United States east of the Mississippi River. He has no capital to finance the expansion, so he intends to break with company tradition and policy and use independent local dealers to distribute his dog food. Excellent has hired Jim Anderson as its new marketing director to head up this expansion. Jim's principle experience is with companies that distribute their products through independent dealers.

Bob Seaver was a salesman/truck driver for the distributor of another dog food. This distributor operates from Wheeling, West Virginia in a large territory that includes southeastern Ohio, northern West Virginia, and eastern Pennsylvania. Bob lives in Columbus, Ohio and runs the route that includes Columbus and southeastern Ohio. He has broken down his distribution area into driving routes so that he can call customers and solicit their orders in the afternoon and deliver the dog food the next day. It takes him two weeks to go through his entire route.

Bob is also required to travel on weekends to dog shows and present his employer's dog food at a booth. Bob is familiar with Happy Pet because Excellent also has a booth at dog shows in West Virginia where Happy Pet is distributed. Excellent's contacts have suggested to Jim that Bob is an intelligent,

2. This role play was developed by Richard J. Snider, Esq., and is reproduced in this book with his permission.

ambitious, hard working young man who might be interested in setting up his own pet food distributorship with the right product and some backing. Jim has visited a dog show and arranged to meet Bob.

After several meetings, Jim proposed that Bob become the distributor of Happy Pet for all of southern Ohio, including Columbus, Dayton, Cincinnati, and Marietta. Bob had asked for a territory that included all of Ohio, including the populous industrial cities of Toledo, Cleveland, and Youngstown. Bob argues that Ohio is crisscrossed east and west by Interstates 90, 80, and 70 and north and south by Interstates 71, 75, and 77, making it possible to service the entire state from a single, central location in Columbus.

Jim tells Bob that Excellent has no current plans to expand into northern Ohio for at least the next year. Jim says that if Bob does well in southern Ohio during that time, Excellent may expand his territory to include northern Ohio. These statements are repeated and expanded in a series of letters and meetings between Jim and Bob, and later, in a more general way, at a meeting with Bill Clowson in Atlanta where Jim, Bob, and Bill shake hands on an agreement.

Bob agrees to set up a warehouse in Columbus, Ohio at his own expense from which he will he will distribute Happy Pet in a territory that includes all of Ohio south of Interstate 70 including Columbus. Bob organizes a corporation called Happy Pets of Ohio, Inc. Then, he leases a building and outfits it with proper shelving and materials handling equipment, including a leased forklift truck. Bob also leases a delivery truck. Excellent agrees to supply Bob with its dog food products and to provide a line of credit of $50,000 for the purchase of Happy Pet dog food, personally guaranteed by Bob and his wife. The line of credit is to be reduced $10,000 every six months, beginning one year after the commencement of the agreement.

A month after Bob has quit his job, opened his warehouse, and received his first truckload of dog food, the attached distributorship agreement arrives in the mail. The agreement makes no mention of Bob's option or right of first refusal to expand his territory into northern Ohio. When Bob asks about this, Jim tells Bob that Excellent's attorneys will not permit him to make a forward promise like that, but he reassures Bob that they have a handshake agreement on these terms. Jim reminds Bob that the entire plan was discussed and affirmed with Bill at headquarters just a few weeks ago, and therefore the very highest authority, the owner of the company, approved the deal. Jim tells Bob that he and Bill were roommates in college and have been friends for more than 10 years and that Jim knows that Bill is a man of his word who can be trusted to keep his promises. Jim also says that it would hurt Excellent's entire expansion plan if the company got a reputation for not honoring its commitments. Jim offers to put Bob in touch with other distributors who will tell him how well the company has treated them.

Bob is not sophisticated in these matters and, after what his lawyer charged him to set up his corporation, he decides he cannot afford, after all his other start up expenses, to ask his attorney to look over the distributorship agreement. In addition, he has already quit his job and personally committed himself on the warehouse lease, the fork lift lease, the truck lease, and $50,000 worth of dog food which he has no way to pay for except from the sales of dog food. He decides he has no choice but to sign the agreement without any changes.

Bob's distributorship initially does well. Almost all his old customers whom he knew from his route in southeastern Ohio with the other company agree to try his product. Their initial purchases give him strong cash flow. Encouraged, he hires an experienced salesman-driver from another dog food distributor already driving a route in southwestern Ohio to develop that part of Bob's territory. The new salesman/driver is also able to persuade most of his former customers to carry Happy Pet and again, there are strong initial sales. Bob gives up his route and hires a driver for it so that he can devote all his time to the office.

After the first blush, however, the business begins to deteriorate. Happy Pet sells poorly out of the retail stores. Bob's customers complain that it is an unknown brand and is overpriced. They suggest the company should advertise more and reduce its price. Some of his customers do not reorder, telling Bob that they have limited space to display dog food products and can only carry those that turnover rapidly.

Other customers complain that the new driver does not rotate the product when he makes his deliveries—*i.e.*, by failing to put the new delivery on the bottom and the older product on the top. They also say that sometimes he is a day or two late getting the delivery to the store. In addition, when Bob asks his driver about the sales display materials from Excellent that Bob gave him to use in the stores, Bob learns his driver has not set them up.

Excellent is also not satisfied. Jim keeps pushing Bob to increase sales. When Jim sends an agent to examine Bob's operation and territory, the agent returns with reports that there are complaints from retailers about stale food and late deliveries. Bob answers that this is a temporary problem related to the driver and will be solved as soon as he fires the driver and trains a new one. The agent also reports that he cannot find in the retail stores the sales materials the company has asked Bob to use, including sales brochures and free sample packs.

Bob answers that he has already distributed all the literature and samples the company gave him when he started and that he cannot afford to buy more. Bob complains that no one in Ohio knows the product and asks the company to do some advertising. The company says it has been selling its product well without major advertising for years in its original territory and thinks Bob needs to be a better salesman, or better yet, that he should hire an additional salesman to develop his territory.

To improve his cash flow, Bob begins selling Happy Pet in some cities north of I-70 and outside his territory. Also, to make his sales appear as though they are increasing and to reduce the price he has to pay Excellent for dog food, Bob begins to sell Happy Pet to Happy Pet dealers in West Virginia and Kentucky. As a new dealer, Bob gets a special price. Also, his discount increases based on the volume he sells. The dealers outside Bob's territory get his special price and he keeps the volume discount. All of this, however, proves insufficient because the basic problem is that Happy Pet is a gourmet premium dog food that sells low volumes at high prices. Consequently, Bob begins to distribute another, more modestly priced dog food in his territory without saying anything to Excellent.

Bob's troubles reach a crisis at the end of his first year when Bob is not able to make the first $10,000 repayment on the line of credit note. In fact, Bob has been unable to pay for his deliveries for several weeks, and now owes Excellent more than $100,000, including the original sum borrowed. At about the same time, Bob learns at a dog show that Excellent has set up a separate distributorship in northern Ohio that includes some cities where Bob has distribution. Worse, he learns that this dealer thinks its territory also includes Columbus, Ohio, and that it has been offering Happy Pet there at a price lower than Bob's.

Twenty-two months into the 36-month distributorship agreement, Bob receives a certified letter from Excellent terminating his distributorship immediately, without notice. At a dog show the next weekend, he learns that Excellent has awarded his southern Ohio territory to the new, northern Ohio distributor. In addition, he learns the new Happy Pet distributor in his territory is the salesman/driver who formerly worked for Bob. Worse, it becomes apparent to Bob as he travels his territory that his former salesman/driver must have a copy of Bob's customer list. A secretary overhears him express his concern in a telephone conversation, and then she tells Bob that she saw the driver copying the route books (which show the name of the customer, the decision making buyer at that retailer, and their history of purchases, as well as other proprietary trade information).

Bob consults his attorney. He feels that Excellent breached the distributorship agreement by not providing him adequate support, particularly advertising support. He also thinks Excellent's sales goals were unreasonable causing him to expand too rapidly. He is also upset that the northern Ohio territory was set up without first offering it to him as Excellent had agreed. He is especially angry that Excellent hired his former driver to run the new territory and that his former driver seems to have stolen copies of his route books.

Excellent, of course, says that it had every right to terminate the agreement. Bob was performing poorly, his payment history was laughable, he was distributing outside his territory and he was distributing a competing brand of dog food. That the new dealer is Bob's former driver is mere happenstance. The information he used to contact the stores could be found in any phone book.

Bob's lawyer suggests that both parties attempt to resolve their conflict before starting any litigation. Excellent's lawyer agrees.

The Agreement to distribute Happy Pet dog food that was entered into between Excellent Pet Foods and Bob Seaver for his Company, Happy Pets of Ohio, Inc. was as follows:

AGREEMENT TO DISTRIBUTE HAPPY PET DOG FOOD

THIS AGREEMENT is made at Atlanta, Georgia this 10th day of November, YR-2, by and between Excellent Pet Foods Company of Atlanta Georgia, a Georgia corporation hereinafter referred to as "Seller," and Happy Pets of Ohio, Inc. of Columbus, Ohio, an Ohio corporation hereinafter referred to as "Dealer."

WHEREAS, Seller is in the business of manufacturing and marketing branded pet foods; and Seller desires to grant a distributorship for the sale of Seller's brand of Happy Pet dog food to Dealer and Dealer desires to operate a business to distribute Happy Pet dog food.

NOW, THEREFORE, in consideration of the mutual promises and covenants contained in this Agreement, the parties agree as follows:

1. Appointment: Seller hereby appoints Dealer as the sole and exclusive distributor for the sale of Seller's branded dog food products at wholesale.

2. Territory: The exclusive distributorship shall cover the following territory, to wit: all of that part of the State of Ohio south of Interstate 70 including all of the territory within the city limits of Columbus, Ohio.

Dealer agrees that Dealer will not sell any of Seller's dog food products in any other Territory without the prior written consent of Seller or the exclusive distributor in whose Territory the sale is contemplated.

Seller agrees to notify, in writing, all other distributors of its dog food products that Dealer has the sole and exclusive right to sell such products at wholesale in the Territory.

3. Price: All purchase orders by Dealer shall be on forms furnished by Seller. Seller agrees to exert Seller's best efforts to supply Dealer's needs in the regular course of its business within three (3) days of its receipt of any order. All orders will be shipped freight prepaid to Dealer's business address by the most economical system of transportation selected by Seller.

The purchase price of the goods shall be established by the Seller. The price list currently in force is attached to this Agreement. Seller will give Dealer ten (10) day's advance notice in writing of a change of purchase price.

Dealer shall pay Seller net cash within thirty (30) days from receipt of Seller's invoice or shall be entitled to a five percent (5%) discount for payment within ten (10) days from receipt of Seller's invoice.

Dealer may return any products that are defective within fourteen (14) days of delivery thereof, and Seller shall replace all such defective products at Seller's expense with Dealer's next order.

4. Dealer Representations: Dealer covenants, warrants, and agrees:

Dealer is a corporation duly formed and in good standing in the State of Ohio.

Dealer will use its best efforts to market and sell at wholesale the branded dog food products covered by this Agreement in the territory specified during the term of this Agreement.

Dealer will maintain an inventory of the products at all times adequate to satisfy, for a period of ten (10) days, the demand therefore in the territory covered by this Agreement.

Dealer shall use such advertising material as Seller may, at Seller's option, require and will promote Seller's product in any manner Seller shall deem necessary.

Dealer will not sell products of a similar nature manufactured by the competitors of Seller within the territory or in any place within one hundred (100) miles of the outside boundary of the territory at any time during the term of this Agreement, or for a period of two (2) years after the termination of this Agreement, regardless of the cause of termination.

Dealer shall not at any time, except in performing the responsibilities of this Agreement, divulge, or use for the purposes of Distributor, any confidential or business information relating to the business affairs of Seller.

5. Seller Representations: Seller covenants, warrants, and agrees:

Seller is a corporation duly formed and in good standing in the State of Georgia.

Seller has not granted and will not grant, without prior written consent of Dealer, to any person, entity, or organization, the right to sell or market the products covered by this Agreement in the Territory covered by this Agreement and will not itself or by its employees or agents make any such sales.

Dealer shall have the right to use and, unless otherwise instructed by Seller, shall use the trade name Happy Pet, for the term of this Agreement. Dealer shall obtain necessary licenses, registrations with appropriate governmental authorities, and a telephone listing under the trade name in the territory assigned to Dealer. The trade name registrations including telephone numbers will automatically become the property of, and revert to, Seller on termination of this Agreement.

6. Training and Assistance: Seller shall furnish to Dealer, at Seller's expense, such assistance and instruction as Seller deems necessary or appropriate to assist Dealer in developing its business including not less than six (6) days of field training each year.

Dealer shall agree, and shall cause any associate, to participate in all training programs, seminars, and field training provided by Seller.

Seller shall furnish Dealer without cost all promotional and advertising materials and supplies set forth in the list attached to this Agreement.

Dealer shall obtain prior written approval from Seller of any advertising copy, promotional material, or other written or printed material used by Dealer in promoting sales of Seller's goods and not provided by Seller.

7. Term: The term of this Agreement shall be for three (3) years beginning on the date first written above and subject to the following:

Provided Dealer is not in default in this Agreement, Dealer may elect, by written notice to Seller at least sixty (60) days prior to the end of the original term of this Agreement, to extend this Agreement for one (1) additional year on the same terms and conditions including this right of renewal.

If Dealer is in default in any payment to Seller for a period of thirty (30) days after demand for payment from Seller or if Dealer defaults in performing any of the other terms, conditions, or promises of this Agreement, and continues in default for a period of thirty (30) days after written notice thereof, Seller shall have the right at the expiration of the ten (10) days notice of default, to terminate this Agreement upon giving written notice of the termination at the expiration of the notice period.

On the termination of this Agreement for any reason, Seller shall have the option to repurchase the products then in the possession of Dealer, and available for sale, at prices originally billed to Dealer plus actual freight on the shipment of them to Dealer, and with deductions from monies due or to become due to Marketing Agent under this Agreement. As to any of Marketing Agents products not repurchased by it within ten (10) days of such termination, Dealer shall have the right to dispose of such products in the regular course of its business.

Dealer shall have no right after termination of this Agreement to use the name Happy Pet or any similar name that may confuse or tend to confuse the general public.

8. Miscellaneous: All notices under this Agreement shall be in writing and shall be deemed to have been duly given on the date of service, if served personally on the party to whom notice is to be given.

Any and all claims or controversy that may be attributed to the contractual agreement and are not resolved by mutual agreement of the parties, including breach of agreement, will be settled by arbitration according with established rules utilizing the American Arbitration Association, and then judgment may be entered in a court of law.

If any legal action or other proceeding is brought for the enforcement of this Agreement, or because of an alleged dispute, breach, default, or misrepresentation in connection with any of the provisions of this Agreement, the successful or prevailing party or parties shall be entitled to recover reasonable attorney fees and other costs incurred in that action or proceeding, in addition to any other relief to which it may be entitled.

This Agreement constitutes the entire Agreement between the parties pertaining to the subject matter contained in it and supersedes all prior and contemporaneous agreements, representations, and understandings of the parties. No supplement, modification, or amendment of this Agreement shall be binding unless executed in writing by all the parties to this Agreement. No waiver of any of the provisions of this Agreement shall be deemed or shall constitute a waiver of any other provision, whether or not similar, nor shall any waiver constitute a continuing waiver. No waiver shall be binding unless executed in writing by the party making the waiver.

This Agreement shall be binding on and shall inure to the benefit of the successors and assigns of the parties to this Agreement.

This Agreement shall be governed and construed according to the laws of the State of Georgia.

IN WITNESS WHEREOF, the parties have executed this Agreement at the place and on the date first above written.

* * *

(13) Solomon Clinic v. Carr (Breach of Employment Contract)

The dispute between the parties is represented by the following pleadings:

STATE OF NORTH CAROLINA	:
COUNTY OF DURHAM	: IN THE GENERAL COURT OF JUSTICE
SOLOMON CLINIC, P.A.,	: SUPERIOR COURT DIVISION
Plaintiff,	: YR-0 CVS 00871
v.	:
MOREY J. CARR, M.D.	:COMPLAINT
Defendant.	:

Plaintiff, Solomon Clinic, P.A., through its attorney, complains of the Defendant, Morey J. Carr, M.D., as follows:

PARTIES

1. Plaintiff Solomon Clinic, P.A. ("Solomon Clinic") is a North Carolina Professional Corporation organized under the laws of the State of North Carolina. Solomon Clinic's principal place of business is in Durham, North Carolina.
2. Defendant, Morey J. Carr, M.D. ("Dr. Carr"), is a resident and citizen of the State of North Carolina, residing in Chapel Hill, North Carolina.

JURISDICTION AND VENUE

3. Jurisdiction and venue are proper in this Court pursuant to N.C. Gen. Stat. §1-75.4(5).

FACTUAL ALLEGATIONS

4. In YR-2, Solomon Clinic and Dr. Carr began negotiations for Dr. Carr to work as a plastic surgeon for Solomon Clinic.
5. As a result of these negotiations, on August 29, YR-2, Dr. Carr entered into a written Employment Agreement ("Agreement") with Solomon Clinic to provide plastic surgery services.
6. Dr. Carr signed the Agreement and agreed to abide by its terms. The Agreement was effective on October 1, YR-2.
7. Among other things, the Agreement sets forth the amount and method of calculating Dr. Carr's compensation. The Agreement provides that Dr. Carr shall receive monthly advances based on her estimated net income, which the

Agreement defines as income collected, less direct and indirect expenses and necessary tax withholdings. Any overages or shortages to the estimate are to be reconciled at the fiscal year's end. In pertinent part, the Agreement states the following:

> 3(a) The compensation for Employee [Dr. Carr] shall be determined by a formula based on gross fees collected by Corporation [Solomon Clinic] resulting from professional services personally provided by or attributable to Employee less Corporation's direct and indirect overhead and other costs of rendering such services.... Employee acknowledges that the determination of direct and indirect overhead and other costs among all physicians employed by Corporation requires some judgment and discretion on the part of the Corporation's Board of Directors and its management, and further may be changed or amended from time to time by the Board. All determinations regarding fees, costs and allocations of overhead expenses shall be made by Corporation in accordance with the compensation formula established by Corporation's Board of Directors for physician employees, and all such determinations shall be final and conclusive.

8. The Agreement further describes the calculation and payment of earned compensation at the close of Solomon Clinic's fiscal year, including the offset of advances. In pertinent part, the Agreement provides:

> 3(b) The amount of the monthly advances against compensation shall be subject to review and adjustment at the end of each fiscal year by Corporation, and at other times during the term hereof with the mutual agreement of Employee and Corporation.... In the event that Employee has received advances against compensation in excess of the earned compensation (said difference being hereinafter referred to as a "Negative Balance"), then such Negative Balance shall be reimbursed by Employee to Corporation within 30 days following the notification to Employee by the Corporation of the Negative Balance....
>
> Anything contained herein to the contrary notwithstanding, in the event that Employee's employment with the Corporation shall at any time terminate for any reason, the Employee shall reimburse to the Corporation the Negative Balance within 30 days following the notification to Employee by Corporation of the Negative Balance.

9. The Agreement also provides that Solomon Clinic has the right, notwithstanding anything contrary contained in the Agreement and at any time during the term of the Agreement, to reduce the amount of monthly advances should it reasonably appear to Solomon Clinic or its management that Dr. Carr would have a significant Negative Balance due to low productivity or collections if the current rate of monthly advances continued.
10. On August 3, YR-1, Dr. Carr notified Solomon Clinic that she would not be renewing her Employment Agreement upon its expiration on September 30, YR-1.
11. As provided under the terms of the Agreement, Solomon Clinic withheld Dr. Carr's August, YR-1 monthly advance due to a significant Negative Balance amounting to $132,367.00.
12. In a letter dated September 22, YR-1, Dr. Carr informed Solomon Clinic that she protested the withholding of her wages and further disputed any amount due and owing to Solomon Clinic under the Agreement.
13. According to the Agreement, however, Dr. Carr agreed that, upon termination of the Agreement for any reason, she would be obligated to reimburse to Solomon Clinic the Negative Balance within 30 days following notification to her by Solomon Clinic of her Negative Balance.
14. On October 4, YR-1, Solomon Clinic notified Dr. Carr in writing that her Negative Balance of $132,367.00 was due and owing. Dr. Carr, however, has not paid the Negative Balance of $132,367.00.
15. In addition, Dr. Carr agreed under the terms of the Agreement to refrain from practicing plastic surgery for a period of two years after September 30, YR-1 and within a 35 mile radius of and Solomon Clinic medical office (which offices are in Chapel Hill and Durham, North Carolina) after termination of her employment with Solomon Clinic for any reason.
16. Upon information and belief, Dr. Carr currently practices plastic surgery at the Surgery Institute of North Carolina located in Cary, North Carolina, which Institute is within a 35 mile radius of the Solomon Clinic offices located in Chapel Hill and Durham, North Carolina.

COUNT ONE—BREACH OF EMPLOYMENT AGREEMENT

17. Dr. Carr entered into a valid employment agreement with Solomon Clinic.
18. Solomon Clinic has demanded payment from Dr. Carr for her Negative Balance as provided under the terms of the Agreement, and the Clinic has performed all conditions precedent to Dr. Carr's performance of the Agreement.

19. Dr. Carr has failed and continues to refuse to repay to Solomon Clinic her Negative Balance as provided under the terms and conditions of the Agreement.
20. Dr. Carr has violated and continues to violate the express terms of the Agreement by practicing plastic surgery within two years after September 30, YR-1 and within a 35 mile radius of Solomon Clinic's two offices.
21. Dr. Carr has therefore breached the express terms and conditions of the Agreement.
22. As a direct and proximate result of Dr. Carr's breach of the Agreement, Solomon Clinic has incurred monetary damages in the amount of $132,367.00.
23. Solomon Clinic and Dr. Carr entered into a valid written Employment Agreement containing a valid and enforceable restrictive covenant, wherein Dr. Carr, for reasonable consideration, agreed not to practice plastic surgery within two years and a 35 mile radius of any Solomon Clinic office following the termination of the Agreement.
24. Solomon Clinic will likely be successful on the merits of its claim against Dr. Carr for breach of the restrictive covenant contained in her Employment Agreement with Solomon Clinic.
25. Further, there is the likelihood that Solomon Clinic will sustain irreparable loss, and its rights will be violated unless a preliminary injunction is issued.
26. No adequate remedy exists at law to compensate Solomon Clinic for Dr. Carr's violation of the restrictive covenant contained in the Employment Agreement, therefore entitling Solomon Clinic to a permanent injunction.

WHEREFORE, the Plaintiff prays for relief as follows:

1. That pursuant to Rule 65 of the North Carolina Rules of Civil Procedure and N.C. Gen. Stat. §1-485, Dr. Carr be preliminary and permanently enjoined from working for the Surgery Institute of North Carolina or any other plastic surgery practice for a two year period and within a 35 mile radius from any office of Solomon Clinic;
2. That Solomon Clinic recover from Dr. Carr damages in the amount of $132,367.00, plus interest;
3. That Solomon Clinic recover compensatory damages from Dr. Carr in an amount that includes, but is not limited to, damage for lost patients and reputation and other losses Solomon Clinic has incurred and will incur by reason of the breach of the restrictive covenant contained in her Employment Agreement, as shall be determined by the trier of fact; and
4. That a trial by jury be had on all issues triable.

* * *

STATE OF NORTH CAROLINA	:
COUNTY OF DURHAM	: IN THE GENERAL COURT OF JUSTICE
SOLOMON CLINIC, P.A.,	: SUPERIOR COURT DIVISION
Plaintiff,	: YR-0 CVS 00871
v.	:
MOREY J. CARR, M.D.	:ANSWER & COUNTERCLAIMS
Defendant.	:

Defendant, Morey J. Carr, M.D., through her attorney, answers Plaintiff's Complaint as follows:

1. Defendant admits the allegations in Paragraphs 1 through 10, 12 through 16, and 19 of Plaintiff's Complaint.

2. Defendant denies the allegations in Paragraphs 11, 17, 18, and 20 through 26 of Plaintiff's complaint.

FIRST DEFENSE AND COUNTERCLAIM FOR BREACH OF EMPLOYMENT AGREEMENT

3. Defendant incorporates by reference all the admissions and denials in Paragraphs 1 and 2 above as if fully set forth herein.

4. Plaintiff and Defendant entered into an Employment Agreement on August 29, YR-2, which was effective on October 1, YR-2.

5. Pursuant to the Employment Agreement at Paragraph 3 (a), Plaintiff's Board of Directors was required to establish a compensation formula.

6. Pursuant to the Employment Agreement at Paragraph 6, Plaintiff was required to "furnish [Defendant] with an office, stenographic services, medical supplies and equipment and such other supplies, equipment, facilities, and services suitable to [Defendant's] position and adequate for the performance of [Defendant's] duties."

7. From October 1, YR-2 through September 30, YR-1, Plaintiff breached the Employment Agreement in that:

(a) Plaintiff's Board of Directors did not have or establish a compensation formula as required by Paragraph 3 (a) of the Employment Agreement, but rather based compensation on ad hoc decisions of accounting department employees who from time to time consulted individual members of the Practice when a question arose about compensation.

(b) Plaintiff did not provide facilities and services adequate for the performance of Defendant's duties as called for in Paragraph 6 of the Employment Agreement, in that, among other things, Plaintiff provided unsuitable support personnel, inadequate management services, failed to collect Defendant's billings, and otherwise generally failed to operate the business of the medical practice in an efficient, reasonable, and competent manner adequate for the performance of Defendant's responsibilities.

8. As a consequence of these breaches of contract, Defendant was and is not obligated to pay Plaintiff for any "Negative Balance" as that term is defined in Paragraph 3 (b) of the Employment Agreement, and Defendant is entitled to recover damages from Plaintiff in the amount of Defendant's gross fees properly collected by Plaintiff less Defendant's share of direct and indirect costs properly allocated to Defendant by Plaintiff, which damages are to be calculated by the trier of fact.

SECOND DEFENSE AND COUNTERCLAIM FOR FRAUDULENT MISREPRESENTATION AND CONCEALMENT OF MATERIAL FACTS

9. Defendant incorporates by reference all the admissions and denials set forth in Paragraphs 1 and 2 above as if fully set forth herein.

10. Preceding the making of the Employment Agreement and as an inducement for Defendant to make the Agreement, Ms. Clara Adkins, Administrator and Executive Vice President of Plaintiff's corporation and an agent, servant, employee, and officer of Plaintiff, negligently and/or intentionally made certain positive assertions and representations of material past or existing facts, which representations were recklessly or falsely made when Ms. Adkins made them and Ms. Adkins knew or should have known that such representations were false, intending that Defendant would rely on such representations, which Defendant did rely upon to her injury and detriment.

11. Preceding the making of the Employment Agreement and as an inducement for Defendant to make the Agreement, Ms. Clara Adkins negligently and/or intentionally concealed material past or existing facts, of which concealed facts Ms. Adkins had or should have had knowledge and which Ms. Adkins failed to fully disclose when there was a duty to disclose, and which were recklessly or falsely concealed when Ms. Adkins knew or should have known that such concealed facts were material to Defendant's making a decision to enter into the Employment Agreement, intending that Defendant would rely on the

absence of disclosure, which Defendant did rely upon to her injury and detriment.

12. The misrepresentations of Ms. Adkins referred to in Paragraph 10 included but were not limited to statements that:

(a) Plastic surgeons in the Chapel Hill-Durham area customarily earn $250,000 to $350,000 per year and Defendant could expect to earn at least that amount within a reasonable time, and that Defendant would be one of the highest earning physicians in the practice.

(b) Defendant could expect to have a Negative Balance after the first 3 months of the term of the Employment Agreement but none at the end of the first year of the term of the Employment Agreement, excepting only special equipment purchases made by Defendant, which purchases Defendant could control.

(c) Plaintiff would manage all business aspects of the practice and would "pamper" Defendant by providing her with a receptionist whose primary responsibility would be to schedule Defendant's appointments, and by providing her a new office with new carpet, wallpaper, and furnishings.

(d) Defendant would have the benefit of offices in both Durham and Chapel Hill, and Plaintiff's other physician employees would provide internal patient referrals to Defendant which would be a "tremendous benefit" to Defendant.

(e) Plaintiff would "team up" Defendant with Dr. Joel Smith, a general surgeon in the Practice, and promote the team as a "breast reconstruction specialty" of the Practice.

(f) Plaintiff was "a very [financially] strong entity" capable of "carrying" Defendant until her practice was established.

(g) Plaintiff would make a "tremendous financial investment" in Defendant's practice, and Plaintiff would promote Defendant's practice by spending at least $5,000 on advertising and organizing seminars.

(h) The plastic surgeon previously employed by Plaintiff has done "very, very well [financially]."

13. On information and belief, the material facts referred to in Paragraph 11 that were concealed from Defendant and about which Defendant made inquiry but did not receive a truthful response included but were not limited to:

(a) That most doctors newly hired during the several years preceding Defendant's employment had Negative Balances after the first and often after the second and third years of employment.

(b) That the plastic surgeon previously employed by the practice had not done well financially, had left the practice under a cloud, and was in YR-2 engaged in litigation over his Negative Balance with the Plaintiff.

14. By reason of the foregoing, Defendant is entitled to void and set aside the Employment Agreement and to receive damages in an amount equal to the fair market value of her services to Plaintiff during her employment, which amount is to be determined by the trier of fact.

THIRD DEFENSE AND COUNTERCLAIM TO VOID COVENANT NOT TO COMPETE

15. Defendant incorporates by reference all the admissions and denials in Paragraphs 1 and 2 above as if fully set forth herein.

16. This court has jurisdiction over this counterclaim pursuant to N. C. Gen. Stat. §1-253 et. seq. and North Carolina Rules of Civil Procedure, Rule 57.

17. The Employment Agreement contains at Paragraph 22 a restrictive covenant prohibiting Defendant from practicing plastic surgery for two years within 35 miles of any medical office operated by Plaintiff, and Defendant is and has been practicing plastic surgery in Cary, North Carolina (which is within 35 miles of Plaintiff's offices) since the time of the termination of the Employment Agreement on September 30, YR-1.

18. This covenant is unreasonable as a matter of law as to scope, time and territory, and violates public policy by creating a risk of substantial harm to the public because of the public interest in the choice of selecting a plastic surgeon, the shortage of plastic surgeons in the restricted area, the potential impact of Plaintiff establishing a monopoly on plastic surgery services in the area, and the need for the availability of a plastic surgeon at all times for emergencies.

FOURTH DEFENSE AND COUNTERCLAIM FOR VIOLATIONS FOR THE N.C. WAGE AND HOUR ACT N.C. GEN. STAT. §95-25.1 et. seq.

19. Defendant incorporates by reference all the admissions and denials in Paragraphs 1 and 2 above as if fully set forth herein.

20. Defendant was a salaried employee of Plaintiff earning $10,000 per month, payable in arrears on the first business day of the month following the month worked.

21. Defendant worked the entire month of August, YR-1.

22. On and after September 1, YR-1, Plaintiff, wrongfully and without prior notice, withheld and refused to pay Defendant her wages for the month of August YR-1 in violation of N.C. Gen. Stat. §95-25.6.

23. Defendant worked the entire month of September YR-1, and terminated her employment on September 30, YR-1.

24. On and after October 1, YR-1, Plaintiff wrongfully withheld and refused to pay Defendant her wages for the month of September YR-1 in violation of N. C. Gen. Stat.§95-25.7.

25. Plaintiff withheld Defendant's wages for the months of August and September YR-1 without proper authorization as provided in N.C. Gen. Stat. §95-25.8.

26. By reason of the foregoing, Defendant is entitled to her wages in the amount of $10,000 each for the months of August and September, YR-1; and for damages as provided by N.C. Gen. Stat. §95-25.22 in an amount equal to the wrongfully withheld wages, plus costs and attorneys fees—all as authorized by that Statute.

FIFTH DEFENSE AND COUNTERCLAIM FOR VIOLATIONS OF THE N.C. UNFAIR AND DECEPTIVE TRADE PRACTICES ACT N.C. GEN. STAT. §75-1.1 et. seq.

27. Defendant incorporates by reference all the admissions and denials in Paragraphs 1 and 2 above as if fully set forth herein.

28. Alternatively, the Employment Agreement between Plaintiff and Defendant constituted a joint venture between the parties and did not constitute an employer-employee relationship.

29. Plaintiff's fraudulent misrepresentations and concealment of material facts described in the Second Defense and Counterclaim for Fraudulent Misrepresentation and Concealment of Material Facts constituted unfair and deceptive acts and/or practices in or affecting commerce in North Carolina in violation of N.C. Gen. Stat. §75-1.1 et seq.

30. Plaintiff's wrongful acts were intentional and undertaken for the purpose of deceiving Defendant and had a natural tendency to deceive and injure Defendant.

31. Plaintiff's wrongful conduct proximately damaged Defendant in that Plaintiff's acts deprived Defendant of her earnings and what she would have earned as a plastic surgeon but for the joint venture between the parties.

32. By reason of the foregoing, Defendant is entitled to recover actual damages to be determined by the trier of fact, plus treble the actual damages, plus

costs and attorney's fees—all as provided by the Unfair and Deceptive Trade Practices Act.

WHEREFORE, Defendant prays the court as follows:

1. That this cause be tried by jury as to all issues triable before a jury;

2. That this court enter a declaratory judgment voiding the restrictive covenant or covenant not to complete in the Employment Agreement;

3. That Plaintiff have and recover nothing from Defendant and that the Employment Agreement be declared void and set aside;

4. That Defendant have and recover of Plaintiff damages for breach of contract as proved at trial and that the same be set off against any damages awarded to Plaintiff;

5. That the Employment Agreement be voided and set aside and Defendant have and recover the reasonable value of her services to the Plaintiff in an amount proved at trial;

6. That Defendant have and recover wages in the amount of $20,000 and damages in an amount equal to the amount of wages awarded plus costs and attorney fees as provided by statute, and that the same be set off against any damages awarded to Plaintiff; and

7. That Defendant have and recover actual damages for unfair and deceptive trade practices, that such damages be trebled, and that Defendant recover costs and attorney fees as provided by statute, and that the same be setoff against any damages awarded to Plaintiff.

* * *

Solomon Clinic timely filed a Reply to Dr. Carr's Answer & Counterclaims. That Reply admitted Paragraphs 4, 5, 6, 16, 17, 20, 21, and 23 of Carr's Answer & Counterclaims, and denied all of the other allegations.

The parties agree that none of the claims in the Complaint or in the Answer & Counterclaims are subject to dismissal for failure to state a claim upon which relief may be granted. They further agree that all claims are triable by jury, except that the issues of (1) the validity of the restrictive covenant (or covenant not to compete) contained in the Employment Agreement and (2) whether there has been a violation of the North Carolina Wage and Hour Act are solely matters of law to be decided by the Judge. Finally, the parties agree that each side has properly pled the correct measure of damages for the various claims.

Appendix B

General Suggestions to Mediators for How to Mediate a Case

Because this book does not focus on teaching how to mediate a case, which is a mediation or alternative dispute resolution course, provided below are some general, step-by-step suggestions about how to conduct mediation if you are called upon to serve as the mediator in any of the cases contained in Appendix A. These suggestions should be read in connection with the discussion in Chapters 11 and 12 about what mediators do.

[I] Introductions and the Mediator's Introductory Remarks

At the outset of the mediation, in a joint session attended by all participants, introduce yourself as the mediator, and then have all participants introduce themselves to one another if they have not already done so.

After these personal introductions, you should make some brief (no longer than ten minutes) introductory remarks to all participants that describe your role as mediator and the overall mediation process. The following is an example of such opening remarks (after the personal introductions):

> The lawyers here are no doubt familiar with the mediation process, and they may have already explained to you a bit about what we will be doing. However, for those of you who have never participated in mediation before, I would like to take a few minutes to share with you my role and generally how the process works.

Let me emphasize at the outset that I am completely neutral and impartial in this case. I have no first-hand knowledge about its facts or circumstances, [but I have read the pre-mediation materials that each side has provided to me]. My role in this mediation is to try to assist you in reaching a possible agreement. My role is to facilitate—not to dictate a solution or to serve as a judge in the case. In this process, you own the problem, the means for solving it, and any agreement you might reach.

It is important to know that the mediation process is confidential. With very few exceptions, whatever is said or done here remains confidential, and cannot later be used by one side against the other in subsequent litigation of this matter. In addition, when one side shares information with me that they specifically instruct me to keep confidential, I am prohibited from revealing that information to the other side. Also, I am prohibited from revealing anything that goes on in this mediation to anyone outside of this room, unless all parties give me permission to do so or unless required by law. You should also know that, even though I am a lawyer, when I am serving as your mediator, I am ethically prohibited from giving any legal advice.

The format of what we will be doing consists of two phases: first, this initial joint session (and perhaps another joint session, if that might be useful); and second, private caucusing. In this initial joint session, I will give each side an opportunity to share whatever they would like to say about the case, either through an opening statement by counsel or a statement made by counsel and his/her client. I may ask some clarifying questions after each opening statement or after we have heard all opening statements. At the conclusion of the opening statements, each side might also wish to ask some clarifying questions of the other. In this way, we can bring to the table at the outset as much non-confidential information as you might wish to share with one another.

In the second phase, the private caucuses, I will meet privately with each side. It is likely I will hold multiple private meetings with each side. These private sessions are often useful to clarify information, and to discuss your underlying interests, feelings, objectives, possible solutions to the dispute, and particular proposals that might resolve the case. It is during these private sessions that you might wish to share with me confidential information. Even though I am prohibited from disclosing confidential information to the other side without your permission, knowing such information often helps me better understand your particular interests and needs, and may lead to more mutually satisfactory proposals to resolve the case.

Please understand that the private caucuses might take some time, and the amount of time I spend caucusing with any one side does not mean that I favor one side over another. During the private caucuses, I might ask a number of questions and even play "the devil's advocate," so to speak—all in an effort to better understand your side of the controversy, and to help you evaluate whether your negotiating positions are realistic. Again, it is not my purpose to be judgmental or to dictate a solution to your case. But experience has shown that if ample time and patience are devoted to fully exploring all aspects of the controversy from the perspectives of both sides, the prospects for a mutually satisfactory settlement are greatly enhanced.

Finally, if a settlement is reached in the case, we will reconvene in a joint session at which I will detail the terms of the settlement, and we will agree upon any technical arrangements for executing the settlement. If, after giving this mediation process a fair chance to work, it appears that no agreement can be reached, it is my duty to declare an impasse. If that happens, that does not mean you might not resolve this case later on. Indeed, parties more often than not end up resolving their disputes by agreement even after an initial mediation was unsuccessful.

Before we begin, do any of you have any questions about my role or the mediation process?

[II] The Parties' Opening Statements

After making your introductory remarks, give each side an opportunity to make an opening statement. As a matter of common practice, usually the claimant is called upon first to make an opening statement. Unless it is absolutely necessary, it is undesirable to interrupt any side during their opening statement. If you need some clarification about the facts or have other questions about the circumstances of the case, for example, the status of any prior settlement discussions or the status of the litigation, ask about these matters after each opening statement is complete or after you have heard from both sides.

After the parties have finished their opening statements, you may wish to give them the opportunity to ask clarifying questions of one another. Don't allow this to turn into an inquisition or cross-examination. The limited purpose of this opportunity is to allow the parties to exchange relevant information that they feel comfortable sharing in a joint session.

Sometimes, particularly when the parties deliberately take a non-adversarial and noncompetitive approach to the mediation, both sides may begin discussing or even negotiating the case during the initial joint session. If this happens, and for so long as it remains productive, there is no need to end the joint session and begin private caucusing. However, in most situations, you will find it appropriate to begin private caucusing shortly after the parties have completed their opening statements.

[III] Private Caucusing

In most cases, mediators hold the first private caucus with the claimant. Then, private caucusing continues with meetings alternating between one side and the other for the remainder of the mediation. Sometimes, although rarely, you may find it useful to interrupt caucusing and bring the parties back together in another joint session. For example, this might be appropriate if the parties express a desire to reconvene in a joint session, or if exchanging certain information or discussing a particular proposal would be more efficient in a joint meeting.

Generally, you should use your private caucuses with each side to:

a. Ask questions to clarify the facts or obtain additional relevant information;

b. Ask about the parties' underlying interests or needs (*e.g.*, emotional, psychological, economic, physical, or social);

c. Listen to the parties without interruption, and allow them to vent if necessary;

d. Find out about the parties' primary, secondary, and incidental objectives, and the reasons for them;

e. Identify the issues;

f. Understand how the parties evaluate the case legally and factually, and what assumptions underlie those evaluations;

g. Explore potential solutions or proposals (both non-monetary and monetary);

h. Discourage the parties from disclosing their bottom lines (resistance points) to you until late in the mediation process after several offers and counteroffers have been fully considered;

i. Probe the reasons supporting particular proposals, offers, and counteroffers;

j. Discuss the risks, costs, and alternatives to not reaching an agreement;

k. Help the parties understand one another's points of view;

l. Play "the devil's advocate" to help the parties to evaluate whether their negotiating positions are realistic;

m. Clarify what information is to be kept confidential from the other side;

n. Make sure you understand the extent of the parties' authority to make or accept an offer or proposal;

o. Communicate to the parties the various proposals, offers, and counteroffers you are asked to communicate and, as appropriate, the reasons underlying them;

p. Suggest alternative potential solutions, if appropriate;

q. Give the clients and their attorneys ample opportunity to confer alone if they wish;

r. Engage in appropriate mediator tactics and techniques to facilitate a possible settlement (*see, e.g.*, §12.03 in main text).

[IV] Concluding the Mediation

If an agreement is reached, bring the parties back into a joint session. Then, carefully detail all terms of the agreement, and ask each side to confirm their understanding of those terms. Be sure to ask whether there are any other matters that need to be included in the agreement. Once all terms are understood, make sure the parties understand the steps that will be taken to effectuate the final agreement. Everyone should understand who will prepare the settlement documents, when those will be prepared, and how they are to be exchanged.

If the parties have not reached a settlement, it is usually desirable to bring them back into a joint session at which you might briefly summarize any points of agreement that have been reached by them. In addition, you might indicate that you would be willing to resume the mediation at some later time if the parties desire. Finally, you should thank the parties for their efforts and express your hope that they might still reach a mutually satisfactory agreement at some future date.

Index

[References are to pages.]

A

Abdication
Negotiation technique, 69

Adjournment
Negotiation tactic, 170

Admissions, Requests for
Negotiating during litigation and, 210

Adversarial Model
Generally, 30
Advantages, 45
Bargaining leverage, differences in, 37
Competitive style and, 41
Cooperative style and, 41
Defined, 30
Disadvantages, 45
Face-to-face negotiations (*See* Face-to-Face Negotiations)
Factors affecting utility of, 35
Future dealings between parties or negotiators, 37
Nature of dispute or problem, 35
Other side's negotiating approach, 36
Pressures to reach agreement, 38
Resistance points, establishing, 30, 93, 98, 130, 131
Stages of negotiation, 30
Target point, establishing, 30, 93, 98, 130, 131

Aggressiveness
Negotiating technique, 70

Anger
Negotiating technique, 70

Answer
Negotiating during litigation and filing, 208

Anthropology
Negotiating, anthropological approaches to, 17

Attorney-Client Privilege
Confidential information in mediation, 263

Attorney's Fees
Contingent fees (*See* Contingent Fees)
Judgment, making offer of; treatment of attorney's fees, 213

Authority to Negotiate
Lack of or limited, 80

B

Blaming
Negotiating technique, 71

Blocking Techniques
Negotiations, 74

Bluffing
Negotiating technique, 71

Boulwarism
Negotiating technique, 72

Bracketing
Negotiating tactic, 78

C
Caucus
Negotiation tactic, 70

Civil Litigation, Negotiation During
See Negotiating During Litigation

Coalition
Negotiating tactic, 72

"Collaborative Law" Agreements
Civil litigation, negotiations during, 218

Company Policy Excuse
Negotiating tactic, 72

Competitive Style
Generally, 38
Advantages, 44
Adversarial strategy and, 40
Cooperative-competitive style
  Generally, 40
  Advantages, 45
  Adversarial strategy and, 41
  Disadvantages, 45
  Preparation outline for negotiation, 132
  Problem-solving strategy and, 43
Disadvantages, 44
Preparation outline for negotiation, 132
Problem-solving strategy and, 43

Complaint
Negotiating during litigation and filing, 208

Computer Software
Valuing cases, 102

Condemnation Case
Appeal, role plays in case on, 285
Valuing cases; holistic analysis example, 114

Conditional Proposals
Negotiating technique, 83

Confidential Communications
Confidential information in mediation, 263

Contingent Fees
Contract
  Sample contract, 58
  Writing requirement, 56
Defined, 54
Ethical considerations, 54
Limitations, 55
Negotiating, 54
Reasonableness of, 54
Writing requirement, 56

Cooperative Style
Generally, 39
Advantages, 44
Adversarial strategy and, 41
Advantages, 45
  Adversarial strategy and, 41
  Disadvantages, 45
  Preparation outline for negotiation, 132
  Problem-solving strategy and, 43
Competitive-cooperative style, 40
Disadvantages, 44
Preparation outline for negotiation, 132
Problem-solving strategy and, 43

Counseling (Generally)
Importance of, 3
Learning by doing approach, 4
Process of, 4

Covenant Not to Compete
Breach of, role plays, 302

Criminal Case
Prisoner's dilemma and game theory as negotiating technique, 8

Criminal Proceedings
Threat of criminal prosecution during negotiations; ethical considerations, 65

D

Deadlines
Negotiating tactic, 73

Debt Collection
Unfair, role plays, 298

Delays
Negotiating tactic, 73

Depositions
Negotiating during litigation and using, 210

Discovery
Negotiating during litigation and, 210

Discrimination
Employment discrimination; role plays, 276

Distribution Agreement
Breach of, role plays, 305

Divorce
Premarital agreement; role plays, 268
Separation agreement; role plays, 270

E

Economic Theories
Cost-benefit approach to negotiation, 12
Distributive bargaining, 14
Integrative bargaining, 14
Negotiating theory, 12
Pareto-optimal settlements, 14
Settlement-Option Quadrant, 14
Trial Option Quadrant, 14

Employment
Role plays
- Contract for employment, breach of, 314
- Discrimination case, 276
- Noncompetition agreements, breach of, 302
- Wrongful discharge, 293

Ethical Considerations
Generally, 49
Aggregate settlements, 52
Civility in negotiating, 63
Contingent fees, 54
Criminal prosecution threat during negotiations, 65
False statements of material fact or law, 59
Material fact or law, false statements of, 59
Personal opinions on merits of case, 59
Puffing, 61
Settlements
- Aggregate settlements, 52
- Attorney's authority to settle and advise client, 50
- Contingent fees, 54

Truthfulness in negotiating, 59

F

Face Saving
Negotiating tactic, 76

Face-to-Face Negotiations
Generally, 172
Adversarial bargaining
- Generally, 485
- Communicating offers, 188
- Concessions, making, 189
- Counteroffers, making, 188

First offers, making, 186
Offers, making, 186
Persuasion, forms of (*See* subhead: Persuasion, forms of)
Problem-solving bargaining and, combining, 200
Agenda, setting, 177
Answering another question, answering question by, 184
Answering question by asking another question, 184
Argument as form of persuasion, 194
Attendees, 175
Body language, reading, 179
Broad open-ended questions, asking, 181
Changing topic, 183
Client's role, 175
Concessions, making, 189
Concluding negotiations, 202
Counteroffers, making, 188
Crucial information, insisting upon necessity of receiving, 183
Elaboration, questions calling for, 182
Emotional appeals, 195
Exchanging information, 180
Exhibits, 195
Ignoring question and changing topic, 183
Listening attentively and patiently, 182
Location of, 174
Obtaining information, 181
Offers, making, 186
Out of bounds, ruling question as, 184
Over-answer or under-answer question, 184
Persons with whom to negotiate, 173
Persuasion, forms of
Argument, 194
Emotional appeals, 195
Exhibits, 195
Promises, 196
Threats, 196
Place for, 174
Problem-solving bargaining
Generally, 197
Adversarial and, combining, 200
Brainstorming, 198
Concessions, 199
Counteroffers, 199
Interests or needs, identifying and sharing, 197
Offers, making, 199
Promises as form of persuasion, 196
Protecting information
Generally, 183
Answering another question, answering question by, 184
Answering question by asking another question, 184
Changing topic, 183
Ignoring question and changing topic, 183
Out of bounds, ruling question as, 184
Over-answer or under-answer question, 184
Revealing information, 185
Silence, use of, 182
Specific questions, asking, 182
Threats and promises, 196
Time for negotiating, 174
Tone of, setting, 176

Fait Accompli
Negotiating tactic, 76

False Demands
Negotiating tactic, 77

False Emphasis
Negotiating tactic, 77

False Multiple Concessions
Negotiating tactic, 77

False Scarcity
Negotiating tactic, 78

Family Law
Premarital agreement; role plays, 268
Separation agreement; role plays, 270

Fault Finding
Negotiating technique, 71

Federal Rules of Civil Procedure
Judgment, making offers of, 212

Fees
Attorney's fees (*See* Attorney's Fees)
Mediator's fee as element of settlement, 332

Floating Trial Balloons
Negotiating tactic, 78

G
Game Theory
Negotiating, 8

Good Guy-Bad Guy Routine
Negotiating technique, 79

H
Hardball Negotiating Style
See Competitive Style

Holistic Analysis
Valuing cases, 111

I
Injunctions
Negotiating during litigation and use of preliminary injunctions, 209

Interrogatories
Negotiating during litigation and, 211

J
Judgment, Offer of
Attorney's fees, treatment of, 213
Negotiating during litigation and making, 212
Sum to be paid, specification of, 212

L
Lock-In Positions
Negotiating tactics and techniques, 81

Low-Balling
Negotiating tactic, 81

M
Mediation
Generally, 223, 225
Attendance at mediation, 248
Bashing strategy, 230
Bottom line, disclosure of, 264
Cases to mediate, 233
Client, conferring with, 265
Client preparation, 250
Concluding, 266, 329
Confidential information, specifying, 263
Cues and clues from mediator, listening to, 263
Effective advocacy during, 253
Evaluative, 228
Ex parte meetings with parties (*See* subhead: Private caucuses)
Facilitative, 228
Favorable situations for, 234
Hashing it out strategy, 230
Information, obtaining, 239, 260
Introductory remarks, 225, 325
Mediators
  Bashing strategy, 230
  Conferring with mediator and opposing counsel, 265
  Cues and clues from mediator, listening to, 263
  Ex parte meetings with parties (*See* subhead: Private caucuses)
  Hashing it out strategy, 230
  Information, obtaining, 239, 260
  Movement in negotiations, creating, 242
  Perspective on case, inviting mediator's, 262
  Private caucuses (*See* subhead: Private caucuses)
  Selection of, 236
  Solutions, generating and discussing, 240

Specific proposals, assessing, selecting and communicating, 241
Strategies, 229
Styles, 229
Suggestions to mediators for mediating case, 325
Tactics and techniques, 237
Terms of agreement, forging and finalizing, 244
Traditional negotiating, 237
Trashing approach, 229
Movement in negotiations, creating, 242
Opening statement during, 256, 327
Outline for, preparing, 245
Parties, 225
Patience with mediation process, 265
Perspective on case, inviting mediator's, 262
Pre-mediation conference with mediator or between counsel, 247
Preparation for
Generally, 245
Attendance at mediation, 248
Client preparation, 250
Outline, 245
Pre-mediation conference with mediator or between counsel, 247
Private caucuses
Generally, 226, 259
Bottom line, disclosure of, 264
Client, conferring with, 265
Conferring with mediator and opposing counsel, 265
Confidential information, specifying, 263
Cues and clues from mediator, listening to, 263
Information, assisting mediator in obtaining, 260
Perspective on case, inviting mediator's, 262
Pros and cons of case, discussing, 261
Settlement offers, making reasonable, 264
Strengths and weaknesses of case, discussing, 261
Weaknesses and strengths of case, discussing, 261
Process of mediation, 223
Settlement offers, making reasonable, 264
Solutions, generating and discussing, 240
Specific proposals, assessing, selecting and communicating, 241
Strength and weaknesses of cases, discussing, 261
Submission, preparation of pre-mediation, 254
Tactics and techniques, 237
Terms of agreement, forging and finalizing, 244
Traditional negotiating, 237
Trashing approach, 229
Unfavorable situations for, 235
Weaknesses of cases, discussing, 261

Medical Malpractice
Role plays, 289

Misstatements
Negotiating tactics, 82

Mutt and Jeff Routine
Negotiating technique, 79

N
Negotiating During Litigation
Generally, 205
Admissions, requests for, 212
Answer, filing, 208
"Collaborative law" agreements, 218
Complaint and answer, filing, 208
Deadlines, using, 213
Depositions, using, 210
Discovery, using, 210
High-low agreements, 217
Injunctions, preliminary, 209
Interrogatories, using, 212

Judgment, making offers of, 212
Last minute settlement, 216
Preparation, considerations for, 206
Pretrial settlement conferences, using, 215
Pretrial strategy and style, 206
Production of documents, requests for, 210
Temporary restraining order, 209
Timing and deadlines, using, 213

Negotiating (Generally)
Generally, 7
Academic approaches to understanding, 8, 28
Adversarial model (*See* Adversarial Model)
Anthropological approaches, 17
Civil litigation, during (*See* Negotiating During Litigation)
Cooperative style (*See* Cooperative Style)
Credibility, importance of, 42
Defined, 7
Economic approaches, 12
Ethical considerations (*See* Ethical Considerations)
Face-to-face negotiations (*See* Face-to-Face Negotiations)
Flexibility, importance of, 42
Game theory, 8
Hardball style (*See* Competitive Style)
Importance of, 3
Learning by doing approach, 4
Mediation, during (*See* Mediation)
Overview, 3
Preparation for (*See* Preparation for Negotiation)
Prisoner's dilemma and game theory, 8
Problem-solving model (*See* Problem-Solving Model)
Process of, 4
Psychological approaches and factors (*See* Psychology)
Settlements, generally (*See* Settlements)
Sociological approaches, 17
Softball style (*See* Cooperative Style)
Strategies
  Generally, 38, 42
  Adversarial model (*See* Adversarial Model)
  Combinations, 41
  Competitive style (*See* Competitive Style)
  Cooperative style (*See* Cooperative Style)
  Problem-solving model (*See* Problem-Solving Model)
  Selection of, 41
Styles
  Generally, 38, 42
  Combinations, 41
  Competitive style (*See* Competitive Style)
  Cooperative style (*See* Cooperative Style)
  Selection of, 41
Tactics and techniques (*See* Negotiating Tactics and Techniques)
Telephone, over (*See* Negotiating Over Telephone)
Valuing cases for negotiation and settlement (*See* Valuing Cases)
Writing, in (*See* Negotiating in Writing)

Negotiating in Writing
Generally, 149
Advantages, 150
Authority to represent, identifying your, 151
Certified mail, sending letter by, 151
Copying letter to other persons, 151
Course of action, conveying specific, 153
Damages summary, 159, 168
Demand letter, sample, 154
Disadvantages, 150
Effective correspondence, techniques for, 242
Facts, statement of, 157, 160

Facts and law, highlighting pertinent, 152
Initial demand, 159
Liability, statement of, 157, 160
Lost earnings, summary of, 158, 160
Medical treatment, summary of, 158, 160
Pain and suffering, summary of, 158, 160
Permanent injury, summary of, 158
Proposal, conveying specific, 153
Registered mail, sending letter by, 151
Settlement brochures
  Generally, 156
  Contents, 156
  Cover letter, 157, 160
  Damages summary, 159, 160
  Defined, 156
  Facts, statement of, 157, 160
  Initial demand, 159
  Introduction to, 157, 160
  Liability, statement of, 157, 160
  Lost earnings, summary of, 158, 160
  Medical treatment, summary of, 158, 160
  Pain and suffering, summary of, 158, 160
  Permanent injury, summary of, 158
  Sample, 160
Style and tone, adopting appropriate, 151
Time frame for action and consequences for inaction, stating, 153

Negotiating Over Telephone
Generally, 150
Advantages, 150
Disadvantages, 150
Effective negotiations, techniques for, 168
Errors or misunderstanding, correction of, 170
Misunderstanding, correction of, 170
Outline, use of, 170
Pace of voice, adjusting, 170
Tone of voice, adjusting, 170
Unavailable to take call, 169

Negotiating Tactics and Techniques
Generally, 68
Abdication, 69
Absent-mindedness technique, 80
Adjournment, 70
Aggressiveness, 70
Anger, 70
Authority, lack of or limited, 80
Blaming, 71
Blocking techniques, dodging question through, 74
Bluffing, 71
Bracketing, 78
Boulwarism, 72
Caucus, 70
Coalition, 72
Company policy excuse, 72
Conditional proposals, 83
Deadlines, 73
Deflecting tactic or technique by ignoring it, 94
Delaying negotiations, 73
Demands, false, 77
Disingenuous or inappropriate tactics or techniques, dealing with
  Deflect, 95
  Expose tactic, 95
  Ignore, 95
  Respond in kind, 95
  Rule out of bounds, 94
Drafting document or single negotiating text, 74
Dumb, playing, 83
Emphasis, false, 77
Escalating demands, 75
Excessive initial demands/offers, 75
Expertise, display of, 88
Exposing tactic or technique, 95
Face saving, 76
Fait accompli, 76
False scarcity, 78
Fault finding, 71
Floating trial balloons, 78
Good guy-bad guy routine, 79
Inappropriate tactics or techniques, dealing with, 93

Inexperience and meekness technique, 80
Limited authority, 80
Lock-in positions, 81
Low-balling, 81
Misstatement, 82
Multiple concessions, false, 77
Mutt and Jeff routine, 79
Nibbling tactic, 82
Off-the-record discussions, 82
Out of bounds, ruling inappropriate tactic, 94
Personal attacks, 83
Preconditions or conditional proposals, 83
Problem-solving (*See* Problem-Solving Model)
Publicity, 84
Questions
  Facilitate agreements, questions to, 86
  Socratic method, questioning by, 87
Responding to tactic or technique in kind, 95
Reversing position, 88
Salami tactic, 88
Socratic method, questioning by, 87
Splitting difference, 89
Surprises, 89
Take-it-or-leave-it approach, 90
Threats, 91
Time pressure, asymmetrical, 70
Timing, 91
Two against one, 92
Walkout, 92
Word-smithing, 92

Nibbling Tactic
Negotiations, 82

Noncompetition Agreements
Breach of, role plays, 302

Nursing Malpractice
Role plays, 296

O
Objectives, Client's
Preparation outline for negotiation, 128, 129

Off-the-Record Discussions
Negotiating tactic, 82

P
Personal Attacks
Negotiating tactic, 83

Personal Injury Case
Automobile accident case, 281, 290
Contingent fee (*See* Contingent Fees)
Ethical considerations (*See* Ethical Considerations)
Medical malpractice, role plays, 289
Nursing malpractice, role plays, 296
Role plays
  Automobile accident case, 281, 290
  Medical malpractice, 289
  Nursing malpractice, 296
Settlements (*See* Settlements)
Valuing cases (*See* Valuing Cases)

Premarital Agreements
Role plays, 268

Preparation for Negotiation
Generally, 124
Adversarial approach, outline for, 136
Advising client, 148
Alternatives to negotiated agreement, list of; step 5, 130
Factual and legal leverage points, list of each party's; step 6, 130
Information to obtain
  Generally, 124
  Client, from, 125
  Law, information about, 126
  Opposing negotiator, about, 126
  Other party, information about, 125
Leverage points, list of each party's factual and legal, 130
Litigation, negotiation during civil, 205

Offers or proposals, list of each party's; step 10, 132
Outline
Generally, 127
Adversarial approach, 136
Alternatives to negotiated agreement, list of; step 5, 130
Factual and legal leverage points, list of each party's; step 6, 130
Format for, 134
Interests of parties, list of; step 2, 128
Leverage points, list of each party's factual and legal, 130
Objectives, list of each party's; step 3, 129
Offers or proposals, list of each party's; step 10, 132
Perspective of each party, information to obtain from; step 1, 127
Problem-solving approach, 129
Revising all foregoing matters throughout negotiating process; step 12, 134
Solutions for each party, list of; step 4, 129
Strategy for negotiating, identifying; step 8, 131
Style for negotiating, identifying each party's; step 9, 132
Tactics used by each party, considering; step 11, 133
Target and resistance points, identifying each party's; step 7, 131
Telephone, negotiating over, 169
Problem-solving approach, outline for, 142
Revising all foregoing matters throughout negotiating process; step 12, 134
Role of client, 148
Solutions for each party, list of; step 4, 129
Strategy for negotiating, identifying; step 8, 131
Style for negotiating, identifying each party's; step 9, 132
Tactics used by each party, considering; step 11, 133
Target and resistance points, identifying each party's; step 7, 131
Telephone, negotiating over, 171

Prisoner's Dilemma
Negotiating theory, 8

Privileged Communications
Mediator, private caucuses with; specifying confidential information, 263

Problem-Solving Model
Generally, 33, 84
Advantages, 44
Bargaining leverage, differences in, 37
Brainstorming session, 33, 198
Competitive style and, 42
Concessions, 33
Cooperative style and, 42
Defined, 33
Disadvantages, 45
Face-to-face negotiations (*See* Face-to-Face Negotiations)
Factors affecting utility of
Future dealings between parties or negotiators, 37
Nature of dispute or problem, 35
Other side's negotiating approach, 36
Pressures to reach agreement, 38
Stages of, 33
Zero-sum controversy, 35

Production of Documents, Requests for
Negotiating during litigation and, 211

Professional Responsibility
See Ethical Considerations

Psychology
Generally, 22
Framing effects, 24

Reactive devaluation, 27
Reference points and framing effects, 24
Risk aversion, 22
Sunk costs, 26

Publicity
Negotiating technique, 84

R
Resistance Points
Adversarial model for establishing, 30, 98, 130, 136
Holistic analysis, 111
Valuing cases, 97, 104

Reversing Position
Negotiating technique, 88

S
Salami Tactic
Negotiating tactic, 88

Separation Agreements
Role plays, 270

Settlements
Attorney's fees (*See* Attorney's Fees)
Contingent fee (*See* Contingent Fees)
Economic theories of negotiation, 12
Ethical considerations (*See* Ethical Considerations)
Mediation (*See* Mediation)
Negotiating tactics and techniques (*See* Negotiating Tactics and Techniques)
Valuing cases (*See* Valuing Cases)

Sociology
Negotiating, sociological approaches to, 17

Socratic Method
Questioning by, 87

Softball Negotiating Style
See Cooperative Style

Surprises
Negotiating technique, 89

T
Take-It-or-Leave-It Approach
Negotiating technique, 90

Telephone
Negotiating over telephone (*See* Negotiating Over Telephone)

Temporary Restraining Order
Negotiating during litigation, 209

Threats
Negotiating technique, 91

V
Valuing Cases
Generally, 97
Average verdict expectancy, calculating, 107
Computer-generated, 102
Economic analysis, 103
Expected outcome, computation of, 103
Fair settlement range formula, 107
Holistic analysis, 111, 114
Intuitive case worth analysis, 100
Motivations, client's, 109
Resistance points, 98, 104
Risk aversion and motivations, analysis of client's, 109
Rule-of-thumb valuation, 102
Target points, 98
Traditional economic analysis, 103

W
Walkout
Negotiating tactic, 92

Word-Smithing
Negotiating tactic, 92

Writings
Contingent fee agreement, 57, 58

Negotiating in (*See* Negotiating in Writing)

Wrongful Employment Discharge
Role plays, 293